For Comrade and Country

For Comrade and Country

Oral Histories of
World War II Veterans

Edited by ROBERT G. THOBABEN

McFarland & Company, Inc., Publishers
Jefferson, North Carolina, and London

On the front cover: United States Marines (PFC Don D. Barrett at right) Britain, with trophies captured during patrols into Japanese lines on Cape Gloucester.

All photographs are from the personal collections of the interviewees except as noted in the text.

Library of Congress Cataloguing-in-Publication Data

For comrade and country : oral histories of World War II veterans / edited by Robert G. Thobaben.
     p.   cm.
     Includes index.

     ISBN 0-7864-1396-4 (softcover : 50# alkaline paper)

     1. World War, 1939–1945—Personal narratives, American.
2. Oral history.   3. World War, 1939–1945—Pacific Area.
4. World War, 1939–1945—Europe.   5. Veterans—United
States—Interviews.   I. Thobaben, Robert G.
D811.A2F57   2003
940.54'8173—dc21   2003011425

British Library cataloguing data are available

Manufactured in the United States of America

Front cover background image ©2002 Comstock

McFarland & Company, Inc., Publishers
 Box 611, Jefferson, North Carolina 28640
  www.mcfarlandpub.com

To Janet

"Marriage is the perfection which love aimed at,
ignorant of what it sought" (Emerson)

And to the men of the Third Battalion,
111th Infantry who served in the Pacific in World War II

Acknowledgments

It has been said that the pen is mightier than the sword. This may or may not be true, but what is unquestionable is the debt all writers owe to individuals who offer support, encouragement and assistance in producing a manuscript. Two women deserve special mention in my case. Janet Thobaben, my wife, and a stalwart in the Centerville–Washington Township Historical Society (C–WTHS) for years, filmed every one of the interviews while she patiently taught me the importance of the pre-interview dialogue and the interview process itself. She endured it all—I know not how. Pat Aldrich, another dedicated worker for the C–WTHS, meticulously transcribed all forty-two interviews from videotape to paper and then typed up every one of the edited interviews for the final editing. Along the way she provided invaluable suggestions, help and encouragement.

I owe a debt to a number of other individuals. Lynn Russell, former director of the C–WTHS, suggested that I initiate a series of interviews of World War II veterans living in the community. This idea was the origin of the project. Donna Schlagheck, chair of the Department of Political Science at Wright State University, provided support for some of the copying expenses. Joanne Ballmann of Wright State typed up the original manuscript for the Preface, and Leslie Kepler, help desk analyst at Wright State, solved every computer problem I had and did it in a friendly and delightful manner.

I owe a special thanks to Carl Becker, professor emeritus of history at Wright State University, my colleague and friend, for his advice on a host of matters associated with this book and his heartening reassurances.

I offer my heartfelt thanks to all the veterans of World War II who gave of their time and who supplied me with pictures and answered questions. Perhaps the dedication expresses my feelings best.

Not every interview could be included in the text. Space is limited and choices must be made. The names and duties of the men and women whose experiences have not been included appear in Appendix A. Their contributions are deeply appreciated.

Many people supported my effort, but I alone am responsible for factual or interpretive errors in this book.

Contents

Preface

In April of 1999 I received a letter from the director of the Centerville–Washington Township (C–WT) Historical Society asking if I would be interested in interviewing World War II veterans living in the Centerville–Washington Township suburb of Dayton, Ohio. The total population of fifty thousand people is divided almost equally between the two political communities. Centerville and Washington Township share the same school system, fire protection and many other services. C–WT is essentially one community.

The director wrote to me because she knew that I was a veteran of the Pacific conflict, had participated in three campaigns in the Central Pacific Theater (Gilbert Islands in 1943, Marshall Islands in 1944, Palau Islands in 1945) and had co-authored a memoir of my service with the 111th Infantry Regiment in *Common Warfare: Parallel Memoirs by Two World War II GIs in the Pacific* (1992, McFarland).

I agreed to take on the assignment and began interviewing veterans of World War II living in the C–WT area. The interviews were filmed on 8mm film and later transferred to VHS videotape for transcribing. Each interview ran from forty-five to sixty minutes. The plan was to create a series of videotapes for the society's library so that future generations could see and hear for themselves the stories of those who fought in this terrible struggle. Every personal account is different. Every story is unique. Among the many people I interviewed there were no great heroes, no celebrities—just ordinary people involved in an extraordinary human event. It was a fascinating experience. After conducting about fifteen interviews, I found them so gripping that I decided to go beyond the original project and try to develop a book.

Thirty interviews constitute the bulk of this text. I edited each veteran's story as faithfully as readability allowed, carefully preserving each interviewee's original wording. A data sheet was completed on each veteran before the interview began, which provided me with each individual's important social relations, economic activity, military records and associations, both before and after the war. In every interview, the veteran brought old photographs, souvenirs, sometimes a diary and frequently parts of their old uniforms. These were very helpful.

1

First a few comments on the men themselves. Some of them were eager to tell their stories, while some found it difficult to talk of the old days. Some were extremely articulate, just marvelous storytellers, while a few found it a painful process to reconstruct their lives fifty-five years after the fact. If social class is composed of income, education and residence, then in general the people interviewed in this book would probably be considered middle class or in some cases upper middle class. At the time these interviews were conducted their average age would have been about seventy-five. Most of these veterans took advantage of the GI Bill of Rights, married, had children and began careers that kept them occupied for about thirty-five to forty years.

One thing the veterans all showed in common: they knew the difference between right and wrong. Their backgrounds may have been different, but they had this common bond.

Because space was limited, only thirty of the forty-two interviews conducted are included here. In choosing which stories to include, I focused on those that were the most intense, exciting and revealing.

The purpose of this book is to see the war through the eyes of its ordinary fighting men as well as those in the military who supported them. The war was a life-changing experience for virtually everyone. I know it was for me.

For those who had to meet the enemy in direct combat, the war, no matter its elemental meaning for freedom, was brutal and terrible. The infantrymen who fought in the hedgerows of Normandy, the Marines who clung to the bloody beaches of Iwo Jima, the pilots who flew through a gauntlet of fire over Germany, the sailors who exchanged gunfire with the Japanese fleet—all suffered the psychological and physical wounds of battle. If any men wanted to embellish their days in uniform "to remember with advantage" what feats they did, they had the right.

Other soldiers and sailors, though, engaged the enemy at a far remove and seldom were participants in the fighting for blood and ground. These were the support troops—driving trucks with food and ammunition, securing and mopping up areas captured by the assault troops, servicing the machines of war and manning desks on the home front. Though theirs was not the blood of frontline battle, they believed, or at best hoped, that they were instruments of success, that they had something to do with victory.

Whatever role they played in the war, those men and women knew that they all shared to a lesser or greater degree in a flawed and frustrating crusade. For they could not escape the ironies, the incongruities, the absurdities inherent in the massing of men for gigantic ventures. In retrospect, as the years passed and they searched for meaning in their lives, they might invest their experiences in war with the sheen of nostalgia or excitement. But they might also place it in a realistic perspective, tinting it gently with the cynicism of age and reducing it to its proper perspective.

The thirty men interviewed in this book all have abiding recollections of the days of their youth when they stood ready to die for the nation. Measured by any one of the several adjectives—ordinary, typical, common, conventional—their interests and abilities seem to be of the millions, those of Everyman in uniform. And their memories spring from the ordinary routines and relationships of servicemen. Their recollections strike no grand chord of decision-making by generals and admirals reviewing the numbers and strategic depositions of soldiers, sailors and marines.[1]

Servicemen who have been in battle have a special obligation to "pass the word along"—to document their experiences in the military. And this burden, this special obligation, is borne not only by those who stood in harm's way because of enemy action, but by all who served in the military. The form matters not—it might be literature such as Norman Mailer's *The Naked and The Dead* or James Jones' *The Thin Red Line*; drama as exemplified by Shakespeare in Henry the Fifth's speech to his troops just before the Battle of Agincourt; *history* captured in the making, like Samuel Eliot Morison's fourteen-volume series on the U.S. Navy in World War II; or journalism like Ernie Pyle's that captured the life of the infantry soldier in North Africa, Italy and Okinawa. All forms are useful. The important thing is to tell the tale—to pass the word along from one generation to another. In his Nobel lecture in 1972, Alexander Solzhenitsyn said, "The sole substitute for an experience which we have not ourselves lived through is art and literature."

This book purports to be a microcosm of American veterans of World War II. That is, if the same procedure employed in this book for the collection and reporting of data were to be utilized in any residential suburb of a city of two hundred thousand or more people such as Dayton, Ohio, the results would be similar. It is primarily this feature of my book that distinguishes it from the two other major oral histories of the war—namely, *The Good War* by Studs Terkel and *The Greatest Generation* by Tom Brokaw. Terkel's book involves about one hundred and nine oral histories of which fifty-two are military men and women. They run from one to ten pages and average about five pages. Brokaw's book includes the accounts of fifty-one people, forty-one of whom are military. Here the accounts run from one page to ten pages with an average of six pages. This book is different from Terkel's and Brokaw's in a number of important ways. In this book, (a) all interviewees are former members of the armed forces; (b) all live in one small Midwest community, Centerville–Washington Township; (c) all accounts of individual veterans include a biographical sketch so that the reader knows something about the person telling the tale—before and after the war; and (d) all testimony of the veterans is *in their own words* as they respond to the interview questions.

It is important to record the narratives of great heroes, celebrities, famous politicians, wives of servicemen, and others who experienced World War II. But if we are to inquire deeply into the psyche of those who fought the war, it is critical that we understand the mentality of the millions of ordinary men who distinguished themselves in battle.

There are a host of "reasons why" it is crucial to chronicle the experiences of men and women in the military. From the historical perspective, those involved in combat should pass the word along to the next generation in some form, because if one has not experienced war, the only way to get any insight into its nature is through the written word. Human beings yet unborn can know the truth of what, where, why, when and how such an event occurred. For example, much of what we know about the Navy's role at the Battle of Midway and the Marianas Campaign we owe to Samuel Eliot Morison and his work. Morison, former professor of history at Harvard, went to government officials when the war started and persuaded them that there was a need for a history of the Navy written while the men who fought in it were still alive. Morison participated in many naval actions and visited areas of ground combat while the fighting went on.

Marines and infantrymen ought to shed light on what war and ground combat is like. More needs to be written about the tedium of daily life, more eyewitness accounts of coming under enemy fire, more of the human side of technological struggle—more about war as the common soldier experiences it. Consider Ernie Pyle's *Here Is Your War*. Pyle's book is a journalist's effort to document the allied invasion of North Africa. Pyle writes from the perspective of the infantryman—from "the bottom up." E.B. Sledge's memoir *With the Old Breed* is devastatingly powerful in its description of an assault Marine in the battles at Peleliu and Okinawa. Sledge is especially honest. He writes with passion about his thoughts as his assault craft heads toward shore: "Everything my life has been before and after pales in the light of that awesome moment when my amtrac started in amid a thunderous bombardment toward the flaming, smoke-shrouded beach for the assault on Peleliu."[2] This memoir by an assault Marine may well be the best literature by an assault serviceman to come out of the war. It is important to disclose the feelings and actions of the average soldier—the fear, anger, hate, regret, relief, pleasure, hope and anxiety of experiences in the service. Only this facet gives a story the ring of truth, and yes, the genuine amusement implicit in some tales. Stories such as these mince no words, spare no pain, disguise no truth.

Whether World War II veterans realize it or not, they were at the center of one of the truly cataclysmic events in human history. The stories and history of the war will command books and chapters for a hundred years. Just consider the consequences of this struggle—fifty million killed, two hundred million injured, the genocide of the Holocaust, the fighting on six of the seven continents of the world. There was even suicide on a mass scale—read *The Divine Wind* by T. Nakajima and R. Inoguchi to learn why and how thousands of Japanese youth consciously gave their lives for the Emperor and the Empire.

Socially, military life teaches young men that "life is a profound and passionate thing." It is a profound thing to face sudden death directly at age nineteen. It is staggering to realize that the enemy's goal is to kill you at nineteen. Life is supposed to be beginning at nineteen—not ending suddenly and violently. And this experience is, at times, a daily reality. Only through the written word or possibly a painting can this reality be made available to a host of people. The significance of life is only clear and lively when objectively one faces its antithesis—death. I don't mean "living on the edge" as young people today say they do when they bungee jump or ski a difficult slope. One may die because one is just a damn fool, but at least no individual, group, or nation has as its goal to bring about one's death.

Life is passionate in the level of fear, anxiety, relief, and pleasure that one experiences at nineteen. Few human beings reach so many affective heights, so early in life, as soldiers do. These affections occur to all human beings, but normally in a rather slow progression as one experiences life over three score and ten. In the military, the number and level may be telescoped into a five-minute experience when all the passions noted above, and more, are realized at a level never again to be attained. Some of the best examples of this passion and profundity may be seen in the war art by American, British, and German artists of World War II and by the artists who covered the Vietnam War in the 1960s and 70s.

We learn from novels, memoirs, poetry, movies, and journalism that men can transcend, *in a group*, their alienated, isolated and estranged lives as civilians. It is not an everyday happenstance, but it is also not uncommon for soldiers to risk their lives—nay, give their lives, for their comrades. Soldiers do their duty in the vast majority of cases, do it when they know their own life is at peril. In the military, one is a part of something—something that exists as an organic unit; something with a head, hands, and legs (to employ a biological metaphor). How else can one explain the behavior of veterans at the "Wall" memorial in Washington dedicated to the Vietnam veterans? A military unit (squad, platoon, company) exists—it is a functioning entity. And it is an extraordinary thing to be a part of something that goes beyond the individual. The military group can accomplish things no individual can hope to realize. One example: read *Sole Survivor* by Lt. George Gay (Midway Publishers, 1986). Read Gay's account of his role as the pilot of a torpedo bomber during the Battle of Midway and of the speech to the pilots of Torpedo Squadron 8 given by the group's commander the night before the battle. The Japanese were not alone in the concept of sacrifice during wartime.

Only in the written word can we transmit the power of the bonding between men in the military—a bonding that transcends anything that a civilian can ever experience. The reminiscent wish of Sergeant Berry Benson, a Confederate soldier in the American Civil War, perhaps says it best:

> Who knows, but it may be given to us, after this life, to meet again in the old quarters, to play chess and draughts, to get up soon to answer the morning roll call, to fall in at the top of the drum for drill and dress parade, and again to hastily don our war gear while the monotonous patter of the long roll summons to battle? Who knows but again the old flags, ragged, and torn, snapping in the wind, may face each other and flutter, pursuing and pursued, while the cries of victory fill a summer day? And after the battle, then the slain and wounded will arise, and all will meet together under the two flags, all sound and well, and there will be talking and laughter and cheers, and all will say: Did it not seem real? Was it not as in the old days?

Ethically, it is incumbent on those who survive a war to honor those who have fallen in battle. Only through the varied forms of literature along with music and art can we call attention, over time, to our pride and reverence for those who died. Maybe in this way they live again.

The polished black marble wall in Washington, D.C., dedicated to the service men and women who gave their lives in the Vietnam War bears poignant witness to the nation's effort to honor its war dead. The nearly sixty thousand names engraved in the stone are touched with the trembling fingers of friends and relatives. Each visitor, in so doing, seeks to bridge the gap between the quick and the dead. The flowers, mementos, letters, poems, and the things they carried in battle move many to tears. Few can walk away without swallowing hard. The bronze monument is a moving sight, but the wall with its thousands of names is eloquent in what it says: "Honor the fallen."

Through the written word we are able to express, on the one hand, respect for the veterans gathered to hear and to read of events of bygone days. This respect would be to those with whom we served and, yes, to those who served against us. This theme dominates Henry V's speech on the significance of St. Crispin's Day to those who fought with him at Agincourt. On the other hand, through writing we can make known our disdain for those individuals who, employing deceit, stood aside when the call came for commitment. As Oliver Wendell Holmes said, "Invisible in war, Invincible in peace."

Finally, only through the written word can we learn about men in combat who did their duty—did it under adverse circumstances. Soldiers see little of cowardice and still less of heroism. What they do see is other men going beyond fear and behaving responsibly under stress. The fear doesn't end, but it is somehow manageable. Soldiers today do their duty not so much for country, freedom or flag, but to get along with their fellow soldiers. Doing your duty means pulling your own weight, doing what is right, taking your turn—on a combat patrol, for instance. You don't goldbrick when a time of peril arises. You don't buck for a section 8 overseas. You do your duty and you do it to get along.

Of all the veterans I contacted, only two simply could not or would not consent to be interviewed. The vast majority want to tell their families what the war was like for them. Frequently we hear somebody say, "Oh, he never talks about the war—he doesn't like to talk about it." But ultimately, given the right circumstance, veterans will. In some ways the exercise of the interview enables the veteran to relive the old days—to almost, just for a moment, be nineteen again—a slender boy in khaki uniform, bell-bottoms or green fatigues. The interview permitted these veterans to relive those bygone days, to go back to a time when life was just beginning and to places where it almost ended on occasion. What a paradox to be a young serviceman.[3]

A French philosopher, poet and fighter pilot killed in World War II wrote the following: "It is the savor of bread broken with comrades that makes us accept the values of war" (Saint-Exupéry).

What cannot be answered in this introduction is who these men were on an individual basis that fought in the war, where they came from, how they conducted themselves during the war, and what happened to them after the war. Only the thirty stories that comprise the text of this book can answer these questions. There each individual comments on his life prior to military service, the rigors of basic training, what the *life-changing experience* of war was like for him, and finally what he did after the war.

What *can* be done here is to suggest some of the exacting questions raised time and again about war by both professional and amateur historians and then hint at the inexact answers that may be revealed in a thoughtful reading of the text. It is, after all, the questions that demand the most reflection as they constitute the condition for the answers. What then are these essential questions of the world of warfare? Perhaps a review of some literature can give us some guidance.

Why do men fight?

Explaining behavior is central to this question and the usual responses of social theorists focus on either the social or psychological basis of behavior. To date, most explanations of why men fight have been made in terms of two aspects of the social "reasons why"—namely, for cause or comrade. There is little doubt that cause (or ideology if you prefer) and comrade probably constitute the mentality of the vast majority of the veterans who served in World War II. And this includes the veterans of C–WT as their voices appear in the pages of this book. However, the reader will see in some of the stories narrated here dimensions of the psychological and, yes, perhaps even the biological aspects of behavior. These facets of the "reasons why" men fight have often been ignored by historians and are only recently being recognized by some as significant. Since the social facets of why men fight are by far the most influential, these will be discussed first with the psychological and biological factors later in this section.

Oliver Wendell Holmes, Jr., in his memoir *Touched by Fire*, reflects in his letters and diary the mentality of men in the Civil War who fought for cause when he says, "But if it is true that we [the Union Forces] represent civilization ... we may be sure it will stand a better chance in its proper province—peace—than in war.... I am, to be sure, heartily tired and half worn out body and mind by this life, but I believe I am as ready as ever to do my duty."[4] Holmes served for three years as an officer of infantry and was seriously wounded three times. In 1862, the same year he wrote the words above reflecting the North's cause, he also wrote, "I see for the first time the Regiment going to battle while I remain behind, a feeling worse than the anxiety of danger I assure you. Weak as I was I couldn't restrain my tears."[5] Here Holmes passionately states the other end of the cause-comrade spectrum. He had been seriously wounded just a few days prior to the regiment's departure and he wished to be with his comrades.

It is instructive to think about this question as one reads these stories of World War II veterans. Why did they fight? Was there any difference in the minds of Civil War and World War II veterans regarding this all important question? If there was a difference, which way does the serviceman "tilt"—cause or comrade, ideology or social relationship?

Gerald Linderman in his book *The World Within War* writes about the appeals of battle—of spectacle, danger, and destruction as alluring features of conflict. Linderman draws on J. Glenn Gray's book *The Warriors* in discussing these "secret attractions of war."

Lt. George Gay, the only survivor of Torpedo Squadron Eight at the Battle of Midway in June of 1942, surely the turning point of the Pacific war, was shot down and watched this great battle while floating, wounded, in a life belt in the middle of the ocean. "I noticed that the Zeros [Japanese fighter planes] had stopped strafing me and I wondered why.... Then I saw why the Zeros had left me. Our dive bombers were coming down. There is no way I can describe what a beautiful sight that was.... They were magnificent and I did not see a single splash indicating a miss. They laid those bombs right where they belonged and caused the most devastating damage possible.... It was unbelievable, but I was seeing it ... three Jap carriers wiped out."[6]

In James Jones' *The Thin Red Line*, Sgt. Welsh comments on combat on Guadalcanal when he says to his company clerks, "'You don't know how to appreciate nothin'.... It was really a beautiful world he thought.... The truth was, he liked all this shit. He liked being shot at, liked being frightened, liked lying in holes scared to death and digging his fingernails into the ground, liked shooting at strangers and seeing them fall apart."[7]

The sights of war are a once in a lifetime episode where beauty, danger, camaraderie, destruction and the sheer spectacle of war combine to overwhelm men. Consider this setting: a clear warm night on a Pacific island with surf rolling in the distance, palm trees waving in the gentle breeze, the ceaseless breeze, and overhead bright stars and a luminous full moon beaming above. Then the wail of the air-raid siren, the sight of enemy bombers moving slowly through the sky, the searchlights slashing across the sky (some catching the enemy planes in their grasping glow), the sound of bombs dropping some distance off, but getting ever closer as the planes traverse the night sky—and all this shared with a buddy in a slit trench. Then the swoosh and the crash of bombs hitting very close—the earth shaking and men being tossed about like rag dolls in the shelter—sand everywhere, hands gripping the ground, ears deafened by the noise. All this in just a few minutes. How can one internalize all the sights, sounds, sensations, smells and feelings. The event occurs in a few minutes. The scene lasts in the mind for fifty-five years.[8]

All this plus the biological basis of behavior associated with concepts such as aggression and territoriality. Aggression is intentional injury to person or damage to property. Aggression is seen by many psychologists as an innate human characteristic. Such behavior is patently present in Sgt. Welsh. Territoriality suggests a love of country. Evidence of this may be seen in the struggle between Palestinians and Israelis over Jerusalem. And can anyone doubt the passionate love of the Japanese people for their island homeland? What human and property havoc would have been wrought had the invasion of the home islands occurred as planned in October of 1945. There would have been millions of casualties on both sides.

How do men cope with battle?

James Jones in his book *World War II*, published in 1975, writes about the evolution of a green recruit to a seasoned veteran. Jones was himself a member of the 25th Infantry Division. He fought in Guadalcanal, was wounded there shortly after his unit went in the line, and returned to it later for a short time. He writes, "Every combat soldier, if he follows far enough along the path that began with his induction, must, I think, be led inexorably to that awareness. He must make a special compact with himself or with Fate that he is lost. Only then can he function as he ought to function, under fire. He knows and accepts beforehand that he's dead, although he may be walking around for a while ... consciously or unconsciously we accepted the fact that we couldn't survive."[9]

Jones says that not all men can accept this at first, but they can and will accept it as their units keep going and staying longer at the front.[10] And there are men who like to live in this manner. There are true warriors who just keep fighting, wounded or not, and you will read about them in this book. Some have labeled the ability to cope as a kind of "numbness." Others have found a way to cope with battle by looking at war as a job—to just do one's duty and finish the job at hand.

In *The World Within War,* Gerald F. Linderman says, "In contending with their initial experience of battle, soldiers grasped, or gravitated to, a diversity of methods for coping"[11]: knowledge of the battlefield, intuition, numbing-coarsening, fatalism, and "the concept of the job." Get the job done—that's the way to get home. All these and more created the condition for coping with battle. Readers will see every one of these mentalities in the stories to come.

There is an excitement in being under enemy fire. At times battle scenes may even be beautiful, and there is a special brightness to days, normal days, that follow some dreadful nights. But some men simply cannot cope, and they sometimes become "section 8s"—candidates for a medical discharge. Trying and failing to cope is one thing. Not to try is quite another in the eyes of veterans. And this subject too will be found in the stories at hand.

What are the ethics, if any, of war?

Perhaps everything is relative when it comes to war. Consider the case of Germany in World War II. How can a nation of 90 percent baptized Christians, a nation that produced a Luther, Bach, Kant and Goethe, blindly follow Hitler; permit the horrors of Auschwitz, Sobibor and Dachau; participate in the Lebensborn program of racial breeding; and murder over a hundred American prisoners at Malmédy? How can they do such terrible deeds? Religion is a powerful force in human life, but it could not stand up to Naziism for the majority of Germans.

Gaven Daws in his book *Prisoners of the Japanese* reports on the behavior of the Japanese Army that took one hundred and forty thousand prisoners after Pearl Harbor. Twenty-five percent of these prisoners died at the hands of their captors. The Japanese denied the prisoners medical treatment, starved them, looted relief shipments and sacrificed prisoners in medical experiments. They stood passively by as tens of thousands died of beriberi, pellagra, scurvy, malaria, dysentery and cholera. The ones that survived were then worked to death. Had the war gone on for another year none would have survived.[12] And at this writing the Japanese still refuse to take responsibility for their atrocities. Finally, the conduct of the Japanese military at Nanking, China, shocked the world: two hundred and fifty thousand civilian casualties—the so-called "Rape of Nanking."

Is there any code of conduct, any ideology, that can stand as a barrier to and limit such behavior? Such does not seem to be the case. Some have argued that the U.S. atomic bombing of Japan was wrong. These people say it was unnecessary, that Japan was prepared to surrender anyway. They argue that the U.S. should have given warning, waited and perhaps used the available weapons in demonstration bombings to convince the Japanese leadership that a new and terrible weapon was ready for use against them. Ethics concerns itself not only with what is right and wrong, but also how one goes about achieving one's goals. Ends are important, but means are of equal import in the area of ethics.

World War II has been called the "Good War" by many historians. They contend that if there ever was a just war in history, the Allies' struggle against Germany, Japan and Italy in the war of 1939–45 meets the criteria set out by St. Thomas Aquinas (1225–1274). He set out three conditions of a just war: just authority—war can only be declared by the sovereign; just cause—the war must be defensive only; just intentions—there must be good motivation behind the war and never, never revenge.

What is the nature of the relationships of men in combat?

Saving Private Ryan, Steven Spielberg's 1999 Oscar winning movie, is a stunning film because it sheds light on what war is really like for the common soldier, bears witness to the daily life of the American infantryman, and gives testimony to the fact that soldiers (and servicemen of all branches) do their duty to get along with the other men in their immediate group—but more than that, they are internally related to their follow comrades in uniform.

Consider the case of E. B. Sledge, who dedicated his book *With the Old Breed* as follows: "In memory of Capt. Andrew A. Haldane, beloved company commander of K/3/5, and to the Old Breed." (The foregoing refers to Company K, 3rd Battalion, 5th Marine Regiment, 1st Marine Division; the Old Breed refers to the Leathernecks, the Old Timers—the Old Breed of regulars who regarded the service as home and war as an occupation. They then transmitted this mentality to the new Marine recruits who served in World War II). Captain Haldane "led Company K through most of the fight for Peleliu. On 12 October 1944, three days before the Marines came off the line, he died in action. The Marines of Company K and the rest of the division who knew him, suffered no greater loss during the entire war."[13] What more could one say about a comrade than that said here by Sledge.

There is no more important question than what we as individuals think constitutes human nature and psychology. Without a conception of what it means to be a human being one can say little about mankind and society. It is clear from Sledge's comments regarding his company commander that he considers human beings as something more than a package of genes existing for no special purpose. Sledge sees the spark of the divine in Haldane and his relationship with him is not mere friendship—it is more. Perhaps more than even family.

In my interviews with these veterans I have heard them say as much. Perhaps this very special relationship can be revealed only in war where men endure hardships and angst unknowable to those who have had no such experience.

This special relationship occurs also in the ranks of the enemy. In *All Quiet on the Western Front,* by Erich Maria Remarque, the central character, Paul Baumer, and his close friend Stanislaus Katczinski (Kat) have weathered almost four years in the trench warfare of World War I. As the book draws to a close, Kat is seriously wounded and Remarque (a German soldier in that war who was wounded five times) writes about Baumer carrying Kat back to a medical aid station suffering from a leg wound. Upon arrival at the medical center Kat is found to be dead from a tiny head wound suffered on the way back. Baumer is crushed. "When Kat is taken away I will not have one friend left.... [A medic asks Baumer if he is related to Kat].... No, we are not related.... All is as usual. Only the Militiaman Stanislaus Katczinsky has died. Then I know nothing more."[14]

Perhaps one more example is needed to make the case. In January of 1944, Ernie Pyle wrote what many believe was his best column ever, "Soldiers Made Shadows as They Walked." In the column Pyle tells about the reactions of soldiers to the death of their company commander, Captain Henry T. Waskow, during the Italian Campaign. Waskow was in his middle twenties and his body was brought down the mountain on a mule train at night and then simply laid on the ground in the shadows of a stone wall alongside the road. Pyle stood close by and noted what each soldier said and did when he saw his dead leader. One looked down and said, "God damn it," and then walked away. Another spoke directly to him as if he was alive and said, "I'm sorry, old man." Another squatted down, took the captain's hand and just sat there for five minutes holding the dead hand. Finally, he put it down, "reached down and gently straightened the points of the captain's shirt collar ... then he got up and walked away."[15] Men in combat ofttimes transcend self-interest, and this willingness to forgo simply caring about oneself generates behavior such as Pyle notes.

Are combatants so hardened that they are immune to feelings?

The war in the Pacific was a savage affair and fifty-five years of peace between the U.S. and Japan have done little to soften the images of that conflict—images founded on Pearl Harbor, the Bataan Death March, blood-soaked island fighting, the suicidal resistance of Japanese troops, the kamikaze planes, the atomic bombing of Japan and the treatment of prisoners. John Dower's book *War Without Mercy: Race and Power in the Pacific War* holds that while Naziism had a strong racial dimension, the struggle in the Pacific against Japan was whipped by racism on both sides.[16] Dower argues that racism was fiercer in the Pacific than in Europe and as a result there was a callousness on both sides that resulted in savage behavior on both sides— particularly the barbarous treatment of prisoners and really the unwilling-ness to take prisoners. American racism denigrated the Japanese. Japanese racism stressed their purity and superiority. Americans saw Japanese as buck-toothed, pint-sized monkeys while the Japanese saw themselves as almost a different species of human being destined to lead the world to a new higher civilization. As such, soldiers on both sides were insensible to normal feel-ings of compassion and sensibility. No quarter was given by either side to the other.

Fighting the Germans involved more restraint—there was some adher-ence to rules and accepted patterns of behavior, particularly toward surren-der and prisoners. The Germans on the Western Front made some acknowledgment of aidmen in their work to save the wounded. American medics in Europe "carried neither pistols nor rifles." This was not the case in the Pacific war. There were some exceptions to the "rules of war" in Europe and these involved snipers and SS soldiers. These enemy soldiers were often shot on sight. Prisoners were killed by both sides, but the savagery of the war in Europe never approached that in the Pacific.[17]

Cruelty and injustice seem to be necessary conditions of warfare. The vast majority of men under fire by the enemy are scared. They are living moment to moment in combat and their level of anxiety and fear is always present, always high. As such their view of the enemy is benumbed by these feelings and they care nothing about the enemy being killed—on land or water or in the air. One can watch Japanese planes shot down and be totally indifferent to the fate of the stricken crews. In fact many would cheer with glee as they saw tracers smash into enemy bombers. "Look at this, look at this," we would holler to the guys in the shelter as a Japanese plane burst into flames and crashed.[18]

The five issues briefly discussed herein are surely not the only questions associated with men involved in combat, but they certainly constitute some of the great issues of warfare for those whose world is for the moment the world of war.

It is my hope that this book will be an educational resource. It is simply an addition to the thousands of history books on World War II. However, truth can best be revealed by the personal thought, memory and action this work features.

Notes

1. Becker, Carl, and Thobaben, Robert, *Common Warfare: Parallel Memoirs of Two World War II GIs in the Pacific*, Jefferson, N.C.: McFarland, 1992, pp. ix, x.

2. Sledge, E. B., *With the Old Breed*, New York: Oxford University Press, 1981, p. 52.

3. Thobaben, Robert G., "Documenting the Army Experience," *Army Magazine*, April 1995, pp. 14–18.

4. Holmes, Oliver Wendell, Jr., *Civil War Letters and Diary*, edited by Marle de Wolfe Howe, Press, Cambridge, Mass.: Harvard University, 1946, p. 80.

5. Ibid.

6. Gay, George G., *Sole Survivor*, Midway Publishers, 1986, p. 125–126.

7. Jones, James, *The Thin Red Line*, New York: Scribner's, 1962, p. 357.

8. Becker and Thobaben, *Common Warfare*, pp. 138, 143, 144.

9. Jones, James, *World War II*, New York: Grosset & Dunlap Publishers, 1975, p. 54

10. Ibid.

11. Linderman, Gerald F., *The World Within War*, New York: Free Press, p. 48.

12. Daws, Gavan, *Prisoners of the Japanese*, New York: William Morrow, N.Y., 1994, pp. 17–29.

13. Sledge, *With the Old Breed*, p. 38.

14. Remarque, Erich M., *All Quiet on the Western Front*, New York: Heritage Press, 1969, pp. 218–219.

15. Pyle, Ernie, "Soldiers Made Shadows as They Walked," *Dayton Daily News*, April 18, 1945, p. 34.

16. Dower, John, *War Without Mercy: Race and Power in the Pacific War*, New York: Pantheon Books, 1986, p. 24.

17. Linderman, *The World Within War*, pp. 90–141.

18. Becker and Thobaben, *Common Warfare*, p. 148.

Part I

The Pacific Theater of Operations

Military Timeline

1941

December 7	Japan launches a surprise attack on Pearl Harbor
December 8	The United States declares war on Japan
December 11	The United States declares war on Germany and Italy
December 25	Hong Kong falls to Japanese Troops

1942

January 2	Japanese forces occupy Manila: MacArthur retreats to Bataan
February 15	Singapore falls to Japan
April 9	American forces on Bataan surrender
April 18	U.S. B-25 airplanes bomb Tokyo (led by Col. Doolittle)
May 4–8	Battle of the Coral Sea
May 6	Gen. Wainwright surrenders U.S. forces on Corregidor to Japan
June 3–6	Battle of Midway—U.S. Navy wins a major victory over Japan
August 7	U.S. Marines land on Guadalcanal and a six month battle begins

1943

February 7	Japanese troops evacuate Guadalcanal
March 2–4	Japanese naval forces lose the Battle of the Bismarck Sea
May 11	U.S. forces land on the Aleutian island of Attu
November 20	U.S. Marines invade Tarawa while Army troops invade Makin Island in the Gilbert Islands

1944

February 2–7	U.S. Army and Marines invade Kwajalein and Roi-Namur in the Marshall Islands
April 22	MacArthur's troops land at Hollandia
June 15	American forces invade Saipan in the Mariana Islands
June 19	First Battle of the Philippine Sea (the Great Mariana Turkey Shoot)
July 21–23	Marines and infantry land on Guam and Tinian (Mariana Islands)
August 10	American forces secure all Mariana Islands

September 15   American forces invade Peleliu (Marines) and Anguar
                (Army) in the Palau Islands
October 20   U.S. forces land in Leyte in the central Philippines
October 23–26   The Battle of Leyte Gulf

1945

January 9   American forces land on Luzon, Philippines
February 19   U.S. Marines invade Iwo Jima
April 1   American forces invade Okinawa
April 12   (Franklin D. Roosevelt dies and Harry Truman becomes
                President)
June 21   Victory over the Japanese on Okinawa
July 4   MacArthur announces the liberation of the Philippines
August 6, 9   The U.S. drops atomic bombs on Hiroshima and Nagasaki
August 14   Japan surrenders unconditionally (Hirohito remains as
                Emperor)
September 2   Surrender signed on board the USS *Missouri* in Tokyo Bay

Jack Hobday

Albert J. "Jack" Hobday graduated from high school in Cincinnati, Ohio, in 1935 and completed one year of study at the University of Cincinnati prior to his entrance into the Army Air Corps. He and his wife, Ginny, have three children, Rodney, Susan and Deborah, nine grandchildren and five great-grandchildren. Jack is a member of the Pearl Harbor Survivors Association and the VFW. After the war he worked for Wagner Electric in St. Louis for eight years, Krogers in Cincinnati for ten years, and the Defense Electronics Supply Center (DESC) in Dayton, Ohio, for eighteen years. He served four years and nine months in the Air Corps—one year of which was in the Pacific Theater as a navigator on a B-17 bomber.

Where you were born and raised, Jack?

My home was in Cincinnati, Ohio, and I graduated from high school in 1935. And as you remember, that was about the height of the Great Depression, and jobs just weren't available. But, I managed to get a job. I found a job at Wright Field, a civil service job in Dayton. And I got a job as a draftsman, engineering draftsman, and I did electrical work on military airplanes.

Often I had to go out and measure up on the flight line, and I got to meet some of the pilots out there, the air corps pilots. We got pretty familiar with them.

Well, the thing in Europe, the war, was going on and everybody knew we were eventually going to get into the war. So I got to thinking, I wonder if I can get into the Air Corps. The pilots told me about the flying cadet program. And that was the program that if you had a year of college, which I already had, and could pass the physical examination, I'd be eligible to go into the flying cadet corps. So I did that, and I left home on February the 12th, 1941, which is my birthday, for pilot training. And my first station was Sikeston, Missouri, for primary flight time.

I finished forty-six hours of flying, and I wasn't progressing fast enough to suit the instructors—I wasn't a real good pilot I don't think. So I washed out of that. And they suggested with my background that I could go to navigation school and be a navigator. So I was sent to Maxwell Field in Alabama to await a class starting in Coral Gables, Florida. I think we arrived in Florida around May of 1941. Now there was a Pan American school of navigation in Coral Gables, Florida. We had old navigators from Pan American flights teaching us celestial navigation. And our actual training was in some of the old clippers out over the ocean. We took star shots and everything. We had to get three star fixes all the time. Very accurate. So I finished up in November and we all graduated in November of 1941. Besides navigation we had weather training, and we had aircraft maintenance and stuff like that.

After a short leave at home a lot of us were assigned to report to the 7th bomb group in Salt Lake City. I remember it was around Thanksgiving time when we arrived there in '41. Well, when we arrived there they were equipped with B-18 airplanes. But they were getting brand new B-17 airplanes which are bigger and more powerful. And the rumor was that we were going to go overseas—leave for overseas to the Philippines. Well, that turned out to be quite true. I was assigned to a crew in a brand new airplane, and we left Salt Lake City around the first of December for a shakedown. This is the first flight I ever had in a B-17. We had ten people on board—four officers and six enlisted men. The pilot and co-pilot were the officers, and the navigator and the bombardier were officers. Gunners and the radio operator and a flight engineer were all enlisted. Ten people. Occasionally, we would carry a photographer which would be the eleventh man. Of course we were well armed— we had gunners all over the place. We had side gunners and tail gunners and upper turret gunners, lower turret gunners. We had plenty of guns on board. Well, anyhow we started out from Salt Lake City, and this was gonna be a long tiring flight what with the fuel consumption, and all that kind of stuff. So we flew south to Las Vegas and over the Hoover Dam which was new at that time. And then we turned east and went over into Texas. Then we turned and went west out of there and we finally ended up at Hamilton Field in California. That's near San Francisco on Oakland Bay. There were a few little things that had to be done, oh, maybe change the spark plugs, something like that.

Well, on the sixth of December 1941, they had a big meeting out there and all the bigwigs were out there. General Arnold was there, he was chief of the Air Corps. And we were given maps. Of course I was still a cadet at that time. I was still a cadet, I'd finished my schooling, but to be an officer you had to be on active duty for six months. That was the rule back then. And after six months, if you did all right, you were given a commission as a second lieutenant. Well, we were still cadets then.

So, we spent all that day charting; they gave us a whole bunch of maps. And I had charts that I never knew—South China Sea, Borneo and the Indonesian Islands. I had no idea where we were going. But anyway, our first stop was going to be at Hickam Field on Hawaii. So we were up all day preparing and getting our charts all in order.

So, we left about 8:45 or 9:45 in the evening. We had twelve planes, but we didn't fly formation or anything. We just took off at five minute intervals. Everybody on their own. We're told not to radio, we're supposed to keep radio silence on the way over. And we did. It was a beautiful night, a perfect night for flying. We had an undercast below, so we couldn't see the water, but it was very calm. All the stars were out. Beautiful. So, we had no problem at all. And everything was working swell. We'd take a shot [of the stars] about every hour, hour and a half, and every fix showed us right on course. So, about midway I got pretty busy. We had to figure out if we had enough gasoline to get over there, and if not, then we would turn around and come back. That's the point of no return, they call that, and I and the pilot had to get together on that. He had the fuel consumption, and I had the position and knew exactly how far we had to go. So, about that time he came down to my compartment and we decided, yes, everything's ok, we're going on. And everything was working great. About daybreak we could pick up, a little before daybreak actually, one little radio program—hula music going on. We could just picture these hula girls over there that we were going to see, and all that stuff, you know. And the radio direction finder pointed right ahead. So, a little after dawn, I guess it was, we could see the islands in the distance. We saw the mountains and everything.

We were going about one hundred and eighty miles an hour. Of course we had throttled way back for fuel conservation. The plane could go faster if you wanted to, but you use a lot of fuel that way. But anyway, we saw on the horizon all this fire and thought, "What's going on there?" So, our radio operator, Sgt. LaLancet who had been in Hawaii before, he was an older guy said, "Oh, nothing to worry about, on Sunday mornings they have target practice, the navy gets out there and starts shooting at targets, and all that kind of stuff. That's what they're doing." So we went in. I thought, well, they're celebrating we're coming in, they're going to give us a big arrival celebration. Well, that wasn't what was happening. As we approached Diamond Head which was right on the edge of Hawaii, the pilot started calling the tower, Hickam Tower, requesting landing instructions. And there was no answer, no answer, he kept calling, but no answer, no answer. Finally, we looked down and we're flying right over Pearl Harbor and we could see all the damage down there. The ships were burning and there were still airplanes flying around and shooting going on down there you know. Finally, they broke in and said, "We're under attack, land at your first convenience." So, we had to pass up the main runway because that was all littered with burning airplanes. So, we went around and we landed on a short runway heading into Pearl Harbor. Well, we were going awful fast, about one hundred and fifty mph, when we hit the ground.

We should have landed going towards the north. But that was all littered. So, we went around, and we came out here and landed on this short runway. And we got to the end of the runway and we're still going over one hundred miles an hour, so the pilot's just jamming on the brakes, particularly the left brake, and it just blew the tire out and ground-looped the plane and we got stopped that way. And as soon as we got on the ground we all jumped out of the airplane. This was about 8:15 I think. It was right at the end of the first raid. The raid began at 7:55 and they had done a lot of damage. All these ships were burning as we went over. And we could see, well, we didn't know which was which but we could see all the ships burning. They [the Japanese] are still bombing and strafing us. In fact, they chased a couple of airplanes that were on our tail coming in to land.

We didn't have any ammunition. We had guns aboard, but in order to lighten the airplane for our long flight we dropped off all our ammunition at Hamilton Field which we could have well used there. But we jumped out of the airplane and everybody ran in different directions. And it's a good thing we did because the Japanese planes came down strafing then. And we were just lucky nobody got hit. I hid under a thorn bush which wasn't any cover at all. I got scratched on my face and I was bleeding I think. Later on a nurse, when we got towards the hospital said, "Are you wounded?" I said, "No, no, I just scratched my face, or something." But, we saw the second attack. I was still out by the airplane when the second wave come over and they bombed again. That was about 8:30, I would think. We were on the ground, and I saw these level bombers coming over and they bombed the barracks and the mess hall at Hickam Field. It's just like they raised the whole thing up and then just dropped it. So anyway, after it was all over, we were still out in the field. I don't remember much about getting fed or anything, or getting any

rest, because we'd been up all day
the day before and all that night
and we were tired out. I'm sure
we got some rest and some food,
but I don't remember that.

But I do remember a ground
crew coming out and we dropped
the bomb bay tanks. Instead of
bombs in the bomb bay we had
carried extra fuel in there—in the
tanks. And they dropped those
out, put bombs in, loaded us up
with bombs, and that afternoon
they sent us out on a mission to
see if we could find where the
Japanese were. And we flew again
that afternoon with bombs.
Well, we went out, we were out
maybe about four or five hours,
I think. We came in about 11:00
p.m., and of course, everything
was blacked out. We had a
different pilot that night, but this
guy was familiar with the area. I
didn't know where the field was
or anything, all I knew was
where the island was. So, I got to
the island and the pilot said,

Jack Hobday

"Well, I know where the field is." They put on the runway lights for maybe
ten seconds at a time so we could line up the airplane to land. Then everything went out. Here we were landing blind, landing blind, I was scared to
death. The Japanese were all long gone. Anyway, we got to sleep that night
out in the field. We had to sleep out on the field, and they had cots and mos-
quito bars for us and everything.

But, I was still in cadet blues. A blue uniform. So, the next morning
they came to me and says, "If I were you, I'd go over to quartermaster and
get you some khaki clothes because I think the Japanese wear blue uniforms."
So I got out of my khakis, or rather my cadet blues, and got into khakis
then.

But then we stayed around Hawaii for about six or eight weeks, I guess,
and finally, we left in February of '42. We were on alert there. We would go
on search missions all the time because there was a fear that the Japanese were

coming to invade. So we would fly and we would be on duty every other day. We would fly one day, and the second day we would just stand alert in case something came up. On the off day we were able to go into town, go to the beach, and all that kind of stuff. So, we had a pretty good life over there. We flew missions quite a bit out of Hickam Field.

And then we finally got orders to continue our trip. We were still on our way to the Philippines at that time. The Philippines were in pretty bad shape so we weren't going there. They detoured us down to Australia, and we left on February 10, I think it was, to our first stop which was Christmas Island which was directly south of Honolulu. And that's a small island, about three miles long, a beautiful island. We had no trouble finding it, and we stayed there overnight. And the next day we went to Canton Island which was even smaller than Christmas Island—a miserable place. Oh god, it was terrible. I remember we slept in tents there, of course, no lights or anything and they fed us. They had a mess hall there, but by then we were so tired we just collapsed. I knew there was something crawling around, so I had a flashlight and there was these land crabs crawling all over the place and rats crawling all over. Oh, man. I was just so tired it didn't bother me. So, the next morning we finally got out of there. It was my birthday. We crossed the international dateline on my birthday, about eleven o'clock, so I had a little ceremony when we went over the dateline. I said, "My birthday's over, I only had half a birthday." I was twenty-five. Yes, I was born in 1917.

Our next stop was Fiji. Beautiful place. Two big islands and a whole bunch of small little islets, and they had plantations, pineapple plantations and banana plantations and stuff. We stayed there for about three or four days and the natives were very friendly. They'd bring us in pineapples from the field and trade for a cigarette. Give them a cigarette and they'd bring you a whole sack full of pineapples right out of the field. And from there we went to New Caledonia—island of New Caledonia—which was a miserable place. We didn't like that. And then finally we got into Brisbane, Australia.

But our flight from California to Hawaii was our longest flight. That was over two thousand nautical miles. We had about, oh, another hour of flying from the time we got there. We weren't briefed on any alternate airports, and I thought that was kind of funny, because they're always pretty careful about that, you know, if you can't get into one, your primary, you go to another one. The only one I knew about was at Hilo, Hawaii, which is on another island, and I knew we didn't have enough gas to get there, so we had to land at Hickam Field.

But anyway, back to my story. We got over to Brisbane, and we stayed there a couple days and then we headed north. We went up to Townsville which was going to be our main base of operation in Australia which is up the coast from Brisbane.

What group were you assigned to now?

They formed the 435th Reconnaissance Squadron in Australia. The symbol is a kangaroo with a spy glass and a bomb. We carried bombs as well as cameras. We took pictures. This picture was shortly after the Coral Sea battle because I had my mustache then. That's when I raised my mustache, during the Coral Sea Battle in May of '42. That's supposed to be the first naval battle where neither fleet saw the other fleet, it was all aircraft and aircraft reconnaissance.

This photograph is of our group that was over in Australia. Here's Carmichael who was our group commander. And here is General Kenney who was a general in charge of the air force over there. These are all our crews and this appeared in the *Cincinnati Inquirer* sometime in '42. My mother cut that out for me. Now, here's a picture of my crew in the day room in Townsville, Australia. That's our entire crew there. We were in shorts. They gave us some shorts over there. There's Bob Thacker the pilot, John Geer was the co-pilot, and Tex, I forget his name, he was our flight engineer, a good, good flight engineer. That's Sergeant Buck, a side gunner, Sorenson, this guy I met recently down in Texas. He was a non-com. Here's our little tail gunner, Zeke Zens, little guy. This is Sergeant Hoehn, he was our photographer on board. Later on, on one of our later missions, he got wounded very badly and he was in the hospital. When he recovered in Australia they sent him back to the States. He wanted to be a pilot, so he went to pilot school. They sent him to pilot school. And he crashed his plane and was killed—on Galveston Island. Nice guy.

What happened next to you and your crew?

Well, we would fly mainly reconnaissance missions out of Port Moresby on New Guinea. We were, as I said, based at Townsville, Australia. But we would sometimes go a week at a time and stay overnight in Port Moresby on New Guinea which is another five hundred or six hundred miles closer. And early the next morning we would take off and fly a reconnaissance mission.

Now, our main goal was to monitor these little islands, New Britain and New Ireland, where the big Japanese naval bases were. Rabaul was a huge naval base, way up there on the tip of New Britain. We would often fly up there. Kavieng was another naval base on the top of New Ireland, over here. We would take off from Port Moresby and usually go up by Lae and Salamaua on the north coast of New Guinea. The Japanese usually had ground troops there. They didn't have too much naval power there, but they had ground troops there and air force. We would go there and bomb once in a while. Then we'd go out and go to Kavieng just to see the different ships that were coming in, or how many ships they had and so on. Then we'd go down through the Solomon Islands and come back. Those were long missions. We would fly maybe fourteen hours a day on those trips. The Japanese had very good anti-aircraft fire at Rabaul. They had navy anti-aircraft fire, so we had to fly at a high altitude there. Rabaul was also a beautiful harbor bay. So, we went over there rarely—mainly on reconnaissance missions. Once in a while we would get jumped by Zero fighters at Rabaul particularly and also at Lae. They had a bunch of Zeros at Lae, and we'd run into those and we'd have dog fights with them. Luckily, we got hit only once in a while. Here's a picture that shows a hole, a cannon hole, in the tail assembly of our plane. And when those things hit, they explode and the poor tail gunner who was in the compartment there got splattered with shrapnel. And he was wounded pretty badly on that flight.

This is our pilot Tex Simmons; he's passed away now. This guy was a RAF sergeant, Australian sergeant. They were running out of pilots and the Australians wanted to give us some help. He was a fine sergeant and they were good pilots too. Here I am. I got a jacket on there. This is Tex our, well I can't remember his name, flight engineer. Zeke Zens, he was our gunner, and here's another bombardier, a different bombardier this time. We'd come back with a lot of bullet holes—several times we'd get wounded people. We did mostly reconnaissance, not too much bombing, but when we had a chance we did bombing.

On one of our missions we took off and one engine, I think it was the number three engine, which was the one on the inside, on the right hand side, was acting up. It wasn't running right so rather than go on to complete our mission we came back to get it repaired. Well, we landed and our main mechanic said, "Well, it needs a complete engine replacement." They didn't have the facilities to do that in New Guinea, so we decided we'd just take the prop off, take off on three engines and fly back to Australia, six hundred miles on three engines, which was no big problem, and have it repaired there.

Well, we started down the runway, and I could see a truck barreling alongside us, going down there fast as we were going, and he turned and got right in our way at the end of the runway, and he stopped, he wanted to watch us go right over. Well, we didn't go over, we hit him, and that was the result. We crashed the airplane there. Again, we were awful lucky. Nobody got hurt except the co-pilot, he jammed his thumb on the throttle, trying to shut the throttle down, and he was the only casualty. Now, whether this guy was Australian or not, he was in a two and a half ton truck—a big two by six. I don't know what ever happened to him. He may be still running, I don't know.

What happened then after this crash?

Well, we flew a few more missions and I think it was in November when we started hearing of rotation. They were going to replace our crews with other crews, and the guys that had the most flying time, the most missions were the first to go. I was on the second group, I had a bunch of missions. I flew fifty-seven missions over there, and I was about the second highest navigator, so I was on the second group to come back.

But they wouldn't let us fly our planes back, they sent a B-24, a converted C-87, I think it was. So they brought us back to Hawaii. When we landed in Hawaii, all of a sudden, we were given an airplane, a B-17, and we were supposed to fly that back to the States. Well, I thought that was kind of silly because that was the longest leg, and the most dangerous leg. But we did—we flew it back and landed. I think it was around my wife's birthday, November 13th. I remember I called her and told her I was back in the States. I'd be home, but we had to go to the Pentagon first to be debriefed, but then I'd be home.

So, I went home in late November I guess. And then we were married. See, we were engaged when I was overseas and she arranged it with the priest and everything to get a hurry-up marriage. He was sort of reluctant, a little bit, because it was another wartime marriage, but we'd been engaged for two years. So we were married the day after Christmas of '42. Then I spent the rest of the time, rest of the war, instructing navigators all over Texas. I know every base in Texas except San Antonio. Never did get there. Kansas, we were in Kansas, and in Galveston. We had some nice bases. Galveston was nice but Dalhart wasn't so nice and Tyote, nobody ever heard of Tyote, Texas, down in the middle of Texas. The main thing that we stressed was that these cadets or these young pilots and navigators were just like we were, I guess, when we got out. We were the best; nobody could hurt us. And you had to get rid of that cockiness a little bit, because you get shot down if you get too cocky. They had to learn to maintain good formation. They were gonna go to Europe and they had to teach them that they had to fly very close formation, so they have all that fire power to concentrate on the enemy. I did that till the war ended.

My wife traveled around with me. We had some experiences. Living conditions weren't very good. We had to rent a room, maybe, once in awhile. Hotels—we stayed in a lot of hotels. But, we had a lot of fun—we had a good time.

When you heard about the atom bomb, what did you think?

Oh boy, that was great. See, I was always afraid I was going to be assigned to a B-29 and bomb over there. I had enough of that bombing stuff. I didn't want to do that anymore.

Yes. I was tickled I'll tell you. When Roosevelt died that was one of the worst days of my life. Because, I thought, "Oh my god, this guy Harry Truman doesn't know what the hell he's doing. He'll mess that up, and we'll be in a war for another three years." He turned out to be a great president. My last station was Colorado Springs which was a nice station. General Doolittle was there; actually he was the commanding officer out there. I'd see him everyday up there. Then they sent me to Camp Atterbury in Indiana for discharge. Came through there, and they explained the GI Bill of Rights, and all that stuff, you know.

I made up my mind. I talked to an old boss in Cincinnati I'd kept in contact with. He was an electrical contractor and I worked there off and on before I went to Wright Field. And I told him I wanted to go back to school and get my degree. He said, "Well, if you need any help, you know, working or anything, I'll have a job for you." I went to the University of Cincinnati. Co-oped. That was the hardest four years of my life. Boy, I'm telling you. I was thirty-two years old when I graduated.

What's this last photograph you have?

That's in Townsville, Australia. That day General MacArthur landed there. He was on his way to New Guinea, I think, and they were changing a tire or something on his airplane. So he stood there about an hour and a half, or two hours, and just posed with his corncob pipe and his bamboo walking stick.

The G.I. Bill was great. They supplied everything—all the books and all the tuition and everything, and I graduated. But it was rough. We were married, we were buying a house, we had a baby, and ninety dollars a month, you know but it went pretty far back in those days although it didn't go quite far enough. I was working hard too.

Could you comment on how World War II may have changed your life?

Oh, yes. I tell you what my mother always said, because she remembered the first world war. Her brothers, "Went to war as boys and came back as men." Well, that's what happened to me. And I matured awful fast, and I guess I wasn't afraid of anything after that. If you live through a depression, the Great Depression, and live through World War II, there's not much else can happen. And of course we had the worst of everything, but we survived and we did real well. I wouldn't have missed that for the world. It did me a lot of good. And luckily, I survived. A lot of poor guys didn't. That was a great experience. I enjoy talking about it too.

Al Allen

Ulys S. Allen, better known as Al Allen, is married and has four children. He was in the Navy throughout World War II serving a total of seven years, four months and nine days. Of that time, he spent six years overseas and only one year and four months in the States. He is an active member of the VFW in Centerville and a member of the Pearl Harbor Survivors. He was born in Pulaski , Virginia, moved to Bluefield, West Virginia, and went to Beaver High School there. After graduation he worked at a gas station earning $10.00 a week. Allen decided he was getting nowhere and his father agreed to sign the papers for him to enlist in the Navy. He was nineteen at this time.

What did you do in basic training?

Well , I went through training at Norfolk Training Station—recruit training. And then after that I went to class A electrical school which was four months long. This is in 1939. We did close order drill and march, march, march, and fired weapons. But we fired, I think, only five rounds. They couldn't afford it. See, that was back when they were running short of money. But we fired five rounds on the rifle range, and I didn't hit anything. We were using a thirty-ought-six, and I'm left handed. So, I couldn't work with that arrangement—it's a bolt action rifle. You had to put it on the right shoulder otherwise you'd break your nose. So, I did no good on the rifle range. And then we did guard duty. We did not have KP in recruit training.

Then I went to a preliminary electrical school, basic theory and a little practical work, preparing us for a job in the electrical department rather than going as a seaman up on topside just pushing a mop. Or what they called a swab. Then I was taken, as just a passenger, on the USS *Nashville*, a light cruiser. We shipped out of Norfolk down to Guantanamo Bay, Cuba. And from there we went through the Panama canal, and up the west coast to San Pedro Harbor where I was transferred to the *New Mexico*. She was a battle-ship in Division 3. Well, when I started out I was a striker, or a helper, in the electrical department because if you go to electrical school you're sure of getting to go in the division you want.

I'd been there about two or three weeks and there were only three mess cooks in the division, and one of them got into trouble and got put in the brig, so I had to fill in his shoes. So I was a mess cook for six months. Now in those days a mess cook would carry the food. We were on the second deck, about amidships, and the galley was on the boat deck level which is two decks up and about one hundred feet aft. We'd carry the food down and we had mess tables down there. They did not stand in line with trays.

And I remember one incident bringing the mess gear. You'd have twenty-four plates, twenty-four bowls, twenty-four cups in racks, I was carrying all three at one time like a knothead. Fell down a ladder right on top of all that. Broke all but about two or three of the items. That was something.

Well, that was about the time they took us down across the equator to allow this rear admiral, who was chief of staff or our commandant, to say he crossed the equator. Then we were going out on maneuvers and back. You go out during the week and come in over the weekend.

Then in, I think it was in about December of '39, they sent us to Bremerton Navy Yard for a three month overhaul. It was up near Seattle. And in three months we did not see the sun. Rain, rain, rain. From there they sent me to San Diego to sound motion picture technician school. I was there six weeks (1940) and then came back. The *New Mexico* was out by then, so I went out on a transport and got back aboard ship in Pearl Harbor, on Oahu in the Hawaiian Islands. Now the *New Mexico* was in what would be called the middle lock of battleship row. Battleship row was down the line along side Ford Island where the naval air station was.

Well, I was in heavy power which took in all the cranes, boat cranes, power steering gear, the anchor windlass, and also all the turrets. The *New Mexico* had around two thousand people. It had four acres of deck space all combined. Now, of course, that's in several decks. And it displaced thirty-five thousand tons. It carried four mounts, triple mounts, fourteen inch, fifty-five caliber in length. That was the main battery. Then it had, I think, it was eight or ten broadside, eight inch, fifty-fives. Then it had five or eight anti-aircraft guns. Then they had machine guns. We usually figured about ten percent of those on the ship were officers.

Well, this is 1940, the war hasn't started yet. What were you doing during this year?

Well, I was working in heavy power equipment, and they wanted people for mine warfare school. Well, I thought I'd like to go back and see what it's like. So I applied and, lo and behold, they selected me. Sent me back to the mainland and on to Yorktown, Virginia. And I was in the first class of the warfare school in Yorktown. We were there about four months and then they sent us back to the ship we came from. I would have gone back to the *New Mexico*. Now this would have been about May '41.

In the meantime the *New Mexico*, the *Idaho*, and the *Mississippi* were transferred to the east coast for some reason. So I got out to Pearl Harbor on Oahu, and they sent me to the *California* which was the commander of battleships at the time. And it was a nice ship, good crew. They said, "Why not stay here." So, I asked for permission to stay and I got to. Why send me all the way to the east coast again? Anyway, that's the way it all started. I worked in the interior communications crew. We had telephones, a public address system, an engine order telegraph, all of the various communication equipment.

Did you ever have any leaves?

Oh, you'd get ashore about one day in four. Oh, yes. I'd go in quite often. It's much different from now. Actually, I remember one little incident. We were going in by bus, crossing what was a canal going through Honolulu and there was a little kid there, looked about six years old. He had a hammerhead shark, holding it by its eye sockets, and it was taller than he was. He dragged it up out of the canal. And I remember going out to Waikiki, seeing these ladies take the diapers off little year old babies, and let them go out and swim in the surf. They were babies and they were swimming! Went to the Sheraton Moana—used to go out on Sunday afternoon when they had *Hawaii Calls* and broadcast it back to the mainland, and they had such beautiful music in the Banyan Court. This was out at the Moana in the Banyan Court out on the seaward side of the Moana. Beautiful place. You could hear the surf and everything. I remember that very well.

It's 1941, did they take any special precautions or anything on the ship ?

We had armed guards circulating day and night throughout the ship, just as if they expected someone to sneak aboard. But still, we were not really alerted the way we should have been.

On December 7, 1941, I'd just finished breakfast. I was down in the IC room getting ready [the interior communications room] because we were going ashore. But we didn't get ashore. I was about half dressed when they sounded general quarters. We said, "Another Sunday drill." Anyway in about thirty seconds they said, "Stand by for torpedo hit." Maybe it was two minutes. I don't know. And so it sure banged in. That hall rang like a bell. We were hit right away—maybe five after eight. Something like that. See, when you're excited time has no meaning. I was right down at my battle station. That's where I kept most of my clothing—about twenty feet below the water line. The torpedo hit in the main radio room which was the next compartment over. And the bulkhead was split and water was spurting through, but not too bad. So we made a tent out of wiping rags to keep the saltwater from hitting the switchboard, because it was drawing fire every time the saltwater would hit it, it would fire and flash up.

Did you have any idea who was attacking you?

They did not say anything about that. In fact, I did not hear anything about the Japanese attack until, oh, it must have been thirty minutes later. I don't know. We stayed aboard for probably another hour at least and we secured all of the switches and so forth on the IC [interior communications] switchboard. It was as big as the size of the room there, because if water gets in there it starts electrolysis and eats up the brass, so we thought it might be a good idea to disconnect them because they weren't being used. Then we began to evacuate the ship. We went about two-thirds of the way up the fore-mast—right up the conning tube. That would be right up the mast. And then we had to come back down to the main deck to get off. And we were wait-ing—we were gonna wait for a power boat to take us to shore. But they said, "Get in the water, get out of here." So, I jumped in.

There was a lot of oil, and the oil was deep on the water. In some areas there was fire but it hadn't gotten to us yet. The ship then began to list badly, but we had a very fine damage control officer who planned all of this stuff—anchoring it around the pier so it would just settle down.

Now the *California* was here and the *Oklahoma* was behind us. Then behind them was the *Arizona*—the one that blew up. The *Oklahoma* capsized because they were unable to get it settled straight down, and they lost a number of men. The *California* went down slowly. In fact, we kept it afloat for a few days. But we could not get any way to get repaired. So they decided to let it settle down without turning over and then come back and pump it out and repair it later.

How many torpedo and bomb hits did the California take?

I don't know for sure, but I heard three torpedoes hit us and one five hundred pound bomb. We were like sitting ducks. We left the ship between nine or ten in the morning—I don't know exactly. I saw lots of enemy planes. That was the end of the whole shooting match. There was five Japanese planes going back over Aiea Heights which would be back down at the end of bat-tleship row. And there was one that was knocked down up at Hospital Point near the harbor entrance. That was the only one I saw that got knocked out.

Pearl Harbor was black with oil. All the water was coated with oil and there were fires breaking out all over. The oil was catching fire. And of course you get in there and the fire gets to you and you can't breathe anymore. Anyway, I dog paddled, I'm not a swimmer, I dog paddled over to Ford Island and got over there and I was so pooped out I couldn't get out of the water. Laying there half in and half out of the water. But I finally I got out.

Then after about a couple or so hours we started stripping all the good equipment we could off the ship. We got out all of the food that was in the ice machines, you know, frozen food. And I helped carry the battleship payroll ashore. There was four sea bags full of money. I was told it was four million dollars. I have no idea. I carried one of the sea bags. After that they transferred all of the excess personnel to the receiving station for reassignment.

They had my orders written up for me to go to the USS *Chicago*, a cruiser. And I asked about the mine depot. "Oh, are you mine warfare?" They tore up the orders, wrote me some new ones and sent me to the ammunition depot. Well, the strange thing about that was that in the first battle of the Solomon Islands, the *Chicago* was damaged severely. And in the second battle it was sunk. So, I missed it again.

Later I was assigned to a shore base at the West Lock of Pearl Harbor. We'd go out on a campaign and then come back. That's the reason I got in some of those islands in the South Pacific. Well, there were four campaigns, and I think the first one I was involved in was the battle of the Solomons. And we were there with a mine detachment. We had three hundred magnetic mines, each one containing one ton of torpex which is about forty percent more powerful than TNT. We hid those in forty acres of coconut trees.

This is the Asiatic-Pacific Theater ribbon and medal. There were four campaigns I was involved in. First was the Solomon Island Campaign in the southwest Pacific. Guadalcanal is a part of the Solo-

Al Allen

mons. And the next one was in the Marianas campaign which is about mid-Pacific. And that was where they had the Marianas "turkey shoot" (Saipan and Tinian and Guam where the Japanese lost almost four hundred airplanes). I was aboard ship there. The third one was, well let's see, Iwo Jima—yes. They needed Iwo Jima for a landing base for the B-29s. That was a bad one—the marines took the worst beating there than in any other place in the war. And it was a crime. But that was the only way they could get it. And the last one was Okinawa.

What are these other two medals?

The Purple Heart—that's from Okinawa. Well, by that time my battle station was in the engineer repair group. My room was two decks up. I had giant hives, and the chief engineer, my boss, said, "You might as well sleep in if we have another attack or another alert." I just couldn't do anything. Less than two minutes from the time I left my bunk it disappeared. Explosion. I was just sitting down in the engineer's log room. I had just gotten into the engineer's log room. The place where I normally sat was over near the entrance. There was someone else there so I went on back to the end of the log room and sat on a high stool. It wasn't one minute, I don't think, and there was a loud explosion—everything was total darkness, total quiet. And I thought, "I must be alive because my foot hurts and so does my head." So I jumped down off this stool. I must still have part of my foot 'cause I could stand up. I know it's weird, but you get weird ideas. Two days or so before this happened I put a flashlight in a basket behind me. I reached around and got it just as if it happened thirty seconds ago. Shined the light around the room, and here's a man with half his head gone, and that's where I would have been normally sitting. And another man, his legs were all battered up.

So, I got hit in the foot. Shrapnel in the foot. See, that's what hit us, it was a kamikaze [suicide pilot]. We lost seventy ships damaged or sunk in a matter of about three weeks at Okinawa. But they were using young very poorly trained pilots. They just come in and dive on you. That's it.

This is the emblem that goes onto my grave marker. It's the one that's provided by the VA, and there's a little ring at the top and that goes into it. Pearl Harbor survivor is what it amounts to. And let's see over here, I think that's American Theater. This yellow one, I can't remember—maybe American Defense (that was prior to the war). And the one on the end is American Theater. That includes the two battle stars there, one is for Pearl Harbor and the other is the battle of Midway. We were not up at Midway, but we were nearby. This ribbon was authorized by the Congress of the United States for Pearl Harbor survivors. They were issued to us up at Columbus at the VA center in November.

After being wounded they evacuated us to a hospital ship because all of our medical department was killed. All the pharmacists mates, the doctors, everyone. But later in the day they got a doctor aboard so they brought us all back; we were called the walking wounded, and we went ahead with our regular duties. Then we headed back. We had a twin screws ship, but one of them was knocked out. One engine room was completely knocked out, so we could only do twelve knots coming back from Okinawa to Pearl Harbor. But we were happy. We were going home. Then we went back to Kaiser yard there in Richmond [California]. Then from there up to Mare Island. We were there about two months.

I was in the Navy for seven years, four month, nine days, and when the war was over they were going to pay us for our terminal leave and I started calculating, I had roughly six years out of the continental limits of the United States during that time. Now, of course, it wasn't all right in the battle zone. In fact, we crossed the date line, I think, seven times.

We were in Mare Island getting ready to get under way to go back to the forward area when the atomic bomb was dropped. We were so excited, we said, "Well we won't have to go back." Well, we did. And we had to stay there repairing. See we were then a repair ship, and we were repairing mine sweepers, and so forth, keeping them going because we had twelve thousand mines around the Japanese homelands.

This at one time was classified. They were called influence mines. You've heard of the magnetic mine. We had the acoustic mine. That's where the noise of the ships props and engines would fire it. And then we had one called the pressure mine. The pressure of the ship going over it on the water would actuate it. So some of these have triple firing mechanisms. And it was called Operation Starvation. But they had twelve thousand of these mines around the Japanese homelands, and anything over six hundred tons could not go through. It would sink it. And they were about starved.

Where were you when the surrender was signed on the battleship Missouri?

We were under way from Mare Island navy yard heading back to the forward area. We got there about two and a half weeks later. We were providing small craft with fresh water. We could make 50,000 gallons a day out of salt water. We were also providing them with fuel, and they'd even come aboard and get cokes. We even had a coke machine there. We had two units. That was part of my crew that did that. And we had ice cream. They'd come, some of those guys would come, aboard from those LSTs and they hadn't seen ice cream or a coke in ages. They just thought they were in heaven.

At the time I had dual status—I was a chief mine man, and I was an ensign. Had to revert back to chief before I could get discharged and had to wait for my orders from the bureau of naval personnel. So I got that about the first of January 1946. I was discharged in San Diego, January 21st, 1946. My wife was in Long Beach, California. So I'd go down to San Diego, and I'd spend a half a day, then come back. I wasn't in no hurry now. I dragged it out about four or five days. Then we went back to West Virginia, but only for a short stay. Then we came to Dayton, Ohio. Been in this area ever since.

Looking back on your long service, how did World War II change your life?

First of all, it gave me a trade. I had nothing when I went in the Navy. It gave me self confidence. And I guess that's about it primarily. I belong to the Pearl Harbor Survivors Association, Chapter 7, which is located on Wilmington Pike at the VFW up there. We have about thirty-five now, but we're losing them fast. We have at least one to two funerals every three months. There were forty-some originally, and they're down to about thirty-five. In fact, most of them are Army.

Don Barrett

Donald D. Barrett enlisted in the United States Marine Corps on January 7, 1942, thirty days after the attack on Pearl Harbor. He participated in three campaigns in the Pacific against the Japanese—Guadalcanal, Cape Gloucester, and Peleliu, where he was wounded. He was discharged from the Marines in June of 1946. Barrett graduated from Catonsville, Maryland, high school, earned a Bachelor of Science degree from the University of Baltimore and an MBA degree from the University of Dayton. After the war he was involved in different sales jobs and spent twenty-eight years with Frigidaire. Later he began his own consulting business—Don Barrett Associates. He and his wife, Eleanor, who was also in the Marines in World War II, have six children—three living in Texas, two in the Dayton area, and one in Virginia. During his service with the Marines, Barrett was with the 1st Marine Division—1st Platoon, A Company, 7th Regiment.

Why did you join the Marine Corps?

Action. Looking for some excitement. Combat. Thrill of defending my country. It just seemed like the right thing for me to do. It was January of '42, thirty days after Pearl Harbor, and I was in the Corps. I enlisted in Baltimore and was sent to Parris Island to go through boot camp. At that time they were so anxious to train men that the training program was condensed. I believe it was thirty-seven days that we were in boot camp from the time we arrived in Parris Island until we were shipped out to our first station and duty. The day began about four o'clock in the morning and I was so tired at night I forgot what time we quit. It was just sheer exhaustion. Go, go, go all the time. Things moved so fast in boot camp that you hardly had time to remember many incidents, but I will not forget my experiences on the rifle range. When we went out to the rifle range you had to learn to fire a Springfield '03 rifle in all the different positions from kneeling to sitting. And for some reason my left foot wouldn't bend properly to suit my rifle instructor. So he got provoked one day and took the bolt out of my rifle, threw it as far as he could, and made me crawl down there, pick it up in my teeth, bring it back and put it into my rifle. It was so covered with sand that I had to kick the bolt open and closed every time I wanted to fire. He stood over me and he jumped on my back. It was recruit abuse if there ever was any. I came so close to killing a man right then that I swore that if the day ever came that I crossed swords with him again I would get my revenge. Ironically, it happened on Guadalcanal the day I landed there. We were in a loading party and he was not a sergeant now but a private. He was doing something on the beach when an air raid sounded and the Japs came in and bombed and strafed us. That bastard got killed or I would have finished him off. This happened right in front of my eyes. This was my first taste of combat, my first day on Guadalcanal.

I was not in the original invasion of Guadalcanal. We came in a little later. My first night on Guadalcanal I was assigned a submachine gun. I'd never fired a submachine gun, or a light machine gun in my life. The sergeant whose platoon I was assigned to said, "Get down in that hole and if anything happens just squeeze the trigger." Well, the foxhole had about two feet of water in it. It was one of the most miserable nights I'd ever spent in my life, and of course nothing happened that night. The next day I was assigned to a squad and from then on it was patrol, action, patrol, action. This would have been in November of '42.

Where were you on Guadalcanal?

Well, we were near Henderson Field, on Bloody Ridge, and then we were sent up to Kola Point to meet the Japs when the first raider battalion drove into us. The raider battalion met them out there and wiped them out. We had no combat, but we were on the Koli River—the Gima [Malimbu] River at Koli Point. And we were told that the river was twenty feet deep and as the Japs came across the river all we had to do was shoot them. I'd contracted malaria, but unless your temperature was over 102 you stayed on the front lines. So one afternoon when it got slow I slipped into the river to cool off, and I found out that it's three to four feet deep. So I reported this and said that, "If the Japs come across that river it's not going to be a case of shooting ducks. They're gonna come across mad, and running, and fighting." Fortunately, the raiders intercepted them, wiped them out, and we went back. Again I came down with malaria and this time yellow jaundice, and I was so sick that I was a dishrag. I was sent to the hospital and on the morning of New Year's Eve I was evacuated from Guadalcanal, with malaria and yellow jaundice, to a naval mobile hospital on [the] New Hebrides.

Guadalcanal was the beginning of the road back. There were so many stories we were told about the Japanese army as being the true imperial army — that they were supposed to be invincible. There was no question that they were fanatics. Their love of country was so intense that they would rather die than dishonor themselves or their family or their country. I've seen Japs come charging into us getting as close as twenty-five feet away full knowing that they were going to meet their maker. This was a different type of person that you were in combat against, unlike [in] the European Theater. This was just a fanatical, rabid enemy. I think the other important thing, and history bears it out, is that we generally knew what was going on while the private in the ranks of the Japanese army had no idea, no idea. They were completely left in the dark about everything. They didn't know where they were or what they were doing. All they knew was the marines were out there and if they got you they were going to kill you. One of the stories that we picked up from a Jap that was captured was that in order to be in the Marine Corps you had to either kill your mother or your father. Another one that they took prisoner said that he was told that every man in the Marine Corps had been taken out of prison for a major crime and put into the Marine Corps. So the Japs really didn't like us and didn't have a whole lot of respect for the Marines, but after they learned what we could do they did fear us.

Here's a photo taken in Melbourne, Australia, after I'd completed commando school. I had regained fifty pounds from the time I was evacuated from Guadalcanal until the time I finished commando school with the Aussies. Actually, I went from Guadalcanal to the New Hebrides aboard the hospital ship [USS] *Solace*. Then I went on a naval mobile hospital in Auckland, to a naval mobile hospital in Wellington, and then they commandeered a navy transport going to Sydney, Australia. We ended up in an army camp two and a half days later aboard the train from Sydney to Melbourne, Australia.

I rejoined my outfit the day before they began a heavy training schedule, but I had whipped malaria and gotten over the yellow jaundice by then and was almost human. I was with the 1st Marine Division, A Company, 1st Battalion, 7th Regiment. At this time I was a PFC. I went overseas as a rifleman. On Guadalcanal I was a rifle grenadier—carried an apron full of grenades and a three pound metal trumpet that I attached to my Springfield '03 rifle. Ironically, we trained with M-1 rifles, the Garand rifle, in boot camp and carried it all the way to my first station of duty at the naval ammunition depot in Hingham, Massachusetts. When we got to Camp Elliott in California, we turned in our M-1s and drew 03 rifles that were left over from World War I. I carried a Springfield bolt-action rifle all through the Guadalcanal campaign.

The rifle grenade was a thing that looked like a trumpet—it was an extension that fit over the muzzle of the rifle, and the grenade was about, oh, about the size of a hand grenade, but it was smooth bored and had a hole through the center of it. And you would drop that down into the trumpet and then fire, supposedly a wooden bullet, and the compressed gas behind it would propel the grenade out into enemy territory. It had a range of, oh, maybe one hundred and fifty yards max. The only problem was it was all World War I equipment. There were no wooden bullets and so you had to use a live bullet to project the grenade and you were never sure if they were gonna explode. We only used it once on the Canal. We never had the opportunity where it was called for. But I carried it for weeks on Guadalcanal.

I was not involved in close combat on Guadalcanal. In the other campaigns it was very close. By the time I got to Guadalcanal the serious fighting was over, it was mostly mopping up operations. But when I rejoined my unit in Australia, we began heavy training schedules. We'd spend a day marching out into the boondocks, in Melbourne, Australia, probably twenty to twenty-five miles away, spend eight days running around playing soldier and then march back. We then had a half a day to do our laundry, stand inspection, and then answer pay call. And we were given fifteen pounds, which was equivalent to about fifty dollars in Australia, and sixty hours lib-

Don Barrett.

erty. So for the next sixty hours you lived it up to the max. And then back to base. The next morning another twenty, twenty-five, mile march out into the boondocks, you were so wrung out, hung over, it was sheer torture. But then after running around in the woods for eight days you got all the booze out of your system and you were ready to go again. Back into town for another sixty hours' liberty. Well, that went on for so long and the Marines would just so dissipate themselves that the old man said, "The only way we're going to make this outfit combat ready is to get them out of Australia." Eighty-two percent of the First Marine Division had malaria and the guys would just dissipate themselves and come down with it. So they moved us from Melbourne, Australia, to Ora Bay, New Guinea.

The Japs met us there. The [U.S.] Army had been ensconced there. The day we arrived the Japs bombed the place. The soldiers had built rectangular mess halls and they would sit in there at night playing cards, writing letters, and so forth—perfect targets for a bomber. And the first night they really killed a lot of men. And of course, the Army doesn't like us because they were living a pretty good life until the damn Marines came in and the Japs came. We spent several months in New Guinea training, preparing for combat and doing some minor patrols. There were very few Japs left there. And then on the morning of Christmas day '43 we landed on Cape Gloucester—or December 26, I think it was. This was on New Britain. This was a relatively easy landing. The beach bombardment had driven the Japs inland. The worst part of it was climbing over the torn up beachhead, the mangrove swamps, and everything else. We landed there really without incident. I got strafed there, in fact, my squad was strafed.

We went ashore there in Higgins boats. The Higgins boat was the first landing craft developed by Higgins down in New Orleans. It was made out of plywood, would run right up on the beach, and then drop the ramp down, and you scurried off and out into combat. Lost one man in my squad. If you want to see what a 50-caliber machine gun's bullet will do to a man's foot, he got hit with one and it just smashed his foot—terrible damage to it. I got a little shrapnel in there. We ran into some Japs and they threw a grenade at us. I cowered somewhat to get away from it, but it exploded and I got it in the side of the arm and the face. But it was like getting hit with a handful of sand. You never knew about their grenades. I've seen a grenade land between a man's legs and blow both his legs off, and I've had them land within a few feet of me and do no damage at all.

On Cape Gloucester we hit there in the rainy season. The first twenty-seven days we were there it rained every day—we never saw the sun. Your clothes were soaking wet all the time, your shoes would rot on your feet—it was that bad. We had driven the Japs back. Cape Gloucester incidentally was the largest beachhead taken in the history of war by one division. Our beachhead was twenty-seven miles long. But this was after the fighting was over.

We had known the Japs were out there and early in January they had asked for a patrol to go out and seek them out, and that's where this incident happened. The patrol consisted of Sergeant Dexkrow, he was our gunny sergeant, and he was in charge of the patrol. The rest of us were all privates or PFCs. Here's a picture of the men on the patrol. That's me on the end. We were sent out to patrol and ran into a Jap camp and for some reason there was no one there. So we rifled the camp, stole everything that we thought could be of value—maps, compasses, drawing instruments, all kinds of documents that we thought intelligence might want. While we were in the process of doing this the Japs came back, and we had to fight our way out of there. Couldn't go back the way we came so we went through a swamp. As we were going through the swamp some P-38s were patrolling the area and saw us, and thinking we were Japs they strafed us. Fortunately, none of us were hit. We got back and we were showing this information to intelligence when a photographer from AP who was there said, "You guys get together and we'll take a picture." So we did. The next morning the Japs came up Target Hill. They started at two o'clock in the morning and the battle lasted 'til two o'clock the next afternoon. They got within twenty-five feet of our front lines. Sergeant Dexkrow caught a hand grenade in the middle of his lap and it killed him instantly. The rest of us survived that. Several days later, I think it was January 6, Dick Saylor and I moved up Hill 660. The Jap snipers had us pinned down and Dick came running up to me and he said, "D.D., I see 'em, I see 'em." I said, "Stay back behind this tree stump." But he jumped out and just as he jumped a Nip shot him and just took the top of his eye off. Blinded him in one eye and he was discharged from the Marine Corps. Ike, Ivan T. Smith, was like a professional soldier. Lots of times in combat Ike's machine gun squad was attached to my squad and there were any number of times that I would find him out in front of me carrying a light machine gun across his arm with a belt of ammunition. In this particular instance, Ike had enlisted in the Marine Corps and turned over his produce business to his wife. But she began to entertain the army troops up there, sold the business, enlisted in the WAACs and put their kids in a home. Ike swore that if he lived through the campaign and he found her, he'd kill her. Well, he lived through it, he came back with me, and I assume he went back to Flint. If he found his wife, Lord only knows what happened. Tom Shanahan, the crazy Irishman, lived through it all and went back to Pittsburgh. Quinn, I never heard from him again. He was so deathly sick with fungus and diarrhea that I'm surprised they even let him go on that patrol. And I have never heard from any of them other than Dick Saylor, and I haven't talked to him in forty years. But that was one patrol on Cape

Gloucester. Ironically, just a few days after that picture was taken I was assistant squad leader of the first squad and when we went into combat I led the attack. I was the point. The morning that we went up Hill 660 I was voted the squad leader of the 3rd squad and all of a sudden we were put in reserve. So instead of leading the attack the other two platoons go out on the platoon front. The Japs, in this particular case, waited until we got twenty-five or thirty feet from them. They were in a pillbox so concealed we couldn't see them. Then they opened fire and wounded or killed most of the marines—shooting them in the knees and the legs. The guys were just laying there. Had one little kid by the name of Kenton that was laying there screaming—I can still hear him. And they threw a land mine out and blew a hole in his chest, and he drowned in his own blood. We were finally able to get the living out of there because we got tank support. They came up with a Sherman tank. And they took that tank, put the barrel of it right down into the pillbox, and just blew them up. Well, by this time the serious fighting was over, but I had just a gut feeling that there was still some Japs in there. So I handed my Tommy gun to one of my men, took a grenade off my belt and pulled the pin, and went up along side of that tank. And as I peered over the side of the tank a Jap officer raised up from behind the tank and aimed his revolver at me and fired. And in the three or four inches of space between my head and the tank this slug whis-

PFC Don D. Barrett (far right) and five other members of a Marine patrol on Target Hill, New Britain.

tled by. It scared the living daylights out of me. I could just feel that bullet smashing into my face. And I thought, "God, what a way to die." I threw the grenade and turned around and ran. And I got maybe fifteen or twenty feet away and my squad behind me all began to cheer. I'm so mad, that here I'm about to be killed and these guys don't even shoot the Jap, they're just watching the whole show. Well, that grenade had caught in his tunic. His jacket was open and it just went right down in there, and before he could get it out it exploded. And when the guys saw that, "Oh, this is wonderful," they said. "Yeah, D.D., you did a great job. It was a good toss, good toss."

So after the Cape Gloucester campaign we went back to Pavuvu in the Russell Islands which was a coconut plantation turned into a Marine base. The island was so small it was unbelievably incredible to try and hold maneuvers there, especially when you're walking through the next companies' tents. We had tents after we solved the mud problem. It was so rainy and so muddy that we had to dig coral, make struts out of coral between the coconut groves and then bring in coral to use as the base for your tent. But we spent several weeks there, and this was when we found out what the Red Cross was like. They sent in several Red Cross nurses aids, women, whatever they were and, of course, this meant that now you had to wear clothes all the time. It was just a different life to suddenly find females on an island where it had been strictly male. We spent several weeks in training there, such as it was, but a lot of maneuvers again before we went back to Guadalcanal. I returned to Guadalcanal on maneuvers and we had enough time off to get back up to Bloody Ridge where I went back to my old foxhole.

Incidentally, the reason I got yellow jaundice, I would take my shoes off at night to let my feet air. And the rats would nibble on my toes. I woke up one night and saw rats just chewing on me, and of course I wore my shoes from then on. But it was from the rats that I caught yellow jaundice that put me out of action on Guadalcanal.

So then we went into combat again and my last campaign was Peleliu; I was a squad leader by then. I had nineteen men in my squad including the flamethrower group and the demolition group. The invasion of Peleliu never should have happened. It was one of the greatest, stupidest mistakes in Marine Corps history to ever try and take that island. The truth about Peleliu has never come out yet. It was a total waste of manpower.

Why do you say that?

Because they could have bypassed Peleliu. My squad went on board in armored tanks. I was manning a fifty-caliber machine gun going ashore. I had never seen so much air force, so many naval ships in my life at one time. And I said to my squad, "This is going to be the easiest campaign yet. All we're gonna have to do is go in and bury the dead." And we started for the beach. This was in September of '44.

And about that time machine gunfire raked the side of our tank and believe me the heads went down then. And then they begin to drop mortar shells on us. They hit the tank next to us. We were the first wave of infantry going ashore and it hit that tank, and it was like putting a cherry bomb in a tin can. It exploded, it set the gasoline in the tank on fire. These poor marines were on fire—clawing, screaming, trying to get out of the flaming tank. And as we passed it by I thought, "This is not gonna be as easy as I thought." The Japs had imbedded railroad tracks in concrete pylons and we hit one of those and almost turned over. But we made it to the beach. I jumped out and hollered to my guys, "Follow me," and started inland—the last place on earth I wanted to be was on that beach. We got inland, and of course, it's a mess of tangled brush and shell holes and everything else, and found out we were on the wrong beach. Our wave commander, who had taken marines ashore on Tarawa, saw what was happening and moved the whole wave down, so we had to cross lines to get lined up to move inland. We were supposed to be at phase line O1 or OA at ten o'clock in the morning and we didn't get there until late that afternoon.

So they set up a perimeter of defense and that night the Japs hit us. Art Henry and I were kneeling side-by-side together firing back at them. They came within twenty-five feet of us and threw a grenade that landed in front of us. Art Henry was hit three times in the forehead, knocked us both down, but I never got a scratch. I can remember bandaging him, and you know how a head wound bleeds, so I took my two first-aid bandages and got them tied onto his head to stop the bleeding. We continued the fighting but I lost one of my BAR men. They dropped a hand grenade, or a mortar shell, it had to be six inches from his face. It blew half his head off, so he never knew what hit him. We stopped the attack, and then the next morning regrouped and started across the island. This happened south of the airfield. Another division had the airstrip. We were moving south toward Ngesebus Island.

We ran into the Japs and they were heavily entrenched there, and we ran into a pillbox. We had a Polish guide, a guy by the name of Janduski, and in those days in addition to the fragmentation grenades we had concussion grenades. This was a plastic grenade where you unscrewed the cap and threw it. There was a lead weight on the end, and as it went through the air, the lead weight unwound this tape, and there was a lead ball in there, and when it hit the lead ball, the detonator, it exploded. Well, Janduski took one of these grenades, unwrapped the tape, ran up to the pillbox, and using his hand, tried to force it in. The Japs saw him, and some Jap smacked it just as he pushed his hand in there. And Janduski wheeled around with his arm up and just blew his hand off completely. My platoon leader said, "Don, go get him, you've got the flamethrower." So poor old Chuck Victora, big old sheep rancher from Montana who was my flamethrower guy, and I went up there and I covered him with my Thompson submachine gun as he poured the flamethrower right into the opening. Four Japs came running out the back. There was a Jap officer, there was one with a rifle, one had a grenade, and I don't know what the fourth one was doing. But as they came towards me I picked up my Tommy gun and just walked across their chest and killed all four of them. The one with the grenade threw it and it came rolling towards us, and as I turned it exploded. I got a little burst of it in the side of the face and down the arm, and so forth. But I did get the Jap officer's revolver and carried that for the rest of the campaign. Later on in that campaign another machine gun squad that was attached to me got into trouble. And I went in and pulled them out.

We spent several more days on Peleliu. The Japs had been there for thirty years. They were entrenched in caves one hundred feet deep—all interconnecting. You seal them off and they come up the next morning behind you. It was on Peleliu that I got hit the last time and this time it put me out of action. We were on a combat patrol trying to encircle them and they dropped a mortar shell on us, and the mortar shell landed and blew a hole in my left foot. That morning I had gotten a brand new pair of shoes 'cause the coral was so bad there it would tear up your clothing and even your

Don Barrett in 2000.

leather shoes. And this mortar shell, a knee-mortar shell, went off and blew a hole in my foot with a piece of hot shrapnel. It's your foot and the blood is boiling and it's not very comfortable. And I can remember screaming to the doctor, "Get it out, doc, get it out." And he cut my shoe off, my brand new pair of boondockers, and I was so mad that he had ruined a pair of brand new shoes. But of course my combat was over then. I was able to limp back to camp and went into the sick bay. And I was laying in the sick bay there and I guess I'd been in sick bay two or three days when word came in that we were being relieved. So I went to the doctor and I said, "Would you discharge me," and he said, "I'd be happy to discharge you and get anybody off this island but there's no way that we can get you to the beach." And I said, "If you discharge me I'll find a way to the beach." So he discharged me.

Well it's probably one hundred and ten degrees on Peleliu as I started walking towards the beach, so I picked up an old stick and used it for a crutch. Pretty soon the bandage came loose, and my foot began to bleed, but I was determined that I was going to make it to the beach and get off that island. I was probably just to the edge of the beach when the last Higgins boat was going out to the ship. And I hollered at the guys and they said, "It's D.D., wait for him." Well, I started running and I got maybe fifteen, twenty feet from the beach when I collapsed. And they came out and dragged my sorry butt aboard and we went back onto the ship and off of Peleliu.

How long had you been on Peleliu?

Thirty-some days, I think. We came back to Pavuvu and the Russell Islands. Another incident happened there. While we were on Peleliu the old man, the regimental commander, called up and wanted to speak to Pete Parish who was our company commander. But Pete had gone to regimental headquarters to get some relief. Well, while he was gone the old man called and wanted to talk to him. And they said, "Well, Captain Parish isn't here, he's gone down to headquarters." He said, "Well, let me talk to the next officer in charge." "Well, we don't have any officers in charge. They're all killed or wounded." "Well, let me talk to the senior NCO, senior staff NCO." "We don't have any staff NCOs." "Well, who the hell's in charge down there?" We said, "Well, we got Corporal Barrett here." He said, "You mean to tell me that you've got a corporal that's running a company, what's left of the company?" So I got on the horn and he wanted to know where Pete Parish was. And I said "He's on his way to you to see if we can't get some relief." And he said, "That's why I want to talk to him—you're being relieved. We don't know when, but the army's gonna come in and we're going to get out of here, and I just thought you'd like to have that news." So as a corporal I was a company commander. This happened on Peleliu.

Why did you get a bronze star with a V?

With a combat V, yes. We were in action, I guess, the second or third day there and moving across the island when the Japs hit us with a machine gun. They hit one of my machine gunners, one of the squads that was attached to me. It looked as though they had taken a scalpel and laid his arm open. I've never seen a bullet wound a man like that. So I dropped my Tommy gun and told the guys to give me some covering fire while I went in and bandaged him up—Whitey, Whitey Morris. He was a big rawboned Texan. I bandaged him up and carried him out and while I was carrying him out my squad gave us some covering fire so the Japs couldn't kill us. Anyway, we got back, and I got a bronze star for that. Never seen Whitey Morris since. He survived. They tell me that when we got back somewhere out of combat he was still in the hospital, but before he left he looked all over for me. But never found me. Haven't heard from him since.

Maybe you could tell our readers what these different medals are.

These are miniatures that I used to wear when I was active in the Marine Corps League and we'd have social events. This is the bronze star with combat V. This one is the Purple Heart. It's for being wounded. Believe it or not, this one is the Marine Corps Good Conduct Medal. Presidential unit citations were not ribbons, they were just awards. This is the Asiatic-Pacific Theater. This one is the Victory Medal, and I forget what the other one was. Then of course we had our marksmanship medal with the M-1, or the '03 rifle. With the M-1 rifle I fired expert. There's my old expert marksmanship. I was a corporal.

Three thousand privates climbed aboard the *General William Mitchell* and sailed for home. And while we were en route the word got out that this would not be a very good public relations stunt, so we were all given our grades back. We got back to the west coast and went through reassignment. The sergeant that interviewed me asked me what kind of duty I wanted, and he said, "God, looking at your record you need something." I said, "Nice quiet guard company." The next morning I got my orders—report to Parris Island as a drill instructor. I could have murdered him.

After the war I came back to Baltimore, started back into college, and Eleanor and I got married. I took a job where I could go to college at night and work by day, and eleven years after I started college I got my undergraduate degree. Finally took a job with General Motors, Frigidaire Division of GM, went to work for them in Baltimore and spent twenty-eight years with Frigidaire. Ended up in Dayton. Later I went into the consulting business and did three years of consulting. By this time I was sixty-five and decided that's long enough, so I quit work and I've been able to avoid employment now for eleven years.

Bob Thobaben

Robert Thobaben graduated from Shaker Heights High School, a suburb of Cleveland, in January of 1942, six weeks after Pearl Harbor, at age 17. He attended Ohio University beginning in the fall of 1942, joined the Enlisted Reserve Corps in December of '42 and began active service on June 1, 1943. Thobaben was sent to the Pacific Theater as a member of the 111th Infantry Regiment where he participated in three campaigns—the Gilbert, Marshall, and Palau islands. He received the Combat Medic Badge and was discharged in November of 1945. Thobaben and his wife Janet have two sons and eight grandchildren. After a short time working in the oil industry, he began graduate study, earned the Ph.D. degree, and taught at Miami University, University of Cincinnati and Wright State University (for thirty years: 1964–1994).

I joined the Enlisted Reserve Corps (ERC) in December of 1942, completed my first year of college at Ohio University in Athens, Ohio, was home for one day and then was inducted into the Army. So I went into active service on June the 1st of 1943.

I actually took the oath in Cleveland. I took the streetcar downtown from my home in Shaker Heights and had kind of a crude physical. It's always sort of an undignified thing to take an Army physical—you're out there in a big room and you have to strip off all of your clothes, you're stark naked, and then they give you a physical. But you soon get over any shred of modesty. Then I got on the train at the Terminal Tower in Cleveland and rode down to Fort Hayes in Columbus.

At Fort Hayes there was really nothing to do—I learned how to salute and I got my uniform. I was there about three or four days and I saw that I was on a posting for Camp Wheeler, Georgia. And I knew what that was. That was an infantry training school—marching, shooting all the weapons and practicing military exercises. Very physical.

About ten weeks into the fourteen-week cycle, I was sitting under a pine tree, and I thought, "There must be something better than this." So I signed up for a program called ASTP, the Army Specialized Training Program, and a lot of other soldiers signed up for the test. The United States government felt that they wanted to have engineers and language experts developed during the war so that after the war we could begin the rebuilding process and so we could talk with the enemy, in this case the Germans. So I signed up for that and I passed. And there was about four or five other guys in the battalion who took this and passed.

So when our training ended at the end of the thirteenth or fourteenth week the battalion left, and everybody, except those of us who passed the test, headed out for California. We waved good-bye to them and said, "Go get 'em." Forty-eight hours later, while we were just waiting for our assignment to the college we were going to go to, the government decided they didn't need any more engineers, they didn't need any more language experts, and they just dropped a curtain on ASTP.

The next day we got new orders—a fourteen-day delay en route. I had fourteen days to get from Camp Wheeler, Georgia, to Fort Ord, California. I only stayed at Fort Ord five days and then I was sent up to San Francisco to a place called Camp Stoneman in Pittsburg, California. That's right by San Francisco, and there I joined the 111th Infantry Regiment. I joined them one evening in October of '43.

I was with them for about eighteen hours in the United States and the first thing they said was, "You're going to be in the medics." I really thought there must be some other medical procedure that I had to go through. Then I found out—I was going to be a medic. And I said, "I don't know anything about being a medic—I just finished infantry training down in Camp Wheeler." They said, "It's easy—we'll teach you on the way going over." So, that was it. The next morning we got on a ferryboat and went down to San Francisco Harbor and got on a huge troop ship called the *West Point*.

We found out through the rumor mill that we were going to Hawaii and we finally pulled into Honolulu Harbor, docked right at the Aloha Tower and disembarked. Then we marched through Honolulu to this little train. It was a narrow gauge train, and we took about an eight-mile ride on the train through the pineapple fields up to Schofield Barracks. This is on the island of Oahu in the Hawaiian Islands. It's about eight or ten miles north of Pearl Harbor—it's a big army base.

We went to Schofield Barracks and I was put into one of the quadrangles. After we were there a couple days they said, "You'll have to join one of the battalions." Now there's three battalions in a regiment and they said, "You can join any battalion that you want." So a friend and I decided to stick together. We walked in the line, completely voluntarily, of the 3rd Battalion. It was a very fateful walk because two weeks later the 3rd Battalion went out to be involved in the Gilbert and the Marshall Island campaigns while the other two battalions stayed in Hawaii for a year.

We went on a ship that was called the *Mormacport*. If you've ever seen an old Humphrey Bogart movie it always reminded me of that. It was a cargo ship, probably built to handle about thirty or forty sailors; the problem was that we had probably three or four thousand men on the *Mormacport*. Anyway, we got on the *Mormacport*, and we headed out for what was the first major assault in the central Pacific. The Pacific War in World War II was a divided command. MacArthur was the commander in the southwest Pacific but I was in the central Pacific commanded by Admiral Nimitz. These two drives were like a pincer movement and were supposed to meet up in the Philippines. In any event, we finally got out there, but it took us about two weeks because the Gilbert Islands are fifteen hundred miles southwest of Hawaii—almost right on the equator, maybe one degree north of the equator.

We weren't really in a convoy. It was just our troop ship with two destroyers as escorts. They were to protect us from Japanese submarines. The destroyers were very fast, but our ship was probably going only twelve miles an hour. The destroyers just keep slashing around going back and forth in front of us. We had no duties on the ship at all. But we had one thing happen that was kind of weird I thought. We had boxing matches going on during the trip. They would have an Army guy and a Marine, or an Army guy and a Seabee, boxing in the evening. And that struck me even at the time as rather ironic. Here we were going into a dangerous area and these two guys are up there beating each other's brains out—and they really fought hard.

Anyway, we finally got out to the Gilbert Islands after a couple weeks. We made a couple of stops in between but they weren't important—Canton and the Ellice Islands. And we laid overnight at Tarawa. The battle had just ended in Tarawa, the Marines had taken that in a very tough battle. There were five thousand Japanese on the island. They were all killed except sixteen. The Marines had over a thousand people killed and three thousand wounded. This was the main base for the Japanese in the Gilberts, Tarawa.

But there is an island about one hundred miles north of Tarawa, still part of the Gilberts, called Makin Island. That's where my unit went. We went ashore and the first thing that everybody noticed was the people—the natives. They were a very handsome people but they are living on the equator and so they don't wear very many clothes. And here we saw hundreds of women, bare-breasted women, running around. And as I say they were very handsome people. Well, we were stunned by this. We're all about nineteen or twenty or even eighteen years old.

When we got ashore we were sent to an area down near the airstrip. As soon as the island was seized, we began building an airstrip on Makin Island, or the Seabees began doing that. And it was just operational when we got there.

Our sergeant told us to dig in because we were gonna get bombed that night. The Japanese apparently came over every night and bombed. So my friend and I began to dig in and it

Bob Thobaben.

was very tough digging—roots and coral and sand, it was very tough digging. So we dug a slit trench. That's a trench about six feet long and we only dug down about six inches and then we quit. We were just lazy. And we were eating and drinking coconuts and things like that. I'd never seen those before either.

That night we were sleeping on the ground and at ten o'clock or eleven the air raid siren goes off and a couple minutes later big search lights come on, and pretty soon we could see the Japanese bombers coming in. They caught them in the searchlights. Now there's an ironic thing I want to comment on here. Here we are, we're about to get bombed and it's really rather beautiful. You're on a South Pacific island, nice warm weather, waving palm trees, a beautiful moon out, search lights on the airplanes and the tracers, machine gun tracers, about every fourth or fifth bullet with phosphorus on it lights them up. So when they're shooting at them its kind of beautiful, plus there's 90mm guns, those are anti-aircraft guns. When those go up they explode in a big flash. There was a kind of a strange beauty to this whole thing—it was kind of otherworldly. Anyway, my friend and I were sitting on our shelter, our ankles are protected, and we heard bombs landing. They were far away and didn't have any effect on us at all. And then suddenly we heard this loud SCHUSS and the bombs were dropping real close. We immediately threw ourselves into our slit trench, and right away we know we'd made a mistake 'cause it wasn't deep enough to cover anything. So we left there and jumped into a hole that two married guys had built. It was a big hole and they were down deep in it. And so we leaped in on top of them, and they told us to get out of their hole—in Army language. And we said, "No, we're staying here." But as soon as the raid was over we started digging again. Everybody did.

The next day, we were assigned to a permanent area and we started digging good bomb shelters. You dig down about three or four feet and line it with sandbags. You can't dig down very deep because of water. Then we'd line the shelters with sandbags, and finally we put coconut logs on top of it. And with this bomb shelter we were probably safe from a bomb unless it hit on top of us, and of course, if it does you're not going to be aware of that. But let me tell one more story about the worst experience I had on Makin Island.

I was on K.P., almost finished for the day, when the air-raid siren went off. As in the past, it made my hair stand on end, or a cold chill run up my back and perspiration begin to seep from my armpits down my sides. The sonorousness of the siren's wail—its whine, its oscillation from high to low pitch and back again sharpened my senses and I was instantly transformed from a lethargic kitchen-worker into an alert soldier—a soldier intent on staying alive. December 1943 on Makin Island in the Gilberts was not a great place to be. The island had just been seized from the Japs and they bombed it almost every day from their base on Mili in the Marshall Islands about one hundred and fifty miles away.

"Damn Japs," I thought. "What'll I do? Where'll I go?" It was two or three hundred yards to the shelter my tent-mates and I had built. I knew it could withstand almost anything except a direct hit; but was there time to get there? No, I decided, I'd head for a bomb shelter I'd seen while dumping the garbage and it was only about thirty yards from the mess hall. "Thirty yards is a hell of a lot closer than three hundred," I mumbled out loud as I began to run toward the bunker. The sprint over, I leaped into the narrow trench that led into the bomb shelter and found myself face to face with another soldier. We didn't know each other, but it didn't matter. He was in the hole. It was a pathetic bunker—about 10' × 10' × 3' deep, with no sandbags to hold the walls, not well covered with coconut logs—really just a damn hole in the ground with some logs thrown over it. But it was too late to change now. I knew from past experience that the Jap bombers would be on us in moments.

We waited for five, then ten minutes. "Damn it, I thought, I could-a made it to my own shelter instead of this abortion." "Looks like some-a those fat-ass cooks made the stupid thing," said my nameless shelter-mate. "It ain't worth a shit." Nevertheless, for now it was my refuge, even though it was poorly constructed, hot, and sultry.

Soon we heard the throbbing drone of the Japanese twin engine Betty Bombers. Now we could hear and see the flash and crash of the 90mm anti-aircraft guns. Bam! Bam! Bam! The sharp, repeated sounds, followed by the odor of the gunpowder with its pungent taste, immersed us—surrounded and enveloped us. Then came the familiar swoosh, thud, and crash of the bombs. "Jesus, these went right through the company area," I said aloud. "I know— I saw it too," said the other soldier. "You'all are gonna have casualties," he went on. We pressed our backs into the sand walls of the shelter—trying to become an internal part of the bunker itself. The raid went on and on. We could hear the dull thuds and explosions of bombs landing near the airstrip about a quarter mile away. The P-40 and P-39 fighter planes were up now— finally. We knew the sound of those familiar engines. The combined noise and din filled the air—it was deafening—airplane engines, fifty caliber machine guns, 90mm anti-aircraft, bombs, explosions—all blared out together in a clash of jangled discordancy.

Suddenly, I heard the familiar swoosh, swoosh, swoosh and the almost simultaneous crash, crash, crash, of a string of bombs that seemed like they were on top of us. For the moment, anxiety and fear were replaced by terror as my anonymous comrade and I were literally turned upside down, and thrown about the bunker. As some logs caved in, the sides of the shelter began crumbling and sand enveloped us both. It was in our eyes, mouth, nose, and hair. Breathing was impossible in the vacuum of those microseconds. Chaos ruled. All was featureless—man, matter, and nature became a shapeless, undefined entity. "Jesus, what's happening," I screamed. "We've been hit," moaned the anonymous soldier.

As fast as it happened it was over. Both of us lay on the ground trembling. "Those Japs damn near killed us," I said. "I really thought we were goners," said the other soldier. We lay there for what seemed like an hour, probably fifteen minutes, then the all clear sounded on the siren.

We struggled up out of the obliterated bunker, looked around at what was left and saw five bomb craters about fifteen to twenty yards from our adopted bunker. Together they looked like a giant had taken five great steps right down the beach past the ruined shelter. Each of us walked haltingly back toward his respective area. We never saw each other again. Never spoke. But for each of us, the unfolding process of what it means to be a real soldier had occurred. We had experienced a very close call—faced imminent death. Everything would be different in the future be it enemy bombings, combat patrols, an assault or an ambush.

So, we were on Makin Island for about two months and we were bombed almost every day. And as I think about Makin Island and what we did there, our job was simply to endure. This was the front line in the central Pacific. There was nothing in front of us. The next island over, which is in the Marshall Islands about one hundred and twenty-five miles away, is the Mili Atoll [and it was] controlled by the Japanese. That's where they were coming from to bomb us. We also had to endure dengue fever. Now, dengue fever is a mosquito-borne disease and when you get dengue fever you can't move. At one time we had about half of our thirteen hundred men down with dengue fever. You run a very high fever for about a week and your bones ache. And we had nothing—we gave them only aspirin. And that's what we did. We put up with the bombings and we put up with the dengue fever.

Then in February of 1944 we invaded the Marshall Islands. Now that's about one hundred and fifty or two hundred miles north of us and the assault troops there were the 7th Division. They took the main island of Kwajalein Island. I don't know if you know what an atoll is, but if you took a necklace and threw it on the floor and let those beads represent islands, that's what an atoll is. It's coral islands that are built up over time and they form a lagoon. And the Japanese had fortified one of the bigger ones that had an airstrip on it. And the 7th Division took that island.

Our job in the Marshall Islands was to take the adjoining islands and to guard the island at the South Pass called Ennylabegan. So we took about fifteen islands in the Marshall Islands atoll. Let me note that I had a diary that I kept, and essentially that's what we did in the Marshall Islands for four or five months—taking these adjoining islands. Sometimes on those islands a small group of Japs, maybe twelve or fifteen, had all killed themselves. On other islands there would be fifteen or twenty Japs manning a weather station or a radio station, and then we would usually kill them. We took a few prisoners but not very many. We were there for quite some time doing this. That really was our duty in the Marshall Islands. Kind of a mopping up. We secured the South Pass, we seized the islands, and took about twelve or fifteen islands according to my diary, and we constructed gun and shelter defense systems.

Then the campaign in the Pacific moved forward. We had taken the Gilberts, the Marshall Islands, and then the Army and the Marines took the Mariannas—Guam, Saipan and Tinian.

In August we were sent back to Hawaii. We'd been out not quite a year but the better part of a year, and we were sent back to Hawaii to a rest camp. Then our battalion was sent to the northern most Hawaiian Island called Kauai. We were based in a town called Kalaheo, near the center of the island of Kauai. And it's very rainy. Some places on Kauai they get four hundred inches of rain a year.

After a few weeks we went back to Oahu and Schofield Barracks and the regiment got ready to ship out—we were going to the Palau Islands. When you leave Hawaii going to the Palau Islands you go another five thousand miles. The distances in the Pacific Ocean are just astounding. It took us at least a couple weeks to get out there and we landed on the island of Peleliu. Peleliu was the major island for the Japanese in the Palau Islands. And the assault troops that seized that island were the 1st Marine Division and later on the 81st Infantry Division.

When we got there the assault was over, the island was secured. But the American forces only took the four southern islands: Angaur, Peleliu, Ngesebus, and Garakayo. The Japanese held all the northern islands and there was probably twenty or thirty thousand Japanese soldiers up there. So we had a lot of duties that we had to perform in the Palau Islands. I only, of course, know what my battalion was involved in. Every day we would bombard the northern islands with our

Bob Thobaben today.

cannon company. They had 155mm cannons and they would shell the northern islands. That was one activity that we did during the few months that we were on this island.

The other thing that we did that was a very important activity for us was combat patrols through the mountains. The Palau Islands are volcanic islands, very rugged, very sharp and densely forested. We ran patrols through there every single day. And a patrol amounted to usually about ten men and was led by a sergeant—and there was always an aid man along with them. As our turn would come up, the sergeant would assign one of us to go as an aid man on the patrol. On patrols you try to blend in with the rest of the soldiers. We never had a red cross on our helmet which would have been used as a target by the Japanese, because the war in the Pacific was different than the one in Europe. It was really a war without mercy. There was no quarter given by either side. As an aid man, I carried a carbine. In Europe an aid man didn't carry weapons. In the Pacific we did. We carried a carbine and just wore fatigues on the patrols. We didn't even wear a helmet, we wore a fatigue hat. The patrols would be three or four hours and we would go through the hills looking for Japanese stragglers. Sometimes we found them and there would be a firefight and sometimes we would capture one, sometimes we would kill them. I think the point I'd like to make here is that when your turn came up for the patrols you went. You would never, even if you were sick, go on sick call that day because you take your turn. Because if you didn't take your turn then somebody else had to take it. That was a major activity—doing patrols.

After I'd been there a couple months, we were sent over to the northernmost of the islands that were seized called Garakayo, and there I was running a water station, and I was the aid man for M Company, a heavy weapons company. We had a machine gun outpost on Garakayo. The reason we had that was that the Japanese would build rafts and they would drift down. You have to understand there's no way they could seize the islands back, but they could come ashore and harass and cause trouble. And if they came down then we would shoot them out of the water on these rafts. The machine gun outpost was manned by M Company, a heavy weapons company. We had fifty caliber machine guns, we had 81mm mortars, and we were on Garakayo. I was probably on that duty for about two or three months. It was very good duty.

And one day an unusual incident occurred. I even remember the day it happened—on August the 14th of 1945. Sailors used to come ashore to our island to drink beer and they'd have beer parties because they weren't allowed to drink on the ship. They had to come ashore to drink. And the sailors would always go into the jungle looking for souvenirs; they were souvenir crazy. We never did that. One day I was sitting by my tent and I saw this sailor come running out of the jungle, he's probably one hundred yards from me, and his hair was flying and his arms and legs were swinging and he's hollering, "I saw one, I saw one." Apparently he came face to face with a Japanese soldier and they both turned and ran like mad. That was an unusual sight.

But that day at lunchtime Sergeant Brady who was the head of the outpost came to me and said, "I'm going to set up an ambush for this Japanese soldier. Would you go with me tonight?" "Yes," I said. When you were asked to do something like that you really had to do it, because the most important thing to me and I think to soldiers generally, was you've got to get along with your fellow soldiers and you don't do that by goldbricking. Goldbricking is getting out of a duty, you know, anyway you can.

So that afternoon the sergeant and I went out and we looked things over. We went in the jungle, I suppose two or three hundred yards and we found what we thought was a good place. There was a number of crossing paths and things. We thought this is where we'll set up. So that night after it got dark we went into the jungle, and we set up this ambush, and we thought we had a good spot—that we could get this guy. And probably about eleven o'clock at night, we'd been there about two or three hours, I could look in the distance and I could see a Coleman lamp burning near the tent area I couldn't see the men but I could see the light. And we heard a voice holler, "The war's over, the war's over, Japan surrendered." This was a stunning thing for us. We knew about the atomic bombs because they were dropped on the 6th and the 9th of August, but the Japanese didn't surrender. And this is now the 14th of August, I'm sitting in this ambush about eleven o'clock at night, and this is the God's truth, I mean we heard the guy saying this, "The war's over."

I looked at the sergeant, he looked at me and said, "Well, let's get out of here." So we walked out of the jungle and it turned out to be true—the Japanese had surrendered on August the 14th. And that's where I was when the surrender came.

A little later we were sent down to Peleliu and they said the 3rd Battalion is going to take the surrender of the Japanese troops on an island called Koror. Now we knew about Koror and Babelthuap. They're the two biggest northern islands that we would bombard. And we were all thinking, "Why is it always the 3rd Battalion? Why don't they send some other battalion?"

So we loaded about twelve hundred or thirteen hundred of us on LCIs and we start weaving our way to this island called Koror. This was the capital of the Palau Islands. We went ashore but there wasn't a Japanese in sight. On the dock there was tons of armaments—artillery and weapons of all kinds stacked there quite neatly. We didn't know what was going to happen. This is in late August. And pretty soon from around the corner came a number of Japanese officers and their entourage, maybe a total of twenty-five soldiers.

And they marched down to us, all dressed in their military finery, and they surrendered their swords and their weapons to our officers. And it went off without an incident. We were surprised. Our officers said they must leave this island and go over to Babelthuap which was just across a causeway. There were thousands of Japanese troops, maybe twenty-five thousand on Babelthuap, and we were on Koror. But we allowed maybe two or three hundred Japanese soldiers a day to come ashore to work in the gardens they had there.

So, that's essentially what we did in the Palau Islands. The other battalions were seizing other islands. We had people who were killed and wounded doing this. I knew very little about what the 1st and 2nd battalions were doing.

At that point they began sending troops home who had the points and in late October they said, "OK, Thobaben you have enough points—you can go home." So I went down to Peleliu and the next day I got on a ship and we started home. We finally pulled into San Pedro, California, and I went to a camp called Camp Anza where they just gave us some clothing, and then I got on a train and we took what would be the old Route 66 across the southern part of Arizona and New Mexico, and so on, up to Camp Atterbury, Indiana. And I was discharged on November 28 of 1945 at Camp Atterbury, Indiana. Took the train home to Cleveland, and that was the end of my military experience.

Frank Treadway

Frank Treadway was born and raised in eastern Kentucky and later moved to Dayton, Ohio, where he worked at Frigidaire. Treadway enlisted in the Navy and spent twenty months in the Pacific. He served on the Destroyer Escort (DE-744) USS Kyne as a helmsman and attained the rank of quartermaster third class. When Treadway was discharged from the Navy he went back to Frigidaire but then moved to National Cash Register (NCR) in Dayton, Ohio, and worked there for thirty-eight years. He and his wife, Inez, have six children (three sons and three daughters) and when NCR began to downsize, Frank tried his hand at gardening to supplement his income. He did this because he and Inez thought they would have four children in college at the same time. He is an active member of the Franklin Street Baptist Church and the VFW.

When did you actually go into the military service?

I went on active duty in December of '43. I went to Green Bay for basic training. Green Bay, Wisconsin. I was there six weeks. We learned about discipline—how to salute aboard ship out in the middle of a field. And we learned how to walk your post in a military manner. Our company had one hundred and fifty men. And I hadn't been in the company of one hundred and fifty people before, and I thought, "Well, I can do whatever half of them can do, I can be among the top half." And I really enjoyed it.

We had a little bit of a problem. We had an assistant chief there that we didn't like, and we signed up a petition to get him out. And it ended up we had to stand happy hour. Happy hour is when you stand, present arms, and look at a clock for an hour. And it's not easy. This guy just cracked a whip. He wasn't even fair. And the navy told us there's a right way, and a wrong way, and a Navy way. And when you're here you do it the Navy way. But we thought, they should take another look at him and see if he was doing it our way. And they taught us to quiet down. It was kind of important. He was mean. We didn't like him. And I think they took away the smoking light for three days. The smoking lamp was put out and everybody on that list had to stand a happy hour. He was just too much discipline. We weren't used to that.

In basic training I discovered I had a lazy eye and I couldn't see to shoot right-handed, and they wouldn't let you shoot left-handed—but I passed the test anyway. After that I got a small leave and went home. Then we went to California to an outgoing unit out there, and took aptitude tests. Some people qualify for different schools, and some people feel it's better to go to sea and earn a position as a striker. A striker means you pick out a vocation aboard ship that you are interested in, and you strike for that. And that's what we did. We went to Mare Island, and they had a number of ships out there. We had an outgoing unit of thousands of sailors, but we had ships we could choose from. And me and Graham Lee Walley, we saw the 744. Now seven's my lucky number, and Walley, he's a good gambler, saw this pair of fours, he liked that one 'cause it had a pair of fours with it. So, we chose the USS *Kyne*, 744. There were a number of ships, but we got that ship. Oh, there's big surprises and a lot of good things in life. We think the *Kyne* 744 was the best ship in the navy.

After we got aboard ship we had a speech from our captain, and he said, "You should make this the best ship in the Navy. This ship is your Navy. And your division, you should make your division the best. And as for your unit, you should be the best one in your unit." And I remember he really fired us up, and we believed it, and it worked. We turned out a real crew.

What do you mean by a division?

Well, you have a communication division. That'd be where radar and signal and quartermaster are located. And then you have the engineering division, that's the engine room. And then you have deck division in charge of swabbing the deck or raising the flag or running the whaleboat. Different divisions like that. Specialty division would be welders and carpenters. I was in the sea division—communication. Later, I went on a deck force to start with, but I wanted to be a helmsman. I liked steering the ship and I was real interested in navigation—how the earth's divided up in longitude and latitude, how islands are formed, and I wanted to be a quartermaster. So I transferred to sea division.

We had thirty-eight states and eleven foreign countries represented in our crew. One hundred forty men in the ship's complement. A DE [destroyer escort] is the smallest major man-of-war. There's about a dozen officers, I guess. Every time we got in rough water they'd blame me. They'd say, "Treadway's on the wheel."

I joined my ship in San Pedro, California. She was commissioned a new ship—brand new. We did our shakedown off of San Diego. And then we went to Hawaii and had another shakedown there. We were there in Pearl Harbor, but you have to have a shakedown because you felt like you were on the edge of a big war out there. Some people just cannot take the sea, they can't take the ocean. Some people can't take the fear. So you have a shakedown to see if you can survive that and thrive on it. So we did that. Some of the men, even the officers, had to leave the ship. They had to sign them to land duty. They just couldn't take it—a DE is rough.

How long is a DE?

Now a DE is maybe about 300 feet long, it's not very long. [The World War II DE was 290 feet long with a 35-foot beam.] And they say that in rough water it's in the air half the time and below water half the time. It bobs. It's the smallest major man-of-war, but it can survive where a destroyer won't survive. [A World War II destroyer was 376 feet long with a 40-foot beam.] That's because the DE stores a lot of fuel. It can go thirty days without refueling. And you can fill those tanks with water, and it will not capsize where a destroyer would exhaust her fuel in three or four days, and being top heavy with guns, they capsize much quicker than a DE. It's built for escort duty. We escorted mainly tankers for refueling. We refueled at sea all the time, and transferred mail or personnel.

They claim seasickness is psychological like carsickness and all. But some men cannot cope, some of them just have to go to bed. Some of them can function. We had a repair crew and we were laughing about that during a shakedown. They make believe you're in a battle, you maneuver, and the water's rough, and our leader was not smiling—the officer in charge. All at once he just vomited and it turned out that he could not take the ocean. He was transferred to land duty and never did go to sea. I don't know what the percentage would be but I'd think five percent of the people cannot take rough water. Some people could take a carrier or a battleship, but cannot take a DE. You've got to master that.

When did you first take the helm?

Well it was, I guess, right out of Hawaii. I was on the helm and you alternate one hour on the wheel and one hour in aft steering. Aft steering is in the stern. They could take over mechanical control of the ship. You're connected directly to the rudder. And if all the hydraulics fail, or electric fails, say you're shot in the middle, you can steer with that rudder from the fantail. You are down under-

Frank Treadway.

neath—right over the rudder and it's direct. It's not by hydraulic or anything else, you've got physical control of the ship. So you alternated an hour on the wheel, and then you'd go an hour back there. And that's when I decided I really liked steering the ship and I like all the things you experience as a quartermaster.

You correct all the charts, and you find out about time zones, take care of the clocks, you find out how islands were formed, and that some islands are growing, some were eroding, some were volcanoes. It's fascinating. You learn to get a star fix and do dead reckoning. It's all fascinating to me. Tell where you're at, at all times. Normally, the navigation officer does the star fixes, but you would give him a count and you'd be there with him—and you had to log that. The quartermaster has to log everything that happens on a ship. You have to be aware of the barometric pressure, the cloud cover, and what have you every hour. And you know your speed all during that hour, and you gotta know the ocean current during that hour, the wind velocity, and everything in order to do dead reckoning—to try to determine where you are at the present time. And all that's involved. It's real exciting. Real education. We had a nice bunch of guys with us. Most of them were from the northeast, none of them's from eastern Kentucky, but they just took me in and we made a good crew.

In early '44 we went to the Marshall Islands. I thought we was in the arms of the Japanese and they was going to choke us. But, I don't have a sequence of all the places we went. We was at Guadalcanal, I remember. Robert Streavel, he lives in Dayton, sent me a log of where we went and when we went. It's really great. We went to Pearl Harbor, Solomon Islands, Russell Islands, and Eniwetok in the Marshalls.

Had you run into any combat yet?

The greatest fear of all my life was on the way to the Marshall Islands. That's before I was a helmsman. I was standing lookout on the flying bridge—a sea basket up on top—you know. It was raining, and I've got the phones on, and we picked up a bogie. You're in tune with the radar, radio. And we're closing in—closing in on this bogie. And I died a million deaths. I'm up there by myself. It turned out it was a barge adrift. Nobody on it—just a barge out there. I had all the bad thoughts you could have. That's when I decided that as long as I'm conscious I'm all right. As long as I know what's going on I'm all right. And I still live by that. I lived for the rest of the war and I never got that scared again. Nothing. It's up to the elements and it's up to the captain. And that happened on our first trip down there.

Then we went to the Solomon Islands—around Guadalcanal. We went ashore on Florida Island. Most places we didn't even go ashore. If we did go ashore, for seventeen months we didn't see a car, or a late newspaper or a girl. But they would clear an island of all population and clear it for flies. You know flies are a problem. They sprayed DDT everywhere. Now, you wouldn't do that at all. And then they give us three beers and let us have a party. That's about the most. Even in the Philippines we didn't mix with the natives. They had a little stockade on the edge of the water and we'd go over there for a party and then go back to the ship. So we didn't see civilization. You know you weren't allowed to have alcohol on ship. If we had it, I don't know where they stored that stuff.

What happened to your ship in the Solomons?

We were just on escort duty. We were on Florida Island and Bob Hope put on a show on one of the islands down there about that time. I didn't go, but I went to Florida Island and I didn't know any of the vegetation. You go back there and you go through a path, you see the vines, the trees, the flowers, the weeds. I didn't recognize any of them, and that was an odd feeling to do that. They did have some natives on the island, and the men had built a big fence, barrier, and they wouldn't let us see their women—they wouldn't let us go through. But they already had peroxide blondes and Coca-Cola bottles. Their culture was ruined.

Did you experience any storms aboard ship?

We were in a typhoon. The *Caine Mutiny* was made from that typhoon, and three destroyers capsized in the typhoon. But we rode it out. And I steered most all that time. But there was no horseplay among the crew. I would alternate and go back to aft steering. A lot of guys would not go to their bunk—they were praying, they were scared to death. They claimed we turned over ninety degrees, and they had a picture of our ship tilted. And it felt like it was just going to go on over, but it'd just sit up there and rock and shake and then go back down.

But there was eight hundred men lost in that storm, none off our ship. Three destroyers capsized. The storm was far out to sea—we felt it for, I'd say, about four days. TBS, the talk between ships, is formal. But during that storm it was not formal. They were almost pleading with each other—trying to find out whether to face that storm on the starboard bow or the port bow. Whether to go five, or six, seven, or eight knots. You have to sense or feel a ship, to decide if you're going to go seven degrees, go seven knots, take it on the port bow or starboard bow. And the ship makes a lot of noise when it's creaking. And those big tankers, they're moving and they're bobbing too, and they're really worried. You gotta take it on the starboard bow. And then you've gotta go fast enough to have control. If you lose power you've lost it. Your screw has to be turning enough so you can straighten up after that wave hits you. And the wave is about twice as high as a mountain. And that mountain is coming at you and it's going to hit you at an angle so you gotta turn the rudders so your ship is turning into it. I was at the helm most all that time. They accused me of causing the ship to shake.

Was your ship involved in any of the assaults?

We got eight bronze stars which came from involvement in a major operation. The Philippines was one, Iwo Jima, Okinawa and Palau. I can't hardly separate Palau and Papua. Can you? [The Palau Islands are in the westernmost Carolines while Papua is on New Guinea.] We saw a lot of ships that were hit by kamikazes, and when I see a ship that was hit in mid-ship, that's when I wanted to be in aft steering.

But Okinawa was on April Fools' Day, and they had a storm—had a typhoon then. And we had some marines on our ship, and they got seasick. Oh those guys were seasick. Sailors and marines don't get along, but we sympathized with those marines when we let them off. But that was a terrible invasion. It was on April Fool's Day. That's about when the kamikazes started, and they didn't cease, they just kept doing that. At Okinawa you didn't know where it was going to happen. We saw a lot of ships that had been hit in the bow, stern, or mid-ship.

But Iwo Jima told me a story. We bombed it for ninety-three days, consecutive days, and by then we had complete air superiority. We had battleships and we had planes directing fire and yet, when we went ahead and invaded it, we lost a lot of marines. Dead. [The Marines lost 6,821 men killed and almost 20,000 wounded. The 21,000 Japanese defenders were killed almost to a man. See *Eagle Against the Sun* by Ronald Spector, p. 502.] But our ship was hooked up with a radio system that was directing these guns with a plane, and he would get down close enough that the fire would get close to him, and an old boy from Tennessee was the pilot of that plane, and they said, "We're worried about you." And he said, "I'm worried about me, too." But he was getting in real close. If you multiply Iwo Jima with a number and compare that to Japan, what would it have cost for us to invade Japan? We wouldn't be here. There'd have been a million men killed.

Our ships sailed free right around that island, and we stayed there a long time, and the planes would bomb when they needed to. The battleship's fire would be directed. We just had three-inch guns, but we had a lot of depth charges and K guns. Our main job was we were a screen. We screened for the big ships. We just put up a screen out there in the convoy. The K gun is a little torpedo that you can shoot off in clusters.

After Iwo Jima, what happened then to your ship?

Well, the first time we ever got twenty degrees north of the equator we went to Guam. I don't know the sequence of these. But the biggest explosion that we had was when we were anchored near the *Mt. Hood*. It blew up. That's the biggest explosion we had. One thousand people was killed when that ammunition ship blew. Nobody knows why. So, we really don't know what caused that explosion. But it was the *Mt. Hood*. There was another ship tied up beside of it and they blew up. It was one thousand men that were killed. All on those two ships. Got it in the log—November 10th. Manus Island. We had a party to go ashore and we was all ready to get in a barge on deck, and that thing blew up right over there. And these ships went underneath the water, and the debris went in the air and it just cleared underneath that debris. It was like a big cloud. And then it started raining steel. It peppered our ship with steel. Killed one guy. On the ship next to us it killed about eighteen people. It'll knock holes in the deck. Big heavy steel going up in the air and falling down. This guy was taking out the garbage. Two of them were over in the garbage when one of them got hit with that piece of steel—crushed him.

We were under way fifty-three days in a row when Japan surrendered. We had been down in the Celebes Islands, but I felt like we were saying hello to the same flying fish every morning. We'd go back at night because you gotta go into the current and into the wind when you refuel. That way you can go slower and hold control. And all these tankers and battleships and everything, they have to refuel. They had to get supplies. So, we were a couple hundred miles off the coast of Japan, and we'd refuel a group at all times. And we were out zigzagging in front laying a screen for this operation. And that was escort duty, destroyer escorts, that's what they're doing, they're escorting these other ships. Plus, we thought we was western union. We would deliver a lot of messages, a lot of personnel, at sea. That's the way we got our fuel, that's the way we got our supplies. Now, we did tie up during that fifty-three days, but we got under way the same day. We didn't stay. We were out fifty-three days in a row when we went into Japan—three days after they surrendered so, we went in on August 17, 1945.

Our captain, during this fifty-three days, didn't believe in the atomic bomb. It really disturbed him. He had a brain hemorrhage and he was transferred at sea. And then the executive officer took over as captain. I don't know if the atomic bomb caused it, but he was disturbed, he didn't believe they should have done that. The rumor was then that it'd take one thousand years to clear the sea.

What did you and the troops think about the atomic bomb when it went off?

I didn't know anything about atomic energy, but we heard broadcasts from China about that before it was announced by the United States. And

Frank Treadway today.

then the captain and all got talking about it. We thought there'd be a wasteland for a thousand years because of the radiation. We really didn't know, but we were glad to get the upper hand. Really glad to end the war. The Japanese just wouldn't surrender. They wouldn't surrender. They're willing to give their lives. So I think the sentiment, after it's all over with, is that it saved a million lives—or maybe a couple million.

What I mentioned before was that the executive officer didn't know how to con the ship. To con the ship you pull into the harbor, and you tie up, and the helmsman does what the captain says—"Forward one third. Reverse two thirds. Right 15 degrees rudder." We spent all day trying to tie up. And you shoot lines over to the dock. Ended up we lost all of our lines. He didn't know how to do it and he had a high temper. If you tried to correct him he'd chop your head off. Ended up that evening, they threw us lines and we tied up to their ship and they pulled us in. Just to tie up. We had a strong current and he was just inexperienced. But all you do is what they say.

But then we went ashore in Japan. We didn't speak any Japanese and we went through communities that didn't speak any English, and there's three of us guys going through. And their houses were real clean. They were just shacks, but they were real clean. But we found a cat, and that cat was real friendly. We could squeeze that cat's tail and it would meow, and they would meow, and we would meow, and we had something in common. One lady invited us in, and she had a couple of kids and a picture of her daughter. They was taken in by the Red Cross. And her daughter had hoped to be a geisha girl when she grew up. She was ten years old, but it reminds you of home. Aspirations for your kids. Their floors were so clean that they served us tea, and that little girl went to get tea and spilled some on the floor, and she got down and cleaned it up. But the floor was clean enough to eat off of.

We were out there, we were in and out of Japan, I guess for a couple months. We went to downtown Tokyo and there was no shops open. In the streets where the bombs had hit there was dirt and they had vegetables planted in there. Some beans were growing downtown. People were real friendly, real friendly. And cigarettes, we got them for sixty cents a carton, and you could sell them for twenty dollars a carton. So you'd sneak off all the cigarettes you could. But one guy that was a clown would auction off one cigarette, and he would give it to some woman back there, and he says, she can have it. So, they'd open up a path, had real order, real respect, you know, let her go up there and get that cigarette. But none of them would pay twenty-one dollars for those cigarettes. I never did understand that. They just agreed to not go more than that, and that's what they did. I never did understand that.

After Japan we came back to the States, we came back to Los Angeles, and we were to be decommissioned in Florida. So we went through the canal zone and then up to the Philadelphia Navy Yard. We was up there for the Army-Navy game in 1945 in Philadelphia. That's where I left the ship. In Philadelphia Navy Yard.

And what'd you do then?

I went to Middlesboro, Kentucky. I didn't come back to Dayton and take my old job back. Anyway, we anchored in the Philadelphia Navy Yard and I had a good buddy that I grew up with—he was on the USS *Detroit*. And his mother would tell my mother where he was, back and forth. We knew where each other was all the time. I looked over there and there was the *Detroit* anchored in the same naval yard. So, we had a party aboard the *Detroit*. It was an old cruiser—a four stacker. So I got out of the navy and I went to Middlesboro, and he got a thirty-day leave. And we got together in Middlesboro. And it ended up that we was going to celebrate homecoming, and then we was going to go somewhere in the world and make the world a better place to live.

We decided we wanted wine, women, and song. But we should get us a couple of nice girls that we could go out with on Sunday, and then we could do anything we wanted to the rest of the week to keep our reputation up. So we picked up two girls. And seven months later we had a double wedding. We married those two girls. I married Inez and we have been married fifty-three years. All of our six kids graduated from Centerville High School. And I'm proud of Centerville, I'm proud of Centerville High School, I'm proud of the neighbors. They all helped raise our family. And we're just blessed with the best family in the world.

So, I went back to Frigidaire and they said I could have my old job back. But they said they were going on vacation the next week. So I stopped by NCR and they hired me. So I started working at NCR and I worked there thirty, near thirty-eight years. Then I started gardening. We've been selling vegetables commercially thirty years this year.

What's this hat?

That's my VFW hat. I'm proud of the VFW—Post 9550. I'll just put it on. I was a charter member you know.

Karl Rotterman

Karl Rotterman lives on Springrun Lane in Centerville. He and his wife Anna have two children. His daughter, Diane, is a schoolteacher in Cleveland and his son, Dan, is a schoolteacher in Brookings, Oregon. Karl went to Roosevelt High School and later to Patterson Co-op. He studied tool making and eventually owned his own tool making company for over fifteen years. He was a member of the United States Marine Corps for about three years and participated in three campaigns in the Pacific Theater—Bougainville, Guam and Iwo Jima where he was severely wounded by a Japanese rifleman. He was a member of the 3rd Marine Division, 9th Regiment, Company A.

What were you doing just prior to your military service in the Marines?

Well, prior to my joining the Marine Corps I was in high school. But I dropped out of high school rather young, and talked my parents into letting me join the Marine Corps which I did. I think I was under the legal age—I was only seventeen.

How'd you happen to select the Marine Corps?

I don't know. I suppose because I liked the uniform. I thought it was probably the elite of the military branches, so I wanted to be a marine. That was in October of 1942. The war had been going on for about a year, and I went down to the post office in Dayton and talked to the sergeant, and he decided that if I passed the physical, why, I could go in. So I went to Cincinnati on the train and went through the physical examination and passed it.

And then within a couple days I got my orders through the mail to be at the train depot on a particular date. And after the boo-hoos of mama and papa, away I went to Parris Island, South Carolina. And that's where I started into boot camp. And I'm sure lots and lots of people have seen the drill instructors at Parris Island. Our drill instructor, our main drill instructor's name was Sergeant Feinstein. Looked like a mountain of a man. Had a voice like a cannon. And he ruled the roost. When we went in he said he was going to be our little god for the next four months—and he was. Every word he spoke you jumped.

I think there was like fifty men in the platoon. That's as near as I can remember. Most of them made it, but there were a few who fell out during the course of the boot camp due to sickness. And then at the end of our boot camp time we had our graduation, and the day after the graduation they had an outbreak of spinal meningitis on Parris Island and quarantined the entire island. So we were there a month and a half extra in training.

The rest was the ordinary boot camp type thing. You had to have guard duty and we had lots of long hikes. And back then in the Marine Corps you boxed everyday. And Sergeant Feinstein always put the biggest guy against the smallest guy. Everyday. Every morning we boxed. Toughen you up I guess. But I'll never forget the fellow that he put me against. We called him typewriter. His name was Smith I think, we called him Smitty. Anyway, he was a great big heavyset redheaded fellow about twice my size, and Feinstein would put me in with him. And we only boxed like two rounds, but he beat me something fierce. I never could hit him. But anyway, I lived through it.

What about indoctrination—
building the esprit de corps?

I think that in the Marine Corps from day one they continually hammer that into you. At that time it was hate the Japanese. And they did many things that really built up a hatred for the Japanese. One time we had what they called field days where you take everything outside, all the beds and everything else outside. And you have a bucket, and you take a bucket of sand, and you take it inside and throw it on the floor, and then you take a brick and you scrub the floor with a brick. They call it holy stoning the floor. Then you wash it all out. And it usually happened at one and two o'clock in the morning. So this one particular time we got it all done, and before we put everything back into the barracks, Sergeant Feinstein said, "Everybody empty your bucket of sand." So everybody emptied their bucket outside and he said, "Put them buckets over on top of your head." So we put the buckets over our head. And then we lined up against the walls and he came along with his swagger stick and cracked the bucket on every guy's head. Said, "You look like a bunch of damn Japs." Which was psychological, I guess. Hate the Japs. We were a very close-knit group. You had to be the best and your drill instructor instilled in you continually that you're going to be marines when he gets done with you. When you leave here you're going to be a marine, and marines are known for excellence. And they constantly hammered that into your head, so that by the time you got to graduation you looked sharp and you felt sharp.

Next I went to Cherry Point, South Carolina, because my assignment from boot camp was supposed to be in the Marine Air Corps. So they sent me to Cherry Point and we were in what they called a casual company—waiting for another assignment from Cherry Point. But then they sent me to Memphis, Tennessee, which was the Naval Air Technical Training Center.

And about half way through that school, each day names would be listed on the bulletin board. You were to be on the flight line at such and such a time, and you had to draw a parachute, and they were using Stearman airplanes. And, of course, eventually my name came up and I was on the flight line. And as I said before, I learned to fly an Aronca before I went into the service. So I was a pretty hotshot pilot I thought. Then this sergeant took me up in the Stearman, and by the time I got back down I was so sick that I couldn't even get out of the airplane. He did all kinds of acrobatics—everything. That Stearman, as I'm sure you're aware of, that darn thing can do anything. It can go upside down forever I believe. Anyhow, he did all kinds of fancy stuff and he let me do a little bit, but very little. And when we got back down, like I say, I was sick and I more or less fell out of the airplane.

I finally got back to the barracks and within a day, about two days after that, my name appeared on another list—I was being transferred. And they transferred me to New River, North Carolina, for advanced infantry training. That was the day they decided I wasn't going to be a pilot. From there I went to California for five or six weeks. Then we went to Camp Matthews out of San Diego, California—down toward Camp Pendleton to scout and sniper school, and from there I went overseas.

Did you leave San Diego on a troop ship?

Yes—on the Lurline, a converted cruise ship. We went to Auckland, New Zealand. That ship was so fast that they said we were not in danger of submarine attack by the Japanese. This was [at the] beginning [of] the spring of '43. Anyhow, we went to Auckland and did some training there. When I got to Auckland I was put in a unit and we joined the 3rd Division there. Then we went from there down to Guadalcanal and did a little more training. At that time the Bougainville campaign was ending so that by the time we got to Guadalcanal they felt that we were able to go right on into Bougainville and do some mop up.

Now Bougainville is a small island, very swampy except for the runway which was a fighter strip only. The weather is hot and the island is loaded with every kind of crawling thing. It was Thanksgiving Day, November 25, 1943. I was a member of the 3rd Marine Division, 9th Marine Regiment, 1st Battalion, Company A, 1st Platoon. The company commander was Captain Conrad "Bulley" Fowler, and my platoon leader was Lt. Zimmer (subsequently killed on Iwo Jima).

This was my first experience in combat in what we called the "Battle for Grenade Hill." I carried an M-1 rifle, two bandoliers of 30 caliber ammo, a web belt with more clips of ammo, three hand grenades, two canteens, my K-Bar knife, a first aid packet and we wore light green dungarees. The 3rd platoon was the attack platoon and they were pinned down at the base of the hill. The 2nd platoon guarded the left flank,

Karl Rotterman.

and my platoon, the 1st platoon, guarded the right flank. We did this to keep the Japs from coming around behind us—flanking us. The fighting took place during this one afternoon and all night. The next morning the Japs had left the area. Most of the fighting was done with M-1s and BARs. There wasn't much use of mortars in this battle because of the canopy of foliage that really prevented it and the swampy terrain. Captain Fowler was wounded. We called him "Bulley"—we never called anyone by rank. He wore no rank insignia and neither did we—never. That was my first experience in combat.

On Guam, our next campaign, I was a scout.

What was your role as a scout?

Well, without getting into a whole lot of detail, in the jungle type warfare that we were in, everything is not a straight line. One day you're fighting in one direction, and the next day you're fighting in the opposite direction because the jungle is so thick and so overgrown and almost impossible to get through that you can walk right by the enemy and won't even see them. And the heat is almost overbearing. It's hard to imagine that you can be in such a position and live through it.

The 3rd Marine Division were the assault troops. I think there were some Army infantry in there too, yes. That was a long campaign—that was I believe twenty-eight or thirty days. But then after the Guam campaign, after we declared the island secured, and we made our camps, there was still a great deal going on each day. They'd continually be finding pockets of resistance and holed up Japanese so that they decided that we should do it all over again.

So they broke all the camps and everybody went back, all the troops went back to the beginning beaches that we had started in, and covered the whole island a second time. And we did almost as much fighting the second time as we did the first time. Like I say, you walk right by the enemy and can't even see them. Here's a few photographs that are interesting. Here's one that shows the amphibious assault—where you go in on amphibian boats. And this one is where they're relieving the troops to go back for some R&R—rest and relaxation. If you can relax in the jungles, why, you're pretty good. I wasn't there prior to the invasion, but Agaña, the capital of Guam, was a pretty nice little city before the fighting took place.

What did you think about your air and Navy support during this particular campaign?

During the Guam campaign I thought it was excellent. Back then, not having the communications that we have today, all of it had to be by wire.

The men had to run with rolls of wire in order to go from telephone to telephone. And running through the jungle with two guys holding a pipe through a big role of wire was tough. And of course the Japs are right behind you shooting and cutting the wire in half as soon as you lay it. Communications were tough. But we could communicate with the ships and call for air strikes and bombardment. On Guam they did a real good job. Course on Guam the anticipated point of assault was in a bay on one side of the island. And it was supposed to be a big secret. They sent decoys into a bay to try to make the enemy believe that's where the big assault was going to take place when really it was over on the other side of the island. And so the big assault took place on more or less an area open to the ocean. But somehow or other we all figured that it was not much of a secret because they were waiting on us when we got there.

You were a scout. What does one do as a scout?

Well, the most dreaded call being a scout was when they sent the word out, "Scouts out and draw fire." Now, that means you go out and let the enemy shoot at you. And we do that so we know where they're at. As nearly as I can remember that first campaign on Guam lasted a month. The second one, the second phase of the same campaign, that was probably, oh, a couple of weeks. We simply went back to the beaches, started over, and did the whole thing again.

This paper was really handed out at Bougainville. [Holds up paper] It was given to us. It's basically Japanese phrases for marines—that is, how to tell them to surrender, to lay down their arms, to halt, whatever—all in Japanese. And if you studied it you would probably be able to converse a little bit in Japanese, not much, but a little. They thought it was gonna do some good I'm sure.

What did you think of your officers and your non-coms?

Most of the officers and the non-coms were great people. They were excellent. After the Guam campaign they started getting in some of what they called sixty or ninety day wonders. These were the lieutenants that were coming in to replace the ones that didn't make it. Some of those must have been hurried through officer candidate school or something because they were not the greatest. They did not have the experience and they were trying to be leaders. And some of them tried too hard. They didn't have the experience and they wouldn't rely on the ordinary lowly PFC or private because they were the officers, and they were supposed to be in charge even though they didn't know what was going on part of the time.

We stayed on Guam for six months when I was still in the 21st Marines. We were way up in the hills of Guam where they had carved a patch out of the jungle. And the flying insects and everything else up there in the jungle were terrible. I got dengue fever a couple of times up there and then I got transferred into the 9th Marines as a replacement. Now the 9th Marines had a beautiful spot down on that bay that I spoke of before—right out on the beach. And it was just fantastic. It was just like Waikiki Beach in Hawaii. We had a beautiful spot there and we stayed there six months and did training. One little incident occurred there. One of the new lieutenants who came over had taken over our platoon because our platoon lieutenant had been killed. At that time they were just beginning to get grenade launchers for rifles. Well, we were gonna go out and practice with them, as well as bazookas, and we went out to a range someplace on the island where we were gonna train with these grenade launchers on our rifles. Well, they also made the grenade launcher for a carbine which was a little bitty rifle. And so I was chosen, for what reason I'll never know, to use the grenade launcher on a carbine. You put a blank cartridge in and you put the grenade in the launcher part. I got it all rigged up and I set it on the ground and held it, and I was gonna fire it. But this new lieutenant said, "No, no, no, that's a shoulder fired weapon. You fire that from the shoulder." Well, he's the lieutenant. So I fired it from the shoulder and wound up with a big black eye, a bruised jaw and everything else. And the dag-gone carbine came apart in the process—the stock fell right off. It has a brass ring or something to hold the barrel to the stock but it flew off and the thing flew apart. The grenade went, fortunately, but I sure got hurt. It's a wonder I didn't break my shoulder. But I held it tight because I knew that thing was gonna kick. Boy, it did, and then after that it was decided that maybe you should put that on the ground. I never did see anyone use one in actual combat.

But anyhow, we were on one end of the island after our six months' stay doing training and everything. We put on several nighttime exhibitions of firepower for different admirals that visited the island. And then it came time to leave. Of course they never told you where you was going for your next campaign, but our colonel decided that we should march from our base camp which was on one end of the island to the other end of the island where the ships were waiting to pick us up. It was a pretty long haul. And so we marched and marched and finally we got to the ships.

And after about, I don't know, a couple days outbound they started bringing out the topographies of the island where we were gonna go. And we were scheduled to go to Okinawa. But we were gonna be stand-by for Iwo Jima. It was the 4th and 5th divisions at Iwo Jima, and we floated around out there for a couple of days. But they were running into so much resistance and needed flamethrowers so bad that it was decided that our unit should go in early which we did.

Here's a picture—it could be me, but if it isn't me, that's exactly the way I looked when we went to Iwo Jima. A flamethrower weighs around sixty-five pounds. I weighed about 140.

Were you afraid under fire?

Absolutely. Scared to death. Shook and shaked so much that sometimes I couldn't even eat. I think I was just as scared both places—Guam and Iwo Jima—especially on Iwo Jima. We were trained in the jungles and Iwo had no jungles. Iwo was wide-open, flat volcanic ash. No jungle whatsoever. We didn't hardly know how to act because we were trained in the jungle which I think was a big mistake. And as I said before, we were scheduled to go to Okinawa. That's jungle. But we were up on Iwo where there's no jungle and it was different.

How long were you on Iwo Jima
before you were wounded?

Six days. A rifleman got me in the head. We were prime targets. Carrying that flamethrower is like painting a target on your back because they wanted to get you. The only reason I was there was because they sent the flamethrower units in early. The rest of the division was still on the boat. But they needed them badly, so after being wounded I was put on a ship, I can't even tell you if it was a hospital ship or what it was, because at that time it was nip and tuck.

And we went to Saipan first. There was a hospital on Saipan and they put us in the hospital in Saipan, and we were only there for maybe a week I guess. And then we got aboard a ship and went back to Hawaii, to Pearl Harbor, and I went in the hospital there. Had a couple of surgeries there, well I had surgeries on the ship and then a couple of surgeries in Hawaii. And then I left Hawaii and went back to the United States, San Francisco, and went into a receiving hospital in San Francisco.

And there I was diagnosed with psychoneurosis and locked up. But the psychologist that analyzed me was crazier then I was. They didn't keep me there very long—they called it psychoneurosis anxiety. Then they let loose of that and put me in an ordinary ward. I think I was in the psycho ward maybe three or four days.

And from there they transferred me by train up to Seattle, Washington—to a hospital up there. And up there a Navy captain, Captain Hill, was the chief surgeon, and up there I had two more surgeries. They were starting to put me back together. I stayed in Seattle and that's where they gave me the Purple Heart in a little ceremony.

And I don't really remember how long I was in Seattle. Perhaps three or four months. And all the time, of course, I wanted to get home. Then they finally transferred me to Chicago—to Great Lakes in a hospital there. And while I was in Chicago, in that hospital, the Japanese surrendered. To back up a ways, when I was on my way from San Francisco to Seattle on that train trip, that's when Franklin Delano Roosevelt died. That was in April of '45. That's when he died. When I was on that trip. And of course Harry Truman took over and he decided to drop the bomb. And I was in Chicago when all that took place.

What do you think about dropping the bomb?

I was glad they did it because everything seemed to be pointing towards an invasion of Japan, and that would have been lots and lots more people dead. I was glad they dropped it, even though it was a terrible thing—it ended the war. I was discharged then from Great Lakes in October '45.

Did you take advantage of the GI Bill of Rights?

Yes I did. Back in the beginning, as I told you, I did not graduate from high school and I felt that I needed something. So I took advantage of the GI Bill of Rights. Got everything all signed up and went to Patterson Co-op in downtown Dayton and spent my four years studying to be a toolmaker. And I became a toolmaker. That's all I ever did for all of my working life was be a toolmaker. Eventually I owned my own tool company. I had my own tool company for about fifteen years. But one of the recessions took us down pretty low so I sold out and retired. But the main reason that I retired, at that point in time, I was only fifty-five, was because I developed colon cancer due to the stress of the business. It was in 1985 that they operated on me for colon cancer and gave me one year to live. And this is 1999 and I'm still breathing.

Looking back fifty-five years, how do you think that World War II changed your life?

Pretty dramatic. A total change. I'm not the same person I was prior to the war for lots of reasons. We have a reunion every two years up in Canton, Ohio, where members of the flamethrower units gather. Now our numbers are dwindling. I think there's only four of us left. In the past two years two of them have passed away. So either there's gonna be just two of us this time, or perhaps three, because someone has said that they found another one. So our numbers are getting real small.

After I finished my Patterson Co-op schooling I was employed at Master Electric Company in Dayton as an apprentice toolmaker. And I was assigned to their research and development department which was kind of an exclusive little area in the factory, all enclosed with glass, and we did the research and development. And there was a hallway that ran the length of our little enclosure, and right on the other side of that hallway was the engineering offices. And the girl that I married was a secretary for an engineer in those offices.

And a couple of years later we had our first baby which was Diane. Later we decided that the only way I was ever going to be able to retire was start my own business which I did along with another man. And our tool company was called Triad Mold and Die. And we stayed in business there for about fifteen years.

Ray Hill

Raymond C. Hill was born in Indiana in 1920—a real Hoosier. He retired in 1997 after being involved for fifty-one years with the Seventh Day Adventist Church. He and his wife, Geraldine, did missionary work in the Philippines after the war for ten years. They have four children. Ray then taught agriculture at Andrews University and later was ground superintendent for the Kettering Medical Center. He attended Emmanuel Missionary College (BS in agriculture); Michigan State University (MA in agriculture); and the seminary at Andrews University. Ray was in the U.S. Navy for just over three years, equally divided between domestic and foreign service. He served on a PT boat in the Pacific Theater and was awarded the Purple Heart medal for wounds received in action.

When the war started I didn't want to go to the Army, I wanted to be a Navy person, so I enlisted in the Navy and went to Indianapolis and then to Great Lakes in September of 1942. And then I went from there, let's see, to boot training at the Detroit Naval Armory. My parents didn't say that I couldn't go, and they didn't say that I could go. But they supported me.

Then I was sent to the Detroit Naval Armory to cook and bakers' school. They made a cook out of me. And I said, if they're going to make a cook out of me, I'm going to be as good a cook as possible. There were twenty-three of us; I was the only one that got to be a third class cook because I had excelled in whatever they said that we were to do in the training. And at bakers' school I volunteered for submarine duty, but there wasn't any openings at that time.

A man there said, "How about a PT boat?" "What's a PT boat?" "You'll find out," he said. It was more of a voluntary thing. The PT boatmen were more or less voluntary. And they wanted men from twenty-two to twenty-four. A little older and foolish I suppose you could say. They were told what to do, and they would do it. So that's the way it was.

The PT training was in February of 1943 at Melville, Rhode Island. Melville, Rhode Island, is on Narragansett Bay, in fact it's not very far from Newport. Newport is more or less the head of the bay, and we were, oh, maybe five miles inside the Narragansett area. Training was eight weeks which included commando training and training in seamanship and navigation. Everyone got to operate the PT boat—stand at the helm.

How long and how wide is a PT boat?

Eighty feet long, twenty feet wide, and it carried three Packard 2500 HP engines— there were 2500 hundred horses under each one of them. Former President Kennedy was captain of PT109. We were in his area a year after he was there. But his story is a very interesting story. The PTs go fifty knots which was a mile plus an eighth, about fifty-eight miles per hour—pretty fast in the water.

In Melville, Rhode Island we had eight weeks of training and then we were assigned to a PT boat. The first PT boats, six PT boats, were lend-leased to the Russians and we took those across the Gulf of Mexico. We stopped in Miami and went up the inside passage as much as possible. I remember as we got up there [New York City] we could see the Statue of Liberty and we could see the Hudson River. We went up the Hudson River a ways, and then back and forth—always training to fight the Japanese one-day.

Then we came back to New Orleans and got our PT boats and started out across the Caribbean. We went through the Panama canal and on the Pacific side we waited about, oh, maybe three or four weeks for a ship where we could build a cradle that would fit a PT boat because they picked up the whole thing and put it on the bow of the liberty ship. That's how we traveled when we went on the sixteen-day trip to Seattle.

We got to Seattle and we got ready to go north. We got a lot of sea gear and cold weather gear, went up the inside passage to Wrangell, Petersburg, Alaska, and finally to Sitka, and there they told us to stop. They said, "We do not need you in Attu and Kiska. We're going to send you to a hot place, hot in Japanese, and hot in mosquitoes."

So then we came back to the Bremerton Navy Yard and got everything on the top deck, it was all new. We never had radar before, we never had a 40mm gun before, plus the other twin turrets. Everything was new. So, it took about two weeks to do that and then we went down to San Francisco.

We rode on an aircraft carrier and they placed the PT boat in a cradle again to ride on the top—on the deck of a liberty ship.

While we were down there in the San Francisco area we practiced around Alcatraz. We did it for about a week just to keep in shape; they want you to keep sharp with the operation and everything. Every man at his gun. And about a week later they lowered these PT boats onto a liberty ship, and the crews all went on a troop ship headed to New Guinea. It took us thirty-one days to get to New Guinea.

Then the skipper got us all together, and he says, "Fellows, I'm going to tell you one thing. One half of this crew will not return to the States. One half. In other words eight will not return. Eight will be in battle and will be lost. We'll lose eight of you in the battle." I don't think that he should have told us that. And just about eight weeks later it was true. When our ship was sunk by a kamikaze, eight men were never found. Eight men—it just blew all apart. I came off with about fifty shrapnel wounds and perforation wounds.

Anyway, first we went up to Milne Bay—that was our base. While we were there we would patrol at night looking for the enemy, and we usually found him too. We had one hundred and twenty-nine patrols, and on twenty-five of those we hit the enemy—enemy ships. We would tackle anything from a rowboat up to an aircraft carrier. It didn't make any difference. Course, we'd hide behind an island. And as they got closer we would shoot at their lights.

Could you describe that memorable attack?

Yes. I think on our first attack we were about a mile away—we could see a small craft that was full of supplies and also soldiers. So we opened up. I opened up with my 40mm because they said in any attack the 40mm will surprise and destroy the ship. And then the other guns took the crew. So, that's what happened. We hit the craft and it just blew up—just blew up. And there were people in the water and they were shooting back at us too. I was the gun captain on the 40mm. I was also the cook. I did the cooking and everything. Usually, they would protect the cook. That's about it, but as I opened up and hit it, I had two good hits, the thing just blew up. But the crew, several of the Jap crew, got up so our fifty caliber guns did away with those. Didn't let one go ashore.

See, the Japanese were frustrated because a lot of them had been bypassed by MacArthur. And it was up to us to protect the stern of the task force, and also to stand by if a place had been bypassed to keep the Japs from reinforcing. We had one hundred twenty-nine different missions there including the Philippines. As I said, altogether we hit the enemy, or we escaped from the enemy twenty-five times.

If the enemy was close enough and fired upon us, we would get behind an island. Course, a lot of times they couldn't get close enough, but we could. We could put our bow right up close to shore. We only drew four and a half feet. This was in '44. And we would attack anything from a rowboat on up—didn't make any difference because a lot of times they were gun boats. They were enemy ships or enemy boats with troops. We also carried torpedoes, and there were 40mm guns mounted on the PT for shooting at aircraft and we had twin 50s also.

What happened when you went up to the Philippines?

On the 15th of December they attacked, a whole platoon of Japanese. They had gone inland to get away from the shore. Then when we landed there with our PT boats a lot of kamikazes came. A kamikaze is a suicide plane. They had the idea of killing themselves. The funeral has already been taken care of. They did it for their emperor. They take their lives by crashing into a ship.

On PT300, my gun was a 40mm gun on the stern of the PT boat. We had twin fifty caliber, and 20mm—we were actually gunboats. And what I

remember was placing four shells into the chamber and then ducking my head. This kamikaze plane came right in and hit our PT boat eight feet behind me—right at the gas tanks. We had just filled up with three thousand gallons of hundred-octane gasoline, and it just blew up. It blew up. This pilot just kept boring in even though all the boats were shooting at him. But he would maneuver. Every time we would maneuver he would maneuver. What we would head for was a circle, because this was our protection—one boat protecting another. But we just got to that circle when that kamikaze hit. He hit right here at that gun. I was right there. I actually had to duck my head.

I came to under the water. I could see all the fire around me and I could see the depth charges going off and the guns going off—the shells. I thought I was in hell. That was my first thought.

Ray Hill today.

But then after a while, I was shaking my arms and a piece of plywood floated by about four feet square, and I climbed aboard that. I'm sure that a one hundred and sixty-five pound sailor would have sunk that raft, I call it a raft, but my guardian angel must have held up that raft. That's what I hung onto. I could hardly move, shrapnel wounds and perforated eardrums—I couldn't hear.

I had about fifty shrapnel wounds. After climbing aboard this raft, this piece of plywood, another boat saw me and they threw a line to me, but it burned. They threw another line—and it burned. They threw about three or four, and finally they soaked it in seawater, threw me a line and pulled me out of the fiery furnace. Boy, was I glad because I only had about five minutes left. This was another PT boat. A PT boat usually has about sixteen men. If you have more guns you have more than that. But eight of our guys were never found. Eight were killed and blown apart and eight of us survived. This was December 17, 1944. We had three thousand gallons of hundred octane. We had just refueled, in fact, we were doing that when this plane was sighted.

This piece of cloth was a part of the parachute or the clothing of the pilot of the kamikaze that dived on our boat. Another sailor there picked this up and gave it to me, and I have kept it for fifty-five years. Then I was in the hospital there 'til February 4, 1945—in our Quonset hospital (a small building) on the island of Mindoro. Then on about the fifth day of February I left. They gave me my orders to report to the receiving station on the west coast of the United States. So, I had twelve rides with twelve different planes going from one base to another and finally arrived in Hawaii. I got a complete new outfit, even a little bit of money that I'd lost. And then I got a troop transport to San Francisco. I left San Francisco after a few months, but now I was coming home.

What are these different ribbons?

Well, this one here is the Purple Heart—I got the Purple Heart. That's for being wounded. This is a good conduct ribbon for serving three years in the armed forces. If you're good enough you get a ribbon. And this one is the Philippine Liberation Medal. This is the patch for our PT boat, and this was the one for the cook. I still got some of the wounds in the arms, both arms, both legs, both elbows, both knees. As far as I know, I was the only one rescued aft. I was glad to get home. This was in, let's see, March of '45. I was in Chelsea Naval Hospital in Boston.

What did you think of the atomic bomb when you heard about it?

I thought it was the thing to do to end the war. It saved millions of lives. I was discharged in October 1, 1945. After the war I came out to Walla Walla,

Washington. Went over to Seattle, and I rode a bicycle around Green Lake. And I was watching a couple of young ladies, as sailors do. And I rode around behind them, and one of them had trouble with her bicycle so I stopped to help. They were going to Walla Walla College after the war was over. My granddaughter just talked to me on the phone yesterday, and this lady, this bicycle lady, is a member of her church up in Washington State. But she was saying that she helped your grandfather go to Walla Walla College. Eventually I went to Walla Walla College, and my roommate said, "Just stay by, just stay by a little while longer." I did and the next week I met my wife. We've been married fifty-three years, and we had four kids and eight grandchildren. We try to see all of them sometime during the year.

Did you go to college under the GI Bill of Rights?

Yes. I got a whole lot 'cause I had forty-eight months service. I was also eligible as a public law sixteen-disabled vet. I had forty-eight months of credit coming. Later I earned a master's at Michigan State. Then in the seminary I had training because then we decided we were going to be missionaries in the Philippines. We did that for ten years. I had twenty-eight hundred acres there. It belonged to the school. I was teaching a B.S. in agriculture. That farm later developed into a ranch—two thousand acres into a ranch, two hundred acres into roads and village, and six hundred acres into a farm. I was there from '53 to '63. Ten years. My kids call it home. 'Cause when we first went over in 1953 the boy was two and the girl was four. Two more of our children were born over there.

When we came back I taught at Andrews University. It's our Seventh Day Adventist University and seminary in Michigan—Berrien Springs, Michigan. It's near Benton Harbor, not far from South Bend, Indiana. I taught agriculture there for nine years. We've been down here twenty-seven years. Twenty-seven. And I was ground superintendent for thirteen years at Kettering Medical Center. When I retired, I worked resource, we call it resource. I had worked for twelve years doing the same kind of work, of course—grass and trees, and everything like that. Little different then the farm, but it was very interesting.

Ray Spahr

Raymond J. Spahr was a member of the Fairmont Presbyterian Church and an active member of the Marine Corps League, the VFW and American Legion. He and his wife, Doris, had two grown children—a son living in Cincinnati and a daughter in Avon Lake, Ohio. During World War II, Ray was in the 3rd 155mm Howitzer Battalion attached to the 1st Marine Division. He participated in campaigns against the Japanese on Bougainville and Okinawa. He spent three years in the Marine Corps in World War II—two and one-half years in the Pacific Theater and six months in the States. He attained the rank of staff sergeant in the Marines. Ray Spahr died June 16, 2001.

Could you tell us something about your life before you were in the Marine Corps?

Sure. I was born and raised in Greene County, near a little village called New Jasper. I was born and raised on a farm, and my mother passed away shortly after I was born so I went to live with my grandparents. And I had a great childhood. I graduated from high school in 1940 when I was 16.

Then I sold Fuller brushes for about a year before the war came along. It wasn't long until I got the same fever and fervor of all the other young men and that's when I joined the Marine Corps. Incidentally, I graduated from Xenia High School. The farm I was raised on was a working farm. We milked cows, fed the hogs, and did all those good things.

After I graduated I worked as a Fuller brush salesman and then after a year I went to work at Wright-Patterson Air Force Base. I worked there until I decided to go in the Marine Corps. I tried to enlist in November '42, but they had their quota filled so they just said, "We'll put you off until after Christmas." So it was January 5 of '43 that they sent me down to Parris Island.

Why did you happen to select the Marines?

Oh, I knew a guy that was in the Marines and I liked the color of their uniforms. Good-looking uniforms. Now the Marine Corps has a fairly rigorous boot camp. After we got off the bus, we took a train down to Atlanta, Georgia, and then up to Parris Island, South Carolina. And I remember as we got off the bus there were marines that were on liberty and they were always singing to us, "You'll be sorry, you'll be sorry."

So, they took us off the bus and I mean there was no let up after that. The first thing they did was march us to a barbershop and cut off all our hair. Every shred of it was gone. They do that for medical purposes. They didn't want any lice or anything, you know. And then they took us over to a quartermaster building where everybody was issued some dungarees and shoes and socks and so forth. And then they took us to the barracks. Now in the meantime we're carrying a suitcase, you know, with our clothes. And as soon as we got there we were told to change our clothes—which we did. We put them in the suitcase, sent the suitcase home, put on the Marine duds, and that was it. And then from then on you belong to the Marine Corps, and you really belong to the drill instructor.

We had a really good guy. He was strict as nails. He was ramrod stiff. He had served on Guadalcanal, you know. And he had got wounded there, came home, and they assigned him to Parris Island to train other young men. He knew what he was talking about. Then, of course, they got us up every morning around five. You'd go to the bathroom, brush your teeth, comb your hair, take a shower, get out of there, get in your clothes, and you generally had to be out in front of the barracks in line at 5:45 a.m. They marched you over to the chow hall where you had your breakfast, brought you back, went to the bathroom, whatever you had to do, and a few minutes later you were called outside and you went to the drill field.

And you drill, drill, drill, drill. Then later on you'd not drill so much, but you'd run the obstacle courses and you'd run the bayonet courses, and all that sort of thing. They trained you well. And since this guy had been in combat and was a long time marine, I think he'd been in ten or twelve years, he knew what he was talking about. For example, when he would take us into a thicket he'd say, "Hey, don't get so close together, one little grenade can wipe all of you out. Spread out, you know, get down on the ground." They really teach you what to do. We just fired the rifles and pistols. You don't get into the machine guns, the BARs and mortars, and things like that until you go to New River, North Carolina, which is an advanced training camp. I was there for three months—no leaves. I stayed there for about a month after my basic training was over. I worked at the headquarters office and I was allowed to go into a little town called Beaufort [pronounced Byoofert]. Beautiful Beaufort is by the sea. And we could go there to the shows and the beer halls and what not. The Marine Corps is pretty strict. They don't put up with a lot of stuff—at least when I was there. Anyway, I stayed in Beaufort for about a month. I think they just needed somebody at headquarters for a little bit.

What'd you do then?

I joined a mobile unit, and we went to Cuba, Puerto Rico, the Virgin Islands, and Trinidad. And we started interviewing marines to see what basic skills they had. We worked as a classification unit and gave this information to their commanding officers. You might have a guy that's a truck driver, but he's in a rifle battalion and you might have a radio operator that was in transportation. Anyway, they would review this and then they would try and place these people in spots where they were more vitally needed. But in the Marine Corps everybody is a rifleman. Everybody. And then you go from there.

Then I went to New River, North Carolina, for advanced training. I was there for a couple of months, I guess, and then they put us on a troop train and took us out to California in the fall of '43. Then we were sent over to a ship and we went to Nouméa, New Caledonia. That's a long trip. We were aboard ship for thirty-eight days. And the name of the ship was the SS *Skinner*. It was just one of the old liberty ships. The only thing that distinguished us from anybody else is that we had a platoon of war dogs aboard. And they were really fun. Everybody loves dogs, except these you couldn't pet because they'd take your arm off, you know, they were taught to be a little rough. Eventually we arrived in Nouméa, New Caledonia. I got to go ashore there one afternoon and I think we were there for maybe one day—one evening.

And then we went up past the Gilbert Islands. From there we went to Tulagi, and then we went into Guadalcanal. We went into Guadalcanal for a few days and then they sent us on to Bougainville. That was our first touch of combat. Guadalcanal was already secured. We had taken the area around Henderson Field and the army was in Guadalcanal attempting to mop up the remaining Japs and that sort of thing. There were still thousands and thousands of Japanese there, but it was secure as far as we were concerned. So they sent us to Bougainville—the northernmost of the Solomon Islands.

What unit are you in now?

Well, I went to become a member of the 3rd Marine Defense Battalion on Bougainville. I went over there as a replacement as everybody does, so I didn't go over with a unit that was intact. Then we went up to Bougainville and our job was to hold the island. Bougainville is a huge island. It's the only place I've ever been that has a live volcano. At night the clouds hung low and you could see the fire. You could see the glow, I should say it that way, and it rained almost every night. And there were thousands and thousands of Japanese on that island.

Occasionally they would attempt to come through our lines; but the Marine Corps had taken bulldozers and gone completely around the airfield. We put machine gun emplacements there, and it was only about fifty or one hundred yards from the field where we had our machine gun emplacements. And if any Japs came up there, bingo, they were knocked dead. I worked in an office for the commanding officer, stood guard duty, and did the usual things that any other private would do. I was there for several months and then I was sent back down to Guadalcanal.

Why was that, Ray?

Well, because they were getting ready for Peleliu. And my unit was going to Peleliu, but I didn't go with them because I'd just come off of the line at Bougainville. But they were getting ready to go so they finally sent us down there, and we marched and did all kinds of things down on Guadalcanal. I joined the 3rd 155mm Howitzer Battalion. I told you, they broke up the 3rd Defense Battalion—took the artillery out and sent it down to Guadalcanal. So we all joined the 1st Marine Division. Anyway, I was assigned to this 3rd 155mm Howitzer Battalion that was being formed and being trained and ready for duty. Most of these men had already been in

Ray Spahr.

campaigns, particularly Guadalcanal, and had then gone down to Australia and New Zealand for rest. From there they went to Cape Gloucester and fought in that campaign there. Finally, they brought them over to Guadalcanal to rest and get ready for the trip up to Peleliu.

And at that particular time the 3rd Marine Defense, or 3rd Marine Artillery outfit, had only mortars. But they took away their mortars and gave them artillery pieces. We had 155mm howitzers, not to be compared to the 105s, and we had to be trained to use these big weapons. They were big. They would shoot about fourteen miles. The long guns would shoot about nineteen, but ours went about fourteen. And so we trained there through that summer, you know, the summer of '44. That's when they left for Peleliu. Because I'd been up at Bougainville, they didn't take me. They left me in the rear echelon.

The 1st Marine Division was up at Peleliu for two or three months and they incurred terrible casualties there. One of my dear friends, his name was Henry Pine, was in charge of the motor corps of our little battalion. Henry was on a bulldozer clearing off a spot and ran over a mine. And that was the end of the bulldozer and Henry. And he was a really nice guy. Henry had been in the Marine Corps for a while, and he had a great big tattoo on his arm. It had a snake wrapped around it, and it said on the side, "Death before Dishonor." And then above it, it said, "Mother." And we used to tease Henry, and call him one of the death before dishonor guys, you know, but he did get killed.

And I had a friend that was in the Navy, he was a Navy Corpsman, and his name was Schnibben. I don't remember his first name now, but his name was Schnibben. And my name was Spahr—both guys with German backgrounds. And he called me Von Spahr and I called him Von Schnibben. And Schnibben got wounded and I never got to see him again. They put him on a hospital ship and sent him home. He was at Peleliu. He got shot—got shot in the stomach. I hope he survived it. So, finally they came back from Peleliu and we enjoyed a few months of inactivity—having fun and making stump juice.

What's stump juice?

Oh, we'd steal sugar from the commissaries, get some grape juice, go out in the jungle and make a still. Some of the guys would do this and it came out as clear as a glass of water, very powerful stuff. And you know, everybody's nineteen, twenty, or twenty-one years old, and we just had a good time. I remember seeing a USO show that came to Guadalcanal—a guy named Charlie Ruggles. Although I'm not a Catholic, I remember going to a midnight Mass at Christmas time on Guadalcanal.

But then we were getting ready to go to Okinawa. The landing was on April 1, 1945, April Fools' Day. To get there we went from Guadalcanal to Ulithi atoll. And it was supposed to be the biggest armada ever known to man. A thousand ships and one hundred thousand men. As far as you could see there was ships, and it was something to behold.

The principal thing I remember about that was, after we were out to sea two or three days, one morning I was out on deck, and I looked out to sea, and I saw this huge thing coming toward us. It was a long way off because you could only see fifteen or twenty miles at sea on the ocean. If you're up in the rigging you can see much farther, but down on the deck you can't see nearly that far. I said to a buddy, "What the heck is that?" And he said, "It looks like a big ship." And I said, "Well, it looks like it's coming at us sideways." Well, it came past us and it was the Big Ben, the Benjamin Franklin, and it had taken kamikaze and bomb hits. They lost fifteen hundred sailors. Somehow or other they had this tug hooked on to the Big Ben, and they towed it down to Ulithi. Why, I don't know, but then they took it back to Hawaii. I don't know whether they worked on it there or in the States, but they got the thing back in operation.

The trip from Ulithi to Okinawa took weeks. All those ships, and most don't go over eight or ten knots. That's about ten or eleven miles an hour, you know, and you're going thousands of miles. At any rate, when we got fairly close to Japan, close enough that we could pick up their radio signals, why, Tokyo Rose would come on, and she'd welcome us by units. She'd say, "Here's a message for the 3rd 155mm Howitzer Battalion," "Here's a message for the airmen of VFM number 22." Where she got this data, I don't know. They had spies everywhere, just like we did you know. But I remember they played our music, and she'd say, "Here's some good old American music for you boys. I'll bet you're homesick, why don't you take over those ships and sail them back home." It was funny.

But at any rate we got there and we were scheduled to go in on D-Day. But sometimes things go askew. One thing I didn't like was when we got to Okinawa they made everybody go below. Everybody but the working sailors had to go below. And you'd hear guns cut loose and we could hear airplanes and so forth. But you couldn't see a thing and you could hear bombs dropping. I think these were our airplanes and maybe some of theirs; but there were sure a lot of bombs dropping. And we just hoped they didn't hit our ship, you know, because you're down in that hole and you're not going to have much of a chance if the ship gets hit.

At any rate, toward evening they came down and told us we weren't gonna go ashore until the next morning. This was fine for most of us because we did get good food on the ship. We slept that night and the next day we went to the mess hall and they said we could have anything we wanted to eat—steak, you know. All I wanted was a couple of eggs. But then we had to go over the side down the rope ladder. And these small boats are banging into the side of the ship. So you go down, but you don't want to go very fast. If you do, you'll step on the guy's fingers that are on the rope below you. And if you don't keep going the guy ahead of you will step on yours. So it's a no-win situation. So, anyway you go down and when the small boat comes in, when the landing ship comes up against the ship, the minute it comes in you drop inside of it. Regrettably, some guy's timing would be off. Now keep in mind you've got a heavy pack, a rifle, ammunition, water, canteens of stuff, and you're as heavy as lead, although in those days I only weighed one hundred and seventy pounds. But, if you missed getting the ship, you go down in the water, and then the next time that thing slams in there you'd be in trouble. At any rate, none of our guys got hurt, but I heard that there were many injuries. Remember, there were soldiers and marines.

Anyway, we got in the landing craft and just like you see in the movies they took us out and we went round and round and round and round. Then all of a sudden, bingo, everybody strikes out for the shore. And then they took us right up on the shoreline. We went right up on the beach and the ship handler dropped the front gate and everybody runs out—we scattered just like the old DI told us to.

The first thing I saw when I got ashore was a dead horse. You feel so sorry for the animals and the civilians and stuff. And I remember the first night I was ashore I heard a machine gun going off and when we got up the next morning we saw where some old lady had come down the road, and of course, they told her to stop, to halt, and she didn't. She didn't understand and they killed her. And I saw a dead kid who couldn't have been over fourteen or fifteen. He was in a Japanese soldier uniform, but I doubt if he was a soldier because he didn't have a gun. You see those things the first two or three days.

When we went ashore the army did a feint toward the end of the island and the Japanese rushed all their troops down there. Well, the Marine Corps went north of a river. And the army went south of the river. Anyway, we went north of the river and there weren't many Japs up there. We just sailed right through the middle of that island. We went north on the island, the army went south.

Okinawa is ninety miles long. And I think at its widest it was much less. I could be wrong on that. I remember it was ninety miles long and it wasn't very wide. We marines went north and we swept all the way up to the end of the island. We were up there for a couple of days and nights and I can clearly remember all the airplanes and the dog fights over the water. The Japs were sending planes down by the hundreds. Planes would go down and we'd cheer—we didn't know whether it was American planes or Japanese planes, to tell you the truth, but we hoped it was Japanese. But then in the middle of the night everybody was awakened. And they said, "Get up but no lights." So we walked down the highway and we walked all night long. Toward morning we were walking along this road, we were walking four abreast, and they split us up because a jeep was coming along. And you know who was in that jeep? It was the day before he got killed and I was one of the last guys to see him—Ernie Pyle. Well, he was probably the foremost war correspondent of his day. He had served faithfully and courageously in Europe and he was a genuine American hero. We all yelled at Ernie, you know, and he waved at us. And I think it was the next day or the day after that that he got killed by a Japanese sniper on a little island called Ie Shima which was just off the coast of Okinawa.

After that my artillery battalion set up near the town of Naha which at that time was the principal city of Okinawa. It had been pretty well ravaged by bombs and shells, and stuff, and we started shelling the Japanese positions. Now a 155mm shell was so long it took two guys to put the shell in the breech of the cannon. And then there'd be another guy with a ramrod of some kind that they'd lift up there and he'd shove it in. And then, depending on how far they wanted to shoot the shell, they would put powder bags behind the shell and then close the breech. And then they had some sort of a firebrand that they'd stick in there and it would go off. At it's maximum the shell would go about fourteen miles. But we could also shell them much closer then that. You just don't put so much powder in the gun.

How do you select your targets?

In the daytime you have artillery observers that are either on top of a high hill or a mountain or something. Also in the daytime we had little Piper Cub airplanes that flew over the enemy and called out targets. We had a nice guy who was attached to us—his name was Lieutenant Andy Prewit. He must have had a premonition because he gave a friend of mine his revolver and said, "I can't use this in the plane. You keep it for me until I come back." And officers generally don't give up their weapons like that. But the guy said, "Sure, I'll keep it for you, Lieutenant." And he went up, and he never came back. Somebody said that they saw the plane get hit and there was just a flash. It obviously got hit by a shell, ours or somebody else's, and that was the end of it. But little things like that come back to you when you talk about it.

What'd you do particularly?

Not much. By that time I'd gotten to be a sergeant, and I spent my time checking personnel and directing people here and there—that's about it. I didn't do anything particular or spectacular. We had three firing batteries and one headquarters battery. I was in the headquarters battery. We had marines and infantry in front of us and we were lobbing shells over them.

Now I've never seen this happen, but at Saipan the enemy broke through our cordon of soldiers and marines, and the artillerymen lowered their rifles and artillery pieces and fired at the Japs point blank. They didn't throw their shells they just shot right into them. And they stopped them, but it was costly, of course. There were a lot killed there.

Okinawa was the biggest battle of the Pacific. [Note: 12,000 Americans killed, 45,000 wounded; 102,000 Japanese Military killed and 150,000 civilians killed.] I really felt sorry for the mothers and children and old folks. You just didn't see very many young people of soldiering age because the Japanese had conscripted them all. Our outfit just kept moving up. I remember that after we got past Naha we moved to another place. And I remember going through this one field, one big flat plateau, and that place was filled with burned out tanks. I regret to say that many were our tanks—but you know the Japs had weapons too.

The Marine Corps had a little different philosophy than the army did. The army was known to sit back and throw in a lot of artillery and bombs and stuff, and make these campaigns go on a long time. The Marine Corps' philosophy was get in, get the objective, and get out. And they felt you'd have less causalities doing it that way than the other way. So that's why our battles didn't last very long. We just kept moving south. And then one fine day the commander of the Japanese army realized that the jig was up so he killed himself and a lot of his people also committed suicide. The war, for all intents and purposes, was over. It was about a three-month campaign.

Then after about a month they pulled all the Marine division units together and they went to China. And I always regretted that I didn't go to China with them, but in those days you could come home if you had sixty-five points or something. And I had eighty some points. They asked me if I wanted to go to China, and I would have liked to have gone, but I thought I'd been so fortunate and I had all these points, so I decided to come home.

Tell me what you thought when you heard about the atom bomb.

Well, there was a friend of mine, his name was Pappy Malone, and everybody called him Pappy because he was twenty-nine years old and the rest of us were nineteen or twenty. He and I shared a shelter-half on Okinawa. We got up one morning and he said, "Hey, I hear they've dropped an A-bomb on Japan—some sort of different kind of bomb on Hiroshima." That was on August the 6th, 1945. And then two or three days later they dropped another one on Nagasaki. Yes. What did I think? Well, I was delighted. Anything that would save my life and the life of my comrades made me glad. I am sorry that so many people had to die but, hey, they were making plans right then for us to invade Japan. They estimated there would be a million American casualties if we had to invade Japan. So thank goodness that the emperor of Japan saw the folly of this war and agreed to surrender.

Do you stay in touch with your Marine outfit?

Yes, we go some place every year now. It started in 1990 when I went down to Washington, D.C., and met a bunch of the guys. That's when the 1st Marine Division was down there. They were honoring people that had been on Guadalcanal. I was there, as you know, but I didn't participate in the fighting there. George [H.W.] Bush was president and he came out and so did Colin Powell—and the secretary of defense was there too

How do you think World War II changed your life?

I don't know what I would have become, but it certainly did change it. I had never really been out of Ohio. I think I'd been to Kentucky—just across the river. But then after I came back, I was twenty-one or twenty-two years old and I had been halfway around the world and I've seen a lot of this country. I've seen a lot of the Caribbean, and I'm grateful to the Marine Corps for the opportunities I had. Finally, I'm very, very grateful I didn't get hurt, didn't get shot.

Robert Pohle

Robert W. Pohle was drafted into the United States Army and served as an aid man with the 7th Division, 184th Regiment, 3rd Battalion, Company L during the campaign for Okinawa in the Pacific Theater. He was wounded while in the line and subsequently was awarded the Combat Medic Badge, the Purple Heart Medal and the Bronze Star. When the war ended he served in the occupation of Korea for eleven months. After the war he married Catherine Jean and they had five children. He worked briefly in the roofing business but spent the rest of his career working in a medical care environment. He retired from the Kettering Medical Center. He attained the rank of technical sergeant while in the Army and is still active in the Centerville VFW post. He served a little over two years in the Army—August of 1944 to October of 1946.

I was born in Norristown, Pennsylvania, right outside of Philadelphia on May 27, 1926. There was nine of us in the family. My sisters had four brothers, and I only had three sisters. I'm third to the youngest—the fifth born. Two sisters were younger. My father worked for a Philadelphia electric company as an engineer. Went to school in Pennsylvania, and then in Takoma Park, Maryland. In 1941, we moved to Takoma Park, Maryland, right outside of Washington, D.C. That's where I finished school and graduated in 1944 from Takoma Park, Maryland. After that I did body and fender work for a company before I went into the Army. I learned the trade on the job. I worked for them a few months before I went into the service.

You were an aid man in the Second World War. Did you have some medical training before you went in?

Yes, I did. In our church, I belong to the Seventh Day Adventist Church, they wanted everybody to be medics, rather than go out and take lives, so they had what they called the medical cadet corps. They not only trained young men but women too. We had quite a training session there—took us right through a real hard course of medical aid. Then we belonged to the civilian defense, and we'd have drills at night when they'd have blackouts. Then we would get into trucks and take off to certain areas. When the lights came on you'd find people wounded all over the place, you know, mock catastrophe. It was very real. So that's where my medical training started.

And then when I went in the Army I was automatically put into the medics because of that prior training. This program went on for a good five or six years. Probably longer than that because our son that's a minister now was in it for a while. I think that he was one of the last ones. There's a place up in Michigan that's called Camp Desmond Doss. Doss got the Congressional Medal of Honor. He was a medic, and at Okinawa he saved over 65 lives at one time by lowering them down over an embankment.

Where did this program start?

Well, Washington, D.C., was the headquarters. We trained for probably six months or so. We got in our uniforms and went out there and drilled. Then on August 30, 1944, I was drafted. I took my papers and gave it to them. And luckily, instead of sending us right overseas to be in combat, why, we took more training. I had regular basic at Camp Barkley, Texas. We did a lot of marching and drilling and stuff, and then we went through the obstacle course. Then, they had a place where you'd lay on your stomach and they shot machine gun bullets over your head. You had to watch out for tracers and stuff like that. Of course, being a medic, I didn't have to fire weapons.

So after we had our regular basic we had thirteen more weeks of medical training. We stayed pretty much in the same camp, but I think we moved to different barracks. The training was similar to what medical cadet corps was except it was a little more strenuous. When we finished we got a leave, went home for two weeks, and then we went to Fort Lawton in Seattle. That's when we went overseas.

Were you in a unit then?

No. I was just a replacement. We went from Seattle to Hawaii, and then after about a week in Hawaii we got on a Navy ship and went to Saipan for a week. On the way to the ship on Oahu we rode in little cars that they haul pineapples in. That was a fun experience. Like little box cars or coal cars.

Anyway, then we went to Saipan in the Marianas Islands, got off the ship there and stayed a week. I think we stopped at Eniwetok for a couple days, and they let us swim off shore. We never got on the island, we stayed on the ship. This must have been March. March of '45. Because in March

'45, we were on the ship, and I wrote my niece this letter. I told her three great things happened. I said, I was in the Army on a ship going overseas, President Roosevelt died, and you were born. So, my second niece was born in March. And then my brother-in-law was killed over in Germany at that time. I got that word over in Hawaii when we landed in Hawaii on April the first. In March we would be between Seattle and Hawaii, and then we landed in Hawaii on April one, 1945. That's the day when they invaded Okinawa. I had never heard of the place. So, I "invaded" Hawaii at the time they invaded Okinawa.

I didn't get to Okinawa until May of '45. It's south of Japan, the southernmost island of Japan, probably about 350 miles away—something like that. They say, if the flag raising on Iwo Jima had never been done, Okinawa would have been more publicized than Iwo Jima. It was a very fierce battle.

When did you arrive in Okinawa?

Sometime in May, I can't remember. I was still eighteen years old at the time, but I know I was in battle because I was wounded on the 24th of May, 1945. We must have got to Okinawa around the 15th of May, somewhere in there, I'm not sure. It'd been going on for about six weeks when I got there. I was assigned to the 184th Infantry [Regiment] of the 7th Division, Company L, 1st Platoon. I was a medical aid man and I remember they told me to go around and get acquainted with the troops, you know, so when you're in battle they know who you are.

So, while we were there, when I first joined them, this guy started screaming medics, medics—so we went running. What he was doing, he was shooting himself through the foot, but he missed. It was kind of funny, you know, he screamed medics before he pulled the trigger so we'd be there, but then he missed.

They were back in a rest area when I joined them, so I wasn't up on the line immediately. You know, these guys take so much and then they can't stand it anymore, so they shoot themselves—usually through the foot. But it was an experience.

So then we went on the line into battle—now that was a real experience. On my first casualty they yelled medic, and the wounded guy was up on a hill. Anyway, this guy yelled medic, and I ran up on the hill. This fellow had a bullet that went through his helmet, followed the contour around, went out and hit his back and put a little slit in his back about an inch long. He had been bent over so the bullet just followed it around. That was my first case. So I patched him with a Band-aid as I remember it. I didn't give him a shot because he wasn't that bad. So, while we were up there the Japanese opened up with artillery, and of course we dug in and hugged that dirt.

Were you afraid at this time?

Oh, yes, sure. Artillery was going off all over the place, and when we came down our lieutenant says, "I never expected to see you boys come back, 'cause the artillery barrage was fierce." So then, while we were standing there deciding what to do, one of the guys got shot in the kidney. We were taking care of him, and while we were taking care of him, another guy gave a scream and a bullet went through his elbow.

I was the only medic in L Company—each platoon had their own medic. And you take care of them, of course, and then you give them morphine, or they used sulfadiazine back then. Awful bad on the wounds. This

Robert Pohle.

fellow's name happened to be Duke Ellington. I think he died. Only thing you can do, I bandaged him up and got him back to the first aid station. The litter-bearers would come and get him and take him back. And 'course, the guy that got shot in the elbow was carrying on more than the guy shot in the kidney. The guy shot in the kidney was serious, but the elbow case was hurting. So I patched him up and got him back to the aid station; then we made more moves. This was my first day in combat. It might have been over a couple days 'cause our first push we were in the Naha-Surei-Yonabaru line.

Naha was the capital. Naha was a real nice little town, but we went right through it even though snipers opened up on us. And the next time we come through it, why, it was all bulldozed—gone. Didn't take a chance anymore. I remember that. The snipers were hiding in the village.

I remember the first night out, it was raining like mad, and I happened to look down and there was a thing sticking out of the ground. It was a landmine. I missed that thing by about a foot. It was a good thing it had been raining or I'd have been blown to pieces. And when you saw your first dead person, which for me was Japanese, it made you sick. But when you saw your first dead American it *really* made you sick. I think the most I ever saw dead in one place was probably six or seven guys. Japanese artillery got them.

Then we kept on pushing and I think I was lucky because we didn't have real bad cases of guys getting legs blown off and stuff like that. If they hit a landmine, why they were dead. One guy had a mortar hit his back, and of course he was blown apart—you see them with their heads blown off, chests blown off.

And the day I got wounded, why, this guy yelled medics. Well, we were up on a hill so I ran down and a machine gun bullet had hit his leg—two bullet holes in each leg. I patched him up and about that time a piece of shrapnel hit me in the shoulder which really wasn't that bad. It was a mortar, I imagine, 'cause the Japs were setting off mortars. I was gonna go up on the hill and look for this guy, but they said, "No use 'cause he's already dead." Anyway, I was hit in the back—the back of the shoulder—the left shoulder. To jump forward for a minute, in 1948, I couldn't raise my arm. I went out to the VA and had it x-rayed and they said, "You've got a piece of shrapnel in there." What it did was it worked its way through, and it's lodged in there now. I've seen x-rays of it. It's a little shiny piece of metal. It hurts. But anyhow, I went back to the first aid station, they bandaged it up, and I went back up on the lines.

When we used to take metal out of guys, you know, after they'd get hit, you could see it and you'd dig it out, and stuff like that there. I remember one night they called medic and, this is terrible, somebody back in the States, when they put the grenades in a box, someone pulled the pin. You know grenades are always in a little canister. They pulled the pin, and when these guys took out the grenades, of course, they triggered it. Instead of getting rid of it real fast he held on to it too long and it blew up. It killed him and, I think, wounded four guys. I thought, boy, whoever did that, were they playing a joke or were they doing it on purpose. These guys, when they do this stuff, don't realize the consequences. It might have been some prankster, but it might have been somebody attempting sabotage.

One other time we were bivouacked around a place, I think this was on a patrol, and this guy set up a booby trap during the night. When he went to disarm it the next day it blew up. He had holes in his hands, and his face was almost blown off. He was a mess. Of course, there was another medic there and he took care of him, but I don't think he lived.

How many men would be in your platoon?

I'd say probably forty. Might be a little more or less. The platoon suffered quite a few casualties. Well, one time we were in the same area where the guy got blown up when the grenade exploded in his face, and there was a cave, and we were all standing around there looking, and these guys decided to throw a grenade in. They threw the grenade, and dummy me, I didn't have my helmet on, and all of the sudden I felt this thing brush the top of my head. Of course, if I'd had the helmet on it might have hit the helmet and killed me. That was scary to feel that thing go rushing over your head.

This bullet here in my shadow box reminds me of a story. We were patrolling, we were up near Hill 89. We were dug in, a couple guys and us, just behind a little bank. All of a sudden there was all of this firing and everybody says, "Oh, boy, it must be a counterattack." So we thought we better move to a lower spot. So, about that time I put my helmet on and just as I lifted up my head I heard this conk, and that bullet hit me right in the helmet and put a big dent right in the helmet. Just below the 't' [a patch]. It hit me in the helmet, and put a big dent in it. If I hadn't had that helmet on why I'd probably be dead. So the next morning I went back and looked around, and there it was laying on the ground. I kept it all these years—over fifty years. That was scary. I wished I'd kept the helmet.

Would you explain what you brought today?

Well, I was a technician 3rd grade when I got out. Went in as a PFC, and then I went to Korea for eleven months—that's where I got my promotions. I ended up a technician 3rd grade which is the same as a staff sergeant. This is the Purple Heart. A Purple Heart is a medal given to people who are wounded. This is a very important one here. This is a medic combat badge. And this medal is a Bronze Star that's given for being in combat—because I was a medic. Actually got that fifty years later. And these are what we call dog tags. This is the 7th Division patch—the hourglass division. The 7th Division fought an awful lot of places. I think it started up in Attu in the Aleutian Islands and then went on and fought in Kwajalein in the Marshall Islands. And they were in the Philippines too I believe. And finally Okinawa. And then they went to Korea and fought that fierce war there. [Note: Readers may want to look up *Life* magazine of October 18, 1945. *Life* magazine was trying to show one day in the life of an infantryman, and they selected a soldier from the 7th Division.] And then the 184th Infantry was deactivated.

This is a Japanese flag that I got, I don't remember just where I got it, but I got it off a dead Japanese—it was full of shrapnel holes. The Japanese carried their flag with them in their packs, and apparently the shrapnel went through. I dare say he was probably killed and I got the flag. Here's another one. This one I picked up, it doesn't have any holes in it, it's getting kind of old. This is a saber, a samurai sword, I got on the battlefield. They didn't use it on me. Apparently, most of the Japanese soldiers carried sabers. That blade is just as sharp as a razor. I'm not sure what these are worth anymore, but every once in a while people come to town and want to buy your sabers. It's worth a lot of money, I think. This is a Japanese rifle. That's the bayonet. It's pretty wicked. This one here came right off the battlefield because it has the emperor's seal on it, and I understand that the Japanese didn't want them to get away with that seal on it, so they ground them all off. This one happens to have it on. Anyway, it still fires. My son fired it about a year ago. The bullets go down in there and I think it holds about six bullets. With their rifles you had to cock it each time, but ours was automatic. We had the M1. All of these came right off the battlefield. Here's a bugle I got. It's a Japanese bugle. This is my first Purple Heart; it was pinned on me a year after battle. It was pinned on me over in Korea by a colonel or something. They had a group of us in there—I think it was two hundred and fifty. I have a picture in the book that shows them pinning the medals on us. That was quite an honor. We even had forgotten about it, and one day they said, "Hey, get dressed. You're going to have a Purple Heart pinned on you today."

When did they declare Okinawa secure?

I think it was in June. There were an awful lot of casualties. I don't remember exactly how many anymore. I didn't see the kamikazes, most of that was out at sea. I know on the island, planes patrolled the island continually—P-38s and P-40s. And I fell in love with that P-38. You didn't even have to look up. You could hear that thing, it had just a different sound, it was just a sweet sound. And this here's a Japanese knife I got over there. It was in a kit I guess. I kind of beat it up, I've used it for everything—hammering, cutting. It's a pretty sturdy knife. This is a copy of the "Hourglass Division" paper they put out. It's kind of dilapidated now, but it shows a few pictures of it. Tells about the 184th Infantry Regiment getting deactivated. The 184th went back to Fort Ord, California; that's where it's home base was. Then it became the 31st Infantry.

Did you go back in the line after being wounded?

Right. I wasn't wounded that bad. I was in the line 'til the end of the campaign. The Marines came one way, and we came the other, and we met up around Hill 89, and what the name of the mountain was I have no idea.

Could you estimate for our viewers how many people you might have treated as an aid man?

Like I say, I was pretty lucky, but I'd probably say between 25 & 50. That's an estimate. Might not have been that many, might have been more. Replacements come in and then you take care of other guys too, you know, other platoons that happen to be nearby.

We patrolled a lot. One night I remember in particular, which still bothers me, we were patrolling and we were near a big drainage ditch. Why we didn't put our camp close to the drainage ditch I don't know. Anyway, during the night we could see movement, and I always was trained to yell 'halt' if somebody was behind the lines at night. Well we yelled and nobody stopped, so the guy started opening up, and all of a sudden they were throwing grenades. When that stopped all heck broke loose, and we thought, oh boy, we better get out of here, and get over to where it's safer. So, these guys over there saw us running, and they were going to shoot at us, but, they said, "No if that's the Japs, those guys will get them." Fortunately, they didn't shoot. So, we went up and dug in.

The next morning we went out, and there must have been, oh, I'll say fifty people or more, women and kids laying all over the place, just splattered. It was horrible. I remember I took a baby off of one little woman's back, and she said, "Water, water," so I gave her water, and she died just like that. She was really shot up. Those BARs (Browning automatic rifle)—boy, they can tear you up. I think that was the saddest thing I ever saw in the war, all those civilians. We just didn't know who they were. You see, the Japanese took their families with them when they moved. But, if they'd have just laid still there wouldn't have been any problem. But we didn't know. We patched them up the best we could. Then we found an old man in a ditch and his leg had just about been blown off—just the skin holding it on. Got him some help. Of course, we moved on and the ambulance, and stuff, took them out.

I had one girl, Okinawa girl, and she had shrapnel wounds on her back, just the whole side here, and I started taking off the gauze she had on it, and it was full of maggots which probably saved her life 'cause they go in there and eat out the dead flesh. When I got to that they said, "Leave it alone." I just left it alone and re-bandaged it. I guess our guys took good care of them. We were in Okinawa 'til August '45.

What did you think of the atom bombs we dropped?

Great. That ended the war. I mean, it was a horrible thing. And I think the United States today seems to be trying to apologize to Japan for doing it. But it's like this one Japanese general said, "Don't you think for a minute we wouldn't have used it on the United States if we'd had it first?" He said, "We sure would." The military didn't even bat an eye at using it in Japan; they knew it was the best thing. But that ended the war. Otherwise, we were starting to train to go into Japan, and there would have been more people killed in those battles than got killed from that atom bomb. We were happy when we heard about the atomic bomb.

I got a picture here somewhere that shows Sad Sack digging in because the night the Japs surrendered the whole sky lit up with ack-ack, artillery shells, and gunfire, and we didn't know what was going on. We actually thought the Japanese are making a counter attack again. For example, I was standing in my tent and all of a sudden this red thing flashed by me. I thought it was a tracer and I hit the dirt but it was a cigarette. I think there were three or four guys killed that night, I forget how many were wounded. These were just guys celebrating the end of the war. That was kind of sad, but I guess that happens. And then we stayed in Okinawa for another month or so, packed up and went to Korea.

There was a big typhoon in Okinawa. I just missed that by a couple of days. We went to Korea as occupation troops. We were the first troops in there. Went in at Inchon, I believe. As we marched down the street, the Japanese were all lined up and they turned their backs to us. And all of us were praying, "Please don't let there be a diehard that turns around and starts shooting us." And we marched into their regimental headquarters and the Japanese officers took off their pistol belts and handed them to our officers. It was quite a sight.

And how long were you there in Korea?

I think I was in Korea eleven months. After we left Korea we got on a ship, the *William's Victory*. This is the ship that we came home on. They put us on it in Korea and we went to Yokohama Harbor and stayed there three days. While we were in Yokohama Harbor the Japanese would come out in their little boats and we'd throw them cigarettes and candy bars, and everything. I think there was 1,500 GIs on that ship. When we arrived in the states we went to Fort Lawton and from there we got on a train and went to Fort Meade, Maryland. That's where I was discharged.

When I got out of the army, I worked for my brother who was in the roofing business for a while. This was in Takoma Park, Maryland, outside of Washington, D.C. And then I decided I needed to find a wife, so I went to work for a hospital there, and that's where I met my wife. I worked in purchasing, and she was in nurses' training. So, I met her and we've been married over 51 years now. We had five kids, and we have about fourteen grandchildren now.

Did you ever take advantage of the GI Bill of Rights?

No. I should have, but I didn't. I just wasn't college oriented. I worked for my brother in roofing, and then I came to Dayton when I married her in 1948. I worked for Dayton Power and Light for about a year and a half. Back in those days you had to drop out of nurses' training if you got married. Silly rules. So after a year we went back, and she finished her training. Then we came back and stayed in Dayton because my wife's from Dayton. I went to work for KayWalt Manufacturing as a machinist and worked there seventeen years. Then I got tired of that and went to work for Kettering Medical Center in plant engineering until I retired.

I have sisters who are nurses—wife's a nurse. Our school was called Washington Missionary College at that time; it's called Columbia Union College now. But mostly they trained preachers, secretaries, nurses, and doctors, and that was about it. That's probably the reason I didn't go to school 'cause I'm mechanically inclined.

How do you think World War II changed your life?

It probably made a better man out of me. I was real timid you know. Even when I got out of the Army I was still kind of timid, but I think that experience helped out. Got me out of that timidness. Also, I'd never traveled. Up until the time I went into the Army we lived in Pennsylvania. My parents never owned a car, so everywhere we went we walked or took a bus. And the furthest I ever got from home was sixty miles up to Plainfield, New Jersey, where my sister lived. And when I was just fifteen, I think I saw my first ocean. The next time I saw it, I crossed it. My dad took sick and so my brothers moved to Takoma Park and started the roofing business. And so my dad worked with them up until he died.

Sometimes kids come up and thank you for serving and helping out. Just like my hat says, "I served with pride!" And I did. I would have been very disappointed if I hadn't gotten into that war. Most guys would have, I think. The only thing, if I had it to do over I would have enlisted in the Navy. I wanted in the Navy so bad. And my friend and I when we were drafted, they said, "What service you want in?" We said, "Navy." They said, "You're in the Army." That's like a friend of ours, his dad was in the Navy—rather in the merchant marine, he says, "If the war comes get in the Navy, you'll always have a nice dry bed at night." This friend whose dad said get in the Navy was on an aircraft carrier, the *Ticonderoga*, and it got hit by one of those kamikaze planes, but he's living.

Les Prether

Les Prether was born and raised in the Dayton area and Green County. He was the oldest of nine children and graduated from Xenia Central High school. After the war he married his wife Carol and they are the parents of two children. Prether enlisted in the Marine Corps where he was attached to that service's air wing (night fighters). He entered the service in August of 1943 and served for about two and one half years until his discharge in February of 1946. He attained the rank of corporal in the Marines and is still an active member of the VFW and American Legion. After the war he attended Wittenberg College and the University of Dayton under the GI Bill of Rights. Prether sold cars and trucks, primarily trucks, in the Miami Valley for forty-six years after the war.

Les, could you tell us a little bit about where you were born and raised?

I was born in Dayton and raised in Dayton and Greene County. We moved often according to how much the landlord would handle. We lived on a farm a lot of times, and a lot of times we lived in town. I'm the oldest of nine children. My dad worked at NCR and at different jobs. When we were on one farm we butchered hogs and had a route where we sold meat, mostly in the Belmont area. He was a nice guy, but he'd get in trouble a lot of times and it was kind of hard on the kids 'cause, you know, other kids are pretty cruel about teasing people.

When I went in the service I thought I was nothing, but the service helped me more than anything I've ever done. I mean I went to ordnance school and I was one of the top students in the class even though there were college kids and everything. I went to school at Bellbrook, then Beavercreek, then Xenia Central where I finally graduated.

Were you in any activities in high school— any sports or clubs?

Oh, no, I wasn't. I worked most of the time. One time I worked in Alpha. Then I worked at Marshall Brother's filling station and in a poolroom for several years. I started out sweeping the concrete and cleaning the bathrooms. Then I'd do wax jobs for people and clean their cars. I worked full time there until I was out of school. You know, in our day getting a job was a wonderful thing. It didn't matter what the job was, even if it was simple or working in the service station or poolroom or whatever. At least that's the way I felt. Jobs just weren't that easy to get. And the last thing my father bought me when I got out of the eighth grade was a new suit. After that I paid for all my school supplies and clothing and everything. They always fed me, but it was a different time and different conditions. And it wasn't unusual, my circumstances weren't. But my father didn't finish school. He ran away and went west—he's kind of a maverick. Good personality, but he kept us on the move.

How old were you when the war started?

Let's see. I was fourteen or fifteen, I guess, when the war started. I went in during the year of '43. I was seventeen then, so if it started in '41, I'd have been fifteen. I had a buddy that wanted to join the Marines and we were gung-ho. We thought we were heroes, you know, and so we joined. We had a terrible time getting our parents to approve. You had to get your parent's signature then because we were too young. Anyway, we signed up and we were inducted at Cincinnati.

Then we went to Parris Island in South Carolina. It was pretty rugged training. And the only thing that really happened to me that was bad was I got some kind of fever, some kind of flu, and I passed out once when we were marching. And when you passed out they just marched over you 'cause they knew some people faked this. Then they'd turn around and march over you again, you know, if you didn't get up. But I had to go in the hospital for about a week. I really felt great about the training. They make you tough, you know, and they really make you proud to be a marine.

In most services there was a lot of esprit de corps during World War II. A lot of people felt it was their duty to go to war, to enlist in the war, to serve, and I still think that's very important for everybody to feel this way. And people looked down on you if you didn't go in. But I must say the training was tougher than I expected—definitely. I mean they marched you, woke you up in the middle of the night, you'd fall out, and then they'd march you at night. If they caught you talking or something it was very tough. I had a lot of buddies—always had a lot of buddies. I have a couple of them that I'm still friends with even today. Not from the basic training group but when I went to ordnance school and joined the outfit I served in. I went to ordnance school after two months at Parris Island, that was at Norman, Oklahoma. That was aviation ordnance school.

How did you happen to go into aviation ordnance?

Well, at that age I was finished with school in my mind. I went through the junior year and then I enlisted but they forced me to go to school because of my IQ score. Like I said, I thought I was pretty dumb, but the Marines forced me to go on. In the Marines you take IQ tests—everybody does. Mine must have been pretty good I guess. And there were other people trying to get in different schools. You know, after boot camp they're trying to get into these schools and they wouldn't let them.

I didn't want to go, but I had to, so I was sent to Oklahoma—Norman, Oklahoma. But we weren't at the University of Oklahoma. This was a basic camp—it was a Marine and a Navy base is what it was. They taught naval aviation courses on ordnance which is bombs, guns, torpedoes and that sort of thing. They taught us how to load them, how to break the guns down and repair them, and whatever it takes to keep the guns operating on an airplane. There were fifty-caliber machine guns and twenty mm cannons. At that time they had some basic rocket weapons too but it was very elementary. But anyway, that was the basic training.

Les Prether.

After I got assigned to general duty and when I went overseas I never got out of that—never wanted to get out of it really. I was in ordnance school for sixteen weeks I think. By this time it was the spring of '44. Then they sent me to Cherry Point Marine Air Base, North Carolina, and two months later they sent us to California.

And did you begin working on planes?

No, I didn't. I was on general duty there too. In general duty you do jobs, general things, you know, like I told you. I built a mess hall on Okinawa, drove a truck, got equipment and stuff that we needed—that we didn't have. Like one time when I was on Okinawa we wanted to get fresh meat. Our pilots were night pilots and so somebody some place along the line got brandy issued to night pilots 'cause it's rich in vitamin A. That's the story anyway. And so we had more brandy than we could use. Pilots tried to drink it all but they couldn't do it. So we traded for things. One day we went down to the beach to the army base and got a duck [land/sea vehicle] and went out to an LST [Landing ship tank] in the harbor and traded them brandy for fresh meat. And that's pretty much the way a lot of people did things when they needed something—they just went and got it one way or the other. And so we had a whole truckload of beef sides.

So anyway, we were living pretty high compared to everybody around us. I was really just waiting to be assigned at Cherry Point. Finally I got the assignment to the squadron—the VMF542. These were F6F fighter planes— night fighters. Their nickname was the Hellcats. They had 20mm cannon and about six fifty caliber machine guns—and they could carry bombs too.

What kind of missions did they fly?

Well, they made night raids and they'd go wherever they were assigned. They would also machine gun and bomb Japanese airfields. That's what they'd be after most of the time. To my knowledge this was their principal task. They were not involved in giving close support to Marine troops. They were always flying to another island trying to knock out enemy airplanes on the ground.

After I joined the 542nd we were put on a train out to the West Coast, got on board ship, and went to our first island which was part of the Caroline Islands. We stopped in Hawaii for a day or two but that was very brief. The island was so small that they had to make the landing strip longer so the airplanes could land there because our planes came in on an aircraft carrier.

The Sea-Bees built the landing strip so it was long enough to handle the Hellcats. This was on Ulithi Island. This place was infested with mosquitoes, but they sprayed it with DDT. They sprayed us too. We didn't realize it was as dangerous as it was but within two weeks there was no mosquitoes on any of these particular islands in the Caroline Islands. We went from California to Hawaii and then from Hawaii to Ulithi. This is located in the western Carolines if you look on a map. It's probably about four or five thousand miles west of Hawaii. It's a long distance. Not far from the Palau Islands really. That's where a lot of our ships were harbored. This would be in the summer of '44—something like that.

When we got to Ulithi we had to haul supplies and do just general things. They made the airfield longer and we finally erected our tents—four men in a tent, and that's where we lived while we were flying out of there. And then we got on a ship and went to Okinawa.

How many missions would they go out on in a week?

I'd say they would go out just about every day. They didn't go out usually on the weekend, but during the week it was every day. They went mostly at night. That was their thing. When they trained in the United States they had shields over their windshield so they couldn't see out. They just had to do everything by instrumentation. We lost one pilot before we left because of the shield. He put it on and that got him confused and he crashed.

We had about fifteen planes in our squadron. We lost about four pilots, I believe, after we went overseas in raids against the Japanese. Anyway, we went to Okinawa on April the 1st of 1945. But when we landed there was no resistance. It was quite a sight. There were ships everyplace. It was just awesome. And a lot of our ships were damaged badly, you know, when the kamikazes hit them. They had a harbor on an island next to us and they put most of those ships in that harbor that had their superstructures blown off by the kamikazes.

And then we occupied an airfield, a Japanese airfield, and that's where we flew out of. I never saw a kamikaze crash into a ship in person. We saw hundreds of airplanes when we were on board ship. The harbor was full of ships with a lot of firepower and we had a lot on our field. So they bombed us and strafed us almost daily. Sometimes in broad daylight. When that happened we crawled into a foxhole. I put my tent over a Japanese gun emplacement so I had thick walls. So I didn't get up unless the bombing and strafing got really heavy. And then we built a place in the corner of this dugout and put sandbags over the top of it. Then when it got real bad we had one on the outside which we dug that was deeper in the ground. When it got real bad we went to that one.

The worst thing about the bombing raids was our own shrapnel which was falling out of the sky like rain, you know, these shell heads and stuff were falling on top of us. This was debris from our own shelling. And of course the Japs did some damage by strafing and bombing but not much. They were generally ineffective as far as striking the targets.

Then the Japs landed troops one night right on our airstrip. And they did a lot of damage for the number of their men that made it. 'Cause they'd have charges on their chest and as a last resort, they'd usually been wounded two or three times, they'd jump on one of our airplanes and set off the charge and they'd blow themselves and the airplane up. And so they did a lot of damage for the few men that made it. But most of them we shot out of the sky.

It was almost impossible to fly through there without being hit by our shrapnel. Anti-aircraft fire was heavy because we had the Navy in the harbor and all of our own guns. And so when they bombed us or strafed us they had to be lucky to get through this maze of firepower. But as I said, this one night they landed troops on our field and they were suicide troops. One of our boys got blinded that night and it was his own fault. He went out the next morning to look for souvenirs and there was still a Japanese out there and he threw a grenade at him and got him. We all did things like that but we shouldn't have done it.

The worst thing about going ashore on Okinawa was that you had to go over the side of the ship on nets—right off the side of the ship. And the water was rough so these landing craft would keep slamming against the ship and if you got caught in there you got smashed. So the only thing you could do is just watch and see how high the water brought the landing craft up and hit the ship, and that's when you cut loose and just fell onto the landing craft. It was difficult because we had our rifles and knapsacks and gas masks. After the first landing my gas mask wasn't in the bag, it was full of food.

And the first time we landed in the Caroline Islands we ate those K rations and that was like eating cardboard, it was horrible. Just no taste at all. So when I landed at Okinawa I was ready to eat. And the first night I was frying bacon and sleeping on the beach because I had Sterno with me and canned bacon and I lived very well.

I went ashore on April 1st . This was the date of the invasion. We began using the airfield after just a few days because the Japanese had left—they went south on the island. The United States faked an attack on Formosa so a lot of the Japanese troops had left Okinawa to go to Formosa. We never attacked Formosa, but they thought we were going to attack there. We bombed them and had landing craft out in the water. But we never went ashore—we went further north to Okinawa.

Where was your base?

We were in the center of Okinawa. Then later we went north to a new airfield that we'd built. Then we went to Japan after that. We flew to Japan. I wasn't involved in the land fighting because I was in the air wing. But the line marines were. It was a bloody battle. But in my squadron we were flying missions to enemy islands and enemy shipping. Course there wasn't too much resistance because the Japanese were pretty well on their knees. We bombed everything and finally they dropped the atom bombs.

I was on Okinawa when the atomic bombs were dropped. It was hard to believe, you know, when they described it. It was almost impossible to believe anything would be that devastating. But we flew over those cities and it was horrifying. But it had to be done.

How'd you happen to do that?

Well, they took us on a C-47 just to see it. Like I said, I wasn't usually where I was supposed to be. We went there long before they even signed the treaty or anything. When the war ended we went to Yokosuka which is in Tokyo Harbor. Yokosuka was a Japanese naval air base. That's where we went. Everything was in caves—even aircraft hangars and engines and supplies. If we'd attacked Japan on the ground thousands and thousands of Americans would have been killed. Hiroshima and Nagasaki, even though that was horrifying, saved a lot of men. Trying to occupy Japan would have been futile 'cause they were in caves, and the caves had been there for hundreds of years.

And the Japs had some food supplies in the caves so at night, a lot of times, they would sneak in through some other cave outside of the base and we'd catch them. Tyrone Power, the actor, was the pilot of our C-47 to Japan.

What did you do in the army of occupation?

Well, we had to get things in shape so our planes could operate out of the airfield. And also I was on a detail that was cleaning out these giant tanks; they had fuel tanks in the mountains that had big valves on them. We had to repack all those. And I also drove a truck up there. I drove to Yokohama to get oil for our planes—drums of oil. We had no problem at all with the civilians. Except they'd sneak onto our base at night and steal food, but other than that nothing—they were hungry too. I was in the army of occupation about three months, I think.

Did you learn any new skills that have stood you in well?

Ordnance school wouldn't be applicable because it was guns and bombs. I'll tell you what did help me—to get my self-confidence and self worth. I think it benefited me more than anything. It also saved my teeth, you know, because they have dentists. When I was a boy the only time you went to the dentist was when you couldn't stand the pain. So I still have a lot of my teeth as a result of going to the service.

My Marine Corps duty was very important. Very important. And I knew it at the time. After I got through boot camp I thought I was king of the island, you know? The confidence they gave you—it's just great. And it made you healthier.

I was discharged at Bainbridge, Maryland. Then I took advantage of the GI Bill of Rights—the whole time I was in college. The government paid for that. I went to Wittenberg one year, and then I went to night school at the University of Dayton for three years. But I never graduated. Like I said, the service gave me a lot more confidence in myself. I didn't have any at all when I went in the service. I'm proud that I went and I'm also proud that I'm an American. And if you're not proud you're not paying attention 'cause all those men died for us. And I think that everybody has a duty to serve and they feel better about themselves if they do it.

James Stuart

James M. Stuart was born and raised in Dayton, Ohio, in the Belmont area. He graduated from Fairmont High School in May of

1944. Stuart and his wife are the parents of two boys who now live in Springboro, Ohio, about eight miles south of Centerville. Jim is in a business partnership with one of his sons today. Stuart's career involved work in personnel and industrial relations with the McCall Corporation and later, in the early 1980s, he worked on the floor of the New York Stock Exchange. He ended up becoming a broker and is still doing this kind of work.

Where was your first post in the Navy?

Great Lakes—fall of 1944. I was at Great Lakes for seven weeks. We learned how to fire fight, and how to climb rope, and how to save yourself, and how to handle phones for shipboard communication. And I learned some of the fundamentals of seamanship, very little, but some of communication. Then I was put on a troop train and in four days I was on the west coast— Alameda, California. We went into that center and very quickly we moved out of there, and I was shipped to Bremerton, Washington, and went aboard the USS *Franklin* in December of '44, early December of '44. Our carrier was the largest attack carrier at that period of time.

James Stuart.

Could you say something about your carrier?

We had a torpedo bomber, the Avenger, and that was used in attacks against shipping including Japanese naval vessels. Then we had a Grumman F4F Wildcat. That was a support fighter plane that went with the Avengers and also provided support and fighter protection for the carrier and the carrier group. Then we had the advanced version of the F-4F, the F-6F—a much better plane. Very good in combat against the Japanese. And finally, the Corsair, the most wonderful plane in World War II that I ever saw. It was a beautiful ship, and it handled itself beautifully against anything the Japanese had.

The *Franklin* had been hit in the Battle of the Philippine Sea at Elite

Gulf and was brought back for quick repair and for replacement of about one hundred and ten people that had been hurt or killed. I was a replacement for somebody that had been lost. When I went on board ship we immediately went to sea—headed south and went out under the Golden Gate Bridge. We went to sea with two new air groups that wound up on board. That was a tremendous experience for me because I never realized how many people could get hurt so quickly. That really caused me to grow up in a hurry. Because in those early days at sea, pilots would miss the ship on approach, or pilots would run into the island, or pilots just simply didn't have enough power to get off the deck. And over the course of maybe five or six early days at sea, we lost fourteen people. This was not even in combat. These were training exercises and getting them ready for combat.

We had thirty-five hundred people on board—twenty-five hundred were ship's crew, and one thousand were part of the air groups. And you know, the ship was one thousand feet long—at that time a huge ship. We could run forty-five to fifty knots which, of course, was an amazing speed. We outran everything in the fleet. Destroyers and cruisers could not keep up with us. To this day the Essex class carriers are one of the faster ships that were ever built.

I had the good fortune to be a phone talker right from the very beginning and I also worked as a yeoman, or in other words, in the different offices. I guess, because of some of my work before, I had a great opportunity to really see what was going on. And my duty station was on the bridge as a phone talker. I was there for regular duty. But when general quarters would sound, I was at a battle dressing station on the hangar deck as a phone talker, and I would report injuries and the damage situation. People were brought to this station that had been hurt or wounded and I would report this information to the bridge. That was my GQ station and also my torpedo defense station which was a second level attack mode. I felt very honored and scared at the beginning—very, very frightened.

What was your assignment?

I became a member of the chaplain's office. Somebody in the yeoman's office or in the captain's office said maybe he can do that and that's where I wound up. I had a friend on the *Franklin*—we went through boot training together. His name was Dale Zimmerman, and he was from the Athens, Ohio, area. In fact, he went into the service at the same time I did. And Dale and I went on board the ship together. We were friends for a while and then he was transferred into the airdales, or onto the flight deck, and I very seldom would see him after that. He died on the day that we had all of our difficulties off Japan. And I tried for years to make some contact with his parents, but could never locate them. They lived in some remote area along the river, and we just never could find them at a post office box. I wrote and called, and did everything possible to try to contact them because I saw him die.

We were in Hawaii in early '45—in January. After we were there for only about three days, we headed into what became the very largest battle group ever formed by the United States Navy—58.3 was the battle group terminology. Task force 58.3. We had many carriers, some battle cruisers, and we had cruisers and destroyers. We had everything imaginable. And every day that went by there was a ship hit by gun fire, or a ship that was hit by a kamikaze, or a ship that was hit by bombs, you know, because we were all under attack at that point.

We were headed first to support the invasion of Iwo Jima. And of course, we were getting very close to the Japanese homeland. And their ships and planes did come out. We then were assigned to soften up Okinawa. So we softened up Okinawa, and then we were suddenly diverted from there and sent to the inland sea of Japan. The fleet went in that close to Japan proper for firebombing and for attacks on the Kobe naval air bases, and for the other attacks up and down the Japanese coast. At one time, our fleet was within seventy miles of the coast, and of course, the Japanese were very upset about it. Every day there were fighters out after us. Probably it was good for the crew because an awful lot of us were very young, and an awful lot of us had never seen anything like that before. You never really get fully accustomed to it, but at least you know how to conduct yourself and cope with things.

There was trouble brewing and we really didn't realize it. The carrier *Randolph*, the carrier *Bunker Hill*, and the carrier *Wasp* were all hit very badly. And each one of them probably lost a hundred or more people. This was the day before we were hit. They were hit by a combination of weapons. One was hit by a dive-bomber, and another was hit by a kamikaze. And still another one was hit by some gunfire and kamikaze. Every day we had planes overhead, and even though we had a tremendous number of planes ourselves, they would send everything they had after us. And of course, you know what happened at Okinawa when the invasion actually took place. The Navy took such a terrible beating. But I had my first experience with being strafed, and I had my first experience with seeing a plane coming right at you, and I had a first experience seeing planes being shot out of the sky, and you know, I went through all of that. I grew up pretty quick.

How did you deal with fear— could you cope with it?

Oh, I was frightened out of my wits, but I was able to conduct myself. There's never a moment that you aren't frightened. At least that was my experience. I think for the most part the others acted the same—I mean, you tried very hard to keep your feelings to yourself as much as you could. You tried very hard to do your job without allowing this mental anguish to get to you. And that's what I think it amounted to because, you know, that's just a matter of survival. You do your job. You've got to do your job for the ship to stay afloat to keep *you* safe. That was constantly [drummed into] us. But I think that by the time we actually had our very big difficulty, I think most of us had gotten accustomed to what war was about. I know we were at general quarters for about twenty-eight hours, off and on, for about a day and a half because of air attacks. There was also some submarines in the area, and our people had not been able to drive them away. And so we were at almost a constant general quarters with little or nothing to eat and without any sleep. And you're always on duty and always alert to what was going on around you.

The day that we were on heavy duty, red condition, we had done some firebombing at Tokyo, and most of our planes came back. So the captain decided that this was the time that the crew should be fed, should be taken off of GQ and the crew should be allowed to relax for a little while. This was on the morning of March the 19th, 1945.

Rather than having something to eat, I was so bone tired I decided to go down to the chaplain's office and just stretch out and just kind of unwind for a little, try to relax, because I was in a position that I could always get something to eat if I wanted to. My mother sent me stuff, my girl sent me things. I always had something I could eat if it was necessary. And I stretched down on three or four chairs or a bench. And it was about 07:00 or 07:30, and all of a sudden those of us that were in that room, and there were probably twenty-five or thirty of us, we just absolutely got upset, tumbled, and thrown. And I wound up across the compartment, thrown against the bulkhead or against the wall. It threw me all the way across the room—the concussion of that first hit. But that was probably the luckiest thing that ever happened to me in my life, because I had friends and companions and people that I knew that decided they were hungry, and they just had to have some coffee and some dried eggs—they had to have something to eat. And those same people got wiped out in a flash because we were still at flight operations and planes were being re-gassed, and planes were being reloaded with machine guns, and tiny-tim rockets, and everything imaginable that they carried in those days. And when the first bomb hit about 7:30 in the morning they caused everything under the sun to blow up. And then one explosion led to another explosion to another explosion, and one fire led to another fire until the ship was in very great jeopardy and nearly sank. As a matter of fact, the ship was at a thirteen-degree list and people could not even stand up with that list.

What happened on the Franklin after that first bomb hit?

I was below. And then a second bomb hit us. A lot of my friends were immediately lost because of the flash fire and impact of the explosive. The first bomb went down into several decks and several Marine compartments were wiped out, because the bomb exploded in that area. In fact, if I may just step aside for a moment, a very good friend of mine, a friend for life, Ben Coy from the Dayton area, the old Miami Conservancy head, was a marine on board the *Franklin*. He just happened not to be in that compartment area because he was on duty up in the captain's area and by some fluke he was saved. But many marines on board that day died from that initial impact. But those of us that could, we worked our way out into the passageway which was full of smoke. There was already water awash in the passageway because there were compartments that were being flooded to try to dampen the fire or get the fire put out.

We were down four decks below, and there was no GQ, no torpedo defense, no communications whatsoever, but we all felt that we had to head for our GQ station and mine was on the hangar deck as a phone talker at this battle dressing station. Most of us had GQ stations either on the hangar deck or on the flight deck. So we all kind of headed down the passageway, little knowing that we couldn't get very far. That was exactly the case because we could not get to the upper decks because of the fire and explosions that were going on. The heat was terrible and on one side of the steel compartment you could feel the heat, being generated through the bulkheads. I remember there were some guys, or young people, that were crying for their mother, or whatever. And I remembered that you should rip your t-shirt off, or get your handkerchief, or get something and wet it down as much as you can and get it over your face right away. I did that, and several others followed my suggestion, and we started trying to work our way out of this place. It was a hell hole. And excuse my term, but that's what it was, it was a hell hole. And we worked ourselves around underneath the belly part trying to find some access to the upper decks. Finally, probably after an hour, and I'm not sure because my watch stopped running at 07:25, which apparently was at the time of the initial explosion, we were able to get up a couple of decks by just simply weaving around. Believe it or not, when we were probably about a hundred feet above the hangar deck level we realized that there was some light and some air and we headed towards this opening. I don't know how, but we finally found our way to the fantail of the ship which was aft. This is where a lot of the old gun compartments are held, and it's where the equipment is held—wrenches are there for whatever might be necessary. But there were gun compartments back there—40mms and 20mms. But we were having a lot of trouble with people that were falling aside because of flying metal or, because of explosions, or who knows what other reasons. But we made it, we made it to the fantail.

And there were probably twelve of us left out of the original twenty-five that started out. Now some of them made it to safety other ways, or some of them were very frightened, and they probably didn't make it. Anyway, we got to the fantail of the ship and the one thing that we noticed right away was, of course, the explosions were continuing to go off. The ship never stopped exploding, because it got into all of the bombs, it got into the shells of the ship, it got into the gasoline, and it got into everything imaginable and was on fire or exploding. And we got out there, and we noticed real quickly that these gun mounts or these tubs where some of these wrenches were kept was a perfect place for safety because we were protected. Some of us laid in this oil and grime, and whatever it was, for a few hours. Some people died on the spot trying to move around or trying to leave the ship. But then probably about eleven o'clock in the morning the ship shuddered, and it almost felt like it was breaking up in the middle, and all of a sudden it kind of lurched to the right, to the starboard side, and it had this bad list so that people could hardly stand up. Others, afterwards, said that they expected the ship to roll over. And it should have rolled over, but it didn't for some unknown reason—it didn't. And in the meantime, a lot of people were leaving the fantail and leaving it every time there was some explosion, or maybe they were trapped by fire and had no choice. And I know we were down to the last five or six of us there.

How high is the fantail up from the water?

The fantail is about seventy feet from the water and it's above the level of the hangar deck, but right below the flight deck. In the area that I was on in the fantail, we were trapped by fire. So three of us decided to leave even though we still had not heard any communications, other than word of mouth, that the abandon ship had been authorized. The cruiser *Santa Fe* had pulled along side to help pull people off the ship, and the *Pittsburgh* came along side to help people and to fight the fires and people either jumped onto those ships or were hauled off and put on those ships. A lot of people jumped and didn't make it, they fell in between the two. We saw an awful lot of people in the water, and the water was nothing but fire, oil on fire, and debris of everything you could imagine was in the sea. People were on debris, they were trying to reach debris to save themselves, or they just simply slipped from sight. People were in front of you for a minute and then they were gone. People were there in front of you and then suddenly only a part of them were in front of you. And every sight that man had ever seen occurred that day—at least that's what I saw.

I went into the water after being literally forced into the water. There was a rope, a line, and I climbed it. I still had my life belt, my life jacket, on even though it had been partly torn and shredded by shrapnel. I banged up my hand a little bit and the side of my face, but that was incidental. I had left my battle helmet on, and it had creases in it, but it was firmly attached to my head. Then I hit that water. I had to let loose of the rope about forty feet above the water, and I hit the water with that battle helmet on, and with my life jacket that was only partly good, and everything kind of crunched down on me. I nearly drowned in the first few moments or two that I was in the water, but I was able to get rid of the jacket, got rid of the helmet, and got my shoes off and kicked myself to the surface. And then the nightmare of being out in this sea by yourself began—except other people were in the same situation. It was a frightening experience to see ships coming and going, and ships running around all over the place, and aircraft above shooting, and Japanese planes coming at ships and the *Franklin* slowly but surely drifting away—listing. You didn't know whether it was going to flop over at any time. Destroyers would come nearby and pass you by. And people needed help, some were burned beyond recognition. And I remember one guy, and I didn't tell this story before, I had helped a burned guy get a piece of wood or something that he could hang onto. A few minutes later a man came along, and he was in a real frenzy—he grabbed at me, grabbed at my life belt, and he held onto my shoulders, held on to me, and he was a big guy. I always considered myself pretty big, but he was very, very strong and very large. I finally got free of him, and I told him to get the hell away from me. And to this day I'm sorry that I ever said that to that man because he needed help. But I didn't know what to do. He made it. You know, I was able to push something to him, but he did make it. But I'm sure that my father and my brothers, if they'd known that story, would have, you know, probably not been very proud of me. I was in the water for probably three or four hours, and I really don't know except by the logs of the USS *Hickok* which was a destroyer that picked me up—that fished me out of the water.

What's this log?

That is a page from the log of the USS *Hickok* DD673, a destroyer. Here it says Merton Stuart. They picked me up on this day, Monday, the 19th of March, 1945.

You know, it was a remarkable thing. Well years and years and years after the incident, I learned that the *Hickok* crew was having a reunion in the Midwest. And so I wrote a note to the *Hickok* crew thanking them for their picking me up, thanking them for saving me, and thanking them for taking such good care of me. And lo and behold, I received from some of the surviving crew members, about twenty-five or thirty of them, notes that thanked me, but also said, "Hey, you know, we were glad to be there, and you were great," and everything of that sort. And one of them had gotten hold of the ship's log for that day. And he made copies of it and sent the log to me. And that was just an exciting thing for me to get. But it was about a three or four hour stint in the water and I had lost all of my ability to wave.

How did they fish you out?

Two guys, two guys came down in a net that was hanging over the side of the ship, and the ship had slowed to almost a complete stop but it was floating. And they got as close to me as they could. I could not swim, but we kind of floated together and the two guys down in this net grabbed hold of me, lifted me out of the water, and threw me up onto a board or something, because I didn't have enough strength to lift my arms let alone to help them bring me up. But you know the thing that I think that worried me more than anything while I was in that water was that we were floating towards the Japanese coast, and we used to be told stories about being taken prisoner by one of these torpedo boats, or something, because they'll take you in to be killed. And I didn't want that to happen. I felt like I was going to make it, but I didn't want that crazy thing happening. So, that day the Japs realized that the *Franklin* was in deep trouble, and they threw everything they had at it including some surface ships—they even brought some subs out. So for about a twenty-four hour period there was just organized confusion—lots of gunfire, and lots of bombs trying to sink the *Franklin*. And of course the *Hickok*, being a support ship, was right in close and was right in the midst of all this, so we were going through a second day of tough times. Not nearly as tough times as a marine or an Army guy on an island someplace. They had much tougher times than I ever had, and I felt fortunate to be in the Navy.

How many people were lost on the Franklin?

We lost nine hundred and twenty-one people and we had three hundred and sixty missing in action, and we had about four hundred and fifty that were wounded out of a complement of thirty-five hundred men. The *Franklin* was the most decorated ship in U.S. naval history. Two Congressional Medals of honor, fifteen or twenty Silver Stars and Bronze Stars, nine hundred and some posthumous Purple Hearts, three hundred and fifty Purple Hearts given to people that survived— most everybody was wounded or hurt that day. Everybody in some way. I had a slight burn and I had some metal wounds, but I was lucky, and I've always thanked my creator that I got through that whole thing. It was a remarkable thing. After probably twenty-four hours the ship still floated, and the *Pittsburgh* took it under tow. That was a heavy cruiser, trying to draw it away from the Japanese homeland. And they got it out, probably got it out about one hundred miles from the coast. And someway or another, they got one of the boilers relit, and for a day or two, along with the battle cruiser and four or five destroyers and a couple of other cruisers, it was escorted back towards Hawaii with one boiler running. It was doing about seven knots. And then after several more days it was able to kick up some more speed and it finally made its way to Pearl Harbor.

Later it finally got back to the Brooklyn Navy Yard going through the Panama Canal. All the survivors were taken to Ulithi which was an atoll. There were ships there, and there were lots of things going on. Those people that were petty officers, those people that were very experienced as far as running the ship, and those people that had experience as far as maintenance and electronics, were taken back aboard ship. And there were about seven hundred out of the original thirty-five hundred that were taken back and they took the ship back. The rest of us were left at Ulithi and then transported back to Pearl on whatever means they could find to get us back there on troop ships. We were on a converted LST. We had marines on the LST from Iwo Jima, and we were all put below decks. And this LST one day lost its engines, and another day lost it's steering, and another day it lost its main beam. And there we were still out in front in combat waters, and we had a couple of sub scares on the way back. But we finally made it. But here we all were down below decks with these marines that had been at Iwo for weeks and weeks, and if you don't think that was an experience, being down below with those guys. And you know what I'm talking about. We were brought back to Pearl Harbor. And every one of us immediately got a thirty day R&R. In other words, we were sent to the beach, and we had about all the food we could want, and we had no duty. We could swim. We had very little liberty, but we were allowed the freedom of the beach and just doing whatever we wanted to for thirty days.

And then after that was over I was stationed at Barbers Point naval air station in Hawaii. I was in a casual aircraft service unit there since I had had aircraft service, aircraft carrier service. That's why they reassigned me there. I left after the war was over; they shipped me back to Great Lakes, and I was in the discharge unit for several months discharging other people because I was a yeoman and had the necessary experience to take people out of the service. I was discharged in November of '46. I had a little over two years in the service.

Looking back on the war, did World War II change your life a lot?

Well, I must say that I'm very glad for the opportunity to have been in the Navy, very glad to have been a part of a war effort, because not everybody was a part of it—at least in the forward areas. I felt good about serving my country. I don't know that I'd want to go through that experience again, but it was part of what we were doing. I feel like the Navy certainly gave me more than I gave the Navy. Because it made a person, it made a man out of me, it allowed me to go to school, and it allowed me to grow up, and mature, and to realize a little bit what life was about. And so I have a very soft spot in my heart for the Navy and for the *Franklin*.

Dick Baumhardt

Richard E. Baumhardt was born and raised in northern Ohio (the Elyria-Lorain area) and was very active in high school athletics at Elyria High School. He entered Miami University in the fall of 1940 and after his second year there he enlisted in the United States Marines—in the summer of 1942. Initially, Baumhardt was in the V-12 program at Miami University during the 1942–43 academic year and then was sent to Parris Island, South Carolina, for basic training (boot camp). When basic training was finished he was sent to Quantico, Virginia, to officer candidate school. After receiving his commission Baumhardt went to California and was sent overseas to Guadalcanal where he landed on August 24, 1944. He served on Guadalcanal and participated in the landing at Okinawa on April 1, 1945. Six weeks after landing he was wounded in action, but after recovery served in the occupation forces in Japan. Baumhardt and his wife, Carol, have four children—two boys and two girls. He attained the rank of captain during his three and one-half years in the Marine Corps.

Were you in a regular unit on Guadalcanal?

No. They transported us to the beach and then we were put in trucks and hauled into a coconut grove some distance off the beach. And the rain started to fall and night came on as the jeep pulled into the coconut grove. Now the reason that Guadalcanal was such an ideal training spot was that while the island was secure, in the sense that we did not have any active opposition, there were plenty of stray Japs still trying to stay alive out there. So every day we sent out patrols in any direction just to give training to us, to get us sharp, because we didn't know whether we would encounter any enemy or not. Eventually I was a member of the 3rd Platoon of Baker Company, 1st Battalion, 4th Marine Regiment, 6th Marine Division.

Did you have trouble with malaria or dengue fever down here?

Yes we did. Every morning you would line up your platoon, ask them to take out their canteen, tell them to put out their right hand, and you'd put two atabrine tablets in their hand, and say, "Put them in your mouth, and I'll stand here 'til you swallow them with a shot of water out of your canteen." They tried to hide the atabrine tablets, 'cause it turned your skin yellow. And they didn't like that. You got used to it after a while. But that would be the way you would try to fight off the impact of malaria on your troop strength. And it worked. But it took a little discipline. We didn't experience much dengue fever. Dysentery was common—it was a problem. Guadalcanal is just a breeding ground for bacteria. And although we had a corpsman attached to each platoon they were busy most of the time examining feet because the men would get infected feet from the moisture and wet feet because we'd wade through rivers.

Could you talk about relationships a little bit?

Well, you see there's one advantage from the psychology side of it. You had to read [censor] their mail. Every letter they sent out I had to censor. Hence, I knew who had a happy marriage, who didn't, who had x number of children, who had this amount of alimony problems. But gradually you knew every factor of their private life. And you'd naturally try to counsel with those who were having difficulty because if they were worrying about something back home they weren't any good to me and in combat. But you got to know them very well whether they liked it or not. Although the older officers warned me, in my enthusiasm, and said, "Don't get too attached to anybody because you're going to lose them and then you aren't gonna be able to cope with that." So you had to find a level where you would get close, not too close, and then back off a little.

The officers usually played volleyball in the evening on Guadalcanal. The call would go out at the end of the day when the sun had gone down a little, the weenie roasters will play the regulars. The reserve officers were the weenie roasters and the regular officers were those who were going to make a career out of it. And we'd play volleyball. And there were no rules. But after a few drinks the bets would go higher because there was no place to spend your money. We'd have very vicious volleyball games. They were good—you let off steam. And then you could walk twelve feet and dive in the ocean to cool off. We also played basketball wherever we could arrange to get a level spot.

What about your relationship with other officers?

I only met one man in the course of my duty whom I did not like. In fact, we had nothing in common other than both being men. He was rude, crude, and tattooed, in fact ignorant, and I did not find many redeeming qualities in him at all. Now he sensed that—naturally. And one night, well, other people observed it too—Dave Schreiner particularly. So one night in the officers' mess, I was writing, I was finishing a letter, and he came down the aisle, and he said, "Are you writing mommy, Baumhardt?" And I decked him. I was immediately called to the commanding officer's table and he said, "I'll see you at 07:00 in my tent, lieutenant." I had felt free to deck this guy. An officer had come to me previously and said, "We've observed his treatment of you and none of us like it, so you have our permissions to do whatever you want to do with him."

So the next morning I went to see Colonel Shapely, our regimental commander, a handsome man and built like a rock. He'd been a halfback at Annapolis and his father was an admiral which explains our liquor supply. Anyway, he had a punching bag outside his tent, sweat rolling off him, and I was standing at attention with a guard. And he turned to me and he said, "Lieutenant, when you throw your goddamn right, keep your elbow in because you're dissipating too much of the blow. Now if you have to hit him again, follow up with an equally good left. Dismissed." That was it. Well, I saw him every day which was a little sensitive.

I found I had tremendous admiration for ninety percent of the officer corps that I interfaced with. Particularly, Colonel Shapley who later offered me a very safe position in the regiment. I declined it, and he advised me that I might regret my decision three days later. But he's a wonderful man. In fact, he jumped into a foxhole with a number ten can of pineapple slices and stuck the k-bar into the can to open it. A k-bar is a knife. You carried it on your hip.

Where did you go after Guadalcanal?

We were floating reserve for Iwo Jima. We were at sea in February of '45. We were standing by in case they needed us. When it was determined they weren't going to need our additional support, we just kept right on steaming to Okinawa. But Iwo turned out to be one that I'm glad I missed. The lava conditions and the terrain, with them shooting, looking down your throat all the time. The Marines had seven thousand dead and twenty thousand wounded on Iwo Jima. On the schedule in the Pacific we were to hit Okinawa next so that was a long time at sea. We would get out on the hatch covers and box every day and just horse around and try to stay in shape. Probably about a week before we got to Okinawa we were having orientation meetings. And we had pretty poor pictures really. In fact, in the whole Pacific campaign we really did not have the right maps. We were using National Geographic maps and planning strategies that way. But we had a pretty good idea about Okinawa. Anyway, we were assigned our respective beaches. And you had to memorize what your objectives were. Make sure your platoon members understood where we were going, what we had to do. The Marine Corps worked on the theory that you could end up in command if you were a private. If you were well oriented and well informed, you were expected to be able to rise to that. And that was good because I had some kids who really managed that.

The landing on Okinawa, as you know, was unopposed at the beach. They did not resist until we were inland. This is on April 1, 1945. That being Easter Sunday they did not think that the American forces would desecrate a holiday, which was part of our strategy and it worked out.

Was there a tremendous pre-invasion bombardment?

I would assume so. I didn't see a lot being on the ship. I was designated as a ship loading coordinator. And I had to go on board ship, study the hull conditions, and decide what could be loaded. We had one guy who loaded a whole thing of trucks and the hatch cover came down and snapped off all the pintles for the machine guns. But I also had to supervise the unloading of my battalion's ship. And there I had my major failure. I had one of my good men come up and say, "Sir, we've got x number of boxes of ammunition. What should I do with them?" And I said, "What do you have left on the deck?" And he said, "I have a duck." I said, "Well, load the duck with any extra ammunition." Now a half hour later I see the duck swing out on the boom and there's a driver in the duck, he's waving and they cut him loose and the duck hit the water and he kept right on going down. The weight of the ammunition was so tremendous. So I'd made a bad decision there. But they couldn't find the duck for years so it saved my butt. So we had an unopposed landing, and thank God.

Dick Baumhardt on Guadalcanal, 1944.

Well, at that time we were all replacement officers—at that moment. Bill Hofer led my platoon ashore. He was a halfback from Notre Dame, and he had fiery red hair and wore a red bandanna. He was a hell of a combat officer, but he was not the kind to live that long. He was wounded on the second day. Our company commander was killed on the second day leading the company up a road. A Jap was laying in a ditch covered with camouflage, raised up to a sitting position, and shot Thaddeus Dodds in the head. And so all of a sudden the line up of our team was changing rapidly. When Hofer got wounded I was assigned to his platoon which I'd trained with. That was one of the smart things the Marines had done. I trained with that platoon. I knew them and they knew me and so we both had confidence in each other. So it worked and I took over my platoon. All the time on Guadalcanal and my training with them made the deal. I said, "I am not Mr. Hofer, I am not going to roar 'follow me,' I'm going to keep you alive long enough to keep me alive." Now we had a deal there—"I'll get you back and you get me back." That's my leadership philosophy. And they liked that. And as a result they took good care of me all the time in combat.

What weapon were you carrying personally?

Officers are only supposed to carry a carbine. But the first time I ever shot anybody with a carbine the guy kept on running. And I said to myself that is not the weapon for me. So the first man who went down with an M-1, I got his weapon and kept it with me. I didn't have much faith in the carbine. And you carried a .45 on your belt. We then headed north on Okinawa. I was part of that. That was the Motobu peninsula—I was on top of that after we attacked going up there. And I looked out on the island where Ernie Pyle was killed that day. And that really saddened all of us too. But at the base of the Motobu I stopped to have some crackers with a big blond lieutenant that I recognized by the name of Courtney. And we chatted and then started our attack up the mountain. And he was killed about thirty yards after we started. And I took an English book out of his pack and kept it all these years. I had a captain in the 4th Marines, Frank Kemp is his name, and Kemp was my role model as to what an officer should be and do. And it turns out when I chatted with Frank the last time, I mentioned having this book. He said, "Well, that kid bumped me out of my starting end job at Yale, so I remember him too." Frank Kemp was an ideal officer. He did everything right. He treated his men right, he treated every other officer right, and he got the job done. So I remember him. He got his leg blown off.

What about fear?

I'm sure every one of us was frightened, but we all knew what we had to do and how to do it. So when the time came that you had to move out of that Higgins boat, everybody moved. I didn't see any problem with that at all. It was built into us that we all depended on each other and if we all remembered that we'd all do the job and get out the other end. So you stuck together that way. I only had one man that I thought was a combat fatigue case. He was one of my men. But he came around after about three days' rest. The only other case I saw anybody crack up was an officer who came as a replacement to me and he said, "You killed twelve of my men last night." And I said, "Would you explain yourself." And he said, "Yes, you killed twenty men, twenty-two men." And I said, "I need more information. What are you talking about?" It turned out he had found a horse and he loaded all the heavy stuff on it, ammunition belts and everything on the horse. And we'd shot the horse. And he cracked up at that. He was an Annapolis graduate and at that point I became angry because at first I felt guilt that I'd done something. Then when we discovered it's just a horse that he was using, I really got mad and I got him shipped out of there pronto, back to a hospital. Never saw him again.

I never felt fatalistic. I just felt if we moved smartly, used our heads and worked together we would get through it. But we had one hundred percent casualties in the entire 4th Marine Regiment. Which meant you had people wounded three or four times to get that numerical count. Everybody experiences fear at some time, particularly when you figured you cut the corners too hard to get to cover, or you didn't have the right place to fire your weapon.

What about training and why did you fight?

First, I think the training paid off because if you train hard enough and long enough, your reaction to a situation is automatic. You don't have to think too much. In fact, if you think too much you realize what a stupid way it is to live, or try to live. Anyway, you would react quickly, swiftly, and make sure the guy next to you did too. Now why do you fight? You fight for the guy next to you. That's who you have to count on. If you stopped to worry about ideology you can end up drinking a lot. But you fight for the guy next to you and that's who's going to help keep you alive too.

Did you have any real warriors in your unit?

Not in my command but I was able to see some. For example, there were very few Jewish officers. But I can remember four, all of whom I would truly classify as warriors. They were fighting to get respect for themselves and their people. One was a captain of the Columbia University football team. And another was the guy who I woke up in the aid station with and he was sitting next to me and he was from Cleveland Heights. And he said, "Boomer,

I'm writing your folks right now to tell them you're wounded but you're going to be all right." And he left. His name was Leonard Fribourg and he was the commander of our machine gun platoon. He took more chances because he thought he had to, to maintain his status within the group. And I liked him and he became a general in the Marine Corps. Eventually he passed all the barriers.

When were you wounded and what were the circumstances?

May 22, 1945. Well we all knew that we had to go south eventually, because we were about to be relieved. They had to set up a separate road network to move us to the Naha area. We did this so the Army could move back and take our place on the Motobu Peninsula, because there was a rivalry between services and nobody really had a handle on it.

So anyway, we made that movement and we got down to the Naha area and now we had to attack Shuri Castle. So it was an interesting middle transition because after you finished one phase of the campaign with great relief— you're going home you think—the jobs done. And now you're going the other way and you're told it's gonna be as rough as you had it already. Maybe worse because Shuri Castle is a better defense position. So there was a mixed feeling—like I'm getting a second shot at getting killed. So you had to pep yourself up. And I had one very difficult time.

We were moving to attack Shuri Castle, and going up the road it was raining all the time. I'd given my poncho to make a litter for a wounded man, so I didn't have a poncho. I saw a marine lying in the road. And you carry the poncho on your back on the cartridge belt. And I saw he had a folded, unused poncho. So I leaned over and pulled the poncho out and in doing so I rolled him over to get more freedom and I was looking at a kid that I had gone to Miami with. He was from Cincinnati and he played in the Campus Owls [Miami University dance band]. Nice guy. He'd been in the V-12 unit and for some reason his grades didn't cut it. And so I had one hell of a shock at that moment.

I was lucky to have one of the best platoon sergeants in the Marine Corps. His name was Leo McGinnis and he was a wildcat oil driller from Louisiana. And he was really good. He'd been through several campaigns and he knew the ropes and he understood me. And so he acted as a bulwark for me all the way through. One night a kid from Dayton got hit, and he had an [incendiary] grenade in his pack. Well, the grenade went off. And he fell to his knees and he was burning and screaming. And I really couldn't take it because I knew him, knew he had a wife back here. So I took out my .45 and I was going to shoot him. And Leo took the gun away from me and said, "You can't help him and you can't help yourself if you do that." So he saved me from making a stupid emotional error. Eventually I got him a chance at a commission. In the Marine Corps you cannot be commissioned in the field and stay in your same unit. You have to move to another military unit. So he got switched from the First Battalion to the Second. They were happy to get him. He got a field commission as a second lieutenant. He was a neat guy. In fact, I thank him for everything I did right. 'Cause when I'd make a mistake in training he would take me aside and say, "Now that might have gotten us both killed. Why don't you think about doing this the next time?" So he was a coach for me all the time, making up for my lack of combat experience. He was a great guy too. He made it from the Marine Corps, came back home and got killed in an accident in Louisiana.

My own wounding was like this. First of all a mortar is no respecter of where you are or anything because the stuff is flying. Now Frenchy Asselin, who's my first runner and lives in Rhode Island, he and I had gone up a railroad embankment to see what was holding up Lieutenant Schreiner on the other side of the railroad embankment. And we came down after we made our observation and a radio call. We were just standing above my company headquarters when a mortar round hit and it flattened me. It went through the left anterior chest and luckily it did not come out the front, 'cause the heart was in the way. And so Frenchy and I were immediately put into an Amtrak and they got me up to the other side of the hill where they could put me on a jeep, one of those racks on the hood, and take me down to the battalion aid station. There I met a kid from Wellington, Ohio, that I'd never known before but he, once he identified me, recognized the name because he knows the neighborhood around Wellington. He was a kid named Neil Wise. From there they took me down to the air strip where they were flying the casualties out, and there a giant came out of the darkness and picked me up in his arms, lifted me up, and I recognized him as Bill Osmanski who was a Chicago Bear pro player. He carried me out to where I could be transported to the airplane. He put me in a rack, the whole airplane was lined with racks with wounded, and we flew out of Okinawa to Guam. I was there two months.

They operated repeatedly to take shrapnel out of my chest cavity and make the repairs that they had to make. And they took good care of me. The hospital was near a runway for the B-29s taking off. Made a hell of a racket. But one day I was lying there and Dick Fey from Miami, he was with the Air Corps, took my hand and said, "Boomer, you aren't gonna have to go back." And I didn't understand it. But he knew the atomic bomb was being loaded. So I was happy to hear his words but I didn't know where the hell he got his information.

What did you think when you heard about the atomic bomb?

I was happy as hell. You feel your chances are running out sometimes and going from one theater to another would have been very defeating. After they patched me up we met up again on Guam. The unit had returned to Guam. So, we set up a new camp for the regiment and the battalion. And they rejoined me, and that's when I became company commander.

After the surrender of the Japanese, we were involved again. That was when we took over the Naval Technical Arsenal in Yokosuka, Japan. This was the commanding officer's headquarters. That's a samurai sword, I got there.

Were you on the Missouri?

Yes. I wasn't there because of my rank or prestige in anything. I had a friend, an Annapolis graduate named Price, and he knew the officer on the gangway that day. So I owe it all to Lieutenant Price. Can I show you something? See, that's a Japanese naval gun overlooking the entry to Tokyo Bay —we were detached with our company to circle Tokyo Bay and blow the breechblocks and the muzzles off of every naval gun that could threaten the advance of our ships coming into Tokyo Bay. So as we went around Tokyo Bay that's the first time I ever had my hands on C-2 as an explosive. And it is fantastic. And as we emptied our trucks we picked up beer, out of every beer brewery that we could encounter. We had a roaring good time.

I learned in the military you have to have friends somewhere to get things done. For instance, I needed athletic equipment on Guadalcanal. So I checked the Navy and I said where do I go to get athletic equipment? And they said, "You will contact Commander Francis X. Wilton in the Admiralties." And I said to myself, it can't be but it probably is. He was my baseball coach at Miami. And I knew he had left coaching to go into the Navy. So I sent a radiogram to Commander Francis X. Wilton saying badly need athletic equipment, signed Rabbit Ears. And back came the radiogram, "It'll be on its way." So he sent me everything I needed.

When you were discharged did you go back to school?

Yes. I should have been in the original class of 1943, and would have been in the class of 1944 had I been able to stay in school. So it knocked a few years out of my life. But there were a lot of people in the same boat. I graduated in 1947. Carol came down to Oxford for a little sib's weekend or something and we met there. Thankfully the training I received in psychology at Miami and the school of business led me into the field of labor relations.

In a sense World War II changed the whole direction of my life, the opportunity it gave me for my education and my military experience. It gave me the confidence to do my jobs.

Gene Cantelupe

Eugene B. Cantelupe is the former dean of the College of Liberal Arts at Wright State University in Dayton, Ohio (1971 to 1985). He is a graduate of the University of Buffalo (1942) with a B.A. in literature and art history. Using the GI Bill of Rights after the war, Cantelupe earned an M.F.A. in 1956 from the University of Iowa and his Ph.D. from Washington University in St. Louis in 1958. He then taught and was associate dean at C. W. Post College in New York. Cantelupe has published numerous articles in professional journals and is the co-editor of *Cultures of Mankind*. In the fall of 2000 Wright State University named gallery space in their art museum for Dr. Cantelupe and his wife Jean. He now lives at Bethany Village.

Gene, where were you born and raised?

I was born in Farrell, Pennsylvania—a town in northwestern Pennsylvania, right on the Ohio border. My father was involved in both business and politics. He owned a hotel and hardware and furniture business. Then he got into politics and was elected to office, public office, city treasurer for many years, and that was his career. He was born in Italy, but was brought here when he was about nine years old. But we didn't talk Italian at home—I couldn't talk to my grandparents. I always regret that. I came from a large family, and we pretty much stayed home—we didn't travel much.

What were you doing just prior to your entry into the armed forces?

Well, I was at the University of Buffalo working for a B.A. in literature and art history. Great preparation for the army! I graduated in '42, so I started in, what would that be, '37, '38. I was drafted while I was still in the university and sent as an enlisted man to Camp Pickett, Virginia. This was for medical corps training. We had all the basics, you know. We didn't have firearms because medics were not supposed to carry them. But we studied how to set up field hospitals and organize army records of all kinds. They immediately sent me to clerk school, which was an easy assignment while others were out doing other things, because I could read. My friends called it "jerk school" because they were all jealous. We went and sat all day in classrooms and typed, and that's where we learned army records—how to be a company clerk, payroll, all that sort of thing. And you know we also learned short order drill, did marches, bandaging, and how to carry a stretcher. I think the training lasted about six weeks and then I was sent to Hampton Roads, a port of embarkation (POE) near Newport News.

I was assigned to the office of the port surgeon because a point of embarkation was a very different kind of assignment. The medical facility was directly under the Secretary of War. Everything was secret because we were involved with troops—troops coming in and troops leaving, and pretty soon wounded troops coming back on hospital ships. They would come into our harbor. And that's what we were involved with.

And I was in charge of all the filing of the vast number of records for the port surgeon. He was a regular army colonel, full eagle, and a bastard if ever there was one. I was terrified of him. Remember, I had just come out of basic training. I met him, stood at attention, and he said, "I see that you have a degree in literature," and I said, "Yes." I was also Phi Beta Kappa, but I kept that quiet until later. And he said, "Well, have you ever filed?" And I said, "Well, no." He said, "You will." All the verbs in the imperative mode. And I said, "Well, yes, sir." You know, I'm standing at attention.

And I was assigned to a little room. Oh it was a small room, but filled with filing cabinets floor to ceiling. It was like a prison. And the chief file clerk decided everything. The job had changed, it was sort of a revolving door because apparently, from what I learned, most of the GIs who were deciding how to file these documents did it according to the Dewey Decimal System. The army adapted that for its own purpose and I had to work with a manual.

But the key was that for every document, in order to file it properly, the chief clerk had to decide the content—what is the gist of the document and then pick a number and file it. And too many of the GIs couldn't understand that. Many documents were misfiled because the chief clerk really didn't understand the content of the document. And so then the colonel would simply call out, there were civilian workers there too, to his secretary. Now he had an assistant who was a captain, but the rest were all medical corps, they were doctors, MDs and snotty. You know that's a closed corporation and they looked down on everyone else as being uneducated.

But anyway, the problem was that the filing system was a great mouth that simply swallowed everything that should have been filed and no one could find anything. When I first sat in this little file room with the chief file clerk, he had an assistant who was a former lawyer who was working on army regulations—a bright lawyer from New York. He really knew what to do with those regulations. But it was all the documents, many of them classified secret from Washington, from the surgeon general that was the problem. All those so-called secret documents. No one could find them and the colonel had a terrible temper. He would just shout when he wanted these. And his favorite word, now this is army language, his favorite word was, "Oh, balls." The GIs would sit in this little file room and just tremble. He would just be abusive, and everyone, all the enlisted personnel, were just sitting there paralyzed.

Well I started. I remember the first thing I did, I was newly assigned, I started to open the drawers and look at the files. And I remember the chief file clerk who was on his way out after a series of others, he said, "What are you doing?" And I said, "What is in these files?" And he said, "Leave it, you better let that alone, there's nothing here but brain confusion." That was the filing system. Well, it ended up where I became chief file clerk. They decided I should be a warrant officer, but that didn't go through. And then I needed help, and I had to get a civilian worker, a young girl out of high school who took a business course. I literally dismantled, or rather we literally dismantled, that filing system and started over until we got it in shape, and from that point on everything went all right.

What was your rank now? Had you been promoted from private yet?

I was promoted every two months. I had very few friends in the barracks where I was staying because you had to wait for promotions and they were hard to get. The company I was with were scattered all through the port. It was a vast enterprise. It was an army camp only it was in buildings, wooden buildings, temporary really, and we were situated by the sea. It was very unusual. And I was promoted all the time until I became, what's the highest rank—Master Sergeant—I had all of that in a matter of two or three months.

And then the colonel, I got to know all the officers, said, "You really should go to officer candidate school (OCS)." So I went to officers' training school and became a medical administrative officer in Abilene, Texas. I was a ninety-day wonder. That's what they called them and I came out with a bar. I really had a very easy time.

Well, while I was at the port, we started to get the first prisoners of war from the African campaign. And they were in terrible physical condition— Germans. And mainly, we processed Rommel's Afrika Korps, and oh boy, they were really something. They had been in prisons, barbed wire enclosures, in Africa, and they were all suffering from skin disease and all sorts of things. And there were also some Italians there. The German soldiers just hated the Italian soldiers. They didn't consider them very military. And the port surgeon played a key role because we had to set up a system whereby these prisoners, after they got off the hospital ships, were processed.

The port surgeon, with the corps of engineers, created an assembly line system so that every prisoner who got off the ship started in one section. They even built temporary shelters and so on. They were first interviewed, and from there they had to strip because they had lice, and that sort of thing, and their uniforms and their belongings had to be deloused. We set up a delousing system with mytholbromide chambers. The clothes would go in there and while the clothes were being deloused the prisoners were sent into a

Gene Cantelupe.

vast shower room with jets in the ceiling. And at a signal the jets would just spray everyone and they would wash down. Then as they came out doctors examined them. They were well taken care of. Doctors examined them and prescribed whatever medication they needed. Some were really ill and had to go to the hospital and that sort of thing.

Then after that they emerged to pick up their clothes and the clothes had to come out of these chambers. And the Germans were furious because the clothes were all crumpled and rumpled and they were looking for their medals and that sort of thing. After that they got onto trains and went all over the United States—to farms, factories, and so on. That was the system.

We had visitors from the War Department in Washington and we had visitors from the surgeon general's office. A lot of Washington luminaries were checking on this system which was going to be duplicated at all ports of embarkation in the United States. So, it was the key and I was in charge of all that, all the documentation. But I also, from time to time, was put in charge of GIs who were working at various steps or levels of the process. Because I had the rank, you see, and so I observed this whole thing and wrote about it. I don't know if you remember that. I have a book on the war and I wrote about it. I kept a journal for four years in the Army.

But the Germans, those Germans, were automatons. They liked the assembly line system. And they were so good at it they helped us refine the system. They showed us short cuts. And when it came time to get the clothes out of those chambers, they were so furious at the wrinkles, they kept pressing, and so on, and I observed them after being deloused and then re-clothed. They would check and then they would recheck their appearance by a buddy looking at them and telling them—straighten this. It was incredible. They were fine as long as it was one, two, three, one, two, three. And then when they marched out to go to get onto trains, we had no trouble at all. They were immediately in formation.

We had isolated their officers who were also prisoners of war, and these men listened to those officers. Boy, those officers helped us. And at the end of the process, the whole thing, the Germans coming out of the system, getting on the trains, it became a kind of show, an exhibition for port personnel to come and see. And people, without realizing it, because of their sharpness, and their well, everything they did had precision to it, people would even clap. And I thought about this, and I wrote this in my book. If Rommel's troops lost the battle in, where was it, in El Alamein? they captured the delousing system at Newport News.

Well then a small group of Italian prisoners arrived and they would not follow that system. The whole system came almost to a halt, and the surgeon general was just furious. The whole thing was not working because he had the medical staff, the doctors, and the enlisted men following all that. The Italians, number one, wouldn't listen to their officers, and number two, they didn't care what their clothes were like when they came out of the chambers. They wanted American clothes. They were eager to put on American uniforms. And then when they went into the showers we couldn't get them out because they were having a very good time and they were using these big towels to play games, and fling towels over their shoulders, impersonating Roman senators, you know, statuary, it was beyond belief.

And then when it was time for them to get on the trains, well, they were just a scraggly, irregular group. They didn't give a damn about anything. And I remember someone saying, "Dear me, just look at that, a gypsy band." They had clothes from everywhere—they had wild uniforms—things they had picked up along the way. And they even had a dog, and no one could figure out how that dog got with the prisoners. And they even brought that dog through the delousing system and gave him a bath. And one of them was carrying that dog and a guitar. It was such a difference.

After the POE, where were you sent?

Biwako, Japan, in the fall of 1945. I was supposed to go in with the Army, on the invasion. I was with a medical unit. And instead of the invasion it turned out to be the occupation. And we went in right after the signing [of the surrender documents by Japan on September 2, 1945] to Nagoya.

I saw a good part of the world. Nagoya was an aircraft center, Mitsubishi, a big aircraft center. It was bombed to the ground with incendiary bombs. We used incendiary bombs, not demolition, and because of Japan's flimsy, flimsy architecture, they didn't need to use demolition bombs.

I went to Japan from the Philippines by ship. First we went to Lingayen Gulf on Luzon. And there we staged, I'm trying to think of the vocabulary, because it was a staging area for overseas Japan. And I was assigned to a general hospital unit. The largest medical unit in the army in Nagoya. Then we were sent to Nagoya to move ahead and set up a general hospital to take care of all of the American troops occupying Japan.

In Nagoya, the hospital was in the former telephone company building. We took over any building of brick or stone because, obviously, it didn't burn. And we set this up using the floors of the building for wards of the hospital. And I became adjutant which was the highest rank next to the commander, the commanding officer. I was really his assistant. We had nurses and Red Cross workers and GIs, and so on, and that was a real experience. That's where, I think, I learned about administration—on that job. My office was near the front entrance of the hospital. Anyone coming into the hospital, we had guards all the time, anyone coming in had to come through my office. I had an office, I had assistants, it was like being dean. I even had secretaries and so on.

One day there arrived in my office a very refined gentleman, I could tell right away. His clothes were in tatters, but everyone else's clothes were in tatters. And he was an art dealer. And he, the Japanese, started to show me things—lacquer ware, china, and so on. And I bought some things from him. And then he said, "I'd like you to meet the group I represent." And they were a group of Japanese painters, and there was a poet, a philosopher, and a journalist. A whole group. Well, I went out to meet them one Sunday with an interpreter, and there I met an artist that I became good friends with.

Before I left, he showed me a large painting, as big as this table only square, and it was the only painting that wasn't burned in the bombing. And I liked it so much that he gave it to me which was really quite a gift. And he gave me some documentation. He also gave me, because we were friends, a scroll that is, I think, very valuable. It is a pictorial presentation of twenty-four hours, a day in his life, from the time he gets up to the time he goes to bed. And it's a series of panels, pictures with calligraphy, and I have had it all translated. Now his painting and the documentation told me that he was more than just a local.

When we moved here from our condo in Lincoln Park, which had a cathedral ceiling, that painting had been hung quite high because it was so big, and it was beautiful in there. But when we moved to Bethany, the question was what are we going to do with this painting. And it was fifty-some years ago that I got it. So we called the DAI [Dayton Art Institute], we know the head curator, and he brought along, to look at the painting, his Asian curator, Li Jian, a Chinese, who curated the show at the DAI. She did all the work. Well, she became interested in this painting. But Jean and I said, "We want to give it to you because we have no place to put it. We'll either give it or loan it, whatever condition or category you want." Well, it turned out, she took the few facts I had on the painting from Nomura Shoin—the painter. How she did it I don't know, but she got in touch with Tokyo where this painting won a first prize in one of the first exhibitions of Japanese art after World War II which was exactly what he wanted. And they said, "Yes, we'll take it." So, it's going to hang in the Asian wing.

Because you were in Japan, what did you think of the atomic bombing of Japan, then and now?

That happened before I got to Japan. I was at Camp Beale, and all of us were wonder struck at the capacity of one bomb to destroy a city. And all the more, I was anxious to see if, when I got to Japan, I could see any of the results. Nagoya was a shambles. Nagoya looked like Xenia after the tornado. And one of the things I'll never forget was the smell of burning—the smell of cinders everywhere. It even got into our hair and our clothes, but we didn't realize it until we got home. And our parents and kin smelled us, and even things I sent home had the odor. I did go to Tokyo. I visited there. I saw the Frank Lloyd Wright Hotel which was still standing; it withstood the bombing. And I came home from Yokohama.

When you got home were you able to take advantage of the GI Bill of Rights?

Yes. For my graduate work. I started to teach, but what I started to do first was do some writing because I had this journal I'd kept for four years. And then I thought—well, I wasn't sure what to do because my hometown is a mill town, and that was now boarded up. It's part of that rust belt between Pittsburgh and Youngstown. There was nothing to do there.

So I decided I should do some graduate work and I used the GI Bill. Later I did some teaching for the new emerging State of New York University [State University of New York]. The new state university system. I was also interviewed at Columbia at Low's Library. But I started out teaching at Utica in a branch campus. Then I went to Lake Champlain, another branch, but I felt I had to start my graduate work. So I started at the University of Iowa, working toward a Master of Fine Arts in writing and art history. The Ph.D. came later at Washington University in St. Louis.

How did World War II change your life?

Well, I realized that coming from a small town, and even though I went to a nice university, how parochial and small my own life had been. So the years I spent in the Army I consider graduate study—equivalent of certainly an M.A. and so on. The experience was an opening to a broader horizon to everything for me. Remember, I saw a good part of the world, almost three-fourths by the time I got home. And I learned about other people. I realized how little I knew about other people—the men in the barracks, enlisted men and officers. Finally, I realized the kind of heritage that I have from Italy, a very different kind of heritage.

Ace Elliott

Nevin "Ace" Elliott was born and raised in Centerville, Ohio—a lifelong resident. He and his wife, Celia, have two daughters—Ann and Susan. Elliott spent almost two years in the Navy serving on a merchant marine ship. He traveled extensively in the Pacific Theater of Operations and on one trip went around the world. He attained the rank of seaman first class. After the war, Elliott studied cabinet making at Patterson Co-op School in Dayton under the GI Bill of Rights. He worked for Centerville Builders Supply for years and is a member of the First Baptist Church.

What were you doing prior to joining the Navy?

Well, my dad was manager of Normandy Farms on Normandy Lane, and I worked for him and R. H. Grant. I was rather young when I went in the service. I was in my twenties, but I had never gotten around much, back in those days you didn't travel much. You didn't have money to travel, let's put it that way. Anyway, I was drafted and sent to Great Lakes. I went from Dayton to Lima. At Lima I joined a group of friends, I made friends with them, and we went to Chicago, up to Waukegan to the Great Lakes Naval Training Station. And I spent twelve weeks in basic training. Then in October I came home for a week, or ten days I guess it was, and I got married—Celia and I got married.

What did you do in basic training?

Well, we did a lot of marching—a lot of exercises. We didn't handle equipment very much because equipment that you have on a boat is kind of hard to put on land. It's too big. But we handled machine guns, 20mm machine guns. We went to gunnery school, and we worked with some 450s [four and one-half inch shell]. At that time most of it was rifles and pistols. This would be in July of '44, and I completed basic training late in September, I think it was the 26th or 28th of September, something like that. Then, like I said, I came home and got married. After that I went back to Great Lakes, was there about a week, and was sent from there down to New Orleans. And from New Orleans we went up to Biloxi where we went through heavy equipment gunnery school, 450s, all machine guns in what we call machine gun nests aboard the ship. Had some 350s [three and one-half inch shell] that we used on the bow of the ship—that was an a aircraft and surface gun. The shell on it was about three foot long, something like that. On a 450, it's about four foot long, and the projectile is separate from the casing of the gun that has the powder. You put the powder load in, then you put the shell in, and then you shove it down in. You had a stick that you jammed it down into place [with]. This actually was a four-inch shell. A four-inch and a three-inch shell. The three-inch was on the bow and as I said, it was a combination gun. It was aircraft and surface. And of course those shells, after they got out, exploded at about three thousand feet. Or if you were shooting at a boat it would explode on contact.

We always had to launder our own clothes—we wore whites. And we had a washer that was kind of on an angle. It had a lot of rough surfaces and you had a brush that you used like a washboard. That's how you washed and rinsed your clothes. After basic we went to gunnery school at Biloxi. Then we came back and I got on board an LST. That's landing ship tank. It's a very flat bottom boat. It has a front end that drops down so equipment can roll out of it and men can walk out of it.

We rode that down to Panama. That was my first boat trip and the seas were a little bit rough on such a flat bottom boat. Sometimes we listed twenty-seven degrees one way, and then the other. I wasn't sick, but my stomach was kind of queasy. You weren't doing a lot of eating on that trip. I spent a lot of time in the bunk. But we weren't on it very long because it only took us about four or five days to go down to Panama. We landed at Colón I think it was.

Then I went across Panama, but I never went through the canal. I went across by train and was assigned to a liberty ship. From there we went out to the Marianas in the Central Pacific Area (CPA). Then we went into the islands out in the Pacific. That was almost out to Japan—its way out there. Then we came back and we boarded a tanker, and went to Eniwetok in the Marshall Islands. And I had a terrible experience there. We were transporting a load of fuel for ships, it was a kind of an oil-based fuel, and we were going to transfer the load over to a Navy tanker. Anyway, the captain of the Navy tanker got off base or something and he hit us broadside. I was standing on the bridge and you could just see the ship bend in like that. But by luck it didn't break open. He had a water breaker on the front of the ship, probably about a twelve-inch square. It just took that and bent it—like I took a piece of baling wire and bent it. He was up high and we were down low because we were loaded. When we were loaded at the well deck it was only about four foot down to the water. The bow and the mid-ship and the stern were elevated, but the tank's deck was way lower. But fortunately it didn't break us open—just bent us real bad. I was standing on the bridge and I could look right down and see all this happening, and it made me just a little bit nervous. This was near Eniwetok in the Marshall Islands. When this happened we were out at sea, we weren't at land. We were just unloading from one ship to another at sea. We would pull alongside one another. The ships stayed apart but we had cables running from one ship to the other ship, and then they strung lines on it. These lines were probably six or eight inches in diameter. And that's how we would transfer our load.

The Navy could take it in to a closer place, 'cause see, we were merchant marine, I was assigned to a merchant marine ship, and we weren't really equipped to go into any combat zones. Well, we unloaded some stuff there—I forget what all we had on there. Anyway, the point to make here is we had a lot of trucks that had guns on them—weapons carriers I think. They were all crated up and everything, so we tore parts of the crate off and built ourselves a frame. Then we took tarps and draped them in the frame and made a swimming pool. And so we swam all the way across the ocean—down past Australia between New Zealand and Australia, and up into the Indian Ocean.

After that we went back to Panama where we caught another liberty ship and went back out. Actually, we started around the world. First we went to Australia, went around between New Zealand and Australia, and then on to Perth and Fremantle on the west side—the Indian Ocean side. From there we went up to Calcutta. But we never stayed more than about a week at any one place. One thing I do remember was that in Australia restaurants and any public buildings of any kind were never open on weekends. They were open five days a week and that was it. You couldn't go out and eat on Saturday or Sunday. If you wanted to go out and eat you had to do it during the week. And from Australia we went out to Calcutta and went up the Ganges River. I don't know how many miles we went up the Ganges River, but we went up quite a ways. Went all the way up to the King George Locks.

We were hauling a big load—had a load of trucks and stuff. And another thing we did once, we had one haul that had forty-seven thousand cases of beer on it. We were hauling this up to the American soldiers and others at Calcutta.

Ace Elliott.

Anyway, we went up the Ganges River and there was a lot of these little guys in canoes. They kind of relied upon the sailors and they always had a rope with a stick in it. They would come out, stick it in one of the weep holes in the side of the ship [drain holes for sanitary waste on the ship], and then get towed along. The river was muddy as the dickens, you couldn't see nothing, but you throw a coin over and they would dive down and come right up with it. They could get it even in that muddy water.

When we came back down the Ganges River we went through the King George Locks again. I don't know how far they raised us up going into Calcutta. Another interesting thing about Calcutta was that whatever your dad was, that's what you were. The kid that was working the lift that unloaded our ship, I bet he wasn't ten years old. Oh, he could thread a needle with the lift. And then down below us, down below the ship in the harbor, there was a woman cooking dinner on one side, she was dipping water out of the bay, and on the other side she had a boy who was going to the bathroom. So, you see all kinds of things.

From there we went down to Madagascar and then down to Mozambique. I was about twenty-five at the time. We pulled in there for just about a day—for refueling. Mozambique is on the east coast of Africa. We were there for about a week—just went into port. We didn't really do anything. We went ashore, but you weren't allowed to wear any uniforms. We always just went in dungarees and T-shirts. We did this because it was a neutral port.

And then we went from there down to Cape Town in South Africa. We spent about a week there loading up materials that we were to haul up to Casablanca to unload. It was all Navy and Army equipment. It was surplus, and we were supposed to haul it up to Casablanca where we would have it unloaded. Before we got there we stopped on the Gold Coast which is on Africa's west coast, but still we were headed for Casablanca.

After we unloaded at Casablanca, we came across the Atlantic to Baltimore. We never did have any problems with submarines in all my travels, and generally we traveled alone. My wife and mother picked me up there and we came back home. And that made a full trip around the world. At this point I needed half a point to get out of the service. So I went from my home to

Los Angeles and caught an aircraft carrier and went to Honolulu, Hawaii, and transferred there. I was there about a week, which I spent on Waikiki Beach, and then from there we boarded a troop transport and come back to San Francisco and went under the Golden Gate bridge—never been over it; only been under it.

There we unloaded and came back to Ohio by troop train. Anyway, we came back to Toledo and from there we came home by car and I was discharged from the Navy. That was in February of '46. I had literally been around the world.

How many times did you cross the Pacific?

I've been across the Pacific both ways, going and coming, and I've traveled across the equator seven times. I've been on every continent of the world. My wife and I went to Italy in about 1965 I think it was. I was with Centerville Builders Supply and we won a trip to Italy. And Celia and I went over there and spent about a week in Italy.

What did you think about the atomic bomb when you first heard of it?

Well, actually, we never heard much about the atomic bomb back in those days. It didn't bother us because we were out at sea and we didn't do much communication.

After my discharge I started with Wagner Wood, and later I used the GI Bill of Rights and took an apprenticeship in cabinet making at Patterson Co-op. That took eighteen months.

I traveled a lot and I saw a lot that I would have never seen otherwise. There's one point I wanted to make on Casablanca in Africa. You probably have seen the mahogany coffee table we have—that elephant? That came from Casablanca. I got it when I was over there in the service. I've only seen one other and that was in *Newsweek* magazine and it was being given to the secretary of state—I forget what year that was. It was back in the 40s when it was given to him. It's an elephant coffee table. The elephant is hand carved, it's got a mahogany oval top on it, and it's got tusks and ivory eyes. I bought it and only paid twelve dollars and a half for it. And I put it in a box and put it under my bunk and brought it home. When I got to Baltimore, I put it on a commercial carrier and sent it home. And I've only seen one other one [as] I said and that was in *Newsweek*.

Were you able to correspond with Celia while you were in the service?

Oh, yes. We wrote letters, but there was times when we'd go, well, there was one time we went sixty-some days without ever receiving any mail. We were out to sea all that time. When we had mail call you would get a whole

package of letters and cards and what have you. I threw away all the old letters at the time that I got them because some of them were outdated when I
read them. They were so old. One thing that we did do, Celia knew where I
was at all times. Like in certain letters, or certain words, I would highlight
one letter, and then she'd go down through the letter and get wherever I was,
what island, or Australia, or India, wherever. We had our own code we made
out before I left. I couldn't tell her where I was or anything, but by going
through the letter and highlighting certain letters in certain words she could
take the whole letter and go through it and by the time she got to the end it
would tell her what country we were in, or island, or wherever we might be.

After the war I never have belonged to any service organizations. I don't
know why. I never had any desire to join any.

Why were Navy personnel on a merchant marine ship?

Well, the merchant marine didn't have the personnel and the training for
the guns, and what have you, that we had aboard the ship. As I said, the Navy
placed a 350 surface and aircraft gun on the bow, we had four 20mm machine
guns on the bridge, and on the stern we had a 450 surface gun. A 450 surface
gun had a projectile about four foot long, and the bow of the ship had a 350
which was about three foot long. And the projectile and the shell itself were sep-
arated. The projectile, you put in after you loaded the shell in. And the end of
it screwed off and it was filled with powder or explosives of some kind. It would
explode upon contact. The 20mm machine gun bullets was the same way, only
a 20mm is about eight to ten inches long, and the projectile is already mounted
in there, but it's loaded. The end of it screws off, and it's loaded with powder
and so it explodes on contact. The magazine on a 20mm machine gun will shoot
about sixty rounds per minute which is pretty fast. Now regarding weather, we
had some high winds and stuff like that, but we never had any real mean storms.
Or at least I didn't go through any. The Pacific, most of the time, was as smooth
as cement out there. One experience I did have, it kind of shook me up. I was
standing watch on the bow, and it was one of those days where it was just as
still as anything. Water wasn't even moving, but the sun was coming in, it was
late in the afternoon, the sun was coming in a line on the water, and you couldn't
see anything. And here come an airplane, it went right up over the top of me,
out of that sun. And it happened to be one of ours, thank goodness. He came
right out of the sun. You couldn't see him. That kind of scared me. But most
of the time I spent was on the 350. You had a gunnery crew, you had a trig-
german, you had a guy that pointed it, and then you had two guys that loaded
it and one handled the shells. Had a regular gunnery crew to each one of them.
That's about all there is to tell.

Part II

THE EUROPEAN THEATER OF OPERATIONS

Military Timeline

1941

December 11   The United States declares war on Italy and Germany

1942

August 17   First all-American bombing run in Europe
November 8–29   Operation Torch: U.S. invasion of North Africa begins

1943

January 27   First USAAF bombing raid on Germany—
                           Wilhelmshaven
February 14–25   Kasserine Pass Campaign begins (a loss by Americans)
March 5–20   A crisis of Atlantic battle shipping losses
April 22   American First Army attacks at Bou, North Africa
July 10   Operation Husky—Allied landings in Sicily
July 22   Americans capture Palermo, Sicily
September 8   Eisenhower announces Italy's surrender
September 9   Salerno, Italy—landings by American troops
October 1   Fifth Army captures Naples
October 4   Corsica is liberated
December 3   Fifth Army opens new offensive in Italy

1944

January 22   Anzio, Italy—landings by Sixth Army
January 7–16   German counterattacks at Anzio almost cut lines
May 23   A breakout from Anzio begins
June 5   Fifth Army captures Rome
June 6   D-Day in Normandy for American forces and allies
August 4   Eighth Army enters Florence, Italy
August 15   Seventh Army invades southern France: Operation
                           Anvil
August 25   Allied forces enter Paris
September 12   U. S. First Army enters Germany
September 5, 8, 26   Fifth and Eighth armies enter Pisa, break Gothic
                           Line, cross Rubicon River
December 16–25   Battle of the Bulge in the Ardennes (Patton relieves
                           Bastogne)
December 17   Malmédy massacre of American troops by the SS

1945

January 16	Ardennes salient (the Bulge) eliminated
February 9	Allies break through Siegfried Line
March 2–3	The U.S. Army captures Trier and Cologne
March 7	First Army crosses Rhine River at Remagen Bridge
March 17–20	U.S. forces capture Saarbrucken and Coblenz
April 1	First and Ninth armies encircle German army in Ruhr
April 10	Ninth Army captures Hanover
April 12–29	Belsen, Buchenwald and Dachau concentration camps are liberated
May 7	General Jodl signs unconditional surrender
May 8	V-E Day

Peter Granson

Peter A. Granson was a surgeon in Dayton, Ohio (he died September 23, 2000) and practiced medicine in the area for over thirty years. During his career he was chief of staff at Kettering Memorial Hospital and president of the Montgomery County Medical Society. After high school he attended Cornell University where he graduated in 1939. When the war ended he returned to school where he earned his M.D. degree from Temple University. He and his wife Tee had four children. Granson served three years in the Army (2 years and 2 months overseas and 10 months in the States). During World War II he was company commander of the 107thmm rifled mortar company, a chemical warfare unit. He served 138 straight days in combat in the battle for Italy, much of it in close support of infantry where his mortar platoons fired both white phosphorus (WP) and high-explosive (HE) shells at German troops. He was involved in both the Anzio and Salerno assaults.

Where were you born and raised?

Well, I was born in Canton, Ohio, and lived there until I was twelve years old. Then we moved to New York City and I went to high school there. After graduating from high school I went to Cornell University in Ithaca, New York, where I was a pre-med student. And after leaving New York, we moved back to Canton, Ohio, and I went to work for the Republic Steel Corporation as an industrial chemist. This was in 1940 and I was there until the war started. After Pearl Harbor I enlisted and went into the Army. It was the Monday after, the next day after Pearl Harbor, that I enlisted. Because I know I was inducted on the 4th of January 1942. I was single, but had an A.B. degree from Cornell.

Where did you do your basic training?

At Fort Leonard Wood, Missouri. It was in the Ozarks. In fact when we got there the camp wasn't really completely built. Believe it or not it was an engineering camp. So I was trained as an engineer and when I finished my training there I was sent out to Camp San Luis Obispo in California with the 7th, I guess it was the 7th Division. Yes. Now this was an engineering outfit and I was supposedly a combat engineer. We learned how to blow up things and what have you, and we went through our basic military there.

Then I was sent to the Mohave Desert for desert training. So we all felt we were going to go to Africa. By that time I decided I was going to try to go to OCS—just got tired of doing dishes—I did enough of that in college. Well, not only that, but that's how I got through school, I washed dishes. I was a "potwalloper." That was the guy who took care of the great big pots. But I decided I'd go to OCS and it was in Maryland at Edgewood Arsenal School which was the chemical warfare school. And I thought, "My gosh, here I am a pre-med and I'm going to be doing something in a lab somewhere." But this was not to be.

We left there as second lieutenants and I wound up at Camp Rucker, Alabama, attached to a chemical warfare outfit which had a 4.2-inch mortar. And of course it had nothing whatsoever to do with chemical warfare. Actually, the Germans had a bigger mortar than we had—they had a 100mm mortar, and you could actually see those shells coming through the air. But this was a rifled barrel. That gun could really shoot those shells you know. Our field manual told us that we were only allowed to shoot these about eleven hundred yards. And the first thing we did the first day in combat, we realized that that manual was antiquated, outdated, and useless. So we just got rid of it and we started experimenting with our ranges, and we found that we could really propel that shell a long distance. And I told you we used to shoot the same targets as the 105 howitzers. In this little diary you'll find that we fired some of those rounds over three thousand yards.

When did you finally ship out for overseas?

Well, it was in the spring of '43—we went to North Africa. We landed in Oran. And from Oran we went to a little place called Bizerte that is near Tunis. Then later we shipped out of there for Italy. We were in North Africa from about April to September and then we went to Italy. The North African campaign ended shortly after we got there. We never saw any combat in Africa. None. That war was practically over when we got there so we saw no combat in North Africa.

Well, from there we got ready to go to Italy. We landed at Salerno on September 8th of '43, and then joined the 45th Division which was an Oklahoma National Guard outfit, a good outfit. From there we were attached to Darby's Rangers and went up to Casino, just north of Casino, and stayed there until we went to Anzio.

When we hit Salerno we set up our guns. The field manual said that the company headquarters was to be behind the guns. The guns are supposed to be in front, but we soon realized that that manual didn't make much sense because we were completely at the mercy of all the artillery that they were firing. The Germans were firing artillery all over the place. And this little place had some cactus plants around it, and the shrapnel would just go right through this cactus. It was the only time I really saw Hollywood's version of war. Because, while we were being shelled there was a tank battle going on to our right, German tanks and our tanks just milling around shooting at each other, and then from our rear came our own tanks shooting at us—which wasn't too much of a surprise because they didn't know what was going on. But that was the last time I really saw a so-called Hollywood version of war. After that it was just dirty.

Was it an opposed landing?

Oh, yes. Oh my, yes. In fact, there was a little town, let me think, maybe it's not on this map. It was Agricola. And the Germans could see everything we were doing. And there was a town over here, let me see if that town is Agricola—yes it is. All we had was a foothold on the beach. And the most unusual thing about that landing was when we landed there was this beautiful Greek temple in a place called Piester, that's the name of the town or the area, and the Germans wouldn't shoot at it and we wouldn't shoot at it. It was left intact. It was kind of a rule, and we respected them for that. They would not deface that temple. They could have destroyed it, but they didn't. I don't remember how many divisions were involved, but the 45th was one. We went into action right away, right away, yes. We had forward observers to select targets.

You're an officer, you wouldn't do that would you?

Oh, yes. Oh, my yes. They loved me—especially at Anzio. You simply had to be able to see the German lines. Well, our targets were troops, tanks, artillery, whatever. Whatever we could see. If we could see any gathering of troops we would fire.

Oh, we had adequate amm-unition, but in those days our shells came packed in cosmoline. Do you remember cosmoline? Can you imagine trying to clean those shells because the quarter-master didn't do it, we had to do it. And if we had to really fire a big mission, it took forever to clean that cosmoline off. In fact, sometimes when we couldn't get it all off we'd actually get some fire on those shells. But we were lucky, we only had one hang fire that exploded in the barrel. That was due to defective ammunition. But other than that we got away scot-free. Finally they decided they would clean the ammo for us in the rear areas. So we started getting our shells in these alu-minum containers.

Peter Granson.

My company consisted of two platoons and we had four or five officers and I think there were one hundred and twenty-five enlisted men. We had troops on the guns, we had our cooks, and we had our supply people. Control of the air was really up for grabs. The Germans were more in control than we were at that moment. But it didn't take long before we ruled the skies. And we were not strafed or bombed at Salerno. But the artillery was terrible. Well, number one, you're supposed to dig a foxhole or slit trench. And it's amazing, we had trouble getting the guys to dig slit trenches in the States, but we had no trou-ble getting them to dig them when we got overseas. They were anxious to dig. And as long as you were below the level of the ground, unless it hit right on you, why, you were safe.

What about casualties?

At Salerno? Oh yes, we lost some people. Some we lost even before we went into combat from so-called combat fatigue. Some couldn't take it. Couldn't deal with it. I had one officer who trained with me at OCS. He got sick on the first day that we landed at Salerno and we didn't see him until we got up to Anzio. He came up there, he was there one day, and he got sick again. And he finally came back and I was the company commander then. Well I kept him around the headquarters a couple of days, and finally I said, "Larry you've got to go back to your platoon." I got a call in the middle of the night from the sergeant, the platoon sergeant, and he says, "This guy is out of it." So I said, "Send him back." I wanted to court-martial him, but he got back to the hospital and some psychiatrist got a hold of him, and he got sent back to the States. And he had the nerve, after we took Rome, to come and say goodbye to us. I could have shot him. I felt very badly about this guy because he never tried. I mean, he was never really subjected to combat. He decided he didn't want any part of it.

But I remember I had one officer who at the time was a forward observer, and this was about a year after we'd been in combat. I was going up to his observation post to see him and I saw him coming back towards me, and all he did was just give me his pistol and he kept on walking. Never said a word to me. But I couldn't get upset with him because I knew he'd been through it. But this other guy had never been through it. You didn't have much use, it's a strange thing to say, but you didn't have much use for people that didn't stand up—do what the rest of us did. But, this guy didn't even give himself a chance to find out whether he was a man or a mouse.

This photograph was taken in the field eating my lunch—a little C ration. And believe it or not the K rations weren't bad, particularly if you got the canned cheese. We'd put it on our little Coleman stove and heat it up, and then take those great big bricks that they called crackers and break them up, and just dip our cheese.

We also actually had a company barber. We tried to keep the guys as neat as we possibly could. The only thing I allowed them to grow was a mustache. I couldn't grow it myself, but I didn't complain about the mustache. But I did complain about the hair.

Well, this photograph is a prize—this is my jeep. I called it the *Baltimore Lady* after a young lady that I knew in Baltimore, Maryland. And in fact, we corresponded all through the war. After I got back from overseas we met each other just one time and we knew that it wasn't going to work. This was going no place. Oh, this is, yes, this is [holding up a photograph] Carl Hamburger. Carl was a corporal, and he was an absolutely fabulous soldier. Now we lost a couple of our officers through either rotation or wounds so I gave him a battlefield commission. Now Carl is one of the general partners today of Stanley Blacker, which makes beautiful sport coats, sweaters, shirts, everything. Well, Carl did his job, but he did it better than he was supposed to do his job. And he had the respect of his people. If you didn't have the respect of your troops, you weren't worth a hoot and a holler as an officer. I knew he would do the job.

How many mortars would you have in each platoon?

Four each—a total of eight altogether. I had one platoon that had something I called the million-dollar hole, because we never had a casualty in this platoon on the Anzio beachhead. The other platoon was overrun by the Germans one night, and we lost not only the platoon leader, but we also lost the platoon sergeant. Killed. After that we started moving up the Italian boot. We went way up the boot to a place called Caserta. In fact we went past Caserta. Caserta was the rear area. That's where Mark Clark had his headquarters.

What do you think of him [Mark Clark] as an officer and as a leader?

Well, I had no quarrel with him, you know. You've got to realize that people in the lower echelon of command had no idea what was going on. We didn't know what the big picture was or anything. We just knew who was in front of us and we'd take orders and follow them—that's all there was to it.

Did you make the landing at Anzio?

Absolutely. We landed on the 22nd of January at five o'clock in the morning with the 3rd Division. When we got to Anzio it was at five o'clock in the morning. Not a shot was fired. There wasn't a German within twenty-five miles of us. Well, we were confused because we never made a landing where somebody didn't shoot at us. But we landed on the beach, got all our troops ashore, got our hospital ashore, and then we sat there. At ten o'clock in the morning the Germans sent their first fighters down. In fact I learned, after we took Rome, that the day that we landed at Anzio they were evacuating the city. We could have gone up there and taken that place I think. But our general wasn't going to move. He just didn't move. And that's one time when I wish that we'd had General Patton leading us because he would have gone right up there.

We didn't move far inland then because the Germans had us literally surrounded on three sides. When they realized we weren't going to move they sent everybody down there because they had to protect their flank. They had troops at the abbey at Monte Casino, and they protected them by holding us on the beach. We could have gone, I honestly think, we could have gone right up to Rome that day with the 3rd Division. But that was not a happy place. We took an awful beating; we lost a lot of people, lot of people. Colonel Darby's Rangers were decimated and became ineffective as a fighting force. The Rangers were a very special unit. Elite, yes! It's strange, Colonel Darby after Anzio went back to the States. He left as a lieutenant colonel, but the next time I saw him was just before the war in Italy ended and he was a full bird colonel.

Then I was attached to an outfit that was going up to the Po River to keep the Germans from blowing the bridges, a regimental combat team. And on the way up there the regimental commander hit a land mine and was wounded. Darby was there as an observer. Darby was the senior officer. He took over the command and went up to a little town called Garda which was on the north end of the lake. And they tell me that an airburst came over and killed him. Isn't that fate?

Why do men fight?

You fight to protect each other. That's the whole idea.

Is that a pretty close relationship?

Oh, can't be closer.

Like family?

More than that. It's hard to explain the bond, but you depend on each other. You know. In that little diary you'll read something that I wrote about battles. After we had been shelled, I took a look at my buddy next to me and said, "You know, one second from now we could be dead." That's how precarious your life was. It was just like that—you lived from one second to the next when you were in combat. We were in combat, let's see—it was one hundred and thirty-eight days. Well, in the two years that we were over there we had almost close to five hundred days of combat. They never pulled us out of line.

I was wounded once—yes—just above my right eye. It was either shrapnel or pieces of rocket that exploded when the shell hit. I realized that I was alive, I was bleeding, but I was alive. I had my arms, my hands, my eyes, I felt like I was ten feet tall. I never had such an adrenaline rush in all my life. And

Peter Granson in October 1999.

I knew I was going to live through that war. I just knew then that they weren't going to get me.

Did you ever feel that time was running out on you?

Oh, you couldn't have those thoughts—you couldn't do your job if you did. No. I knew that I might not make it, but I still had a job to do and I did it. And my men felt the same way. I mean, they were at risk as I was, but they still did their job.

I had one sergeant who was an absolute warrior. His name was John Matovsky. He was wounded four times. The fourth time he was wounded I said, "John, I'm gonna get you out of here. I don't want you fighting anymore." 'Cause I figured he'd used up every chance he ever had. And he refused to leave us. And I know at the end of the war when I was in the States, I got a letter from the War Department wanting to know if I would recommend him for a promotion to officer. Boy, I'd do it in a second. I think he was mad too—he was angry with the Germans. He was Polish, and the first time he was wounded was at Anzio. The Germans had broken through the 3rd Division line, and I think John, single handedly, just stopped—blunted—their attack. Next thing I know John's coming back from the OP with about ten German prisoners and he's all bandaged up. And I didn't find out until later just exactly what he did up there, but he just about wiped that outfit out all by himself. And being stupid, really, I said, "I'm going to put him in for a Silver Star"—like that was some big deal. He should have been in for the Congressional Medal of Honor. He actually not only took care of the troops that attacked the infantry, but he also captured all these prisoners and brought them back. And he went back to the hospital, but he wouldn't go any farther back than the hospital. He figured if he went that far back they might send him back to the general hospital down at Naples. He wouldn't leave the outfit. He had a Purple Heart with three oak leaf clusters on it. Four times he was wounded. He just was a remarkable, remarkable man. I don't know whatever happened to him. I hope he got his commission. I'm pretty sure he did, but he may have stayed in or retired. But he was a war hero.

In June of '44 we started off and were involved in the capture of Rome. This was the first week of June, I don't know the exact date. That's where they pulled us out of the line for the first time since September of '43 and I did all the sightseeing. I met these people in Rome who were very good to me, but it's like when we spent the summer watching the Germans build fortifications at Florence, Italy. You know, we were on one side of the Arno River and they were on the other side, and we just spent the whole summer looking at them. We waited 'til they got their defenses built properly so they could attack.

Would you comment on these photographs?

This is at our company headquarters in Anzio. It was a place called Campo Morte, the field of death. How appropriate can you name something? That's the name of the place. This is a photo of the original company commander. I was his executive officer. Here's Florence. After we took Florence we were heading this way and hit that German line that was all fortified. I mean, they just fortified everything, but we had to go through this line. We finally got through the German line and we'd gone up here just south of Bologna to a place called Viarregio with the 85th Infantry Division. While we were there, this is 1944, we got word on Christmas Eve day, the 24th of December, that the Germans had broken through at Leghorn, and they were actually going to capture the city seaport. So I took my company and rushed over to this area, and we got over there and then found out there wasn't anything going on. We spent seven weeks over there with this outfit. I hate to talk about this outfit, but they were useless and only got shot at one time in the seven weeks. I wasn't used to that. But this outfit had a very poor, poor record, you know. It's too bad.

Well, after we left this place called Viarregio, we went back with the Tenth Mountain Division—[Senator Bob] Dole's old outfit isn't it? And we ended the war with them. Then we went up to Lake Garda and there was a tunnel there. The Germans had blown the tunnel and we were waiting for boats to take us up to the north end when the war ended. Well, I couldn't believe it. In fact, the night before I got the message, well, I actually got the message that night but I didn't believe the messenger. I'd gone out and I bought enough Asti spumante to take care of my division. And we had a party in our headquarters—the troops, everybody—and this young soldier walks in and says, "The war is over." And we literally told him, in a very nice way of course, to get out. And then the next morning we got the word from my colonel that the war is over. And believe it or not, I was on my way home on rotation right after the war ended in May of '45. The day after it ended. But Carl Hamburger stayed.

But, you know, the fun started after the war was over. I mean, lots of things to do and see and we didn't have to worry about getting killed or shot—but I was on my way home. And I was sent back to Washington. That had to be the worst duty I ever had. I wasn't used to it. Maybe it was a post-combat depression, but I just felt awful. In fact the day they dropped the bomb and the Germans, or rather the Japanese surrendered, I was in a bookstore in northwest Washington, and I remember, they said, "The war's over." The next day I took my papers and I walked them through—my discharge papers. I had all sorts of points and medals and stuff like that and I was out of the service the next day. And I went home long enough to see my parents and then I went to Cornell and met my wife there. Well, I'd been out of school almost six years, but I was gonna go to medical school. I didn't even know if I could still study, so I went back and took some courses in anatomy and embryology and what have you. They were all medical courses. Went there four years. And we came out here in 1950 because they paid interns—they didn't pay interns in those days. They gave them room and board, but you weren't supposed to be married and have a family. But we had three children and that's how we got to Dayton. We love this place. I was probably the oldest resident they ever had in Miami Valley.

Would you comment a bit on how World War II changed your life?

Well, you know, I've thought about that many times. I think one thing it showed me was that I wasn't a bad man—I mean, if I could put up with that I was doing well. I could stand the rigors of combat without going bonkers. So I can look anybody in the eye. I learned a lot about myself.

Herb Corson

Herbert Corson has lived in Dayton, Ohio, almost all his life. He graduated from Fairview High School and then went to Miami University in Oxford, Ohio, where he worked his way through school and graduated in 1940. He enlisted in the U.S. Army Air Corps shortly after the Japanese attack on Pearl Harbor and served as a navigator/bombardier on a B-26 in the European Theater of Operations. His plane was shot down and he spent over twenty months as a prisoner of war (POW) in Poland and Germany. After liberation at the end of the war he stayed in the service until 1950 when he left as a captain. He then started his own vending machine business and operated that until he retired in 1990. He and his wife Janice have three children who live in the Dayton area. He belongs to the Methodist Church in Centerville.

Pearl Harbor was December 7th of '41, and I got called up the 9th of December '41. I was sent down to San Antonio, Kelley Field. I stayed at Kelley Field about six weeks. And then after I left Kelley Field, they sent me to Parks Air College in Missouri to learn how to fly airplanes.

And after about a week they washed out about half the class. Fortunately, I was still in the running. Then one morning they called us all into the auditorium and they announced that everybody that was still there was going to transfer out of flying school and go back to Texas. This was quite a blow. They told us they were going to give us some tests when we got back to Texas and I qualified as a navigator. All my friends were going to be bombardiers, so I said, "I don't want to do that [be a navigator], I want to be a bombardier." Well, they said, "You're going to be a navigator." So, not being too familiar with the military I began to complain. You shouldn't really do it, but I guess it worked. Finally, after I went to navigation school for about a month or two, I got called out of class one morning and sent to Midland, Texas, to be a bombardier because I'd been making such a wave about wanting to be one.

So I actually graduated in Midland, Texas, in September of '42 as a bombardier. I got my wings and my commission. And then from there they sent me to McDill Field, Florida, which was a medium bomb group, and assigned me to a B-26—a Martin Marauder bomber. And after training at McDill, we were sent to Savannah, Georgia, Hunter Field, for more training. Finally we shipped out of Miami to South America, and from South America we went to the Ascension Islands, and from the Ascension Islands to Accra which is in Ghana, West Africa. And from Ghana we went up to Dakar, and Dakar to Oran, on the north coast of Africa and finally into Tunisia in the battle area where we did our first shooting.

Would you describe your airplane?

The B-26B was made by Martin and had a six-man crew. There was a tail gunner, a radio man–turret gunner, a waste gunner, a pilot and co-pilot, and I was the navigator/bombardier. Six people. The B-25 has twin stabilizers and was made by North American. The B-26 was made by Martin. It was called a medium bomber. The B-25 is the one that went on the Tokyo raid. There's been some confusion on that; it wasn't the B-26. When we got into the Tunisian area, we were assigned to combat. And I have a list of every mission.

The categories in this list of missions include the date, the target area, the number of ships in the group, and what the bomb load was. For instance our first trip was to Carliforte, Sardinia, eighteen bombers, eight, three hundred pound bombs, the target was shipping, and we had a problem. I shouldn't even talk about it, but our gyroscopes toppled and we had a dry run—we didn't drop any bombs. We only were in Africa for four trips. As you may recall, Rommel was run out of North Africa by Montgomery and Patton and our targets went ahead of them. This was on 26 of April 1943. And then we actually did strafing missions at five hundred feet over Tunis and Stax. Here the mission list shows that our target was Bizerte Harbor—it was shipping.

We had eighteen airplanes and we're each carrying six five hundred pounders. We had good results strafing and bombing on the mission.

We completed thirty-eight missions and you needed forty. So I just missed it by one. Villa Littoria, our last trip in Italy, was a railroad yard north of Naples, and our job was to destroy the railroad yards. And we did, but as we dropped the bombs we were hit by anti-aircraft fire, and our right engine caught fire. But we successfully got the fire out. We thought we were trimmed up to sneak home, but the German Messerschmitts noticed the dead engine, and when you see an airplane with one engine gone, that's easy bait. They shot at us again and got the engine on fire, so we had to bail out.

Well, we were hit, and we were really seriously afraid of exploding in the air—I'd seen this happen. When you're hit you have fire in your wings because that's where the gasoline is. So, we wanted to get out and we all six got out. We had to lower our wheels to get out. We lowered the landing gear, and there was a ladder from the co-pilot's seat. You went down the ladder and stepped off into space—the last eleven thousand feet. The gunners went out the back. We opened the bomb bay up and then the co-pilot went out. He had to get out of the way so I could get out. I was in the nose. I had to crawl over his seat to get to the hole to go out. The pilot was the last man to go out.

We were up about eleven thousand feet. I had never jumped before and people say how could you do it? Believe me, you do it. There's no such thing as worrying when you got fire around you. And they always told us, in Florida and Texas, when you do this, if you're in a battle area which we were, you don't open the parachute right away because you're gonna float through a lot of lead, a lot of shooting going on. If you can keep your presence of mind to free-fall as far as you can you fall out of the dangerous stratum. So I don't know how long I held it, but I thought, "Well, I'd better do it." I must have free-fallen three or four thousand feet. I was utterly confused and I suppose partly in shock, but then I finally decided to open the chute because I was afraid maybe I'd pass out and not do it. When I opened it, the little pilot chute comes out first, which is probably the size of a small table. I looked up at that pilot chute, and I thought, "Oh, for heavens sakes, somebody shorted me, this is not gonna work." Then the big one pulled out, twenty-eight feet of silk, and I was OK. It opened up. Then I floated down.

There was another eerie thing on the way down—I was hurting bad. When I opened the chute, it was a chest pack, it yanked me forward and broke my back, and I was in excruciating pain. I was just dangling there, moaning and groaning; when a couple German fighters circled me. I thought they were gonna shoot me as I was just hanging there and floating. But they didn't, they just wiggled their wings and went on. And finally I hit the ground. It is Italy. I'm not moving. Now my landing was a miracle, according to what the doctors in Cincinnati and Atlanta said when I got back to the states. When I hit the ground, I came down into a plowed field that had just been plowed that morning. So it was very soft terrain, and I came down and I lit right on my tailbone. And the doctors said it stove the break. Had I landed differently, the spinal cord would have gone. I didn't know my back was broken and I walked away. Didn't know I had a broken back 'til 1950. When I got ready to get out of the service in '50, somebody said, "Herb, you ought to go to the medics and have a real good physical, because you don't know what might have happened," never dreaming what *had* happened. "And then afterwards you'll have a case if it's a military connected injury." So, I went to Atlanta, and they checked me and checked me in Cincinnati, and they said, "You know, you had a broken back, but it stove." When I hit, I hit right on my tailbone, and it just was a miracle. And I got a little pension, whatever that means. I also got some teeth knocked out, but otherwise, I'm lucky.

They said in training when you hit the ground, get up and fall face down in your parachute so you collapse it or it'll drag you everywhere. So I did that, got unbuckled and was gathering up this pile of silk to dump it somewhere. I wanted to get it out of sight because there were people looking for us. I was carrying this silk to a well, I was gonna stuff it in an open well. But some little girl came out of the olive grove and said she wanted it, I guess for a dress. So I left her and the silk and got into a straw stack, and I hid in the straw stack.

About that time I saw the pilot wandering around dazed. I yelled at him and we both got in the straw stack and just kind of burrowed in tail first. Then the guards, the dogs, and the police were running around but nobody saw us. We stayed in the stack all night trying to figure what to do tomorrow. We knew the allied landing was pretty close at Salerno. If we could just lay low for a couple days 'til the allied landing came in, they could overrun us and recapture us. We'd be safe. This was August 21, 1943, and I think, Salerno was about eight days later.

But anyway, in the morning we thought we'd try to get something to eat, so we went to a farmhouse which was a mistake. The Italians thought there had been a paratrooper invasion. The day I went down there were one hundred and thirty-eight airplanes that went down—German, Italian, American, British—it was a tremendous air battle. And so when all these parachutes come down the Italians were out of their houses with their arms up—they were trying to surrender. But we got in this farmhouse to get some food, and they sent some kid out the back door to go get the police. And I never did get the food.

Then the Italian police took us into Naples to a penitentiary in Naples harbor. And we stayed there for probably a week. It was constant bombing—it was really a mess. Then they took us by truck up the Appian Way from

Naples to Rome. After they had paraded us around Naples in trucks, like in the zoo, showing the people the American gangsters, they took us to Rome and from Rome we went to a monastery north of Rome where they had a makeshift prison.

At that point, the Italians quit the war. A man by the name of Badoglio became president, and made peace between the Italians and the allies. So the Germans came and took all of us off to Germany. They didn't want to miss anything, so they took the whole group by train up through the Brenner Pass, through Innsbruck and into Munich to a little place called Moosburg which was a reception center. Well we stayed there about a week, and then they put us on another train and took us up to what was part of Poland, ninety miles east of Berlin, to a place called Stalag Luft 3. And that's where I spent the next twenty months. I was a prisoner of war for almost two years. This camp was actually part of Poland. It was ninety miles east of Berlin in western Poland. The camp had been established in 1939 or 1940, and there were people there three or four years ahead of us—British that had been captured.

Are these all officers?

All officers—an officers' camp. No enlisted men. In this book *The Longest Mission* it shows the camp. These are the buildings we lived in. These are the security fences and between the fences there was electric wire. And they had machine guns in the towers, and it wasn't really safe to leave. This is a picture of the camp, an aerial shot, taken from a P-51 reconnaissance plane. I was in this building right here—in the center of camp.

Herb Corson.

We had roll call twice a day, about 5:30 in the morning and about 5:30 in the evening. And believe me they were meticulous with the count. We had no duties; all we had to do was make the two roll calls. Then we had to cook our own food because there was no such thing as a central place to eat. They brought potatoes in and we had to peel them. Thank god for the Red Cross, they brought in Red Cross boxes. And our parents sent stuff every six weeks after we got established. We even planted gardens in the summer and got seeds through the Salvation

Army in Sweden. The Germans could never understand why we made cucumber hills so high. In Germany they didn't do that, you know, and a cucumber hill usually would be a foot high in the States. But we made them four feet high, hiding the dirt coming out of the tunnel. We didn't know where else to put the dirt. Well, this is the food that the Germans gave us—the bread, potatoes, cabbage, and they killed an ox now and then and we had gravy off of that. We took turns cooking and they brought coal in.

Some soldiers were killed in the great escape. And the Germans let us have a ceremony—cremate, and bury them outside the camp. People say, "Were you brutalized?" No, we weren't. We were told to understand who had the guns and if you want to get home, be good or you won't get home.

This is our tunnel. There was a movie made called *The Great Escape*, and Steve McQueen and someone else were the movie stars. I guess the movie is still circulating, and the original story came from our camp, Luft 3. The tunnel was dug, and the trap was under a stove. They dug down and out into the woods. They had an air conditioning system with bellows pumping air and they used the German electricity. They had electric light lines in the tunnel and a little cart you could lay on. And actually over a hundred men got out. But the Germans caught them and executed fifty of them. That's why you saw the funeral. And they let fifty of them live. Hitler wanted them all killed and Hermann Göring intervened. There's a little camaraderie between air forces. He said, "Let's just kill fifty of them." Three actually got home.

Did a lot of people work on this tunnel?

There were probably four or five hundred men that were doing different jobs. I didn't dig. I had a unique job; I was to get all the nails I could get to put the shoring together. You couldn't go to Lowe's or Wal-Mart and buy nails. So, every time I look at a wall today or a frame, I look and see if there's a loose nail you could pull out. So my job was pulling nails. I could usually get twenty-five nails a day.

I wasn't slated to go. Very unique the way they got out of this thing. In *The Great Escape* there was an escape committee of people that knew more about the outside and what they were gonna run up against than we did. Unless you qualified with the language, and your health, and whatnot, you weren't allowed to go. We had our own American-British escape committee, and you were selected by your ability to save your life. If you thought you could make it, and they knew you couldn't make it, you were never going to be selected. Most of them were British. The British were the ones they killed fifty of. I was shot down in '43, probably October of '43. I know when we got into the camp we were taken to one side by American and British fellow prisoners, or senior officers, and it was explained to us that things were going on that you don't ask questions about—just keep your mouth shut. So we didn't know it had happened 'til it was over.

What would a day be like in the camp?

Well, you get up at 5:30, go out to roll call which took about a half hour, usually very cold, then we'd come back in the building, make some coffee and eat some German bread. A loaf of bread weighed 8½ pounds. We took the bread and sliced it with a meat slicer and put it on the stove. Put the knife like this and tamped it down so we'd get the water out of it. It was like Melba toast. We'd put margarine on it. Here's a plate I made. This was made from two British Hershey tins and it came through the Red Cross. We cut it and pounded it together with this knife. That was my plate in prison camp. And then I punched a hole in it so I could hang it on my belt when we took the march. And I brought it back with me. These utensils were issued by the Germans. This fork still has a pretty vivid swastika on it. This is my peeling knife. A lot of potatoes were peeled with that. I don't know why they let us keep that but they did.

I might add about the food, and I think this is interesting, we learned how to cook. And it was unique to see a P-38 pilot and a bomber colonel trying to bake a cake. Well, this was an everyday affair. We couldn't get our cakes to raise because the Germans would not let baking powder in. That was an explosive derivative you know, but the British had been there so much longer they knew how to get around these things. They said what you do is put toothpaste in the batter and the cake will raise. Of course the British did it meticulously. Course the Americans do everything in gross amounts—we squirt a whole tube in and stirred it up. We had cake coming out all over the place. It works though, so we made cakes that way. And people would say, "Did you taste the toothpaste?" No. You could get all the toothpaste you wanted, but you couldn't get baking powder.

When the Red Cross boxes would come in you'd go down to the outer logger area, where the boxes came in from Switzerland, and the Germans would open up the box with a knife. It'd never been open, a big cardboard box, and there were all the different ingredients with a manifest of what was in there. And you had to break your own box down to get the food. They wouldn't give you the box it came in because there might be something secret in there. The Germans would take a can out and they'd say, "One can of tuna." Then they'd take a knife and punch two holes in it and hand it to you. That's so you couldn't save it. And the British told us the first thing to do was put margarine in the holes. We did. So everything the Germans did we worked hard to countermand it. It preserved the tuna for some time.

Then we used it for the escape committee people who took it with them so they could survive. But the unique thing about it is you could see the Germans were hungry—they weren't living too well. They never took a thing out of that box. Never took a thing. And they'd see a candy bar come across, a pack of cigarettes and you could see their mouth watering, but they'd give it to you. And you had to check off on a receipt that you got it. Everything the Germans did was done, shall we say, by the numbers. And when our food from home came in occasionally, they would open that box up and search it.

You brought a few souvenirs.
Would you describe them?

This armband was from the SS, German elite, Hitler's elite guard. They were in the camp and this was on a Gestapo member. This man was dead. He was laying in the street. After Patton liberated us they just didn't give up. They had a fire fight right in the camp. And this fellow was laying dead, so I lifted him up and pulled this off his armband. There's a little bit of blood on there yet. Now this armband was what the German civilians wore, what we would call an air raid warden in the States. It says the German People's Arm of the Wehrmacht, German Army [Deutscher Volkssturm Wehrmacht]. It was a people's division like an auxiliary.

I didn't keep a diary in camp. You weren't supposed to, and although I could have I didn't. Some people did. I kept a diary before I was shot down. I kept a diary in Africa, which is illegal too, but I did it.

We had one general come in, an American general, and he made us stand inspection in Germany. We thought it was awful, but the morale went up one hundred percent. Go shave, clean up, wash your face, make your bed, and shine your shoes. The highest-ranking officers naturally represented all of us to the German officers. There were senior American officers in the camp and then each building usually had a light colonel in charge. But there wasn't any, shall we say, rank pulled on people. We lived together, we washed our clothes together, we talked together, we lived together pretty well.

And I have to say this for the Germans, the German guards were practically all enlisted men, they would salute you because they knew we were officers. And we were told, don't ever fail to return it. The Germans are a very unique people. I don't speak lovingly of them, but I have to admire them for their principles, their tenacity in the way they did things. And you would return the salute, and they would salute you. That shocked me to think you'd get saluted by a German guard. But if you tried to get away they'd shoot you.

Could you talk about the relationship that you had with the men on your airplane?

Well, there were six of us as I mentioned earlier, but the three enlisted men weren't in our camp, this was an all officers' camp. Where they went I never knew. By the way, we all made it and they're all alive today. Although, I think the pilot has died. You'd see the enlisted men when you flew, and it wasn't the caste system exactly, but you just weren't supposed to fraternize with them. You know, that was part of the military code, but we all got along fine. In the airplane there wasn't any problem at all.

Now with the ground crew, we never knew them too well. We'd bring an airplane back, shot up kind of bad, and we used to get criticized for not taking care of their airplane—it was their airplane. In the prison camp I made some real friendships. Many I keep in touch with to this minute. We exchange Christmas cards and occasionally we talk on the phone. Nobody else will believe us so we talk to each other. There was a bond established that you can't break. I have nothing against the American Legion, the VFW, and those groups, but the people I was with as a prisoner are just a little bit different. Prison camp makes you a lot closer. You don't argue because tomorrow you have to look at the same fellow. Can't go hide so we just got along. And it was amazing how well we got along.

By the way, we had the news everyday from BBC. Somebody would walk in the door, and if you're playing cards or anything you didn't look up, because the guards could see the activity in the building through the windows. The guy would walk in the door, and he'd say, "Johnny Walker time," and he'd pull a little piece of paper out of his pocket, and he'd read from the BBC. They had a radio in the camp. I never saw it, didn't know where it was, but we had a radio. And he'd read the news including even the World Series scores. And when the evacuation was made from Poland to Moosburg, the radio was taken apart and reassembled and we had a radio the first day at Moosburg. So, American ingenuity was unique.

Now, when we got new arrivals in the camp we got no news for a few days, because you didn't know who was coming in the front gate. Could have been a spy. So we wouldn't get

Herb Corson today.

news for maybe a week at a time because we got a new group of people coming in. And then after everybody was cleared it was ok. Your job as a prisoner was to go down to the gate when they brought the new ones in and see if you knew anybody—was there somebody that you could vouch for. Until we had that completely figured out we had no news.

How many prisoners were in this camp?

About eleven thousand. And when we got down to that second camp where Patton liberated us, there were one hundred and thirty thousand. See, every camp in Germany was evacuated to south Germany—to Moosburg. And I think the master plan was, Hitler was getting us all down there to use us as hostages to negotiate the final end of the war one way or another. It's a little bit northwest of Munich and Dachau was about ten miles from us. This is in Bavaria.

We were in Stalag Luft 3 'til January of '45—about a year and a half. We were moved because the Russian advance was coming from the east. They were in Breslov which was about ninety miles away. And the Germans were afraid that the Russians were going to overrun the place and recapture us. And they wanted to keep us, I repeat, as hostages. And so, the German officers came in one night, and said, "You have thirty minutes to pack. We're going to evacuate the camp." And when we marched out of camp it was twenty-two below zero, and there was German columns going one way on the road and we were going the other. We're heading north toward Berlin. And the German troops were going to the front, southeast towards Breslov. In the meantime, the Russians strafed the road and we all ran and jumped into ditches together, and the snow sputtered up when machine gun bullets went down the road. And finally they took us to trains south of Berlin, put us on these box cars, and hauled us down to Moosburg 7A.

How long a walk was this?

About seventy miles. It took us a few days. Moosburg was a nightmare. See, every camp in Germany was being dumped into this one collection area, and there were British, there were Italians, there were Indians, Russians, Americans—about a hundred-thirty thousand. Patton was in shock when he found it out. He liberated the camp.

We arrived around the first part of February '45 and were there for a couple of months. There were even some civilians in there that the Germans wanted liquidated. Conditions were terrible. Then they were trying to identify everybody which was almost futile. The Germans finally allowed the Red Cross to bring in food. Stalag Luft 3 was like the Hilton Hotel compared to

Moosburg. This new camp was tough. And the food was running out. When I was shot down in Africa I weighed one hundred and seventy pounds. When I was liberated, I weighed one hundred and nineteen. I think our eyesight was even getting bad. That's the first sign that you're gonna starve I was told later. But we made it.

Patton came through the front gate. And typical of Patton's style they tried to negotiate with the Germans, but the SS wouldn't do it so they shot their way in. And instead of opening the gate they simply drove a tank through it like a Hollywood movie. This photo shows the tank, and the third vehicle was George Patton in the jeep. The second was like a Brinks truck—an armored truck. This occurred on April 29, 1945. Patton stood up on the tank, and I've only seen the man once, but everybody in the air force loved him believe me. He stood up on the tank, he got out of his jeep and climbed up the treads of the tank, and he put his hands up like the messiah, and everybody, all these people stopped cheering, he said, "Welcome back to allied control. You've been through a lot. I don't even want to think about it. I'll have you home in thirty days. We'll have medics in here tonight. I'll have you all back home in thirty days." And I was in Dayton, Ohio, in thirty days. I couldn't believe it. I didn't think the military worked that well. Patton looked around and said, we couldn't hear all the conversation because he was talking to a couple of the colonels. "I want to congratulate you, and thank you, and I don't want you running around the countryside drinking whiskey and chasing women, because you're not capable, any of you." He was very right. "If you get in my way I will shoot you, 'cause I'm still killing these goddamn Germans." And he clicked his heels, and he said, "God bless you." He crawled up the tank and I never saw him again.

We were emotionally high. Everybody. People almost cried. Especially when they pulled the swastika down and the American flag went up. We were more boy scouts then. Very emotional. Most emotional part of my life, I think, was that moment. And then, of course, we all went out and tried to drink booze and chase women. He was right.

How do you think World War II changed your life?

Well, it definitely did. I look at the experience, especially in prison camp, and things that happened in airplanes, and think I'm such a lucky person to be here, and nothing in this world bothers me anymore. If I walk out of your home here and I've got a flat tire, I'm not gonna go crazy, because one time things were a lot worse than a flat tire. I rationalize. I guess that's the word. I leaned to rationalize. I don't have a hair trigger temper, I get angry like we all do, but suddenly I think wait, wait a minute, it isn't that bad. So, if anything ever was good from that whole experience it was that. And I learned to know people at close quarters for a couple years in prison camp. And I learned it's better to make peace and try to live with people rather than keep on with vendettas. That hurts everybody. I don't know where I would have ended up if I hadn't done that, but I just feel like I'm a lucky person to be here. So many people I know aren't here, and looking out the window of the airplane and seeing balls of fire that once were friends—it's pretty emotional. I have nothing against the military even though I don't belong to these organizations, like maybe I should. I don't want to claim to be a hero 'cause I'm not, I'm lucky.

Herb Stachler

Herbert H. Stachler and his wife Dorothy are the parents of ten children, seven boys and three girls (one girl deceased). Stachler worked in tool and die shops in the Dayton area before and after the war. In March of 1941, nine months before Pearl Harbor, Stachler was drafted into the Army. Later he transferred to the Air Corps and attained the rank of captain as a P-47 fighter pilot with 102 missions in the European Theater of Operation. After being in the service for about eight months he began training to be a pilot (primary, basic, advanced). Stachler was then assigned to be a fighter pilot in a P-47. Then with about four hundred hours of training he was assigned to the 366th Fighter Group and went overseas to England to begin his combat flying. He was discharged in August of 1945. He is a member of St. Charles Catholic Church and is also a member of the VFW.

Can you tell me about the first mission that you went on?

I remember the first one. It wasn't too much because we didn't go into France too far. I think everybody, all the pilots, including me were scared. 'Cause, you know, it was a strange new environment for us and we had to fly across the channel at the wide part, across Southampton, and parallel to Cherbourg. So we were over water for probably ninety miles, and we had never flown that much over water before. You don't know what to expect because you're going into somebody else's territory. So we didn't go in very far and I don't think we even fired our guns on that first mission. I think it was just a kind of orientation flight to get us a little bit used to what it was going to be like to fly into a combat area. We didn't see any flack at all on that mission. We just circled around in France for about twenty minutes, a half hour, and then headed on back to England again.

But this airfield that we moved to, where we flew all our missions [from], was at Thruxton, England. And it was a real nice airfield. England had many airfields and the houses were built right around the airports. So whenever you came into land, you were just skimming the top of these houses. And I always wondered how much we scared those poor people with our type of flying. But it had to be that way because you want to drop the plane in on the first part of that runway.

Maybe you could say something about your crew?

The mechanic was named Nupen, and the assistant was St. Don. So we had a mechanic and assistant mechanic full time on our aircraft. Then there was the armament man and the radioman but they would crew two airplanes. And sometimes you need more than that to get you on your way with loading your guns and everything. You might have four, five, or six guys working on the plane.

What different kinds of missions did you fly?

Well, sometimes we would escort the heavy bombers. I remember we were on missions where there was probably over a thousand bombers. But when there were over a thousand bombers there was a lot of different fighter groups that would fly escort for them. Sometimes the bombers would even talk to us and thank us for being with them. We flew off to the side at a little higher altitude—stacked at a couple different altitudes. Our job was to protect the bombers from enemy fighters. And you could see the enemy fighters maybe five or ten thousand feet above us. Seems like they were always higher than we were. I don't know how, but you could see them way up there. And they were just sitting there waiting for us to leave which we had to do at different times on a deep penetration mission. The P-47 was such a gas hog, we burned about one hundred and twenty-five gallons an hour in that thing. Well, lets see, we could fly about four hours. But with three external belly tanks, because we carried only three hundred gallons in our main tank right below the cockpit, we could fly on deeper missions. But we were never able to carry the bombers completely into Berlin. And that's where the Mustangs [P-51s] came in later on. They were very, very good, but I always felt so fortunate to be in a fighter when we were over areas where they were doing a lot of firing at you. You see those big bursts of shells all coming up and big black puffs exploding all around. And then you would see a bomber drop out of formation. It made you sick to see that. And those guys in the bombers can use very little evasive action. They may change altitude a little bit or they may change direction just a little. But the Germans could calculate with their radar about what altitude and direction they're flying and so they would just set up a barrage of anti-aircraft fire. If the bombers hadn't done any evasive action at all they'd fly right into it.

Did the bombers have a certain number of missions they had to fly before they could go home?

Yes, most of them were thirty which was a lot of missions for those guys, because their missions were all ten hours or more. For us, well it was supposed to be around seventy I guess—sixty or seventy. But after you're there you just want to keep going. There was so many things happening that they wanted to hang onto you as long as they could because they were just getting replacement pilots coming over who had much, much less experience than we did. A lot of them only had one hundred hours of fighter training time as against our four hundred. Plus the training we got as a fighter group was so good. We lost mostly replacement pilots. I don't know how the Germans could pick them out. They don't know who's a replacement pilot and who isn't, but it just seemed funny that most of our losses were those guys.

Of the seventy-five pilots who went over, I'd say at least seventy-five percent of us returned from the original fighter group. As I said, most of our losses were replacements. Maybe they lost their cool a little bit and the weather was another factor that caused some losses. Many were lost in bad weather just through accidents, diving into the ground, or getting shot down.

Were they shot down by other fighters or anti-aircraft guns?

Most of them by ground fire, but we did lose some of them to enemy aircraft—where maybe a flight of four got caught by thirty-five German planes. I was involved in air encounters only a couple of times. When we saw them, and they had initial speed on us, I just turned into them and I fired my guns. I really wasn't in range to hit any of them, but it made me feel good. Then I put my plane into a steep dive, 'cause I knew that they had the speed on us and we were outnumbered and my wingman did the same thing. We both just headed for the ground, 'cause we knew we could out dive anything in the sky. So we just headed for the ground and then started skimming the trees. Right on the deck. They could do that too, but with the weight of our xaircraft we'd out run them. That's one of the big factors I like about the

Thunderbolt—the speed going down hill. I'd say something like seventy degrees. But if you get to diving too steep, you endanger yourself [in that you might not be able to pull] out.

When you're bombing a railroad track or a bridge, at what altitude would you drop the bombs?

I would say we're probably getting rid of that thing about the time we got down below a thousand feet. Often it was too low because when that bomb explodes the concussion felt like you were hit and the whole aircraft just jolted. To drop our bombs we had a little handle. We did have electrical, but they didn't work very well. So we used all manual releases. You just pull a little handle. The left hand generally was your throttle hand, and you used your right hand for the button for your guns and your stick. You do so many things automatically after a while you don't even think of it—you just do it. We'd be flying, oh, maybe around ten thousand feet and then dive. We might be hitting four hundred and fifty to five hundred miles an hour when we released the bombs. Then we would look for targets of opportunity. When we flew into Germany or Europe, maybe a couple hundred miles or more, we would then head back. We'd fly in at high altitude and then hit the deck coming back shooting anything that's in front of us. Remember, your ground speed is greater at altitude than it is on the deck. In other words, your indicator speed might say three hundred and fifty, but when you're up at ten thousand feet you could add another two percent for every thousand feet to your air speed. So your airspeed is greater at high altitude.

What kind of targets would you strafe?

Well, we'd dive-bomb bridges, trains, and marshaling yards. And with the ammunition in our fifty caliber guns, we'd use that on any moving vehicle—trucks or trains. Now our ammunition wasn't much good for a German Tiger tank, 'cause I'd fire at those and

Herb Stachler in France, November, 1944.

you could just see your bullets bouncing off of them. A lot of us pilots went up near the front lines where they had knocked out some Tiger tanks because we wanted to see what they looked like. They were big. They were twice the size of our tanks. And they have an 80mm shell, you know, their big guns. They could fire a shell straight through our tanks. They knocked out a lot of our tanks. It generally killed the whole crew in the tank, 'cause it sucks the air out of it. We tried to bomb them but it's hard to hit a target that small. I mean, we would do it but we never had too much luck. And when you're flying at a speed like that you're over your target and you're gone and it's kind of hard to look back and check to see what damage you've done, 'cause you want to get the devil out of there. You don't want to hang around too much.

We tried to stay together because you're strong as long as you are with a group. You get by yourself and you're gonna find some Germans flying around—just looking for some stray guys. I got hit one time for not paying much attention to what's going on. We were supporting troops coming in at the beachhead area, but before I do that I'd like to tell you about our trip over on D-Day. Before we went over that night the military sent over gliders being towed by C-47s and paratroopers. They went over at night—went right over our base. During that time all of our aircraft were painted with stripes around them so our troops could identify our aircraft, 'cause we figured there was going to be more of us than enemy aircraft. Anyway, the gliders were dropped at different areas over the beachhead area, and some of the areas were missed. The poor guys—a lot of them were killed in their drop areas. They hit trees and hit buildings. When we flew that morning on our first mission, we arrived over the beachhead area before troops landed—they were still circling out in the channel [this is June 6, 1944]. All the landing craft were out circling in the water and so we dive-bombed some targets near the beachhead area. I don't know how much damage we did, it's kind of hard to tell, but in any event we could see all the gliders that had crashed and the parachutes—there were thousands of parachutes laying all over the place with different colors that designated ammunition or medical supplies. They said there was over five thousand ships on that invasion. That's all there was, thousands of ships. When we flew over that morning you looked down and you just blinked your eyes. You couldn't comprehend how many ships there were—you never dreamed there'd be anything like that. Anyway, when we headed back the landing craft were just heading toward the beach, and I thought to myself at that time, there's going to be a lot of those boys dying because the Germans were wait- ing for them. The big pillboxes they had didn't get damaged much by shells at all. They still had over twenty feet of concrete on them.

And so we went back home, and later that afternoon we flew another mission. They had the beachhead established already, but boy, it looked like chaos down there. Just ships, all type of ships coming into the shore there. The waters were very rough and the Germans had put a lot of obstacles out in the water—big railroad irons in a cross shape. And so a lot of those poor guys that were headed into the beach never got onto the beach because they couldn't reach it. Often the guy that was driving the landing craft had to order them off. So a lot of guys got down into the water over their heads and with all the gear they carried a lot of them drowned—right there.

We did some dive-bombing and strafed as we went along the beach-head, you know, above the beachhead area in Normandy. Other outfits had different areas they were hitting also. We didn't see too much enemy activity. The Germans really didn't realize this was coming off like it did. Then they started moving up stuff. But that morning we didn't see much activity. You didn't see too much stuff above the beachhead area there at Normandy. But it got active a little later when we come back on the second mission. Then we did see some trucks and stuff moving.

But the Germans were very good at camouflage, and there might have been stuff there but you didn't see it right away. They camouflage their vehicles and when they see aircraft coming they pull off the side of the road into the tree areas and you don't see them then. A helicopter could probably spot them, but with us, at our speed, we didn't. We're hitting targets farther back in. What we're trying to do is to hit bridges and things so they can't bring up supplies to the front. So we dive-bombed intersections with time or delayed action bombs—anywhere from two to twelve hour delay.

What would be the size of the bombs that you're carrying?

Well, at first we were carrying just five hundred pounders—one under each wing. And later on we started carrying thousand pounders, one under each wing. That's a lot of weight. We had water injection on these planes so you could increase your horsepower almost five hundred horsepower up to twenty-five hundred horsepower, and we'd use that for take off—to get off the ground. We did that because of all that weight. And we used up every inch of the runway. It seemed like we were just never gonna get any altitude, just skimming over the trees for a good while, before the aircraft developed enough speed to start doing a lot of climbing. Later on that was about all we carried—one thousand pounders.

Were you ever hit?

Well, I've got it marked that about six days after D-Day is when I got hit. We were supporting the ground troops and supplies coming in and

German aircraft came in on my right side on a deflection shot. I never did see him, but he got some pretty good shots at me and hit me on the side of my cockpit area, with 20mm explosive head shells. He hit me in the engine section and then later in the wing, so he must have been right behind me before my element leader yelled at me and told me there's a Jerry, saying, "Herby, there's a Jerry on your tail." At first I thought they were shooting at me from the ground and thought what the hell are they shooting at me for? We were flying about forty five hundred feet I guess. Well, after a little bit I noticed my oil pressure dropping and my hydraulic pressure dropping, and then I felt or rather I saw fluid seeping up through the floor of the plane. Since our main gas tank is down below the cockpit floor my first thought was gas. So I took my gloves off and I reached down and smelled it. No, that's hydraulic fluid. And so I told my element leader, I says, "Hell, I'll never make it back to England like this," 'cause I was getting oil all over the windshield of the cockpit area. And I said, "I spotted a landing field right above the beachhead area"—the engineers had built it. They graded off an area, and they put down what we called chicken wire. About like heavy fencing. They stake it down to the runway, and I said, "I'm just gonna circle back in and land there." So, they circled overhead 'til I got down. And I knew I'd have to come in pretty hot, 'cause I wouldn't have any brakes and my flaps wouldn't work—no hydraulic pressure. And so I landed as short as I could—probably hit at one hundred and eighty mile an hour when I touched the runway. But I got stopped before I got to the other end. There's a lot of drag on the type of runway they had down there. So I stayed there for two nights while they were patching up my airplane. But they couldn't do anything to the one engine mount that was shot through. Your engine mount is mounted on a firewall, and the tubing was shot all the way through the four tubes that are mounted there. They said they couldn't repair that and I said, "I've gotta get back." During the night the Germans would come over and all the guns on the beach would be shooting. I never did see them shoot down anybody. But we had to jump out of bed and run for the foxholes. I thought, "Hell, I'm not getting any sleep here. I got to get out of here." After two nights I said, "I'm gonna just take it easy with the aircraft, 'cause they can't fix it, and I'm gonna try to get back home to England." So I headed back to England and our base where the guys were starting to get ready to move out. They were starting to pack up—they said they were heading for that same strip I just left. So we were the first fighter group in France. But I beat them all there.

Is this some of the shell that hit your plane?

Yes, this is part of the German shell. You see how they break up when they explode? They break up into pieces and those jagged pieces are what tear

Herb Stachler today.

people up. It brushed my pants leg when it come through and exploded up past the firewall. That was the only damage I got.

I found these pieces in my cockpit. Later I had to take my plane to a sub-depot because we didn't do major overhaul—I had to have a new engine.

Finally when they got it fixed, I had to take it up and test hop it because you gotta put so many hours of slow time on them—break the engine in. And so after about six hours, when I thought I was doing pretty good, all at once the airplane quit on me. I was flying about ten thousand feet, and I thought, "Oh my god, now what am I gonna do? I don't want to lose this airplane because it's Lil' Herby." And so I thought, "Well I'm gonna ride it out a little bit." And all at once it caught hold after a few thousand feet and I circled back to the sub-depot again. And I told them what happened—that the thing went out on me. And you know what they did? They said "We'll just take that engine out and put another one in." So I was there a good ten days while they put another engine in.

At this particular base there were also the glider pilots that had come back from the invasion. They'd been in on the invasion and were brought back, and they were madder than the devil. They said they'd never want to fly in another motor less aircraft. I told a couple of them that I met, "How'd you guys like to have a ride in a P-47?" They said, "How can we ride in there, there's only one seat?" I said, "I'll get you in. I can't wear a parachute, so I'll just get you in there, and I'll sit on your lap." I had done that before when I took my crew up. You can't wear a parachute and you couldn't even use your shoulder straps either. I did it because I was the shortest guy and I could take guys up. I took some of the bigger pilot crews up, you know, their mechanic, assistant mechanic—I'd take them up for a ride.

Checking my airplane out once, here come a sergeant out to my airplane and he's from Dayton, Ohio. And I knew him. And he said, "Herby I come out here and I saw your name on the plane and I couldn't believe it." He worked in the battery shop there on the sub-depot. I was the shortest guy in the outfit, and they started calling me Little Herby. There was a comic strip years and years ago called Lil' Herby, so my mom sent me the cartoon of the comic strip to me. I give it to the guy that does the painting, and he put that on. That was my nose art on the P-47.

Well, anyway, I took old Bud McAdoo, from Dayton up for a ride then. When I come back down to the field, I said, "Did you ever do a roll?" He said he never had been in a fighter, he said this is new. I said, "OK, I'm gonna do a roll." I come down over the runway and pulled up and did a barrel roll because with a barrel roll the centrifugal force holds you onto the seat.

Would you explain the equipment you brought?

Yes, this is my helmet, what's left of it. And we got British goggles. We liked their goggles better than ours. And it's in pretty bad shape now after fifty-some years. These are the gloves I would wear when I was flying. The reason I wanted the cuffs on was because in case of fire in the cockpit, you had a little more protection with coverage. This is my A-2 jacket. And these paintings on my jacket represent missions. I had one hundred and two. There were dive-bomb missions, top cover missions, fighter strafing missions, and there were fighter sweeps where we go back into enemy territory and just look for anything. These little umbrellas here are for top cover flying protection over beachhead areas, and other areas where they needed protection. And the little airplanes here, the small ones, represent escort missions. And these are fighter sweeps represented by the small broom. I wore the jacket all the time. This is it—the A2. I wore a flying suit, but I always wore the jacket.

What's this small map?

On the inside pocket here is where we carried our escape kits which included the silk map here. We had compasses, and some other things to aid us in case we were shot down. This silk map is fifty-five years old.

Why are you in civilian clothing in this photo?

All the pilots had pictures taken with just civilian outfits on so that if we were shot down in France they would have some identification to make for us as civilians. We were stationed up near Aachen, on our last airstrip—Y-29. That's when I left the outfit. We were in on the flying associated with the Battle of the Bulge. When the Germans attacked we couldn't get out because the weather was so bad. When the Germans started their last big offensive, they must have planned it when the weather was bad because none of the aircraft could get out so they had a free run at it. But what really killed the Germans on the offensive they started there was lack of fuel. The big Tiger tanks used so much fuel they just ran out. They had hoped to capture more of our fuel, but our people destroyed a lot of our own fuel, so they wouldn't get it.

When did you complete your 102 missions and start home?

I would guess probably in January or February of 1945. Well, I think I was probably a little more scared when I decided I wanted to get a hundred missions in. Course most of the pilots all wanted to try to shoot for that after a while. And once I got my hundred, then the last two I didn't mind so much. But it was that one hundredth one that probably had me on edge.

Why was that?

Because we had one pilot who wanted to fly one more mission to get his hundredth—and he didn't make it back. And I had a friend who wanted to fly his sixty-fifth mission escorting bombers and didn't make it back. Just the way things happen. Well, when I come back I was sent to Marsh Field in California. And since I was behind a few months in flying pay I wanted to get some flying pay, so I went to operations and got co-pilot time on B-17s, B-24s, C-47s, in fact anything I could get time on. Then we were rated as to where we might go. I was supposed to go to Eglin Field, a tactical base, which is what I wanted to do because there you'd fly all type of fighters and you would try to figure out which is the best tactical fighter, and of course we were getting into jets then. But my one eye messed me up and so I was taken off of orders. When I got back on orders again, I was sent to Mission, Texas, to an instrument training school so we could be instrument instructors. But I just couldn't seem to get into it because I always felt that I can be taught, but I'm not a good teacher. But the training we got was good—you could have got an instrument card to fly even when the birds can't fly.

Then they started letting the guys out with so many points. Well, my name wasn't on the list to get out the first time they started letting them get out so I had to keep taking instruction which was good for me. And then when the next list come out, because they were not needing pilots as much anymore, I asked if I couldn't get out 'cause of the number of points I had. And you only needed eighty-some points and I think I had one hundred and eighty-some points. You got so much for all your combat time you know—missions and all that. So we were let go and we went to Indianapolis to a base there where we were discharged. I was discharged and I headed back to Dayton, but I was still in the Air Corps—unattached.

Well, after I was back only about three or four weeks, I was running around to different bars, you know, just having a good time and I just decided this is no good. I ought to settle down. I was already twenty-six years old. I was going with a couple other girls, but I just didn't feel like that was quite my speed. So a friend of mine told me about Dorothy Fackler being single.

She graduated with me seven years prior to that, but I never did go with her. So I looked up her picture in the book and realized what a beautiful girl she was. And I thought, well, I'll take a chance and call her. So I called her up and six months later we were married. We've been married now going on fifty-four years.

How do you think World War II changed your life?

Well, I think it changed my life in that I really appreciate what we have over here in America. How lucky we are that this didn't happen over here, and we didn't get a lot of our people killed and our cities destroyed. And when you look back now it makes you feel bad, because you know there was a lot of lives that were lost. So I really appreciate being from this country here—the U.S.A.

John Thompson

John A. Thompson was drafted in 1942 and shortly thereafter decided to join the paratroopers. He attained the rank of staff sergeant in the 82nd Airborne Division, and jumped into Normandy on June 5, 1944, a few minutes before midnight. Captured by the Germans, he was a prisoner of war and eventually escaped. After World War II he married and worked at Wright-Patterson Air Force Base. He is a member of the American ex-POWs and the D.A.V. (Disabled American Veterans).

Where were you born and raised?

I was born in Austin, Texas, at 2301 Willow Street. I lived in Austin, Texas, for most of my childhood, and went to Austin High School where I graduated in 1937. During that time I worked with my dad off and on. My father was a carpenter and we grew up during the Depression. I worked summertime's mostly with my father building houses. After a few years of that, I worked and earned enough money for my tuition to Texas University and I was there until just before World War II. I studied architecture and later transferred to mechanical engineering. In the meantime I had to take another job to earn some more tuition. I worked for Reed Roller Bed Company in Houston, Texas, and that's where I was when I was drafted in August of 1942.

I went first to a reception center in San Antonio—Fort Sam Houston. I was there for just a short period of time and they sent me to basic training in Camp Walters in Mineral Wells, Texas, where I took my basic training.

During the time I was in Camp Walters a group from the airborne command came in and demonstrated what it was like to be a paratrooper and I signed up for that. And it was in November of 1942 when I was transferred to Fort Benning, Georgia, to the parachute school.

What persuaded you to join the paratroops?

It was the glamour. I was very impressed with their demonstration. They had little shined up high-top boots, and the jumpsuits, and it appealed to me very much. I'd never been in an airplane before and so my first airplane ride was the one I jumped out of.

The training was very intense. The physical training, and the little gimmicks they used to teach us how to leave the airplane and jump—those were very frightening to a lot of people. And the washout rate there was quite high. Some of the guys would just freeze when it came to the mock up towers. They had two hundred foot high towers that they would pull us up on a cable. Then we would have to release ourselves from that two hundred foot high tower and we would float down in a parachute. And they had another training device they called the shock harness. They would raise you up, facing downward, and you were expected to pull a ripcord. It would drop you down about a hundred feet or so and snap you like a whip. That was to prepare us for the open shock of the parachute when we actually jumped from a plane. It was very intense training. And at the end of each day we would be very torn up and very tired. I tell you, we would sleep real well during the night.

I made my first jump after about five weeks. We were required to make five jumps from a plane in order to qualify for the parachute infantry. I took about five weeks for that, and after about six weeks I finished jump training and got my parachute wings. After that, they put me back into another course and I took more training at Fort Benning for another six weeks.

What was it like to jump out of a plane?

Actually, the first jump was about the easiest jump that I made. The training that we had taken had pretty much prepared us for what we were going to do. I really wanted to do this very badly because I felt, like so many other people, that we had a war to fight and whatever we had to do in order to win that war we were willing to do. The first jump was about fifteen hundred feet above the ground and I barely felt the opening shock when my parachute opened. That was a little higher than most of the other jumps we made later on. Our jumps were normally made from around seven or eight hundred feet off the ground.

There were a couple of jumps that I made that were quite interesting—particularly the one in North Carolina where we dropped the entire battalion of about three hundred men into a small L-shaped field. It was about five hundred yards long and two hundred yards wide and the assembly area was the intersection of the sides of the L. So we got the green light and dropped out of the door of the airplane and we were all aiming for this little intersection of the L. About one hundred feet off the ground I heard some commotion above me. I looked up and there were two other paratroopers tangled in their chutes and they landed right on top of my canopy. We all fell the extra hundred feet to the ground on one parachute. I want to tell you that it was a pretty rough landing.

Did you have any control over these chutes?

We were able to steer by climbing the risers. If you wanted to steer in the right hand direction you'd pull the riser down, we called it climbing the risers, and your chute normally would go in that direction. But it was a very limited amount of control. The parachutes they use for skydiving now are much larger and they're more controllable than the ones that we had.

We started our training in Fort Benning about November of '42, and by the end of the year we were pretty well finished. Then there was some additional training, specialized training, that they gave me after I completed my basic paratrooper training. We were really in great shape when we got ready to do the Normandy invasion. An example of that was that we did a five-mile run before breakfast in the morning.

I was assigned to the 508th Parachute Infantry Regiment after my training at Fort Benning and we moved to North Carolina—to Camp McCall. We took our unit training there which lasted from that time until the time we invaded Normandy.

Then in December of 1943 we went to New York and we were shipped over to a little town in Northern Ireland—way up on the northern tip. There was two little towns there, one was Port Rush, and the other was Port Stewart, and we had a camp in between those two little towns. This was now February of '44. We stayed there for about three months and then we were shipped to England where we did some more unit training.

This training was in an area around Nottingham and our camp was immediately adjacent to Sherwood Forest. You remember the story of Robin Hood and his merry men don't you? We were not quite so merry as Robin Hood, but that's the location. And we did a number of parachute jumps from that base. Actually, a lot of those jumps were night jumps because the jump we were going to make into Normandy was to be just before midnight on D-Day, and so we were practicing hitting a target and doing it all at night.

When we went into Normandy, though, we were not able to stay together because the unit that was supposed to drop down and set up the radar were unable to find their target. And so we just had to kind of wing it you might say.

What happened to you and to your unit just before D-Day?

I think it was in May of 1944 that they moved us away from the camp near Nottingham. We were moved to a staging area. It was interesting when they moved us out of town. They asked us to not do anything unusual—don't show any emotion, don't wave to the people as we go by, because they didn't want the people to know what

John Thompson.

was coming up. And it felt a little bit silly to ride on those buses when everybody in the town was out waving and telling us goodbye. I think they knew more than we did, where we were going and how we were going to get there. But we went to the staging area where we stayed for several days.

It was about June 4th when they had planned originally to send us out to the airstrip, but the weather got pretty bad and they postponed it for another twenty-four hours. So it was actually June the 5th when we went to the airstrip and assembled and got on the airplane. I had a lot of equipment. I was in communications and I carried a radio, probably a dozen hand grenades, and five or six hundred rounds of ammunition for the carbine. And I had a land mine in my backpack. And I weighed about, oh, three hundred and twenty-five pounds including all of that equipment. Actually, the night we were waiting to board the airplane, we were all just stretched out on the ground and we had to have a little help getting up because of the weight of our equipment and everything. We would not have been able to get up by ourselves. Fortunately, there were some people that helped us up off the ground so we boarded the airplane.

There was about twenty, eighteen to twenty, paratroopers for each jump. Now that doesn't sound like very many, because I think the airplanes they have now are much larger and they carry a lot more men. But there were about eighteen to twenty paratroopers on the airplane that we flew.

It was very quiet on the plane as we left the airstrip. Then there was a period of assembly for the airplanes—they had to rendezvous out over the English Channel. This was a very quiet ride. There was not much conversation that night because we were pretty serious about what was happening. I think we were all apprehensive. I know I was apprehensive. Some of the comments that they made demonstrated that.

But we went ahead with the ninety-minute ride, and as we turned in toward the Normandy coast I have never seen such fireworks in all my life. As we approached the coast of Normandy, the 101st Airborne Division preceded us into Normandy. By the time we got there they had everything going pretty well, and as we crossed the coast of Normandy, if you could forget for a few moments what the Germans were trying to do to you, you have never seen such fireworks in any 4th of July celebration. It looked like solid tracer bullets coming up at us. I was a little concerned about those tracers catching the parachute on fire, but fortunately it didn't.

Our jump was only about a six hundred foot drop and we were on the ground pretty quickly. It was near the little town of St. Lô, and there was a town Sainte-Mère-Eglise that was rather close—it was right in here at Carentan, which was right north of St-Lô—we were to assemble in Sainte-Mère-Eglise. But as it turned out I was off the map—I landed about fifteen miles away from Sainte-Mère-Eglise. That happened because there was a lot of confusion because of the lack of radar on the ground. There was a lot of confusion and the Air Force, or the Air Corps at that time, were doing the best job they could without any radar on the ground. They were just kind of flying by the seat of their pants there. They had the compasses and all that, but it was not very accurate. And for that reason there were a lot of us scattered all over the peninsula there. After we left the airplane the ground fire was still being aimed toward the aircraft. Actually, I was out of the ground fire just a short time after I left the airplane, and it was all rather quiet. It just took a few seconds for us to be on the ground because it was such a short, low drop. We were supposed to have assembled and have our units together in order to link up with the ground troops that were coming in on the beachhead. As it turned out some of the guys did get together. They did much better than I did.

Our battalion commander was Lt. Col. Mendez, and I heard later on that he jumped from a height of about twenty-one hundred feet and got lost for several days before he got back to the unit. He was quite an interesting man. He was a West Point graduate. He was a full-blooded Indian and he really did a good job of directing that battalion after he finally got back. He was an interesting person.

What happened to you after you landed?

It was dark. I didn't know where I was. I tried to listen to hear some of the other guys from my unit. But it got so quiet that I didn't hear anything much. It was really dark. And so I used my compass to try to head toward the north. We were supposed to assemble and try to link up with some of the ground troops the next day, but I didn't get very far. The next morning I found this elderly Frenchman and I thought he might be able to tell me where I was, but he was frightened and ran away. I wasn't able to ask him anything. So I just kind of stayed in that area until daylight and then I started going in the direction I was supposed to go.

And it was about noon that day, June 6th, when I finally found some of the other paratroopers. And those were the first American GIs that I had seen, and so we got together. We got together because they heard the firing of my carbine. I found a target over across the field—a German soldier. I emptied about half my clip into him and these guys heard my firing, and they came running to see what was going on. But it was all over with by then. So we stayed together until about four o'clock that afternoon. By four o'clock that afternoon we had about twenty people gathered together and there was a second lieutenant who had kind of taken command of our group there.

We were all pretty weary and we wanted to stop and rest by the side of the road there. This turned out to be a bad mistake because the wooded area right next to that road gave the Germans a lot of cover. There was a German flanking unit for an artillery battalion that was located in that woods. All of a sudden they opened up with all of their automatic weapons and we were just completely devastated. I tried to leave the group and go out across an open field to where I could get away from the woods. There were two of us, another sergeant and I, and we got about halfway across the field, but the machine gun fire was just horrible. So I asked him, "Do you think we ought to stop here and give up," and he agreed.

So I took my helmet off and laid it on the ground. We were out in a completely open field. And the Germans had already gotten about half of our group there—they were casualties. Some of them were wounded and some of them were killed. And we really didn't have any chance of getting away from them. At that point I was doing a lot of praying. I thought the end was here, and I didn't think I would be able to survive. But somehow I managed to survive without getting wounded.

And so they took us prisoner. There were several soldiers in their unit and one of them was a young German who looked like he was about sixteen years old. His rifle was taller than he was. And the only thing he would say was, "Hands up, hands up." And so they disarmed us and took us back to an assembly area near an old barn, and that's where we stayed the night. I still

John Thompson today.

had my landmine, which I took out of my backpack, and laid on the ground there and they didn't even notice it.

The next morning a chicken came along and started pecking at that landmine. I decided to clear out and wait because I was afraid that chicken would set off the landmine. But from there on we were just hauled around in two-wheel carts or trucks or whatever they could find. We never really got to a regular POW camp until about September. It was just wandering around because they couldn't find a place. Eventually there were probably about, oh, two hundred prisoners. It was quite a group of them. And they just kept taking us from one spot to another until finally in September they got us into Stalag 4B, which was near Muhlberg on the Elbe River. And that was my first POW camp.

In the meantime my parents didn't know where I was—I was just missing in action from June until September. But there was a navigator from a B-24 who came from my hometown of Austin. When he heard a broadcast by Axis Sally that there was a John Thompson who had been captured he wrote that home to his family. He wrote home to his parents and they looked up my family and told them that he had heard this broadcast. So that was the first indication that my family had that I was still alive.

What happened after you got to this POW camp?

It was an old British camp—pretty well established. Most of the guys there were captured in North Africa, Italy, and Sicily. Most of them were British and they were pretty well adjusted to the life of a POW. But somehow I was never able to adjust. I wanted desperately to get away and escape— get back to allied lines. That's what I was there for. There was one of the POW guys that was a private, and he was scared to go out to the farm on a work detail. His name was Elmer Bartel, and so I arranged to trade places with Elmer. I was going to go out on the farm and try to escape from there. As we were getting ready to load up on the trucks, there was a German officer checking each one of us out. When I started through the line he held up his hand and said, "Halt, you are not Bartel. Stand over there." And from that point on my home was in this little solitary confinement place about the size of a broom closet. That's where I stayed for the next few months. I was there from September until December. The American Red Cross came in and made an inspection, actually it was the International Red Cross. Anyway, they made an inspection of the camp and they talked to the commandant and said, "You have to do something with this man; either try him or send him back into a unit." So the commandant called me in and he was a very friendly person. First thing he asked me was, he knew that I was from Texas, "Habla usted el español?" And I said, "Poquito, no mas." And so he had a document he wanted me to sign and he pulled it out and showed it to me. It was written in German. I said, "I can't sign this, I don't know what it says." So he smiled and pulled out another document that was written in English. I read it, and it told about all the bad things that I had done that caused him to put me in isolation. And actually, after I looked at it, I was kind of proud of it—so I signed it.

Then a short time later they transferred me to Stalag 3A, up on the Oder River near the town of Frankfurt. Now this was wintertime, and the Polish border is really cold at that time of year. So we stayed there until about March of 1945. On the eastern front the Russians were coming closer and closer. And when the Russians began to move into that area, the Germans wanted to move us back away from the Russian front so they started putting us on boxcars and carts and moving us back toward Berlin. And it was about early in April when they marched us into a little town near Stendahl on the Elbe River, actually it was a little east from the Elbe River. And we were supposed to stay in an old beer garden for the night because we'd been going for quite a while.

Well, we went back about halfway in that building and we could hardly believe our eyes when we saw a big hole in the wall—probably put there by an artillery shell. So we had a quick meeting among some of the guys in the group, and ten of us decided we were going to go through that hole. There was no guard on the outside of it. So we just crawled through the hole and started back to the Elbe River. We were heading west towards the Elbe River. We knew the allies had pulled up to the Elbe River and that there was some kind of political arrangement where the Russians were supposed to take charge of the area up to the Elbe River. So we knew that our guys were there.

We had a little underground radio and we were able to keep up with the BBC announcements on the radio. But it took us several days to get back to the Elbe River from there. There were just ten of us.

We were stopped one night by a German sergeant. He wanted to know who we were and what we were doing. I think at that point they had us pretty well dead to rights, but they just put us into an old air raid shelter and since there was only one of the German soldiers that was guarding us, and there was ten of us, we managed to take charge and then continued on our way towards the Elbe River.

We got into a group of evacuees—hundreds of people that were walking together, moving away from the eastern front. And we walked with the group for a little while until we saw a Russian spotter plane that was flying over. Well we knew what was about to happen so we left the group. We were only about fifteen minutes away when the Russian artillery began to shell that whole group of people. We could see the smoke, columns of smoke, but we kept on towards the Elbe River.

And it was on April the 25th that we finally reached the Elbe River and saw the U.S. flag on the other side. It was an American unit. So we yelled across the river for somebody to come and get us. And later on we found out that some of the guys were getting ready to open up on us because they didn't think we were who we said we were. But their colonel was looking at us through the field glasses and he said, "I believe those guys are legitimate." So he brought a motor launch over, picked us up, and said, "Welcome home fellows." That was one of the most emotional times I ever had in my life. It's hard to explain the feeling that you had at a time like that.

But they took us back, airlifted us back to a ship in the channel, and transferred us over to an ocean liner. It took us several days to get back to Boston, Massachusetts. And that's where I called my mother and told her everything was all right. This was probably on about the 30th of April of 1945. I think it was early in May when the actual war was finished.

Then what happened to you?

Well, I took a train back home. They gave me a sixty-day leave to recuperate from the ordeal I'd been through and I went back to Austin where we had a big reunion. It all worked out pretty well. Later I was reassigned to another infantry unit which was a little surprising because I was a paratrooper. I'd been trained to do that and so I asked for a transfer back to the paratrooper unit. So they assigned me to the airborne command at Fort Benning, Georgia, and that's when I went back on active duty. And then they interviewed me to see whether I was eligible for a discharge. I didn't have quite enough points for a discharge. But I asked the company clerk if they could arrange to give me another battle star because the trip out of Germany was a little bit tougher than the one going into Germany. Ultimately, they agreed with me and I had enough points for a discharge. So it was in October of 1945 that I was discharged.

Would you comment on the effect that World War II had on your life?

It made me glad to be alive. I've never stopped thanking the Lord for bringing me through all this. Some of the things that happened during the time I was a captive were pretty horrible. At one point before we got to the first camp, some of our own P-47s came over and strafed the column and tore us up pretty badly. It was a rather horrifying thing. All during that time, from D-Day until September, we were bombed and strafed by our own aircraft, 'cause they didn't know who we were or what we were doing. It was several days after we had been captured. They put us on trucks and were hauling us back away from the front when two P-47s came over and started to attack the column. And if you've ever had somebody fire eight 50-caliber machine-guns at you at the same time—[each plane had eight 50-caliber machine guns] that was a pretty horrible experience.

But after everything was over and I got back to civilian life again, there was some adjustments I had to make. It was more difficult going from military life to civilian life than it was going from civilian life to military life. They didn't have a lot of orientation or counseling at that time. It took me about five years to really recover from the experiences that I'd had. But I've also been grateful, and I think it was a positive thing, 'cause it makes me appreciate more the things that we have in life now.

Karl Pauzar

Karl Pauzer is 77, a forty-five year resident of the Centerville-Washington Township area. He is Catholic, graduated from Chaminade High School, and was drafted into the United States Army during World War II. He had three and one-half years of active service (two years domestic and one and one-half years of foreign service). He is married to Jean and worked before and after the war at Frigidaire in Dayton, Ohio. During World War II he attained the rank of staff sergeant and is an active member of the VFW in Centerville.

My family has lived in Dayton for the past three generations. When the war started I was working at Frigidaire Division of the General Motors Corporation in their machine gun plant. I was working at what they call the barrel shop where they make thirty caliber machine gun barrels.

When I was drafted I went to Fort Sheridan, Illinois, outside of Chicago. It was in the wintertime, right on the shore, and it was very cold. You'd wring out your washcloths and the next morning you could hammer them on the table like a piece of wood, they were just frozen. Very little in the way of blankets. We used our overcoats in addition to our blankets. We stood outside in the cold, rain, snow, whatever, outside the mess hall waiting to eat and the old coal stove, coal-fired stoves, would pour soot down on our heads.

In my basic training I learned to march, learned how to shoot an M-1 rifle, and things like that. But the weather we didn't like. We never saw the ground. It was snow and ice and we were out there trying to do close order drill. And the cadre, I think, took delight in giving us quick movements, trying to make us slip or something like that. It was not an enjoyable experience at all. Of course the other soldiers were down south in the heat and the snakes and all that, but we were at Fort Sheridan.

What happened to you after basic was over?

Well, I was called before a board. I didn't know what to expect, but they asked me if I'd heard about [the] Army Specialized Training Program (ASTP) which I had. This was a program they were setting up to produce officers from draftees who did well on the tests. They were to be future engineers and foreign language experts—possibly even to help govern Germany after the war in various phases of government. They said, "Do you want to go to ASTP or do you want to go to OCS?" I had a score high enough to qualify me for either and without hesitation I said, "I want to go to ASTP." You know, I figured I could learn something there that would help me later on in life. So, at that point I was sent to [the] University of Illinois to study engineering. I spoke German, I wanted German, but of course the army always tries to put a square peg in a round hole. So I ended up in engineering at Ripon College which is outside of Green Bay. It's well known in engineering circles and is an old, well-respected engineering school. As I say, then they transferred me to Ripon, Wisconsin, for whatever reason.

But then, due to our infantry losses, due to our losses on the ground, I guess, they decided to wash out the whole ASTP program. So all of us were washed out and I was sent down to Texas and put in an anti-aircraft outfit down there. But then with our air force having superiority over the Germans they no longer needed anti-aircraft, so there I was again—stuck. Finally I was sent to Mississippi for infantry training. I was supposed to get six weeks' infantry training, with the 36th Division—the Texas National Guard. There used to be four regiments in a division but then they cut them down to three. I happened to be in the regiment they left behind—the 144th Texas Regiment. We trained in Mississippi for six weeks. After my six weeks they retained me on cadre duty for a while.

Then the company commander told me he was going to have to put me on a levy (shipping order) pretty soon. The next six or so levies had all gone to the Pacific because they thought they had enough troops in Europe, or in the pipeline, so I said, "Put me on the next one for Europe." So I got on the levy to go to Europe and I was sent to a port of embarkation. There they had some artillery pieces that needed servicing, and due to my experience at Fort

Sheridan on 90mm anti-aircraft guns, I was kept there for a month or so to clean and oil the guns. This was in the early fall of 1944.

At that time, many of the eighteen year olds were going into the service, going straight overseas. Six months after they went into the service, many were killed and they'd never even been home. So at that point, just before that actually, the War Department said you will get a delay in route or furlough or leave prior to going overseas. So I was home at the time of the invasion of Europe on June 6, 1944. Then I left home and went up to the point of embarkation. I was kept there for a month or so, I don't know exactly how long, to clean these artillery pieces and oil them and all. Then I was put in charge of a platoon of younger soldiers because by this time I was a corporal. Then we went overseas.

Just as fast as I'm telling you, when we pulled into England we unloaded onto a train, the train started up, and we went through London. At the time, the buzz bombs, as we called them, the B2 rockets, were being shelled down on London. And those rockets weren't accurate but would hit London just indiscriminately. I remember being on the train and we had to keep all the blinds down because of flying glass.

Well, we escaped that and just as soon as we got to the other end of England we unloaded. There was a ship waiting and we went across the channel to Le Havre, France, in the fall of '44. We didn't go towards Paris. We dropped down somewhere in the area right south of Le Havre. I can't recall the name of the town, and we went to what they called a "repo-depo," or a replacement depot. And then we were sent out—put out in a field. I don't know how many there were of us—we were four deep in ranks and I don't know how long we were there. They just counted down halfway and they said this half goes to the 36th Infantry Division and this half goes to the 14th Armored Division. And of course there were people over here in the infantry that were tank drivers, there were infantry people over here they put in a tank division. That's so much for your classification and training.

Karl Pauzar.

What unit were you assigned to and where was your first big battle?

I was put in an armored division, in the armored infantry portion. An armored division is a third artillery, a third infantry and a third tank. We walked tanks into battle because they're almost blind. They can actually see very little, and we had to look out for them because the Germans would have dead soldiers laying there along with some live ones, acting like they were dead, and at the last minute they would get up and point a bazooka at our tanks point blank and shoot. And then when they got to moving too fast we would jump up on the back of the tanks and hold on while we were going across fields.

Our first big battle was in the Alsace-Lorraine area—near a city called Strasbourg. There were two small towns that were in the path of the Germans who were trying to sweep down through there and go up and secure Antwerp for supplies—oil and so on—and it was a very critical area for them. And we were sent in there to try and stem the tide. And our division was up against three or four divisions of Germans, several of them SS divisions. The weather was brutal. It was cold with lots of snow on the ground. They had one of the worse winters for years over there. This was now December of '44.

Anyway, we were sent there and we were told to take this town up on the hill. And leading to the town was a broad open plain with a creek through it. And our company commander, later on, told me he and a sergeant, with no artillery fire, were supposedly gonna sneak up on them. So here we are in olive drab uniforms with snow on the ground. Anyhow, our sergeant along with the company commander went around to the left flank and observed the Germans on the other side of the hill with artillery concentrated and ready to fire on us. So he went back and told the battalion commander.

The battalion commander sent the executive officer down, but he wasn't able to verify this because the Germans spotted them and drove them off. But any event, we were ordered to do this. My company commander knew it was suicide. He sent all the officers to the back of the platoon and he was out in front. Well, they waited until we got down to the bottom, where this open creek was, and then they opened fire. Well, we lost all our officers that day except one, and he wasn't with us, he was back at division training getting supplies. We probably lost a third of our company at that time. And our company commander was wounded and captured. He lay out there and we laid our artillery down on them while they took cover, and my company commander escaped momentarily, but the Germans recaptured him. Same thing happened again. He was wounded again, and this time they took him back to a triage area where a young German nurse, young and inexperienced, not hardened to the realities of war yet, did what she could for him. To the

German doctors he was just an American, he was an enemy, and they were not going to waste time and all taking care of him. They were going to take care of their own and they shoved him off to the side to die.

But this young German nurse, eighteen years old or so, wasn't hardened, like I say, to the realities of war and did what she could for him and enlisted the aid of more qualified people and saved his life. I didn't know any of this 'til after the war. That's all I knew for the next thirty years—that's the last I knew of him. But in any event she nursed him back to health, evidently, but that was the most dramatic event in my life, I think, over there.

Of course I experienced other things. I was strafed. We were strafed one time by the British because they were gonna strafe the Germans, but we had moved in our position and we weren't where we were supposed to be when we called in the strike—we had not put out the correct flag. There are different colored flags, and every day you put out a yellow or green or red panel to identify that you're Americans so the air force won't strafe you. Well, we didn't do that so we were down at the intersection and these planes came down strafing, but we were in the building so none of us suffered any casualties at that point. That was called friendly fire, happens all the time, and you get friendly fire from shelling too.

I was on an observation point one night, volunteered, and went out on patrol in between the lines. It was the only high ground in the area. Anyway, we were up on top and our artillery would fire, and you felt like it was coming right down at you because you're up high, and it would just barely clear the hill in order to drop down on the Germans.

After that we were pulled back into France to be refurbished. We had to get new troops and new equipment, and so on, because we were ineffective as a combat force anymore. Like I said, we lost all the officers but one who was back in the rear area. So they brought the battalion motor officer up to take over the company. He was a captain, and he called us in and asked us what happened, and tried to piece everything together. So at that point we brought in more troops, gave them some training, were refitted, and we were there in Saessol-sheim, France, for about three weeks, I guess, before we went forward again.

Here's some shrapnel from an artillery shell. It's designed and manufactured in such a way that the shells break up in those very irregularly sharp fragments. Traveling very fast and tumbling, it can cut into you and just take an arm or a leg or whatever off—that size of shrapnel.

After a battle we searched all the prisoners, live or dead, for any information that we could use—any maps, any details, any orders, any instructions, anything like that. And this medal was in one of the Germans' pockets, so evidently he'd been on the Russian front. This was a dead German soldier, and that was of no importance to our military, but all the intelligence and maps and all was sent back to our intelligence section, and so on and so forth.

Would you explain these two pictures you brought?

That is what's left of a building outside of a German ammunitions dump outside of Augsburg, Germany. Its evidently suffered a direct hit from a bomb and that's all that was left of it. Nothing but rubble. This is a picture of the former quarters of the German guards that were guarding what we used to call the DP camp, a slave labor camp. It was a synthetic oil factory in Germany. That's where the workers were housed—in this building that we were bunked up in. It was better than the ground. That's where we stayed several months while we were guarding that DP camp. That was in the Munich-Augsburg area of Germany.

We never knew where we were going, why we were going, or whether we were going forwards or backwards. If they told me to go home at any one time, I don't think I'd know which direction to start.

But anyhow, we were told that there was a slave labor camp up there—a concentration camp. So by then our tanks and all were a little ahead of us. And they came to the camp and the German guards there didn't have anything but rifles. Well they weren't fools, they took off. So when we got there the concentration camp people were free to wander around and so on. We had strict orders not to throw them any food. Some of our medical people were kept there for six weeks to administer to some of those people. In fact, one of these guys still lives in the Dayton area. He still gets counseling about once a month, psychological counseling, out at the VA, and still can't even talk about it—it breaks him up. These inmates were walking skeletons. I can still see them. Once I was driving a vehicle down the side of the concentration camp at Ampfing, and this man was coming towards the fence probably no more than twenty feet away from me—tall, very gaunt, showing no emotions. The only thing that was moving was his feet in a very slow shuffle. He never showed any signs of recognition or nothing. And he was wearing the typical concentration camp garb—striped clothing.

We had another interesting experience at Moosburg. That was the camp where all allied airmen were kept—no matter what rank they were or from what country. There were privates and there were generals, around one hundred thousand. And we liberated Moosburg, and there were many prisoners in there from Russia, from all over.

After the war I went back on assignment and was able to take pictures and contacted some of the people, and I'm still in contact with some of them today. Even one fellow who is a civilian went back and lived in Moosburg, unbelievable or not. There are officers around here from the Air Force Museum and Colorado Springs that have contacted me for pictures. One fellow, he's a dentist, a retired dentist in Indiana, said that with that picture he could identify each building and what it was used for. It was a huge camp. We were sent back there to reinforce it. We had people in it of undetermined identities. They had different I.D.'s, two or three different ones, and they spoke different languages. Some of them were war criminals, some of them were in the black market. We didn't know what they were—but our job was to detain them until the CIC and CID could interrogate them and find out just who they were and if they were wanted, and so on.

Was your fluency in the German language helpful?

Yes. My last two years at Chaminade High School I took German and it wasn't but a short time later that I was over in Europe. I questioned some prisoners during the war briefly. But after the war in Europe ended I was assigned to an engineer outfit with Colonel Westmoreland who later was a general in the 60th Infantry Regiment, 9th Infantry Division. I was working with the engineers, and we had all the material we needed, but we were anxious for the buildings to be rebuilt for the Germans, but more importantly for the American dependents coming over.

So I had to deal with German contractors. We had the bricks and all. We would take German prisoners out to these bombed out buildings and they'd just sit there and chip mortar off of them and stack them. We tried to salvage any of the roofing, any of the plumbing, anything we could salvage. So I had some dealings with them. And then I went with a German girl who spoke no English at all, so that was kind of handy.

I had a very interesting experience. Another fellow and I were dating two German girls and I never let on I knew German. Anyway, we were sitting around a table one night somewhere, I don't know where we were at, but I know there was nothing much to buy. And the German girls, every once in while, would stop talking to us and start talking to themselves—laughing and giggling back and forth, you know. So after about the fourth date, or something like that, one of them asked the other one a question and before she could answer I answered her in German. They were quite shocked trying to remember what they had discussed before.

Later, I signed up and stayed over there in the army of occupation till the middle of 1946. Then I went home. I took a week or so off and tried to put my life back on track, and finally went back to work. I went back to Frigidaire.

How did World War II change your life?

Oh, the Army certainly changed me. It makes you do things that you wouldn't have the opportunity or the confidence to try. It certainly builds your self-confidence up. You're forced into it. It's just like medical advances—they do things during the war they wouldn't dare to attempt to do in civilian life, but they have no other choice: the person is gonna die. But they did tremendous things, and that's the way I feel. I was forced into jobs.

I was put in a spot as a first sergeant. And never in my wildest dreams when I went in the army would I ever think I'd be a first sergeant. I was a platoon sergeant and the first sergeant was leaving and I was called in and they told me I was going to be the first sergeant and I said, "I don't know about that," and he said, "No, you learn it the way I did." I think his last name was Harley or something like that. But they dump you in it and as confidence grows you attempt more things too. You don't have anything to lose. But I thoroughly enjoyed that portion of it. I even got a direct commission as a 2nd lieutenant too—but that was after the war.

That's what most of our young people today need—the discipline that they don't get in civilian life. You get an opportunity to lead and you learn early on that you're responsible for your own actions. No mom and dad—nobody's there to bail you out. What you get yourself into, you're gonna have to get yourself out of, and pay the price. And you learn that early on. Some of them learn right away, some of them take a while, and some of them never learn.

We have a division reunion every year in various parts of the country. It's going to be in Virginia Beach this year—this September, but we've had it in Columbus, Ohio, and we've had it in Louisville, Kentucky. About ten years ago I walked into a hospitality room up in Columbus and there was a fellow sitting there and he looked kind of familiar, and he said, "Hi, you remember me?" And he told me his name and slowly, slowly it started to come back, he was in the same squad I was in. And he said, "I've always wanted to ask you something." "What," I said? "Why did you volunteer for that night patrol?" Remember me telling you on top of that hill? I said, "I don't know. Suicidal, I guess." He laughed. I said, "How did you remember that." There were three of us, I know that. I don't know who the other two were, and if you told me you was one of them I would have believed you." But, yeah, I'm in touch with him. He's out in Omaha, Nebraska, that's where the reunion was last year.

There's a few people you know, but in combat you're spread out so far that people come in at night, they get killed during the night, and you never even saw them. And somebody will tell you, "Yes, so & so, and so & so, got killed, and so & so got wounded." "Well, who are they? Never even heard of them." The only time you're together is the first day and the last day. On the last day, you got a few people that you know, but the rest of them are strangers.

Why did you fight—for cause or comrade?

You end up fighting for your comrades, that's what you've got to do, that's what they stress when you went in the army. Trust. Trust. First day there the sergeant's out in front of us and he says, "If you catch anybody stealing from you, do what it takes to bring him to me; if he isn't able to walk, drag him to me." You fight for your comrades.

Paul Schreiber

Paul Schreiber and his wife, Aleen, live in Centerville, Ohio. Schreiber graduated from Miamisburg High School and was drafted into the Army in April of 1943. He served two and one-half years in an armored artillery unit with about one year overseas in combat in France and Germany. After the war Schreiber went to the University of Dayton under the GI Bill of Rights, took an M.S. degree in electronics from Ohio State and did further graduate study at the University of Cincinnati. He taught for a short time at Centerville High School, the Air Force Institute of Technology and Sinclair College. But his primary career was at the aerospace research laboratories at WPAFB working in the area of plasma physics. Schreiber is a member of the VFW, American Legion and Emanuel Catholic Church.

When did you actually go in the Army?

We left by train from the station in Miamisburg in April of 1943. There were quite a few fellows going at the same time. They took us to Columbus—to Fort Hayes. And there we were issued our clothes. Then we took a train to Camp Phillips, Kansas, and there we found out we were going to be in truck drawn artillery. In a battalion you have three firing batteries—A, B, C, and you have a headquarters battery and a service battery. Of course we also learned how to fire our guns, rifles, bazookas, throw hand grenades, and fire machine guns.

And then we went to Fort Riley, Kansas, for our tests. That was a very miserable night that we spent there. It was twenty below zero. We were out all day and all night. And I actually saw people crying while they were trying to do their job. These were firing tests. So we passed all our tests there and then went on to maneuvers in Tennessee. When we finished maneuvers satisfactorily we went to a camp near the Kentucky-Tennessee border. There we were changed into an armored field artillery battalion. The only basic change was we now had six 105 mm self-propelled guns per battery. Now the M-7 is a self-propelled howitzer. There is also a fifty-caliber machine gun on the tracks.

What's the difference between a tank battalion and armored artillery?

In an armored division you have tanks, which may be out in front, but you also support those tanks with armored artillery. So if you break through the enemy's line the tanks would be out in front. There might also be some infantrymen in halftracks or in armored artillery and other supporting units. And you can travel very fast. This would be part of an armored division. I frequently rode in a type of vehicle that's called a halftrack. And I was the radio operator for the battery commander.

We left from New York Harbor to go to England and we landed at Liverpool. This would be either June or July of 1944. It was probably about a six or seven day trip I'd say. We even had a small aircraft carrier with us. It was a large convoy. We didn't have anything happen on that particular crossing. Then we went by train to Wolverhampton, and from there by truck convoy to a tent camp where we were issued our equipment.

After we had our equipment we went to Wales to calibrate the guns, came back and went to Weymouth on the English Channel. Then we crossed the channel on a landing ship tank [LST] and landed near Utah Beach. It took two ships for our battalion. We also had a big barrage balloon attached to each ship, I guess for protection against dive-bombers. This was around August 15 of 1944 that we landed on the beach in France. They pulled in at high tide and we waited 'til the tide went out and then we just went right off the ship onto the beach. I think they used a bulldozer to push extra dirt and stuff out, but we rolled right off the ship onto the beach.

How many batteries in your unit?

Three firing batteries, a headquarters battery, and a supply group. I was in Battery C, a firing battery. The first night on the beach was kind of interesting. We went into a bivouac area and all during the day I kept hearing guns going off. This turned out to be simply the nervousness of all these guys on the beach. It was mostly small arms fire. Much of it was accidental discharge. Officers carried pistols and the rest of us carried a carbine. That's what I carried. We did have a few bazookas also.

You could see some affects of the landing on the beach, and so forth. There were quite a few ships still out in the water and they were using ducks constantly to bring in supplies. There was still a lot of confusion. Ducks are simply floating trucks. Then we found out we were going to be assigned to the 3rd Army, 7th Armored Division. They had already broken through all those hedgerows and it took us a long time just to get caught up to where the fighting was. We finally did that. The Germans were retreating, so we went south of Paris and at Fontainebleau we fired our first round. This would be in late August of '44. That's where we caught up with the Germans and fired our first rounds.

How did you feel when you first came under fire?

Well, I guess it's like everything else, you're scared. But you kind of get used to it after a while. I can give you an example. This happened later on. They sent a fellow up as a replacement. Every time he heard a shell go off, no matter how far away, he would hit the dirt. He was a nervous wreck and I felt really quite sorry for him. And they decided at that time they needed more people in the infantry. And they had to pick some people from our battery to go to the infantry so they sent him. I often wonder how long he lasted.

He just didn't understand that if you're careful you'll probably be ok. Not absolutely, but you don't have to worry about fire that's going miles

away. In fact, when an 88mm comes in it comes in screaming and you only have a short time to hit the dirt or your foxhole. But, you know it's coming in close to you. It's really a screaming sound coming in. You might be familiar with mortars. But an 88mm, it's *bang*, it's just like that. You only have a few seconds I would say.

We began to inflict damage on the enemy. And things were really in a tremendous state of flux. When we came to roadblocks, sometimes we'd just go around the roadblock. The Germans would often set up a roadblock but we'd just go around it. And then sometimes the free French would come in and take care of what remained there.

What were you really doing during these battles?

I was on the radio listening for directions from battalions and reporting what

Paul Schreiber.

the battalions were saying to the battery commander. Of course, he may not be around and I'd have to write it down. We had two way communicating radios. We did have three tanks—actual tanks. They would mix in with the other tanks and act as forward observers and radio back fire direction. Then they'd make corrections—bring it down to where they would get close to the target. And we had other forward observers also. In fact, we had two cub airplanes that would act as forward observers.

As we went through towns that were just liberated it was kind of interesting because the women, and what men there may be around, would come out, shake your hand, give you wine, and the women would give you flowers and kisses sometimes. They were really happy to get rid of the Germans. As we went on the Germans were in tremendous disarray.

We were up around Rheims one night and there was no moon, stars—no lights at all. I don't know if you've ever been in that situation, it's almost as bad as being in a room with no lights at night, you just can't see anything. And we were moving on the road and we had little slits for lights to determine where the other vehicles were. I had a flashlight which I had painted over the glass so it only showed a very small amount of light. And we were stuck on a road—we were having a terrible time moving. It was right at a crossroads and I heard a rumble, rumble, rumble coming down our way. So I told the halftrack driver to back up. So he backed up. I got my flashlight out and waved several trucks through the crossroads. I found out later on that I had waved through several German trucks. You just can't imagine how dark it can be—like I say, it was great confusion.

Then we went down near Verdun, which is a famous World War I battle site, and later we got the Verdun Medal—our outfit did. And somewhere we crossed the Moselle River. They had pontoon bridges across the river, and as we crossed we were under tremendous artillery fire. I was sitting on one side of the halftrack and this other fellow was across from me and I heard this big bang. And I looked down in my lap and I had this huge piece of shrapnel in my lap. And what had happened, the shrapnel came down over the halftrack and hit him on the helmet, put a dent in his helmet, and it came to rest in my lap. But fortunately we made it.

What about relationships that you had with other enlisted men and officers? What was that like?

Since I was a radio operator I was naturally on the radio most of the time. So the people I really knew well were the people who rode in the halftrack. And so with those people I had a nice relationship—even with the battery commander, a nice relationship. It's kind of strange, because before we went into combat the officers were here, they slept here, they ate here and so forth. And the enlisted men were over there. No social interactions whatsoever. But once in combat that all changed. We were all in the same boat and I was with the battery commander all the time as his radio operator. We ate together, played cards together and the separation between officers and enlisted men ended in combat.

So, now we went toward Metz, France. And there we ran out of gas. We were also very low on ammunition. This gave the Germans enough time to regroup and we ran into a stonewall there. There were tremendous fortifications there. We went into a position which I thought was kind of a dumb position, on the forward slope of a hill and there we set up our guns. And we were getting quite a few rounds from German 88s into the area and a goofy thing happened. I had the door of the halftrack open and I had a pack of cigarettes on the seat. I lit a cigarette and an 88 came screaming in and I hit the dirt. And when I got up and went over to get another cigarette out of the pack, I pulled out a piece of shrapnel. Kind of strange. If it took a direct hit, we're finished, but you really get protection from shrapnel if you're inside.

We had one fellow that never wanted to wear his steel helmet, and the battery commander would give him the devil. So he finally made him put the helmet on. One day he's walking away, a shell went off, and a big piece of shrapnel hit his helmet, put a dent in it, and you couldn't get that helmet off of him afterwards. But the helmet itself was kind of interesting because it was used for a lot of things. It was also used as your washbasin. And sometimes in the mud I'd use it as a seat because there was so much mud around there wasn't any place to sit down. And then I've seen it used, in the halftrack, you can imagine if you're traveling all day long in the halftrack and you have no chance of getting out, I've seen it used as a pot —as a urinal.

Anyway, we were at this position one day and they fired a smoke round behind us, on the left, on the right, and in front of us. So we knew that they were gonna really zero in with a lot of artillery on us. So we quickly exited that position, and boy they threw everything in there, but most of us made it out. We went to a new location which was really much safer.

How do you think most soldiers coped with battle—how'd they deal with it?

I think it depended somewhat on their age. I think younger people could cope with it better than the older guys. I mean that's from my experience. I think you just took every day as it came, you know, maybe say a few prayers now and then. It was not pleasant but you had no alternative.

After we were there sometime it was really a muddy mess so we went back to an old factory to kind of clean up our equipment and maybe clean ourselves up a little bit because the opportunity to take a bath was sometimes months at a time. And back at this factory where we were staying we were inside which was kind of nice. We were cleaning our guns and the halftrack driver in our halftrack was sitting here and the battery commander was sitting there. He was cleaning his gun. It accidentally went off and I looked up and above the head of the battery commander there was a bullet hole three inches above his head.

What kind of food would you usually have when you're in combat?

Since we were on the move quite a bit, we had K rations and C rations. Well, there were three kinds of K rations—breakfast, lunch, and dinner. For breakfast you had a little can, about the size of a small tuna can, filled with chopped egg yolk, some meat, and about six crackers. And then there was coffee, instant coffee, and maybe a little candy or something and that was it. You had the same diet for lunch except the can contained cheese. And the same diet for dinner except it was hash. You ate it cold. Now, a much better ration, and we had this most of the time, was a C ration. And you got two cans. You had a good-sized can of maybe hash or something like that. And another pretty good sized can with bigger biscuits in it and sometimes they even put some cigarettes in it and things like that. Now the way we got that food hot was we put the cans, with something like hash, on the manifold of the halftrack. And that would heat it up, really heat it up nicely. And we had a little Coleman stove which we used all the time to heat up water for coffee and also for shaving and things like that. That was a very handy little stove. You could use gasoline in it. In the morning we usually would heat up some hot water and dump it in the helmet and kind of clean up our face a little bit—try to shave.

So, after we cleaned up our equipment and everything, we went to a new position. I think it was just over the German border. And we took over a barn and house—they were actually connected together in Germany. You walk out of the kitchen and you walk right into the barn. And they pulled the halftrack into the barn and there was a hayloft above the halftrack and some fellow went around looking for eggs. A premium, you know, a little extra treat. While he was poking around in the hay he hit a German soldier. This German soldier jumped off and down onto the halftrack. So we got one German soldier there.

Did you personally have to deal with any prisoners?

Well once I took a little walk outside—I don't know why I did this. Anyway while I was walking in the field away from the house and barn, I noticed two German soldiers in the field. And when they saw me they put their hands up. And I took those two as prisoners. I was always armed—my carbine was my constant companion. I never went anyplace without it. Slept with it. And they threw their hands up and were really very happy to give up, you know. They probably were around fifteen or something like that.

So after we were there for a while we went to another position just on the German border, and one night there was a fog. We were down a little depression, our guns set up, and there was a fog. I was on the radio and I heard this forward observer, all excited, trying to contact the battalion and he couldn't get the battalion. So I took his message and he said there was a huge counter attack developing and he wanted to put fire on the Germans in the counter attack. I couldn't get the battalion either, but I had a wire to our executive officer. So I transmitted the fire directions to the executive officer of our battalion. And he had contact with the battalion. So they then gave the message to battalion and the forward director directed the fire. While we were firing a tremendous number of rounds, the fog just dissipated from all the firing. Finally they did connect with the headquarters fire direction. I was out there carrying ammunition, because everybody was carrying ammunition to keep the fire on this counter attack.

Shortly after that I was out in the dark and someone hit me up here—in the shoulders, and I fell back and cracked my leg. Somebody just sort of dove at me and hit me in the shoulder. I don't even know who it was. But it broke my leg.

In the morning I looked at my leg and it was really swollen up. I showed the battery commander and he says, "I want you to go down to battalion headquarters anyway to find a radio 'cause we're having trouble with ours. While you're down there see the battalion surgeon." So, I had a big stick and I hobbled along with this stick to the jeep and they took me down to the battalion surgeon. He looked at it and said, "Well, you ought to soak that in hot water."

There was a group nearby that had a big fire under a barrel washing clothes. Another use for the steel helmet. I filled my steel helmet up with hot water, tried to get my foot in it and soaked it all day. Went back the next morning and it was just as bad if not worse. And the barrack commander said, "Well, go back to the battalion surgeon. Try another day of soaking it in hot water." Next morning—still swollen up. And worse. He said, "Well, you better go back." So I went back and the battalion surgeon said, "Well, I think you should have an x-ray. We don't have any x-rays here, but there's a field hospital back someplace that has a small x-ray machine." So I got in the jeep and they took me back there. I walked in and it was total confusion and they said, "Sorry, we don't have an x-ray. About a mile down the road there's another field hospital that has a full x-ray machine, but we don't have any transportation." So I took my stick and hobbled down about one mile to this other field hospital, went in and asked if they had an x-ray machine? They did. So they took an x-ray of my leg, and the nurse came out and held it up. The doctor came over and looked at it and said, "Stretcher bearer."

I was there for a while and then I was put on that gooney bird, the DC3, to England. And that's where I wound up—in a hospital in England. It was right before the Battle of the Bulge—mid December, 1944. I was in the hospital for at least a month I would say, or more, then they sent me to a rehabilitation center where you gradually work back up. You might take a one-mile hike and later on two and ten, and so forth.

After that we went back to Southampton and got on another ship to cross the channel. Then in France I got on a train. Now the trains are not too good at that time and what I rode in was a 40&8—forty men or eight horses. But I think they had more than forty men because it was hard to find a place to lay down. But the train traveled fairly rapidly to the German border. And I spent about two or three days on the train. I camped there for a little while and then got on another train to take me back to my outfit. The railroads in Germany at the time were in one horrible shape and I think it took us two weeks to go across Germany in this train eating K rations all the time. And you know, you have hygiene problems like where do you go to the bathroom? How do you wash? One thing we discovered was the trains stop so many times we'd go up to the engine, and the engineer would pull a little string and hot water would come out into our helmets. That was kind of convenient. So eventually I rejoined my unit right on the Austrian border. That would be June of '45. The war was over. The war ended on my trip back.

We were there at least for a month or so. And we did get a trip to Berchtesgaden—Hitler's crow's nest. That was interesting. Then we eventually got on trucks and went all the way back to Cherbourg to get on a ship to go back to the States. There were three groups. If you didn't have many points they were going to send you directly to the Asian Theater. If you had an intermediate number of points they sent you back to the States to regroup and have a furlough. [If you had a sufficient number of points, you would be eligible for a discharge.] I got home in August of '45, I think. The war with Japan was still going on. Then when we heard about the atomic bomb everybody was highly excited. Of course I was extremely happy that the war was over.

Finally I was sent to Texas, Camp Bowie in Texas, and there it was a very relaxed atmosphere and nobody really took things too seriously. And sometime, I think in December, I was discharged at Camp Bowie, Texas. My highest rank was a T5, technician 5th grade.

How do you think World War II changed your life?

The biggest change probably was the GI Bill, 'cause I wouldn't have had enough money to go to college. And it gave me an opportunity I probably never would have had otherwise. So I think that it really had a tremendous effect on my future life.

Louis Blank

Louis E. Blank lives in Washington Township on W. Rahn Road. He is a widower with two grown children—a daughter living in Champaign, Illinois, and a son living in Columbus, Ohio. He spent twenty-two months in the Army in World War II—ten months Stateside and twelve months in the European Theater of Operations. After his discharge from the Army he worked for a short time in his father's plumbing business, but then in 1948 he enlisted in the United States Marine Corps where he served for twenty-two years—until 1970. As he says, he served in the Vietnam War also, "But that's another story."

Lou, how did you happen to get in the Army?

Well, it was a very short decision on my part as I always remember looking at my father's uniform from World War I and the books that he brought back from Paris. He fought the battle of Paris, I think. But I always wanted to be a soldier. Strangely I did. I just looked forward to the day that I could go down and enlist.

I was born in Dayton. I went to grade school at Jefferson and then from Jefferson I went to Colonel White. From Colonel White I had to turn around and go west to Roosevelt. But I graduated in 1943 and then I enlisted in what was called the Enlisted Reserve Corps when I was seventeen. When my eighteenth birthday came I was called to active duty—about November of '43.

Well, I first went down to Cincinnati and then went from Cincinnati over across the river and through the woods to Fort Thomas, Kentucky. And I think almost all of the young men were draftees. Although I wasn't drafted, most of the men were. Anyway, we went down to Fort Thomas where we were given our uniforms and our further assignments.

Where did you go for basic training?

After I got my uniform and our assignments were read off to us, I was assigned to go to the infantry-training center at Camp Croft, South

Carolina, which is no longer there—they decided that I would be an infantry-man. Those are the ones that are pretty dispensable. I think we had thirteen weeks of training there, very good training, as I remember.

It was a huge place. And we had to march a lot. When it was time to fire a rifle we went out to the rifle range, marched out there. Ten miles there and ten miles back in the evening. So, there was twenty miles a day we marched. We fired the heavy machine gun, fired the light machine gun, fired the rifle grenades. Then, of course, the basic rifle, the M-1, and we fired mortars. I was in pretty trim shape, I didn't weigh but maybe half as much as I do now. I remember we had a sergeant, Guido DiPamphelis, and he had a voice. He could stand in the center of the parade ground and wake somebody up in the bar-racks that was furthest down the line. There were some good NCOs, of course, but they weren't none of them combat veterans. But they were kept because they had pretty good control over men. They had good physiques and were bayonet instructors and instructors in various and assorted other things.

Did you have to pull any details like KP or guard duty?

We had one of the finest mess halls that I encountered, and this is not exaggerating, in my twenty-two years of military service. I can never remem-ber a better feeding mess hall then the one I had at Camp Croft. We ate fam-ily style, big long tables, and once I forgot to be polite, I guess, and I said too loudly, "Pass the potatoes." And the mess sergeant came over, and he said, "Was that you?" and I said, "Yes, sir, that was me." "Well you're on KP for a week." So he drags me into this kitchen for talking too loud and for not saying please. He didn't like it—it was too loud. And we had in that mess hall, oh, about four or five cooks

What happened to you after your basic training ended?

Basic training ended and then as infantrymen we got on a train, I imag-ine at Spartanburg, and were transported up to Camp Shanks, New York. Now Camp Shanks, New York, was what was called a POE, port of embarka-tion. We stayed there and they found me for KP. First time I ever had twenty-four hours of KP. I was in the mess hall and my job was to clean gizzards. You slice the gizzard open, empty the sand and gravel out of the gizzard, wash it off and put it in a barrel. So, twenty-four hours of chicken livers. That was about enough for me.

And from there we got our orders and were put on another train and went down to Bayonne, New Jersey, and were put on a transport. It was a

German vessel, of all things, and had a civilian crew—merchant type. They put us down in the hold, way down below, and they steamed away and we went to Greenock, Scotland. We went over in a convoy, thank goodness, and of course the German submarines were pretty well taken care of by this time and I don't think we lost any vessels. From Greenock, Scotland, we went down to England. Now, I don't know the name of the place, it was this transient camp somewhere in the woods to prevent V-bombs or German aircraft from spotting us.

We were only there a little while and then we were assigned to the 30th Division. I think it would have been in England. When we went to the continent we came down a ship's cargo nets and went into an LCM and proceeded onto the beach. Of course the beach was cleared, but we still came in on a landing craft at Omaha Beach. I'm sure it was Omaha Beach.

We were all replacements. Then after we got ashore we formed into a column and marched inland about, oh, ten miles, and we could hear artillery fire, or bombs, or whatever it was, you could hear that, but it was close to St. Lô and this was a replacement camp. And in this camp we were broken down into whatever organization the 30th Division had. They broke it down into regiments. Then they broke it down into battalions, and then they even went down into companies. That's the way they did it—whoever needed the replacements according to MOS—military occupational specialty. Mine was as an infantryman and that's what they needed. We were there just a short while. We saw our first real action there in this replacement depot. It was under cover of trees and this was as much camouflage as the American soldiers had.

One thing that I would criticize at that time was the very poor fire discipline, despite the fact that everybody was told you shouldn't shoot at the airplanes. Well, the Germans would send a reconnaissance airplane over almost every night. And of course they probably knew where we were anyway, and they dropped small two hundred and fifty pounders I guess, and killed a chaplain—the regimental chaplain. And that was the first time I was under fire. After that I left there to join the 120th Infantry Regiment and I was assigned to the 2nd Battalion in G Company and I went up and joined the squad—all the way down to the squad level by this time. Now G Company is a rifle company—D, H, and M companies were the heavy weapons companies. And then we moved step by step towards the front.

After we landed on the Normandy beach, we came down through Calvados. They make very good wine there. Calvados is an apple brandy. Very dangerous. And we came down slowly and had several skirmishes with mostly German units. We were pretty fragmented at that time and we came down in the direction of Mortain. Now here is a town, Tessy-sur-Vire on the Vire River, and as you can see this peninsula goes up to Cherbourg. This divided

Louis Blank.

the Brittany peninsula from the other part of France. The Germans had been attempting to cut that in two. They didn't succeed in cutting off the troops from the Brittany peninsula and the other part over to the west. But that's what they were trying to do in the action at the time.

Anyway, we came down then to Avranches, not far from the Vire River and Mortain. It's a fairly good-sized town. This would be for me in July and August of 1944. Well, at Mortain our battalion set up a defensive position after having relieved the 18th Infantry of the 1st Division. They moved away somewhere else and we moved in, and we made a big mistake, I think. We relieved during the daytime, and you don't relieve during the daytime, you relieve, if you can, at night. See, because the Germans knew that one outfit's going out and the other outfit's coming in. Well, whenever you do that you lose an amount of cohesion between the separate organizations. Anyhow our job was on Hill 314. Hill 314 overlooks the city of Mortain and the Germans were in control of Mortain, but we could look down into Mortain.

We dug in our positions on one side of the hill, and they really didn't have too much to tell us about what was going to happen or what was happening. So we dug our hole, my buddy and I. We dug our hole and set up there. We had a real good camouflaged position. And long about three o'clock in the morning the Germans struck our positions there. And whenever that happens, of course, there's a great deal of confusion about this, that, and the other thing. And then later it all quieted down.

So we got out and were going to our squad which was too strung out. Again, we didn't have much communication between our next unit or our next people. But anyway, we got out and we were going to try to find the outfit or find the next group. And so we started up the hill. We were on kind of a reverse slope and started up the hill, and here was our corpsman, not corpsman but aidman in the army, laying there—he'd been killed. And there were quite a few dead soldiers as we were going up the hill—quite a few dead out there. And we went up almost to the top of the hill. On the top of the hill was a road, and the road went to our right and up to a chapel, a little church. And as I looked down towards that church I spotted a machine gun, and it wasn't any further from me than that tree right there [Blank points to a tree about thirty-five yards away] maybe a little further, and three or four German soldiers standing around this tree. Well I was quicker than they were and I fired at one and he went down. But I knew it'd take only a matter of seconds before they'd spin that machine gun around. It was pointed down the slope. So we ran. And we ran over to a hedgerow and got down on the ground there. When I think back it's kind of funny—we took our hand grenades and put them up there, put our bandoleers up there, took our clips out and had them up there. I guess we had kind of decided we're going to make a stand here. And we thought that they would come towards us, but they didn't—nobody came. And so we figured we better hunker down there before we go on. But unfortunately there were German soldiers on the other side of the hedgerow, and we were quiet we didn't say nothing, but there was a break in the hedgerow and we decided we're gonna play like we were dead. And this German soldier came over the hedgerow. He had his machine pistol on his shoulder and he came down. I knew all he had to do was take that machine pistol off his shoulder and we're done, you know. We lay there. I didn't move and neither did my buddy. And he come and kicked me, he kicked my foot and said, "Stand up." And that was the end of the ballgame for me. We were captured and he motioned us to go down that road toward the chapel. We got down there and went down below it. There was a big cliff and up here was the chapel, and we had to come down by rocks—huge rocks. Then there was a command post of some description there. These were SS soldiers and one of them was gonna kill us because he knew that I was the one that killed his comrade out there. And he picked up an American carbine and was gonna hit me with it. But he didn't because one of the officers, or non-commissioned officers, told him, "Don't do that." So then we were made to sit down there and this German officer, he didn't speak English, but I understood some of what he was telling us, he said, "There will be somebody to come and pick us up." And then it was all quiet. An airplane would fly over every once in a while. And we were led down to a road, down at the bottom of Hill 314. And there was a jeep down there and it had an SS driver, and I noticed his cuff title. German SS men wore a cuff title, and it said his unit. And the cuff title on this soldier was SS Nordland. And SS Nordland weren't German soldiers, they were Norwegians. And we got in the jeep and sat in the back. Now by this time we were getting hungry, we hadn't eaten for about three or four days, you know, and I found some bread somebody had left down on the floor of the jeep and ate that. Tasted good. And then I reached in my pocket and what did I have in my pocket but a hand grenade. I could just see me putting that grenade up next to the driver, but I just didn't have the moxy to do that. So, I just dropped the grenade off to the side, you know, just threw it away. That was the beginning of the journey back to the main prisoner of war camps in Germany—August 10, 1944.

When were your parents notified that you were missing in action?

They had received the missing in action telegram from the Department of the Army. Later, the German authorities gave us all one of those postcards. And on there we were supposed to answer, well, they had it all printed out— "I'm in good health and I have been wounded or I have not been wounded." And this went on then to my home on Oxford Avenue. [It was received by his parents on November 22, 1944.] So it took that long to determine my fate, what happened to me.

The first area that we were gathered together with other prisoners was at Alençon, France. Now at Alençon, France, I would imagine they had about five hundred men from the various areas where the Germans had captured guys. And we moved from there by truck, and it was a very harrowing experience driving down any street or highway in France at that time. If a P-38 saw you, or P-51, look out. Well one did. He came down and looked us over first and I guess he kind of determined that Germans wouldn't have acted like that, you know, they would have scattered. So I guess he determined that those were prisoners in there. But he fired a burst and when he fired that burst I fell through the floor of the truck. Good thing it wasn't going, it wasn't moving, it was just sitting there. And of course I scrambled back up again and then we proceeded on.

Then we got to Châlons-sur-Marne, that was another gathering place in an old French artillery barracks. By this time we were getting hungry, although we did get some food at Alençon. And we also got some food at Châlons-sur-Marne and at Châlons. Those barracks were four stories tall and most of the guys couldn't have made it to the fourth story if they had a bunk up there. They slept on the stairways 'cause they just couldn't quite make it up there—too much exertion. There we got raspberry jam and bread in the morning and then some sort of soup. And it wasn't very nice, but it served the purpose I guess.

Then from Alençon we got on the train again and went down to where we were strafed again by P-51s. The cars, the French railroad cars, were not designated POW or anything. They didn't hit anybody in our car. But it went on and we wound up in Paris. Then we were put on trucks again and I was there in Paris on August the 21st. And had I been able to jump over the railing and run someplace to get away, that would have been the place to do it, but nobody did. And they were shooting in the streets at that time. The brave Frenchmen were shooting soldiers, German soldiers. But on the 22nd, if I'm not mistaken, the next day, Paris was free.

What are these things you brought with you?

OK. These are just standard GI dog tags with a name and a service number. And I believe this is a T40, no T44. I received tetanus shots and that's on there too. And your blood type—these are just regular GI dog tags. This is a German dog tag that was issued to us and it told the camp number, Stalag 7A. That's in Moosberg, Germany. And again I got a number, 85509. And this—that's a can opener. And we had all kinds of assorted names for it, but they came in every C ration and every K ration. If you didn't have one of these things I guess you'd just starve to death, or eat the can, but that was a nifty thing. Very small. And whoever invented it was pretty neat. With the American dog tag, if the man is a casualty or killed in action, one of these tags is removed and the other one stays with the body. And then these [the German dog tags] are much the same way because this is just broken in two, snapped in two, and one goes with the body and one goes home.

I didn't spend much time there. That was the main camp. I was moved out of there with twelve other prisoners. We left there and went down into Bavaria to what was called a commando. Now a commando is a group of men who are going out on a work detail. The Germans, of course, weren't so dumb as to leave all these healthy young men in a camp someplace not doing anything—they're going to put these guys to work. So enlisted men were required by the Geneva Convention to work. Officers could volunteer to work. But since I was a PFC, I had to go to work. So, they transported us down to a little town called Schrobenhausen. Now, Schrobenhausen is in Bavaria, fairly good-sized town, and we were quartered in the county jail. And then in the mornings we would go up the street to a farmer's house, I believe his name was Schmidt, we went there and he fed us breakfast and then we would march out and go in the potato fields. The farmer had a nice yoke of oxen. And I got the job of driving the oxen. And I learned how to say left and right and what to do if it didn't move. You hit it in the nose with a big club. And we gleaned the fields. We were gleaners. And we picked up all the potatoes no matter how small, and put them in the wagon, took them back. We worked for the farmer for quite a while. And one evening meal, you know, at just an ordinary meal, a little meat was served which was welcome. He was very nice to us. And we finally found out from the daughter, a pretty girl, that her brother was in Camp Swift, Texas, as a POW—a German soldier. And he would write home that the Americans treated them so well. That was good for me.

Then we left the farmer and we were transferred by a little march out to the forest. And they had a beautiful place there. It was built for Italian soldiers or prisoners and somehow we got to use the place. It was like an ideal log cabin in the woods. Only we had bunks for twelve and then had a kitchen with a big stove, a tile stove that radiated heat. The place was always warm in the winter. By this time my shoes were giving out and my uniform was tattered, so the Germans gave me a Yugoslav uniform. I also didn't have any socks by this time. So they gave us what was called "Fusslappen," and that was nothing more than a square of flannel. You put your foot in the middle, fold it over, fold it over, fold it over, and put your foot in. But the nice thing about wooden shoes was, when it was snow and cold on the ground, that cold didn't go up into your foot. Well, I still managed to get frozen feet, but it wasn't all that bad.

We had a cook and we had potatoes to cook, and then we would go out to the forest and cut. The forester, who was a little old German man, would mark trees that we were going to cut down. And he showed us how they cut the tree in Germany. They don't cut it down like we do, they cut it down with a shorter stump. That way they didn't waste anything. So, we cut trees down—big ones, little ones, all fir or pine.

And then it was getting toward spring of 1945 and each one of those logs that went down we shaved the bark off. Then it was numbered, it was measured in diameter, and all put down in a book, and when that was over we planted little trees. The guards were never bad to us. One was a young fellow who was a, what's called a "Gebirgsjäger," mountain trooper. And he was nice. Oh, he'd always say, I hope the wars over tomorrow and we can go home.

But anyway, then we started our march again. We had to get out of there because the Americans were just down the road. And off we went with all our possessions—our worldly goods. And we were lousy—we had lice so bad. And it was just a mess. We were sleeping on the ground and sleeping in the straw sacks in that nice little cabin. Nobody was really sick, but the lice was the worst things.

And then we went down and we met up with a German company, German soldiers who were older men. I had no idea what kind of soldiers they were. When we had to sleep, we slept in the barn of this family's house. And then they gave us bread. Anyway, we were in the barn and a German officer came in and said, "We're going to give up, we're not going anywhere any further." The Russians were over on the other side; how far, I don't know. And he said, "You're in charge," not to me, but one of the prisoners. And so they piled all their weapons up, and all of them started to cry. And I was talking to one of the German soldiers and he was crying, he was one of our guards—we only had three guards. And he started crying because he didn't know where his wife and family was, and what's going to happen to him. Well, who knows, you know, but then our guys went into the house and got as much wine as they could find. And one guy was missing and he was down in the potato cellar, he couldn't move. And that was about it.

We went down to the nearest town and this was a town called Au. A tragic scene went on while I was there. We went into this pub and there were several people gathered. Ex-prisoners, by this time, on the front stoops of the place and a drunken American was gonna go over and shoot some German soldiers that were in a barn across the street. And a British soldier, he'd been a prisoner since Africa, went up to him and he says, "No, don't do that." And the guy shot him and killed him. Can you imagine the day he got liberated some drunk shoots and kills him.

Then the Americans came. I don't think we even wanted to leave. We wanted to see what was going on. So, we went to a German family's house and lice and all we slept in their feather bed. There must be lice in that featherbed yet. But then we caught up with the American soldiers. Then they took us on back to the hospital and then we went back to the states.

What was the first thing you did when you got back home to Dayton?

Well, I went from one hospital to another. I was in a hospital in New York, and then I went to a hospital, Billings General Hospital over in Indianapolis, Fort Benjamin Harrison, and they kept me there for a while because I had hepatitis and I had frozen feet and I weighed only ninety pounds. They said, "You gotta stay in bed." And I guess I was the only one that stayed in bed because all the other guys went out at night. And we would race around on wheelchairs, had wheelchair races. And finally the doctor said, "You can go home now on leave." So they gave us thirty days compensatory, or whatever kind of leave they call it, and then I came home. I walked out the main gate and hitched a ride to Englewood. And then got a ride back into Dayton. I wanted to surprise my mother and father. And I did. And that was it. They finally discharged me, and I went home. That was the end of my World War II.

Later, I went into the Marine Corps. At first I learned a trade after I got home. My father had a business, a plumbing business, a very good plumbing shop. And I learned a trade. But I got mad at him, and I told him, "I'm not gonna work here anymore." And I went down and joined the Marine Corps. Well, I guess we had a good relationship, no matter what, but he was a rough old cookie and you'd better do what he told you to do. And then I joined the Marine Corps and then had another career. Had another war, Vietnam, but that's another story.

Nick Engler

Nicholas A. Engler was born and raised in Troy, New York. He and his wife Delores had five children—three boys and two girls. He served in the Army for a little over three years. His highest rank attained in the service was corporal. He was in combat in the European Theater as a rifleman with the 95th Division. He was wounded seriously in action in Germany. After the war he took advantage of the GI Bill of Rights and graduated from the University of Dayton (U.D.) with a degree in physics. Nick did graduate work at the University of Cincinnati and then returned to U.D. as a professor of physics. He taught and worked in that institution's research institute from 1952 to 1986 when he retired.

I was raised in Troy, New York, and went to a Catholic high school in Troy. From there I went to Notre Dame for two years as a major in accounting. Then one day in August my mother came down and said, "Dad lost his job, you're not going back to school." So then I got a job as a junior accountant at GE in Schenectady, New York.

When did you go in the army?

The war began at Pearl Harbor in December of '41, and I was drafted in October of '42. I was sent to Camp Upton and then to Camp Breckinridge, Kentucky, for basic training.

I spent my basic training in a line company doing infantry training, obstacle courses and hiking. Athletically, I was in very good shape. I'd always played tennis, I ran, and I was in good shape. I could outrun everybody. I never dropped out of a hike and I never dropped out of double-timing. But the captain hated me—hated. And we were jogging along one day, and he came up to me and said, "When are you gonna drop out, Engler?" And I said, "Right after you." So that wasn't too good.

But at any rate I got into basic training at Breckinridge, and just hated it, it just was awful. Go to a lecture and the sergeant would say, "This here mortar is gooder than that there one." You know, stuff like that. After basic training was over I applied for ASTP, Army Specialized Training Program. I had two years of Spanish at Notre Dame and thought I was

Nick Engler.

going to do language. And I went to do the language thing and it was all closed. And I didn't want to go back to the infantry so I said, "What else is open?" And they said, "Engineering." Now we were all New Yorkers. And we just knew we were going to go to Harvard or Yale or Princeton, or something like that. And they came out and said, "You're going to go to the University of Dayton." And we said, "Where in the world is that?" We never heard of it—never heard of the University of Dayton. Now this is in '43.

At any rate, I spent six months at U.D. in the Army Specialized Training Program in engineering—I just loved it, loved it. And we got an aptitude test to go into pre-med and I said, "I don't want to go to pre-med, I'm happy where I am." And they said, "You've got to take the test." So I did and they sent me to the University of Illinois in pre-med and I passed everything. But they cut the shipping orders on the basis of my midterms, and I was shipped back to the infantry.

Then the call came for people to volunteer to go overseas, and there were about twenty-four of us that volunteered to go overseas. So they pulled us out of that division and sent us to Fort Dix. We shipped out from Fort Dix in September of '44 to go overseas. We went on board the ship the *Lucitania*. Didn't see much because I pulled latrine duty for seven days, never saw the ocean, and then we landed in Coventry.

On the first morning it was real foggy and I couldn't see anything except a bunch of rubble. And then the fog started to lift, and you could see more rubble. And then the fog lifted some more and you could see even more rubble. And the fog lifted completely and all you could see was rubble. It was absolutely amazing. Coventry was leveled.

So any rate, then we trained in England and had lots of night maneuvers. We used to shoot dice, I shot a lot of craps in the army, and I loved craps. And one day, right before we were going over to France, we got in this crap game and I just got lucky—I got pass after pass. And this guy went and he said, "Engler, you make one more pass, and I'm gonna kill you." And he went and he got his gun and he comes back to the crap game and he's got a gun. And I made the pass and he said, "I'll get you when we get in combat." So any rate, I sent home three hundred bucks, you know, from the crap game.

Later we got a pass to Stratford-on-Avon, and this one guy that I know loved Shakespeare, so we went to Stratford-on-Avon. We had this three-day pass and I had all these English pounds in my wallet. You know how pounds are, they're much bigger than your wallet. And we get to the box office and it's in open air—and I pull a pound out. But the corner was crimped and all the pounds came out and they scattered—you know. And the Englishmen in line got all the pounds back for me and kept muttering—"Damn rich Yankee soldier." Any rate, we had a good day in Stratford-on-Avon.

Then we went over to France in a LST. And we had to get off the LST onto another smaller boat but the sea was very rough—very, very rough. And you're carrying a pack and gun and you got to climb down the side, and I was just absolutely petrified. This was on a rope ladder. One guy got killed when the boats came together.

We landed at Utah Beach and it was in late October of '44—after D-Day. There was still all sorts of vehicles lying around and lots of debris. The cliffs were steep, and you couldn't imagine how those guys would take that— just couldn't imagine how they climbed up those cliffs. And any rate, we then progressed, we rode on a 40 & 8, a boxcar for forty men or eight horses. I think we were on that train for a couple days, I don't know. Then we got off and made our way through St. Lô.

I remember St. Lô vividly, just utter destruction. The smell of a town that's been bombed is just awful—just smells dusty. Any rate, we went through St. Lô and then got to our new division, the 95th Infantry Division. Met with them on one side of the Moselle River. The company I was in, Company C, was on the other side of the Moselle. There were twenty-seven of us and we got together in a schoolhouse that night and we were given our instructions. We were gonna go across the Moselle on a boat and rendezvous at the outskirts of this town and then take the town. And none of us had ever been in combat before, none of us. We were green. Any rate, I'm sitting there and the sergeant yells, "Does anyone know how to work a 301 radio?" And I'm saying to myself, I'm gonna stay on this side and I'm gonna work the radio communication with the guy on the other side. I ain't gonna cross any damn river. So I said, "I can work a 301." He said, "Good, we need one, take it." So, I had to pick up the 301 on my back and along with my pack and my rifle, and take the thing across the river. So, that's how smart I was.

You're going into combat for the first time. What were your feelings?

What I did was, I didn't think about it. I kept telling myself, "Oh, this isn't real, nobody's gonna shoot." But I was just petrified, absolutely petrified. I was frightened the whole time I was in combat. There was twenty-seven of us, and thirteen of us got in one boat, and the other fourteen got in the other boat. The one that had the fourteen we never heard from again. They were hit and were all killed, but we got across. I'm in the end of the boat and the engineers who were driving the boat said, they didn't want to mess around, "Get out." So I jumped out and you know, I jumped into a hole—the Moselle was flooded. And I went under because I had all this weight. So I reached up and grabbed the boat and worked myself back into the boat. So I got out, and Duckor and Fishenburg and Epstein were there.

So any rate, we get across the river and it's like two or three o'clock in the morning and we're waiting 'til dawn. And I couldn't stand up because I was all wet and I have this radio on my back plus my pack, and I couldn't stand up. So Duckor and Fishenburg would stand me up, and then I'd slowly sink to the ground. Oh, to hell with it, I just sat there.

So, any rate, we sat and we waited 'til dawn, and then we crawled up to the fence and Fishenburg took his bayonet out. "What are you doing that for?" I said. He said, "Hand to hand combat." "Oh, god," I said. But those damn Germans came out of that building and surrendered. They didn't know that we were twenty-seven guys, well not twenty-seven now, only thirteen of us were left, and that we hadn't ever shot a gun in our life, it was amazing. But any rate they just surrendered. Oh, twenty or twenty-five of them. Amazing. And Duckor shot one of them 'cause he started running—Duckor just shot him. I asked him how it felt. He said, "Don't ever ask me, don't ever, ever ask me."

And then the Germans came back, and so Duckor and I and Fishenburg and Epstein hid in a pigpen. It was nothing more than a pigpen. And it was only like four foot high, but it had a store of raw potatoes. And we were there for three days. We couldn't get out. The Germans ran the town and we couldn't get out. So we ate the raw potatoes.

And then finally these tanks would come down the street, and we'd drop grenades on them as they came down the street. We could see out the window where to throw the grenades. But any rate, finally the American soldiers came back and we got rescued. We went on our way to combat. It was our first combat experience. Yes. And it was—it was unreal. It was, I really can't define it well. We were scared. We were petrified, but I just kept telling myself this isn't real, this isn't part of life. This is something else. But as I think back on it, I know I was scared—I know that. But, you could function. We had to really.

And so we went through a couple of towns and I carried a bazooka— you'd have to take turns carrying the bazooka. And so one day I'm carrying the bazooka and the rifle and we came to a tank trap which is just nothing more than a big ditch and it's raining—it rained all the time. I slid down, and then I got back up—just gotta keep those muzzles up. And I'm trying like hell to get into this town and there's a little barbed wire fence and I trip going over, but I still got the muzzles up. So I got up but I fell again and still kept the muzzles up, and the sergeant yelled, "Engler, don't be so goddamn scared." Well, I was scared, but that isn't why I fell.

I ran to the front yards area of the town, and the lieutenant is across the street and he's motioning us across. And I said to the guys, "The lieutenant wants us across the street," and I run across the street, and everybody follows me, and the lieutenant says, "Good work, Engler." I said, "What do you mean?" He said, "The Germans have the road zeroed in." The guys knew that the road was zeroed in and they wouldn't go across the road. I didn't know the road was zeroed in so I went across the road. That's how I got the damn Bronze Star. There was no firing. I wouldn't have gone across the road if they were firing. So I got the Bronze Star.

What were your feelings the first time you came under enemy fire?

The scary thing was when there wasn't any fire. If you walked down a road which you knew the Germans had zeroed in and nothing was happening you were petrified. Once the shells started to come in you felt better because now you knew where the shells were going. It was almost a funny relief. Not really funny, you know, finally seeing the shells burst. And so it was a peculiar sensation because obviously you're in more danger when there are shells coming. But you get used to that. You could tell where the shells were going to come in by the noise. You could tell whether they were near you or away—whether they were artillery or mortar. We had more artillery than mortar. Mortar you couldn't hear, but artillery shells you could—they whistle. I remember walking along the road one time, and the shells were coming in and we had a new lieutenant, and every time he heard one he'd crawl in the ditch. And we finally said, "Hey, watch us, when we go in the ditch, you go in the ditch." We could tell from the sound how close they were coming to you and whether you should get cover. Doesn't take very long. And it better not.

And then we got into Metz, and we had one helluva fight in Metz—it was very brutal. You crawl over dead bodies and that sort of stuff, and lots of shells. The Germans had all of the buildings mined, and when they saw us go in they'd bomb them. Once Duckor ran out into the street and the building blew up. So Duckor and I got under a jeep. Then we crawled out from under the jeep and Epstein got hit by a two by four, and he was flat and out. We rolled him over and he just looked up. So they took him back. Then later, I'm sitting up against a wall, leaning up against a wall, and there was a guy next to me I didn't know. I'm looking up at a barn, and all of a sudden a German helmet appears, and I'm reaching for my gun. I wasn't quick enough, and he fired at us and he hit this guy but he missed me. So I dragged this guy into the building we're leaning on and called a medic. The medic comes, and I say to him, "Should I stay?" He said, "No, get out of here." I got out and that damn building blew up.

So any rate, Duckor got hit by a stone in his foot and said, "I gotta go back." And I said, "Duckor, don't go back. Fishenburg's gone, Epstein's gone, now you're gonna be gone. I'm gonna be all by myself." "I gotta go back." I talked to him later about that and he said, "Nick, I was so goddam scared I had to go back." And that sort of made me feel better, 'cause I was scared, but I wasn't that scared. I mean, I wasn't gonna give up.

Eventually Metz was over and then we went on—four or five days later, I guess. It was three o'clock in the afternoon and the captain calls and says, "OK, we're going on the attack, guys. Our company is the point company, and our platoon is the point platoon, and our squad is the point squad, and you, Engler, are the first scout." That means I'm the first guy—the first guy. "So what do I do?" "Just walk up ahead and see what you see."

So I'm walking and it's foggy, and I looked back, and I don't see anybody behind me. And I look ahead and I don't see anybody ahead of me. Oh, what the hell is this? So I hit the ground. A mortar shell comes in here and a mortar shell comes in there. And I think they're aimed at me—Engler. And I got on my hands to get up and the next one got me. And it got me here in the shoulder and went and hit the collarbone and broke it—I went down. Missed the lung and went down in the 4th, 5th, and 6th ribs, and lodged in the 6th rib of my spine. And it paralyzed me. I could not move except for this arm [right]—I could move this arm, but otherwise I couldn't move. Now this has got to be like four or five o'clock in the afternoon, and it's getting dark and a medic comes out and says, "Can you move?" And, I say, "No." "Are you hurt?" "Yes." Then the sergeant came up, and the sergeant says, "Are you hurt?" And I said, "Yes." He says, "I'll go get some help. I'll get you out of here."

So I lay there and it got dark and nobody came. This was about five o'clock on the first of December. I can reach out and I can get apples. I'm in an orchard and I can get apples, and I can eat the apples, but I couldn't move except for this arm. I lay there and lay there, and then dawn finally comes. I'm thinking, now they'll come back for me. I've been wounded now about twelve hours. And all of a sudden it starts to get dark again, you know, and I think, "Well I'm going, I'm going, I'm gonna die." And it was so peaceful you wouldn't believe how peaceful it was. I'd just like to go home and get a shower, you know? But there was no fear, there was no nothing. I just, hey, that's the way it goes.

And so I'm lying there, and it's dark again, and I feel this toe prodding me. And I have a German blanket over me because three or four day's prior to that I'd found one and I wanted an extra blanket. So when the medic came he put this German blanket over me. So, I had this German blanket over me and I feel this toe prodding me. I thought, well, shit, I'm not gonna say anything—it might be Germans. And I didn't say anything. So finally, I heard this guy say, "Well, he's dead." I said, "No, no, no! I'm not dead." So they picked me up and put me on the stretcher, put my gun on too. I threw my gun off, 'cause I knew you couldn't take guns in medical units in the States.

I was afraid they wouldn't let me in. He put the gun back, I threw it off, so finally, the hell with it—they carried me.

There were shells coming in, but they were miles away. And every time the shells would come in they'd drop the stretcher. I said, "Hey, guys, these things aren't near us." So they finally get me into an Italian aid station and I'm freezing to death, and they put nine blankets over me. So I had this German blanket over me, and I'm getting nice and warm, and all of a sudden, the colonel says, "Attack." So we have to go out. They put me on a jeep, you know, the fender of a jeep and we hit a mine and I go creaming off into the field but luckily I wasn't hurt. The jeep hit a mine, and boom, I was thrown off in the field.

So they got me back and we got into an airplane that got forced down, got into another airplane, and, oh no, no, they got me into a hospital first. They got me into a hospital and put me out into a hall. And I'm lying there thinking come on guys do something, you know. And finally they come and get me, and they bring me in and a doctor says, "Mennen, Mennen." And I say, "What does Mennen mean?" He says, "You're an American soldier?" "Yes." He thought I was German because I had the blanket on—the German blanket on. Mennen means where does it hurt? So any rate, they take the shrapnel out, took it out of my back, 'cause it was lodged there, got me on another plane and I get back to England.

I got into a hospital, clean sheets, I know I'm safe, I know I'm gonna live, and I go into shock. Boom. Just like that. I can go three days and I don't go into shock, and I get into a safe place and I go into shock. The nurse took a look at me and ran out. Then she came back and they hit me with something. I said, "What' s the matter?" She said, "You're in shock." It was three days from the time I got hit, at least three days, maybe four, from the time I got hit to the time I was in the hospital room, you know, it was forty-eight hours after I got hit that I got help.

But any rate, the left arm deltoid muscle was severed, and the first doctor that looked at it said, "The arm is useless. The nerves are gone, you'll never use it." The next doctor came in, and said, "No, no, no, some muscle." And so I couldn't move it and was sent to the hospital where the nurse said, "If you want to use that arm again, you're gonna have to work, and you're gonna hurt." So they put me on a wheel, you know, and god did that hurt. But I did it, and I can use it now. I got 95 percent use of the arm now.

So any rate, back in the hospital—I was in the hospital for four months in England. The shrapnel was taken out of my back. I have a scar on my back where they took the shrapnel out. And, so any rate, I got back along about April. I'm well enough to go back in combat, and I was thinking of all these things. This is April '45. So I'm thinking about all the things I can tell the doctor about why I don't want to go back into combat, you know, my arm

Nick Engler today.

hurts, back hurts. There's a tent, an open-ended tent, on the exit end is a truck. I walk in and the doctor says, "Good morning son, how are you." I said, "Fine." He said, "Next." That's a true story. And before I know it I'm on this damn truck going back to combat. So any rate, I go back to my outfit. Everybody thought I'd been dead—then two days later, V-E Day came. Two days before V-E Day. Duckor was there; Fishenburg, and Epstein were not, but Duckor was there.

Was it a close relationship between the four of you?

Oh, yes. We did everything together. You just, well, you just live with each other. It's hard to explain. We met probably a month or two months before we went overseas. I was lying on my cot and it was a Jewish holiday. I was lying in my cot in the barracks, and the corporal came in and said, "Engler, what are you doing, why are you here?" "What do you mean, what am I doing? I'm here." He said, "You got a pass." It was a Jewish holiday and they thought I was Jewish, and so they gave me a pass. And so I ran down and grabbed the pass and they were just getting on a bus—Duckor, Epstein, and Fishenburg. They were all getting on a bus to go into town for the Jewish holiday. And I say, "Wait for me." So I got on the bus with them. They said, "What the hell are you doing here?" "I got a pass, shut up, I'm Jewish."

What was your immediate reaction to the German surrender?

Nothing. Nothing. There was no reaction—we were sober. I don't mean non-alcoholic sober, I mean just sober—grim. We knew we were gonna go to the States, and we knew we still had Japan. And so we knew that we were far from getting out of the Army. That V-E Day meant nothing to us as far as getting out of the Army was concerned, nor did it mean the end of combat. And there was actually no celebration. None. Just sat around and looked at each other. I got letters saying aren't you glad for V-E Day? Why?

So any rate, we went to a Polish displacement camp and guarded [it]—made sure the Germans didn't come in and the Poles didn't get out. And I did that for, I don't know, two or three months. We were guarding it. We had to make sure that the Polish guys didn't get out because this was in a German town and they were Polish displaced people. And we had to make sure that the Poles didn't get out into the town and steal things. And of course they did. Every night they would go out and steal all the German bicycles and bring them back. And every morning we would take the bicycles back, and who cared, we could care less. And they had, I don't know where they got the musical instruments, but they had musical instruments and they had a dance every night. The best polka you've ever heard. And the barn would reverberate and they just had a great time.

There was a guy there, an old man who could speak five languages, and he was a former professor at one of the Polish universities, and he and I got together and we talked a lot. And he told me that we had to stay and fight the Russians 'cause they'd be our enemy. And then he said, "You need a girl. Oh. You need a girl." And so he'd parade me through the dorms where all the girls worked. "Want that one? Want that one?" And every night he'd come and I'd say, "No, no," "Come on," he insisted. But I never did—but he was a good guy. He was just slave labor is what he was. He worked on the railroads.

We sailed out of Le Havre in June of '45 and went back to the States. Duckor and Epstein and Fishenburg and Engler marched up Fifth Avenue in New York City with French muskets and nobody stopped us. Marched right up the street. And I got on the train, we lived in Troy, and I got on the train in New York City to go back to Albany for my month's furlough, and I was sitting all by myself.

Then we went back to South Carolina and trained for the Pacific Theater, and the 95th Division was to be one of the first divisions to go in[to] Tokyo Bay. And we were practicing assault crossings. But anyway, then they dropped the atomic bomb in August of '45. And people ask me now, "Wasn't that awful that we dropped the bomb?" And I say, "Oh sure," but I think it saved my life, you know. You know, it saved millions of lives. Yes. Oh, yes. We had combat time in Germany and we didn't want any combat in Japan. We all knew what it was, and we were scared to death, and we just—you talk about cheering. When that bomb dropped we cheered. We cheered because we knew we weren't going, we knew we were safe, we knew we were out of it.

What are these two medals here?

Well, this one's the Purple Heart—that's for getting wounded. And that's a Bronze Star which I got for courageous action. The Bronze Star is very common, you know, the Bronze Star is very common. I have a story about, can I tell the story about the Purple Heart? When my youngest son was about ten we were showering together on a Saturday night about five o'clock in a stall shower in our house, and he looked at my arm and he said, "How did you get that scar on your arm, on your shoulder?" And I said, "I got shot." He said, "If you get shot you get killed." I said, "No, no, no. I got shot in the war, but I'm all right. I got a Purple Heart for it." And I said, "Would you like to see my Purple Heart?" And he said, "Could it wait 'til after dinner?" You talk about a put down.

What happened to you after your discharge?

I got out in December of '45, put the Army overcoat on the floor of the garage, and I said, "Run over that son of a bitch." My dad was absolutely determined that his kids would go to college. And so I wrote to University of Dayton and I wrote to the University of Notre Dame to take me back. Well the University of Dayton answered me first—they said come on back. And so I did.

Now Mary Tuite was the registrar—a wonderful woman. I said to her, "What can I get a degree in the fastest." And she called me back and said, "If you work real hard you can get a degree in physics in a year and a half." And that's what I did.

Then I went to graduate school at Cincinnati, got my master's and was working on my Ph.D. when Schraut called me—wanted me to come back to U.D. and take a job as a professor for one year, and I said, "No, I'm not gonna do it, I want to finish my Ph.D." He said, "I want you back here," and so I came back, and I was interviewed by the president of U.D. and they offered me a fantastic salary, four thousand a year, or something like that. And I said, "Yes, I'll take it for a year." So in 1952 I took a one-year temporary assignment at the University of Dayton as a physics professor and I stayed 'til 1986. But I got into research. I was in the research institute, and I got into that, so I had a very, very lovely career.

Art Ensley

Arthur T. Ensley and his wife Gloria have three children. Two still live in the Centerville-Washington Township area. Ensley graduated from Central High School in Superior, Wisconsin, and shortly thereafter enlisted in the Army Air Corps. He was a pilot on a B-25, an attack bomber, in the European Theater during World War II. He flew all of his seventy-eight and one-half missions from a base in Corsica. Ensley was shot down and with the help of partisans worked his way back to allied lines. He attained the rank of captain and served in the military for twenty-three years. He then flew as a commercial pilot for about another ten years. Ensley is a member of the VFW, the American Legion, and Volabamus, an association of military pilots.

All my life I wanted to be a pilot. So I was one of those people who was blessed with getting the kind of career and profession that I dreamed about and always wanted. I wanted to be Richard I. Bong; I don't know whether you've ever heard of him. He was America's number one ace. He shot down something like forty airplanes. Well, we both came from the same school. He was a couple of years ahead of me and he lived just outside of Superior, in Poplar.

I was accepted as an aviation cadet and I was sent to Maxwell Field in Nashville, Tennessee. And I went through the training there, about two or three months. But what really made it nice was Glenn Miller. That was his last stateside assignment. And when we went out for parade and passed for review it wasn't just some old band playing with a bugle and a drum as most of them did. He put a little jazz into it, you know. We danced to his music several times. This was in the fall of '43. But anyway, that was the highlight of my pre-flight. And then I was sent to the various schools for my flight training.

From primary I went to Cochran Field in Macon, Georgia, and we flew a BT-13 or 15 something, a low wing airplane—a lot of airplane for a kid out of a Stearman to fly. I was twenty-one at the time. They put us in a higher-powered airplane—looked almost like a fighter.

Did you want to be a fighter pilot or a bomber pilot?

Everybody wants to be a fighter pilot. And everybody's working towards it. And I have to admit they took the better pilots for fighter pilots. How they rated them I don't know, but I didn't get a fighter. I got a strafer/bomber which was maybe a consolation prize, you know. Then we got our commission at Moody Field, our wings, and we were officers.

So they sent us out to La Junta, Colorado, and all through the training there the attrition rate and the fatality rate raised. So by the time we got through with our training we had lost fifty percent of them from flying ability and maybe three percent from fatalities. There were a lot of deaths coming through the training. We were trained flying the B-25. But no war time stuff, just how to fly it, take it to altitude and this sort of thing. But it was a nice airplane. Everybody liked it. We lost some crews in it but not many because we were just learning to fly that airplane. We were out there three months, I believe, and when I got that assignment I knew I wasn't going to be a fighter pilot. But I knew there was another program going—one that had a solid nose in the B-25. They had adapted it with a French 75, a French type 75 cannon.

Somebody got the idea we could use one thousand pound GP [general purpose] bombs. We could put four of them in. Then somebody came up with the idea that if the shackles were arranged right we could carry one hundred pound fragmentation bombs—all sorts of different type of armament. Then somebody come up with the idea that we can put six one thousand pounders in. It's a smaller diameter bomb because it's semi-armor piercing. It's half the diameter of the regular one thousand pounder. So they did everything and tried everything and they had that airplane loaded with six thousand pounds of bombs

When we went overseas we came through North Africa, in Talergma, but we didn't fight out of North Africa. I was sent up to a base in Corsica. All our missions I flew out of Corsica. And we were bombed and everything up there. They'd come in at night and run sneak bombs. We had our slit trenches, we'd run out and get in those slit trenches but, you know, flyboys aren't gonna dig any deep slit trenches. And one night Washing Machine Charlie [slang name for night bombers] came in and knocked out half of our airplanes. They threw basketball size bombs out of it. Boy, I tell you, it actually hit the ground and rolled. Well the next day when we got one of those attacks, all these pilots were out digging those foxholes a little deeper.

Tell me about your first mission.

Yes, it was very good. I went out with the pilot. As I say, I wasn't checked out on the bombsite so I flew missions with the pilot in my crew. Then he went home and I started flying as pilot and they gave me a co-pilot, and it went very well. This airplane that we're talking about was *Miss Mitchell.* The airplane had no name, it was a brand new airplane when it started flying. Now it's customary that the crew, or ground crew or somebody, puts the name of their girlfriend or wife or anything else on it. But anyway when I got the airplane, that's when I was married to *Miss Mitchell—Miss Mitchell* the airplane. And I stayed with her through my entire combat career.

When I first got there it was twenty-five missions and you could go home. Hell, you'd get twenty-five missions in a couple months. So they raised it to fifty missions. We were bombing up into France, all the way across Italy, and all the way down Italy. The ground forces were south of Rimini at that time, slugging their way up through the Rimini Mountains, you know. A lot of losses. In fact they were even south of Rome coming up. Theirs was a dirty job. Our job was good. We did lose some airplanes in that mid area of Italy. But all in all, it was thirty, forty, or fifty minutes to the target, drop your bombs, and come home. Well, the day I got shot down I was up to ten thousand four hundred feet. That was my bombing altitude. They were not doing well on the low altitude attacks so they made us mid-range. They tried to get us as high as possible to minimize the anti-aircraft guns and low enough so that the airplane still performed well. They had loaded them down—they were really heavy. So we bombed generally around ninety-five hundred feet, and if you got over thirteen thousand feet you weren't very efficient. That was our range. And the Jerries [Germans] and the ack-ack knew that too. I never made a mission in Italy where we strafed. As I say, the airplane just wasn't that adaptable. Now in the Pacific I understand it was pretty good. But we couldn't take that German ack-ack.

Now on a typical mission the squadron would put up eighteen airplanes. When we went as a group we'd go in multiples of eighteen. Eighteen, thirty-six, I've been on missions as high as seventy-two airplanes. Each leader had his own bombsite and you flew in formation, but each plane made its own run and dropped the bombs and then came out in formation with the other elements so they wouldn't be flying all over the sky. You'd sit out there with your box and he'd drop his bombs and you might just turn over two degrees to make your run. And when he dumped his bombs he's gonna be going, so as soon as you got your bombs out, you took your box and took off to catch him, or to get into that formation. The protection was getting all these top guns together. There's two fifty calibers firing up here, two out the side, and two in the tail. The protection was to get as close together with all that fire power and that discouraged some of those fighter pilots. My wingman would be so close to me that it seemed dangerous. I think they'd clear the wings but they would be sitting right tight in there.

We got the fighters knocked out early. But they were always a threat, and we didn't relax because they weren't a threat. The Germans just either moved the fighters out of the Italian area or whatever. We definitely had air superiority. I think they were running out of airplanes. I [had] probably only been hit by enemy aircraft, not hit with gunfire, but attacked would be the word. They'd fly through our formation, and you'd see how close your wingmen were out to each side of you. I liked this slot, I'd always fly a flight right under the flight ahead of me. We'd be right up so close that you could count the rivets and wave at the tail gunner. We stacked them up there.

Anyway, seventy-two airplanes in our flight was a large mission. But it was always eighteen. I flew two missions in a day with eighteen airplanes. Night was kind of a hectic thing 'cause the only time you'd go up at night is if you had two missions that day and something was pressing. By the time you got home it was real dusky. It was hard. We hadn't practiced much at night, you know, and hell, at the time I probably only had less than three hundred hours.

What speed would you be flying at in a plane?

I'm trying to think of what the bomb run was. I think our bomb runs were between one hundred and ninety to two hundred miles an hour. We'd take more if you could get it, but generally that's about it. You're maneuvering with a formation and you just can't make a turn here because you got all those airplanes behind you and you have to gradually come over. And when you're evading flak you can't duck out easily. You might just gradually start to turn, to feint away, and then when they start to get your range you might just pick it up two or three hundred feet. And they'd all ease up, and then you'd see the flak underneath you. But by the time you turn around they were up with you again. On some of the longer missions and on the more dangerous targets we'd get fighter cover. I never found it too efficient. They didn't have the range. We had an RAF outfit that flew Spitfires and we'd pick them up, oh, maybe thirty minutes off Corsica. But they couldn't stay with us to the target. They could probably only get into Italy and they'd have to turn back. A Spitfire is a very, very short-range airplane. And the long-range airplanes, the American P-51s and P-47s that had the capability, were being used in the war over Europe.

Could you comment on fear you experienced in war?

Well, you'd go for two or three missions and get a little bit complacent you know. And then when you got a bad mission, and a lot of your airplanes got shot up, and you got shot up, you paid more attention to evasive action. And we had certain target areas that were tough. You'd walk in the briefing room and see the target and know its trouble. We didn't get it yesterday and we're going back today. And on those missions, yes, I don't mind saying you had butterflies or bumblebees in your stomach. Anybody that says they weren't concerned, downright scared, something's wrong.

Art Ensley.

Once we had come back from Yugoslavia. It was a bad mission and we got shot up very bad. And we were sitting around having our coffee and donuts. That's the last I ever flew *Miss Mitchell* because we didn't take off on the next mission with her so that was the last time I flew her. In Corsica there's always the hills and the mountains. We were always very aware of those if we were working under a low ceiling or anything. They were a hazard to us, particularly when you're coming in at night and so on, or if we're in heavy dusk.

How about the men in your crew?

Well, we had the pilot, co-pilot and navigator/bombardier. Three up front. Then you got a turret, top turret gunner up in this position. And the bombardier's here and the top turret man is here. They were both killed when we were shot down. Pilot, co-pilot, then you got a radio operator that operates these waist guns. If you're attacked from one side then he goes to that side of the airplane, but he handles both of these guns. Then you got a tail gunner, he's also got a turret. It was a total of six men. Now, if you're on a very exacting target you get hot shot bombardiers. That's if they're really after something—then you take a bombardier with you, a professional bombardier.

What kind of a relationship did you have with the officers and enlisted men?

The enlisted men have their tent area and the officers had theirs. Usually, the enlisted men lived better than the officers because American ingenuity is just something you can't believe. They would make a wooden floor tent with a screen on it—almost like home. Whereas the officers say, "Oh, tighten that up over there," because they weren't gonna be there long. But we had a nice place to live. We went into a bombed out building and had rooms and you could say who'd you live with. I lived with a public relations officer, my bombardier, and my co-pilot lived in another area. And the enlisted crew always stayed in the enlisted area and were probably more comfortable overall then we were. But we didn't live together.

How many missions were you supposed to fly?

Well, when I first started flying it was twenty-five. Then it went up to fifty. And that wasn't bad because the fighter aircraft were being less active and the Germans weren't concentrating their ack-ack unless it was a specific target they were trying to protect. They were really in retreat going out of Italy but they were trying to make the Americans fight for every foot of the way. The ground forces had a rough time coming up through the mountains in Italy. So anyway it went to fifty. And when my crew got fifty I was trying to talk them into staying with me to fly one hundred. I was gonna fly two missions. But I couldn't talk one of them into it. Fifty missions, that's it. They were going home. That was just a difference in make-up—mental make-up. But I stayed on and took another crew, and I also used to fly the make-up crews. If a crew got shot up and there was an odd crewmember that survived he'd go on a make-up crew. I ended up with that make-up crew. I volunteered to stay for one hundred. I liked it. Really, I liked it. And I wanted to be a captain. I was a first lieutenant. Went over as second lieutenant, made first, and I was not ready to come home, you know. So you had to do your homework and get the job done real well if you wanted to be captain.

Tell me about your last mission, 'cause you say you had seventy-eight and one-half missions.

Well, I'm on my second crew and this airplane was the queen of the fleet. The engineer, the ground chief, named that airplane. And we didn't like it but we weren't going to argue with him because we had the absolute best airplane in the squadron. I started with it when it was brand new—brand new other than the flight time over. And with the combination of a brand new airplane and a crew chief, a conscientious crew chief—we'd come in with holes in that airplane and the next morning you'd never see it. We'd be up and gone again. So they'd work at night and do everything. It was wonderful. Just fantastic. Phil Ostlie, came from around Minneapolis, Minnesota. I'm jumping ahead of my story, he's the one that maintained this airplane. When he came back to the States and got out he joined the Confederate Air Force, they picked up an old B-25 scrap that they rebuilt into a new airplane. But I'm getting ahead of my story. I was on the seventy-eighth mission with a relatively new crew. We went out and we were on the rail diversion going into the Brenner Pass—that's what we were trying to cut off—anything going into the Brenner Pass. On this mission my bombardier was killed in action. Also Sergeant Knott was killed in action. Knott was in the top gunner turret. The radio operator and the tail gunner got out. The airplane caught fire—a violent and uncontrolled fire. And you went out on two conditions: if the airplane was unflyable the pilot would give them the bell and out they'd go. But you didn't have to get a bell. If the airplane was on fire, if that dude is burning, which ours was—just infernal—you would get out of it anyway you could. I'm glad you brought this up. How'd I get in this airplane, how'd it get on fire? There's so much to tell and it's just like yesterday. Now this wasn't *Miss Mitchell* that was on fire. As I said when I came back from my seventy-eighth mission we'd been shot up pretty bad. And so the crew chief worked hard and a couple of days later we had it patched and ready to go. Now they did everything except service it, they loaded it with bombs, replenished the fifty-caliber ammo for the machine guns. And that morning before the mission, that's all I had left was the service thing. They brought the service truck up to pump us full of gas—nine hundred and seventy-four gallons. I'll never forget it. In the meantime we were being briefed. We came out in the jeep, dropped our crew, went to the airplane, and as we walked under the airplane there was some black goop coming out of this thing. Well, they had just been working frantically to get the airplane back in service. But evidently there was a hole left up in the upper section of the fuel tank. And we didn't know it leaked until it was filled full of gas. That's the first time they filled it after they'd gone through this major repair. It didn't look quite that bad, but it was seeping enough so that you wouldn't fly the airplane. So anyway, we had to leave the airplane and go with the spare airplane. Well, now this [the plane they had to leave] was the queen of the fleet. It's like going from day to night leaving your own airplane. You'd have flak suits, everything perfect in it, even the needles were perfect. Anytime you'd take off and coordinate something or change rpm, everything was just absolutely perfect. So we went down and got this spare airplane. Now the spare airplane was kind of the dog of the fleet. They'd use it as a spare, but they'd also use it on training missions or if they wanted to go on a trip to Rome or something like that they'd use those airplanes. So this is the plane we went to. And I'm thinking—be off the ground in about twenty minutes. So we hit the spare airplane, and went through it, checked it all over. And although we were not very happy with it, we got it ready to go, cranked it up, made take off time, got our formation behind us and so on.

But anyway, one incident that happened, and there's so many things that could happen I couldn't tell them all to you, was the airplane had flak suits—like a lady would have an apron in the kitchen. Only big flak suits, I mean maybe eighty pounds. And it was a bib over the front of you, a bib over the back of you, and they had snaps up at the shoulders. Naturally if you had to get out, you're parachute, harness, and everything was under that. So these shoulder snaps worked all right and I got my flak suit on and I was so rushed I wasn't sure if I put my parachute on or not. I was young and foolish. I flew some missions in real hot weather and I said, "Oh, I'll get into the parachute if I have to," but I didn't always really follow the rules. I think that my friends knew me for that. But I got into this flak suit and it's got a snap just like you have on a convertible top—a heavy canvas top. Well, I kept trying to connect those at the chest and I couldn't get them to work. So I just took those two straps, brought them around and tied them in a knot, and then I put another knot in because it kept loosening up. So I was literally tied into my flak suit. That was the only unusual incident on getting that old dog in the air. The airplane flew rather well but we weren't pleased with it, you know— this oil pressure would be up here and this one would be over there, and it just wasn't the queen—*Miss Mitchell*. So we went out on the mission and it was a rail diversion going into the Brenner Pass. These were vital. The Germans at this time were trying to pull back as much as they could to save it. They had a lot of fight left in them yet down there and we tried to knock [out] these rail diversions in the Brenner Pass to keep it out of service so they couldn't retreat up out of there. Anyway, we were on this mission to go in and knock out one of those rail diversions, but they really had it protected and we had intense anti-aircraft fire. When we started our mission approach, enemy fire kept going even through we're dropping our bombs. We stayed with it and got our bombs off even though the airplane was all beat up. And then about the time we got our bombs off, the airplane caught fire. It evidently had leaked enough fuel down into the fuselage, from the fuel they had put in the wings, so we got a collection of fuel in there and it was a hideous thing. So anyway, the two guys in the rear bailed out—the tail gunner went right out the back and the waist gunner went down the bottom and out. The man in the turret, when I looked back, was completely engulfed in flames. He couldn't wear anything but a chest type parachute. It's a harness and you have a pack, oh, about the size of a three ring binder, you'd snap on you. Well, he had to get out of the turret before he could put his parachute canopy on his harness. The last time I saw him he had it on one side and he had dumped the door out the bottom. But that's the way they found him in the wreck. But it was living hell in there.

How did you get out?

How did I get out? I don't know. The Lord looks out for you sometimes. But right in the top there's a way the crew chief could open that up and get out to clean things and so on—get to the top of the airplane. It's definitely not an escape hatch. And I have to give credit to my co-pilot. When he looked at the situation he pulled the releases and popped that hood. I didn't have to ask him what he was doing. He was going out the top. And you're not supposed to be able to do that because you have all of these obstructions here. Those propellers are turning, there's antennas going from the tail to the main part of the airplane, and one of those antennas could just cut you in two if you hit that in the slipstream. Well anyway, he'd made the decision to go. He stood up on the pedestal and faced backwards, and I was trying to control the plane. He stepped on my hands a couple of times, but we didn't need any briefing because it's never been done before. There's no procedure to do it. But as he started to hit that position I pulled the airplane up almost to a stall, pushed him, and popped the stick forward. And he said later that he went out of that airplane and it seemed like he had to look way down to see it. Now how did I get out? I have to say I must have done the same thing. I must have climbed up and fought my way out of that. But in the process I was beat up more and I think we had another secondary explosion in the airplane and that might have helped blow me out of it. But I can't say whether I had supernatural strength to get out of it. The Lord was looking out for me because I didn't get cut up by the propellers, or cut up from these top guns, hit by the tail, or hit by an antenna. It's just a miracle I came out of it. But I was knocked out. I lost my consciousness. And I opened my eyes and I saw the horizon and it passed me. And it passed me again, this way. Now in an airplane, if you are in a spin, as you come around you see the horizon, this is the way you right your airplane from a spin. I thought I might be still in the airplane. So, I was reaching for the controls to get with the spin, you know but there were no controls there and I realized I was out of the airplane. I've never been able to determine or never been able to figure whether the seat was with me or whether it was that flak suit that had been giving me trouble, but something was back there and I got rid of that. And I thought, "Oh boy, did I put my parachute on for this mission?" And I reached down and I felt, and I had the parachute. So all I had to do was pull this little release, a quick release, which released these two chest snaps, these two shoulder snaps, and these other two shoulder snaps, and my flak suit would have come off in two pieces. Well, I told you I had it tied with two good knots. And by this time I had been all burned. I was burned from my goggles down to my hands which were burned, the skin was off of them. And I went to untie those knots and it was just almost impossible. I had no feeling except pain, I couldn't tell you where the pain was, but you know what a burn is like. So anyway, I took that first knot and got it out, and there was the second knot and I got that disconnected. Well, normally to get out of that suit you pull this chest cord and it takes these harnesses off. By untying the flak suit, it came up in the back, up in the front, I went on through it, and it caught me in the neck. Well, that didn't really knock me out, but it kind of dimmed me a little bit, you know what I mean? The lights just kind of go down and come back up again. So I pulled my ripcord and I felt that thud. And oh what a welcome thud that was. And I was oscillating because I evidently had my chute open and I was on an angle as the chute opened and stopped my rapid descent. It was still moving down pretty fast 'cause I had a little momentum, I swung like a kid would swing on the canopy as it came down across the ground and up. And on the second oscillation, I was worried how am I gonna stop this oscillating, boom, I hit the ground. And I hit the ground extremely hard. I fractured three vertebras, they were compressed, compression fractures. Anyway, I got on the ground and fortunately there was this farm hand who was definitely anti-German and he waved to me. I didn't know what he meant, but in Italy I think that means come with me. I assumed it was and I was gonna come with him. In the meantime I could hear them shooting at us. We were in the riverbed. We had about three or four little sectors of the river which was not running at a high level, and we had to wade through those to get off the shore. And he kept telling me to come this way, and I was gonna go that way. And I got up and I ran and carried my parachute with me. I got up on the other bank and one of the batteries that shot us down started using ground fire at me on the ground as I was running. I was about done. I was in extreme pain and he kept wanting me to rush and come. But I can't do it. No. And so he took the parachute off me, covered it with a bunch of stuff, and I went a little further with him. He was alert enough to realize that I was spent. They put their hay up with a pole up through the top and it keeps it from the weather. Evidently, this was being partially used so it had some loose hay and he covered me up with that hay and I laid on my stomach in there. I don't know whether I laid there for hours or days. We figured later on that I probably was in there the rest of that day, that night and the next day and they probably got me out the next night. But I dirtied myself and I was bloody, I was hurting, but I laid in that hay and literally slept. I think I must have passed out or gone to sleep. Later he came and got me out.

They were partisan fighters—they were the Ozapos and the Garibaldis. Fortunately, I was with the Ozapos. This was northern Italy. They were still fighting for ground up there, even during the war, you know. These were the anti-Communists. The Garibaldis were the reds, they wore red pants and shorts and red wherever they could put it on, red scarf. The Ozapos wore green, they were the Christians but they were partisans too. And I was with them. They were both against the Germans, but they weren't very friendly to each other. One was supplied by the Communists and the other one was probably supplied by some of our special forces. We had all kinds of secret stuff going on up there. We went to a house and they cleaned me up and I got something to eat and early the next morning they came and got us again. And they brought a bicycle for me to ride. They asked me if I knew how to ride. I know how to ride a bicycle, let's get out of here. Well anyway, my hands were in such bad shape I couldn't do anything but lay my hands up on the handlebars. And you know their bikes have a handbrake to slow them down. So I laid my hands up on the handlebars and peddled along with them, very slow. I didn't have much strength left. I immediately worked myself into just a terrible sweat. And we had a couple of little hills over into another valley and as we went up I found I couldn't do it. I had to get off. So one guy pushed my bicycle up while I walked up—and they even kind of gave me a pull to help me up. When we got on the other side I thought, "Oh, this is fine, I won't have to pedal." So I was ready to go again and they said wait. They knew what was coming and I should have known, but I wasn't very alert that day. One of them went on downhill and he cleared everybody out of the way. So over the hill I went and down on that bicycle with my hands up here on the handlebars—worthless. And I'll tell you, that was a ride. It kept picking up speed. It actually scared me. Not as much as the airplane did, but it did scare me. Eventually we come to the bottom, and then we did the same thing again. There were three ranges that we covered and I felt I was gonna just lay down on the side of the road. I was just completely exhausted. And we came to a place where the fingers of the mountains come out and then we went over this range, and this range, and over this range, and finally there was a pretty good road. So they said to get down and wait. And along came an ox in the road and a wagon. They expected me to follow along on that bicycle, and they had my tail gunner who had been shot through the legs, and he couldn't walk, in the wagon, along with my co-pilot in that wagon. So evidently, they'd coordinated this thing and we met them at this rendezvous. I said, "Keep the bicycle," and got into that wagon. It just moved at a snail's pace. But anyway, they took us up into a safe place and we went through all the routine of the escape evasion. And we stayed out of harm's way, and didn't get captured, and eventually walked out. I stayed there about a week and I was in severe pain and I had to receive medical help for my hands. I couldn't use them, they were wrapped in bandages. I couldn't do any of your personal things or anything like that. It was horrible. And after about seven days, I was gone for forty days, we ran into these special service people who were back there causing trouble by helping the partisans. And there was an English mission back in there too. And there was some English major, a pain, but a nice Englishman, and this individual was a pain. So we got a party together and we were going to walk out. Well, I took my tail gunner and he says, "I'm coming too." I said, "All right," and I took him out and walked around a little bit, but he couldn't do it. So I had to leave him back there in the hands of friendly people. So I left him and I had my co-pilot with me and two others from those special services. This English major, the American first lieutenant, and we two walked out across the lower portion of the Alps and down into Yugoslavia. And we walked into that area and ran into some more partisans. They were just not very nice. They took care of us, got food for us, but they were more on the Communist side. I didn't know this. I was just a kid, I didn't know what a Communist was from a traffic cop, you know. But I knew they weren't friendly to us. They weren't real friendly like the Ozapos. So anyway, we got in touch with a transport outfit in a RCAF Dakota. That's an RC-47, who's gonna come in and pick us out. By this time we had quite a number. So they flew in, and I think there were twenty of us. And they flew in and flew across this makeshift runway and, I'll be darned, somebody parachuted out. I said, "Oh no, they're here to get us and they're going to bail out. Something's wrong with the airplane." Well, their procedure was they flew over the runway, one guy bailed out, looked it over, got on his walkie-talkie, and told them if it was OK to land. So they come in and landed. So anyway they got us out. I was shot down November 18, 1944, at about eleven o'clock, if I remember right, in the morning. I remember the altitude as ten thousand four hundred feet on my altimeter. And from that time until we got into Florence, Italy, where they had moved our Air Corps headquarters, I was walking out.

But on New Year's Eve I was sitting in a bar with my co-pilot in raunchy, mismatched, mis-sized clothes and uniforms ordering a drink. It was New Year's Eve day. They flew us in and we were gonna get drunk. And we'd been eating horrible stuff and neither one of us could hold a drink. But we covered four hundred and eighty miles.

I never took advantage of the GI Bill because I stayed in the military. They promoted me to captain even though I didn't fly my complete second mission. They took good care of me. In fact, I was a captain when I was shot down, but I didn't know it.

Robert Corbin

Robert Corbin went through the Dayton public school system and graduated from Fairview High School. After graduation he worked at the Rike-Kumler Company until he enlisted in the Army in December of 1942. Corbin finished basic training and then went through OCS and was commissioned a 2nd lieutenant in spring of 1943. He joined the 84th Infantry Division and subsequently earned the rank of first lieutenant in the artillery and fought in the European Theater until he was captured after thirty days on the front lines. He was a prisoner of the Germans for one hundred and forty days. After the war he attended Otterbein College in Westerville, Ohio, married his wife Ede, had two daughters, Lynn and Carol, and then worked for Rikes from 1953 to 1979. At that time he went into the food business (catering) as head of Restaurant Management Company. In 1976 he ran for the Ohio State Legislature and was elected to the House of Representatives where he served until the fall of 2000. He is an active member of Normandy Church, American Ex-Prisoners of War, and the American Legion.

When we landed on Omaha Beach, we drove down to Cherbourg, picked up our supplies, and then took off and went to Liège, Belgium, and dropped off our supplies. There were twenty trucks and a jeep and a weapons carrier to take care of any breakdowns we might have. I was the officer in charge, and there was a soldier who was a maintenance non-com for the battery in the last vehicle. This would be sometime in October '44. It was a tremendous experience. Then we went back and joined our outfit, the 84th Division, at Chartres, a famous cathedral city in France. From there we were sent up into the front lines in northwestern Germany—up near Aachen.

This is your first combat? What kind of feelings did you have?

Well, my job as a forward observer was to usually be with the officer in charge. It was thrilling, exciting, scary. Damn right I was scared. I was in the front lines for about thirty days before I was captured. My job was directing fire. One night we supported an attack on a pillbox late at night. So I had to wake up my gunners and have them fire out there. The day after Thanksgiving in '44, I was going up to relieve my counterpart and they asked me if I would go by and pick up the padre at regimental headquarters. He wanted to go up to the front lines. So I drove over, picked up the padre, put him in the front seat, and we went up to this little town of Geronswieler. The OP [observation post] was a schoolhouse and it was located in a little cul-de-sac. But we missed the turn and so we drove down to the end of the street. There was nothing out there except fields, so we turned around.

Just as we were getting ready to start back down the street the Germans threw a mortar barrage at the town. And a mortar landed right there, right behind me, three feet away from me—just missed me. But it didn't go off. And I've often said I'm glad I had the padre with me. Anyway, we went back and found the cul-de-sac and finally got to the observation post. When we got there I contacted Lt. Hendrickson.

Our observation post was on the third floor of an old schoolhouse. As Hendrickson took me up the stairs he pointed out the base points and registration points that were used to direct fire. In other words, the base point is five hundred yards left of the target, and they can then, with a mathematical azimuth, shift the guns over there. Then once we see where the shells are landing we can direct them in on the target. And as I'm going up the stairs I notice these holes in the building—didn't think much about it. When Hendrickson left I'm up there alone and all of a sudden I hear this terrible screeching sound. Now a German 88mm howitzer shell screeched when it came at you. Not all shells did that, they'd whistle, but the 88mm screeched. Anyway, I hear this terrible screeching sound while I'm on the third floor and the shell goes through the second floor. I can tell you that's a little disconcerting. I didn't mind shells going over my head, but when they're going under my feet that bothered me.

I was there about thirty minutes or so and the mortars started again. By this time the roof of the schoolhouse was gone—nothing but lath up there. And I spent my whole day running up and down stairs between the shelling of 88s and mortars. We did a little firing and chased the Germans around, but nothing of any great consequence. That night we were sitting around eating down in the basement of the schoolhouse, and one of the infantry officers came in and commented that they had just captured a pillbox fifty yards in front of our forward elements.

Now you've got to understand where we were in western Germany. We're in the middle of the Siegfried defensive line the Germans built—like the French built the Maginot line. And we're fighting in and around those pillboxes. I was intrigued by the idea of getting in that pillbox. And I thought, if I can make it the Germans can't shoot at me yet I can shoot at them. So, I asked to be allowed to go. The next morning about 6:30, they sent a runner back for me and we started out to go to the pillbox. As we were starting out he says, "Lieutenant, do you mind if we take a short cut because there's a sniper on the trail." I said, "Of course I don't mind, I don't want any sniper shooting at me." So, we went ahead and started across that open area I mentioned earlier. We're actually walking out into this gap in our lines. And we started up this little hill, and the runner says, "I'm not sure we're going the right way. Let me go over and reconnoiter." He goes up over the hill and there's a hell of a firefight takes place up there. I can hear machine guns and rifles, and so on. Well, that's the end of the runner.

About two minutes later we walk up over the hill and there are three guys, a machine gunner and two riflemen, and the pillbox was still over there about seventy-five yards away. We got about one third of the way to the pillbox and out of the dark somebody comes and says, "Hands oop, come out." Now it's funny what goes through your mind in a situation like that. But prior to being in this situation, I'd read the *Stars and Stripes,* and they were commenting that German soldiers wanting to surrender knew only the American phrase, "Hands oop, come out." I thought this guy wants to surrender to me. So I reached for my 45, and I'm just ready to point it at him when he shoots me. Now, he doesn't get my skin, but he rips my jacket. Like somebody rips a hole in your jacket. Then I realized that he wasn't going to surrender. That he had other things on his mind. That's how I was captured. And since I've got my 45 in my hand, he indicates I should get rid of that. Which I did then. Then they took us back to this pillbox. This was the 26th of November 1944.

What happened to you then?

They took us back to the division headquarters, and we were kept there for four days while they interrogated us, and then we were taken to a command post which was the artillery headquarters for the entire western front for the German army. There was a thirty-foot long situation map that had every unit, English, American, German, and French from the North Sea to Switzerland on it. The two officers who were there spoke English and they were very interested in practicing their English. One officer had been a Luftwaffe pilot, Messerschmitt pilot, who had been shot down—had his legs shot up and couldn't fly any more. He was on the staff there. The other one was a fellow who had gone over to Germany to visit his parents in 1939. He was from Brooklyn and they wouldn't let him come back. The other guy had gone to St. Joseph's College in Philadelphia. They both spoke very good English.

All of a sudden a staff car pulls up and a German general came in. He was a colonel general which was the second from the top general. There was another officer with me when I was captured. He was a first lieutenant at that time and I was a second lieutenant. They took him into another room and interrogated him. They were interested in our delayed fuse shell. We had a shell that has a 15/100 of a second delay. It hits and has an initial explosion. It gets inside the metal or the wood or whatever and once it burrows in there there's a 15/100 delay and then it explodes. It's a tremendous anti-tank weapon. And so they were interested in that. We were then taken to a schoolhouse where we slept overnight and guarded by a member of the Volksturm, an old German man, and then we were joined by a couple of 8th Air Force sergeants. We were in Krefeld at the time and then they took us to Dusseldorf which is thirty miles away. We got there by hitchhiking. The Germans didn't have transportation for us so our guards would take the four of us, get on a truck, and we'd ride five or ten miles in that truck until it was going the wrong way, and we'd get off. Then we'd ride five or ten miles on another truck. Finally we got to Dusseldorf. When we got to Dusseldorf we found that the 8th Air Force had bombed it the night before so the roads were all messed up with dud bombs and wreckage. You couldn't drive in the streets at all.

And this one sergeant had an Air Force jacket that had a swastika going up in flames and fourteen bombs underneath it. And so as we're walking through Dusseldorf, people are spitting at us, cursing us, shaking their fists at us, and so on and so forth. We finally said, "Turn that jacket inside out," 'cause we were concerned about getting shot in the back. The next strange thing was they put us on a streetcar to go across the Rhine River. Here's our military trying to get to the Rhine River, and when I got there I rode across on a streetcar.

We were there for several days, and then they took us to Fallingbostel which is up near Hamburg in northern Germany. We were given food like jerky and black bread on the two-day trip. And then they put us on these boxcars. Fifty men to a boxcar, and the conditions were very bad. The latrine was a hole in the floor in the corner. And there were fifty men to a boxcar. These boxcars were only two-thirds the size of our boxcars. So, it was very crowded, very cramped. In order to sleep at night we devised a system: for two hours half the men would lay down while the other half stood up. At the end of two hours the other way around. And that's the way we slept. During the days you'd have one group of people with their backs to the wall, two other groups of people with their backs to each other in the middle. And that's the way you sat. Instead of two days it took four days. And we didn't have any food for a day and a half.

When we got to Fallingbostel there were five thousand French prisoners there. We went in a little officer's area they had there, which was segregated, and there were some half a dozen Canadian and English officers there that had been captured. Altogether there was about eighteen or nineteen of us, I suppose. We were there until the 20th of December, and the Germans bragged about their success at the Battle of the Bulge, which took place on the 16th. They said they needed to get us out of there 'cause they had to make room for all of the prisoners they were bringing in from the Battle of the Bulge.

So we got on a train; there were thirteen or fourteen of us, with about a half a dozen German guards. And we traveled all the way across Germany through Berlin, through Stettin, into Schubin, Poland. It was about a four-day trip, and we went to Oflag 64. We got there on Christmas Eve.

We arrived in Oflag 64 and we were immediately impressed with the organization inside the camp. This was an organized prisoner-of-war camp with a senior American officer and a staff, and we controlled the area inside the barbed wire. In other words, the Germans were on the barbed wire, but everything inside was American. On Christmas Day we conducted a security program there because everybody who arrived had to be cleared for security reasons—so the Germans couldn't slip spies in. And you were cleared by having someone you knew personally, or someone you'd served with, or someone who lived in your hometown, or had served in your outfit vouch for you. And they would post the names of the new arrivals. And then that person would come around and talk to you. And once they talked to you, then you were cleared. A friend of mine, Herb Hayes, who I'd gone to high school with at Fairview, came and cleared me.

Now the prisoners who were at the camp before we arrived had been given a Christmas card they could send home to their families. So at the bottom of his Christmas card he wrote, Bob Corbin walked into camp today. Well, his wife figured out that Bob Corbin was somebody from Dayton. So she got on the phone, the letter arrived the 12th of February, and called every Corbin in the phonebook until she got my mother. And that was the first time my mother and father knew I was alive, because up until that time I'd been listed as missing in action.

And then the Russians began to move through Poland. The Germans decided they were going to keep us as hostages, so we were ordered to get ready to move out, and each one of us was given a Red Cross parcel and any cigarettes that hadn't been used. We built little backpacks for ourselves and took some blankets. It was zero, six inches of snow on the ground, when we were ready to march out. We were sixty miles east of Stettin and they told us we had to walk the sixty miles to Stettin.

So we started out and we would walk fourteen or fifteen kilometers a day or more—I have here a record of all the stops we made. And we ended up walking five hundred and fifty-four kilometers. Now the third day out the Germans took their guards and moved them away. And we were all left alone for one whole day with one German officer. So five hundred of our guys took off over the hill. But I didn't take off. I talked to my colonel, and he advised me to stay put because he thought there was safety in numbers—far better than risking your life in the Polish countryside. So I stayed and the next day the guards came back. They'd gone back and ambushed some Russians, and then came back and picked up their duties.

Instead of walking towards Stettin, as we had originally planned on doing, the Germans took us up to the top of the Oder Estuary—to the Baltic Sea to Swinemunde. We ended up walking five hundred and fifty kilometers which is about three hundred and fifty to four hundred miles. This is now January, February and going into the first week in March 1945. We walked for forty-two days.

How many of you were there in this group now?

Well, there were fifteen hundred that started out, five hundred finished, five hundred escaped, and five hundred went by boat and train to other German camps because they were too ill to go on any farther. After we got into Germany, I drank some water out of a pump one day and got amoebic dysentery and I was sicker than a pup for two weeks. I lost twenty-five pounds in that period of time. I was defecating seven or eight times a day—every day. All you do is just walk out of the column, walk over in a field, relieve yourself and come back. The guards are not too happy with you 'cause they had to wait for you.

One night we noticed some people going by in sleighs with Red Cross parcels. So our officers immediately contacted the Germans and they gave us one Red Cross parcel for each two men. Dallas Smith, who was a close friend of mine, and I shared everything. At night and during the day you buddied up with another fellow. Our food would be some black bread, boiled potatoes, ersatz coffee and ersatz soup morning and noon. Ersatz means fake. And Smitty and I had a system whereby we would take our bread, and we had some margarine, and one guy would cut the bread, spread the margarine on the bread, and then hold it out to the other guy to choose which piece he wanted. So that you don't have one guy accusing the other of stealing the food. At night we slept together, we shared our blankets. We took our shoes off and put them down at the corner of our blankets to keep the blankets tied down, and we would sleep together in the blankets, in hay mounds, in barns, and in churches. Usually we were in barns and large communal farms in Poland. So, Smitty and I were very good friends. This guy was a schoolteacher, he was the epitome of what people refer to as a sissy. But he had shin splints for half the time we were on the road and he walked every bit of the way, never asked for any help or anything.

Finally we got to Stalag 138 in Hammelburg. This is March 6th, or 7th of '45. When we got there they had about one thousand officers who had been captured in the Battle of the Bulge. So, we were back up to fifteen hundred again. There were also thirty-five hundred Serbians there, so it totaled about five thousand people in camp. The conditions were terrible, the food was terrible and there was very little of it. And that was the first time I ever had lice. Now lice is a horrible thing. Every night before you go to bed you take your undershirt off and you pick off as many lice as you can so you can get to sleep. But still they're crawling on you. It was really bad.

On the 27th of March a very important thing happened. An American task force was there to try to get us out. General Patton's son-in-law, Colonel John Waters, was a prisoner of war with me. So Patton organized a task force of two hundred and sixty-six men, sixty vehicles, armored vehicles of the 4th Armored Division, and they fought their way back to Hammelburg. Many people say it was to get Colonel Waters out. He had been shot, under a flag of truce by a German soldier, right in the base of the spine and was in terrible pain. That evening the Americans chased the Germans away and seven hundred of us walked out of camp.

So we got on the half-tracks and we started down the road. Then my half-track conks out—won't run. Finally we caught up with the column and someone came running by with some bread they found in a German PX truck. So I ran up and grabbed two loaves of bread and came back. Later we ran into a German roadblock. So Colonel Paul Good, who was our senior American officer, held a council of war and said, "There's gonna be a hell of a fire fight here in about an hour. If you don't have a gun you better walk back to camp."

I'd always had the theory that if you got outside the barbed wire there was a fifty-fifty chance you could make it if you used your head and were careful. So, I went to Jay Drake who was from Michigan, and I asked him if he'd like to go over the hill with me, and he said, "Yes." So, I went to Smitty and he says, "I'm going with you." So I said, "Come on." And we started out. As we walked through the woods the firefight began behind us. We could hear the shells hitting the trees behind us. All of a sudden we heard a machine gun. So we creep forward and we could see, two hundred yards ahead, this German machine gun sitting there waiting for us. So we decided that we would hide out that day until all the activity ended.

About eight o'clock that night when it got dark, we got up and started walking until finally we came to the edge of the woods about a half a mile from where the Germans were with their machine gun nest. There we laid down and we actually fell asleep until we woke up at midnight. All of the sudden a fog developed and we just walked out under the fog—got away from that area. Then we walked about another five miles, found a group of trees where we could hide and sat down. We had a little something to eat out of the rations from the tankers, and we also had the bread that I had grabbed.

We knew there was a road, a river, and a bridge nearby. The bridge was only two hundred yards away from where we were, but we knew we couldn't walk across the bridge because there were German soldiers on the bridge. We figured maybe we could find a boat to cross the river. So, we waited 'til it got dark that night and we started walking out. We walked to within fifty yards of the road and we saw a whole regiment of soldiers walking down the road. When they passed we ran across the road and got down to the river.

Naturally, we couldn't find a boat so we fashioned a raft for our clothes and our supplies out of two logs. We took our Polish overcoats off, made a raft with them, put the supplies on, and took our clothes off. Smitty jumped into this river, and it was about twenty-five yards across and about five feet deep. It was a mountain steam—colder than blazes. Anyway, he takes the provisions across, and then we grab our clothes, and we start across. Eventually we all made it.

There was a cliff we were climbing up on the other side and when we got half way up we stopped and had some bread. We'd gotten some bacon in a can from the tankers, so we took that bacon and spread it on the bread, and we thought it was like cake—it tasted great. When we got up on top of the cliff we started walking and it started raining. So we figured we needed to find a building. We eventually found this abandoned house that was all boarded up. We couldn't get in, but behind it was a shed, a little shack, like a garage. And it had a ladder and a small place above we could climb in. And so we climbed in, took the ladder up inside, and we were there until we woke up about 9:30 in the morning looking out on a beautiful mountain valley. While we're looking we saw German soldiers about two hundred yards away recapturing some of the Russian prisoners of war that had escaped.

When they left we started back up into the woods, and right behind this little shack was a box that the Russians had looted from the PX full of candy. So I grabbed it, and while I'm trying to run up the hill, I get about two-thirds the way up the hill, I discover I can't go anymore—I'm exhausted. But eventually we got up to the top of the hill and we found this bunch of fir trees out in the middle of the field and we decided to hide out in there. Now this is our third day.

And the next three or four days are spent in virgin forest type territory where there're no people around and we're just walking. Well we walked and walked following the compass that we had and we walked toward the artillery fire. But we always stayed in the woods, we only walked at night, and we never came out in the daytime. Later we heard this tank-like vehicle moving down the road, but it's over a hill and we can't see it. I want to go up and see whether it's an American vehicle or not. But Jay says, "No, no, stay here. If you go out there you're liable to get captured."

But I started anyway. I had only gone about ten yards, crawling on the ground, when a German staff car with three or four German officers in it, four or five Germans on motorcycles, and a truck with a dozen other Germans in it comes right to that spot that I was headed for. And they were there for about fifteen minutes. I was really sweating. But they never saw me and they eventually moved on. By that time the tank had also gone.

By that time it was so dark we couldn't see each other and so we crouched down on the ground. After awhile we just got up and silently walked away. The only person we actually ran into the whole time we were escaping was a German civilian with a big gunnysack on his back. He says, "Morgen" and we say, "Morgen, Morgen" [morning in German]. And he went one way and we went another.

Then we climbed up a hill and found a thicket of pine trees and went to sleep. When we woke up at eight o'clock the next morning, within fifty yards of us, a troop of fifty German soldiers armed to the teeth were walking by us. That night we walked another two miles and we found a barn. We climbed up in the hay mound of the barn, went way back in the corner of the hay mound, put the straw up on top of us, and went to sleep. At six o'clock in the morning we heard the farmer and his two kids getting the feed for the stock. They're about ten feet away from us. But again, we were under-cover and they didn't see us. They got their stock, their feed, and just went back downstairs.

We stayed there all day—'til nine o'clock that night. We had no food, we were out of food, and we were in pretty bad shape. Finally, we went down and took some potatoes out of the barn, peeled and ate them, and started walking again. We were so sick and so under nourished that we could only walk two hundred and fifty yards in fifteen minutes. You know normally you can walk a mile in fifteen minutes. But we kept on going, and we finally ran out of woods. We were in the main river valley at a place called Asschafen-berg.

And we could see down over the valley, we could see this road out there, and there were American vehicles going up and down the road. "My God," Jay and I said, "We made it." Smitty, the old pessimist said, "Naw, those were captured at this Battle of the Bulge; the Germans are using them." I said, "Well the road goes this way and trees go that way, let's walk down there and see if we can't find out whether we made it or not." So we did. We got about fifty yards to the road and a big two and a half ton truck goes by with a big white star on it, and we knew we'd made it.

So we ran down to the road, and remember we're in ten days or better growth of beard, Polish overcoats on, apparitions if you ever saw one, and here comes two officers in a jeep. And we're saying, "Hey, guys, here we are—we made it." "Who the hell are you?" they said. "Get your hands up." We said, "We're escaped prisoners of war, we got back, we're just escaped pris-oners-of-war." They said, "Oh, they been looking for you guys. There's an engineer headquarters about a half-mile down the road. Go down there—they're set up to take care of you."

And so we did. We walked on another half a mile down to the head-quarters, and they were prepared to take care of us, and then we made it back to the American lines.

How long were you in captivity then?

One hundred and forty days. The interesting thing about this is that when we got to this location we had been in the American lines for two and a half days. We were thirty-five miles behind the forward elements of the American army. But we got there and we made it because we were careful. We were three of twenty-five that escaped out of the seven hundred or more that tried. What happened to the other ones, I don't know.

First of all, we had to delouse ourselves and then burn our clothes. And the only thing they had were some tropical uniforms that were in a ware-house there. They wanted to take us to a hospital, and we old macho guys thought, "Naw, we'll go back—we don't need to go to a hospital." But we should have gone to a hospital. It was April 6, 1945, and it had been a nine-day trip. It took us nine days to walk and we covered about fifty miles in that trip.

And so we then went back to what is called the reverse repo-depo route. Repo depot is replacement depot. Those are the outfits that bring replace-ments and supplies up, and so we were to go back when the trucks turned around and went back. We'd ride back with them.

Every time we got to another place and they found out we were escaped prisoners of war we were treated like heroes—they'd give us another PX ration. PX rations are candy, cigarettes, toothpaste and soap, and shaving gear. Then we went to the city of Worms and slept in the mayor's house. And then we got on a train and went to Paris, checked into the BOQ hotel there and ate at the BOQ. The night after we'd eaten at the BOQ, we weren't filled up so we went over to the Red Cross at the Mayflower Hotel and had some coffee and donuts. We were sitting there at the bar and mentioned to the bartender that we were escaped prisoners of war, and how much we appreciated the Red Cross and what they'd done. And a man said, "I'm the director of the Red Cross here— we'd like to hear your story." That's about it. I wouldn't take a million dollars for the experience, but I wouldn't do it again for a million dollars.

Will Frazee

Will Frazee was drafted into the Army in January of 1943 and served with the 69th Infantry Division in Europe as a rifleman. He was in the service just over three years with sixteen months overseas. He attained the rank of sergeant. Frazee and his wife Barbara are the parents of three children. After the war Frazee used the G.I. Bill of Rights to earn his bachelor's degree and a law degree from Ohio State University and later an M.S. degree in economics from Columbia University. Frazee worked as an aide to the mayor of Kettering, Ohio, but in 1958 moved to Centerville where he still practices law. He's a member of the American Legion, Post Five.

Would you comment a little about your life prior to your military service?

Well, I was born and raised in Dayton, Ohio, went through the Dayton public schools and graduated from Parker Co-op in 1941 with a major in tool and die. Then I became an apprentice, an apprentice toolmaker, in a General Motors plant which happened to be a war plant located in the northern fringe of Dayton—in Vandalia at Arrow Products. Arrow Products was making a convertible pitch propeller and hub for the P-51.

When did you go into the military?

I went on active service in January of 1943. First I went to Jefferson Barracks, Missouri. And this was January, you have to remember, and Jefferson

Barracks was an old, old army camp perched on a bluff above the Mississippi River. And it was so damp and so cold that even the marrow of your bones was cold. That was a miserable experience in basic training—to be in hutment at that old army camp. The hutment had lumber sides up four feet high and then on top of that was a tent.

There I had an opportunity to volunteer for airborne. And after I finished basic I went to Westover Field in the 881st Airborne Engineer Battalion. Airborne was all volunteers, they had a very high esprit de corps. It certainly was in contrast to what I experienced in the infantry. It just seemed to be an exciting thing to do. I liked being in an all-volunteer outfit. I thought that would be good and I thought I would experience some interesting combat in the airborne because they were quite active. Also you got to fly overseas instead of taking a boat because the B-17s that they were flying overseas would have airborne troopers in them. So you got to fly to England instead of going on a surface ship and risking the German subs.

There's paratroopers and gliders. Which group were you in?

Slightly more than half were glider troopers—I was a glider trooper. I was not what we called a jump man. I picked gliders. Flights in gliders were part of our training. The flights were terrifying. It was a CG4A glider manufactured by WACO in Troy or Piqua—I can't tell you which. But it was a fabric glider and it had aluminum spars. The front hinged up so when it was in position the air pressure of gliding held it shut. The only way to get out of that glider was to walk to the rear of the tail section where they had omitted some spars and you simply stepped out, the fabric would give way and you would fall out of the glider. Actually, the front of the glider was like a clamshell. That's how you got in, but you could not get out that way. If you had a smooth landing, like on an airstrip, then everything worked, you know, then the front came back up. But if you were airborne, you could only get out by going to the rear of the glider by falling through the fabric. The glider was supposed to hold eight troopers, but if you had a jeep in the glider or another piece of engineering equipment like a small grader or something of that nature then you had to reduce the number of troops

Well, we were getting ready to go overseas, we were in the final stage. Then out of the blue came orders that I was to report for a program called Army Specialized Training Program (ASTP). And so that was quite a lark, but I was only there nine weeks. Then they decided they didn't need twenty-seven thousand engineers and linguists and they sent us all to the infantry as buck privates to start over.

Then I was sent to Camp Shelby, Mississippi. It was late spring of '44. At Camp Shelby we were back in hutments. I was assigned to G Company, 2nd Battalion, 272nd Infantry Regiment, 69th Infantry Division. Well, I trained with them until we left for overseas at the end of October in 1944. I went overseas as a private and in France I was promoted to PFC. I was a rifleman. I was a rifleman in a rifle squad, of a rifle platoon, of a rifle company, of an infantry rifle regiment. It was rifle all the way. They said take care of your M-1 and it will take care of you.

We were in a convoy of ships so big that as far as you could see to the horizon it was all ships. We could not see the edge of the convoy it was so large. It swung south of the Azores in an attempt to avoid German submarines. And when we got south of the Azores which is a little off kilter as far as getting to Southampton, England goes, there were submarine attacks and we were ordered below. And we heard all of these depth charges going off and we hoped that that old freighter could sustain that because we didn't see any possibility of getting up on deck if one of those hit. It took us nineteen days to get over to England

Well, when we got to England we saw our first bomb damage because the warehouse area of Southampton was mostly unroofed and the docks were beat up. We boarded trains and we went to Winchester, England, and were quartered in hedgerows in Nissen huts. Winchester is in southern England, the famous Winchester Cathedral is located there. We were there through Christmas of '44.

When the Battle of the Bulge broke out they took about twenty percent of our personnel and sent them over as replacements. So we were reduced by about twenty percent in personnel and firepower and people who had trained with us. When we got to France they replaced those soldiers with repo-depo people—the replacement depot people. And they sent us cooks and bakers and truck drivers and gasoline tank fillers and a little bit of everything. These were people who scarcely knew which end of the gun the bullet came out of. And so we took those people under our wing and tried to teach them as much as possible because we were going to have to rely on them when we got in combat.

Anyway, we went to Le Havre where we debarked very crudely—at Le Havre that is. We went over the side of that ship on landing nets and climbed down the landing net into an LCI. And the LCI took us there. A few people fell from the landing nets and didn't land in the LCI and those were the first men we lost. They were either drowned or crushed. This was early January of '45.

When we got the division ashore we were put in cattle rack semis and taken to a place near Soisson, France, and they said. "There's a rest camp there and you're going to be in the rest camp." When we got there, there was nothing but a muddy hillside where the quartermaster had thrown tents off into the mud and we had to set up that camp. We had to erect those tents to have protection. It was bitter cold and very windy.

Then toward the end of January, around the 20th, we rode 40&8 boxcars up to a quartermaster truck company in Belgium which took us up to the line, the front so-called, in Belgium. And we relieved the 99th Division which had been shattered by the German onslaught in the Battle of the Bulge. They were down to about a regiment and a quarter of the normal three regiments—so we went into the line and replaced the 99th. We put three regiments in place of a regiment and a quarter, which shows how heavy a build up, was going on in the Battle of the Bulge at that time. This was very late January, probably up to the 25th, 26th, or 27th.

This was our first combat. We were supposed to replace them at 4:00 a.m. in the morning but they were substantially pulled out by midnight and so we took over and in my regiment, by 8:30 in the morning, forty-two men were dead. These casualties were due mainly to German snipers. We were well trained and well equipped but we were combat green. And as a result some men, thinking themselves out of range and being out of normal range, fell victim to German snipers. There was very little artillery fire—although it did claim a couple of people. There was heavy mortar fire but there was no small arms fire at all. So they were lost in various ways. I think it was the penalty of being green troops and assuming too much.

Will Frazee.

How far were the Germans away from you?

Well, they were in the Siegfried Line and from our front we could see the Siegfried Line. We could see the pillboxes, we could see the apertures in the pillboxes. I don't know, a half-mile or something like that, maybe a third of a mile. And there was a gravel road there which was called the International

Highway—a fancy name but not much of a road. And that was the border between Belgium and Germany, that road—the International Highway, so called.

I was frozen stiff for a number of reasons. We had winds of fifteen to twenty-five miles an hour, it was sub-zero, and we had been instructed to heavily dub our combat boots to waterproof them. So we had put on all sorts of this greasy substance called dubbing which did indeed waterproof. The problem was it also penetrated the leather, made the leather very dense, and made it a thermal bridge from the outside temperatures to our feet and to our toes. And having no galoshes at that time to help insulate us our feet were frozen and we were frozen most of the time. The weather was horrendous. It was as much a problem as the Germans. We were losing people to trench foot and we were losing people to frostbite.

What were your emotions at this time?

Well, I think you wondered if you were going to make it. The Germans were awfully good soldiers and certainly had a lot of experience compared to us. Although I will say this, the 69th Division was reputed to have expended more live ammunition in training than any other unit. They were emphasizing that before they sent our units over. And so we had a lot of training sessions with live fire where we would move forward under live fire or we would move forward behind artillery. They did a magnificent job of training us at Camp Shelby. The camp was horrible and the living conditions were miserable—it was full of snakes and chiggers. If you could count on your body four hundred chigger bites you were eligible to go to the hospital. Less than four hundred chigger bites you weren't. But the training itself, in expending ammunition and in putting us in realistic situations, was truly magnificent.

That helped a lot but it didn't overcome our inexperience—we were still green troops when we went in the line. But I'll tell you, you learn quickly or you're not there. For us it was three to four weeks I suppose. Remember, you're highly motivated to learn. We found that the army was very poor about bringing up hot food, they just sort of didn't. They gave us combat rations, mainly K rations. We found that they were always willing to bring up ammunition and we had plenty of it. We found that specialized things like white cloaks to help conceal us in the snow were not available. They were available to the Germans and the Germans wore them but we didn't have them. We found we had no galoshes. We found that a heavily dubbed combat boot was a tremendous conveyor of heat out of our feet and into the air. We found that it was very fatiguing—the heavy packs we carried. I opted for a pack board. I had to carry the squad cooker and the nested aluminum pans in return for getting the pack board. So I had it a little easier, but the conventional packs were not really well designed.

What about fear when you're in combat?

I think you slightly get used to it. Of course the thing you learn is to keep firing whether you see a target or not. Lay down heavy continuous fire. That was the best thing to keep Jerry's head down and to get Jerry in the mood to pull out and retreat and give up what they were defending. So we had to learn that, but we learned it. We'd been told that before, but we lapsed, you might say, when we actually got into combat.

But we did learn to lay down heavy fields of fire and would only save three clips and stop firing when we got down to three clips. We each had to carry two bandoliers of ammunition and each bandolier contained eight clips. And the ammunition came forward to us riflemen in the form of bandoliers. You sling the bandolier over your head, it crosses your shoulder, it is made of cloth, and it contains eight filled clips of M-1 ammunition—thirty caliber.

Then we went in an attack mode and we were preparing to attack the Siegfried Line. We crossed this gravel road called the International Highway and my rifle company walked right into a minefield. And a couple of men stepped on mines and one medic attempting an evacuation stepped on a mine.

So we were ordered back out and we turned around and we tried to put our feet in the same footsteps we had made coming in. And we had an ignominious retreat back over the International Highway and into the woods. So we were there two days and the Siegfried Line was breached about fourteen miles north of us by another outfit that swung in behind it. And finally we were able to go through the Siegfried Line unopposed. And so we regrouped on the other side.

Our first billet inside the Siegfried Line was in a little frame constructed German house that didn't amount to a hill of beans—but it had a basement. So we went into the basement and we found that the concrete wall facing toward Belgium was about eighteen inches thick. And the concrete wall towards Germany was only about six inches thick. And they had stepped the basement windows so that you could fire out at an angle. We were astonished at that. This little innocent house had been converted into a strong point.

Were you in combat until the war ended?

Until the war ended. It ended a little early for my division because we were the first to meet the Russians at the Elbe River. We made the historic link-up. We had captured Leipzig and had advanced past Leipzig and gotten to Torgau, at least a group of four men, a patrol, had gotten to Torgau. The body of the division was still back about eight or ten miles. And we made that historic link-up on the 25th of April. So the war for us was over on the 25th of April. We had met the Russians.

What's the difference for the combat infantryman between fighting in a city and in the countryside?

Well, I would say street fighting is about twenty times more scary than in the open countryside because there's only a certain number of doorways to get into. They can rake those streets with machine gun fire. Yes, it's pretty much pure terror fighting in an urban environment. All the buildings are masonry, therefore if a bullet happens to hit a building, it glances off and it's still active, you might say.

From time to time we would run into tanks, but that was rare. The big thing we would run into would be the 88s. They had ringed their cities with these weapons. Even relatively small villages, like five thousand people, would have emplaced 88mm anti-aircraft guns. And these anti-aircraft guns could be leveled and could send time-fused shells right into us.

So we developed a technique where we would get in place, but stay hidden. And at the crack of dawn, when we could just begin to make out each other and not cause any unnecessary deaths from friendly fire, we would get up, we would throw off our pack, some men even threw off their helmets, and we would race as fast as we could toward these emplacements. We did this because they could only cut the fuse so short, and therefore there was a protective zone from the emplacement out to where they could cut the fuse the shortest. And we had to get up into that protective zone as fast as we could. I would say the protective zone would be, perhaps as much as three hundred yards. They couldn't cut the fuse shorter than that. If we got in that zone we were pretty safe. We wouldn't carry any bandoliers because you had plenty of ammunition in your belt and bandoliers would flop around and all. And we would go up over the emplacement and we would stand there and pour our fire into the emplacements, and frankly kill off all the crews—you know. And it worked almost every time. And those enemy crews, even though they were armed with small

Will Frazee today.

weapons, would never come up to the bank and oppose us. Well, we were usually in overwhelming numbers.

We were strafed once—in my entire combat experience we were strafed only once. And when I say we, I don't mean that any bullets landed near my outfit, my rifle company. But the plane came and was intermittently hopping and strafing and going like a roller coaster. And when he went over us we had no problem with it, you know, because he was not firing—he was going up when he went over us.

When you met the Russians at the Elbe River, did you actually shake hands with them?

Oh, absolutely. They were supposed to stay on their side of the river. That was the diplomatic agreement as we understood it. We were supposed to stay on our side of the river. Well, we went into these towns. I was in Mockrehna which was about eight miles short of Torgau. We would go in and we would take the best houses for our billets, skipping the other houses because there were plenty of houses in regard to our number. Well, the Russians came pouring over the river and they took the houses in between the ones we had rejected. So their company street was our company street. And it was something else.

We found a totally different culture in the Russians. Totally different— as soldiers. They were, shall we say, unrestrained. They had fought the Germans for longer than we had. They had come back through their ruined cities and villages, those the Germans had leveled with demolition [charges] and burned out, and had even leveled the walls with demolition [charges]. They had hatred, a burning hatred of the Germans that we did not possess. And so they treated the Germans very, very badly. They even treated their own troops, we thought, very badly. What happened on our company's street was a Russian officer came back about two in the morning and didn't know the password. The Russian sentry insisted he give the password. The Russian officer didn't know it and couldn't give it. So there was this confrontation, the sentry would not let him pass. So the Russian officer pulled out his side arm, an automatic pistol, and shot the sentry dead. If that had happened in the U.S. army that officer would never have gotten out of Leavenworth.

And also they had these huge cast iron kettles on wheels, they used steel wheels, and they used to build a fire under them. And they would go out in the middle of a pasture with a sledgehammer and knife and they would hit a cow in the head and hit it repeatedly with a sledgehammer until finally the cow would go down. They would then strip the hide off, they would take the entrails out, they would cut up the meat and throw it in this big cast iron cauldron—whatever. Those things must have been eight foot across, you know, eight feet in diameter and they were at least six feet high—probably seven. They would build a fire under it and they would fix their food. Many of them had German army equipment—cartridge belts, and many of them had trousers. They had cotton tunics of the Russian army, but trousers of the German army. They truly lived off the land. We had an elaborate supply chain, you know, we got cartons of eggs. Even when we were at the front we received pork chops, we received all sort of things like that. They lived off the land. They had no discernible supply chain at all for anything.

After V-E Day in May we were told we would go to Marseilles and we would be shipped through the Suez Canal and we would be part of the invasion force for Japan. But of course that never happened with V-J Day coming. So I finally came home and was discharged a PFC. That's not much of a military career, to go in as a private and come out thirty-seven and a half months later a PFC.

Did you take advantage of the GI Bill then?

Yes. I didn't go back into tool making even though I loved the trade, even though I was proud of being an apprentice toolmaker. Still, I thought, the army's gonna pay for this, you know, this country's going to pay for this. And I used every day of my GI Bill. Every single day of eligibility. I went to Ohio State. I took a bachelor's degree in business, I took a law degree, and then I went to Columbia University in New York City and took a master's degree in economics. Then I became a senior research analyst because of my degree in economics. I became senior research analyst for the city of Columbus. And I was in that position for a little over a year.

Then I went to the village of Kettering and I was there sixteen and a half months. Then I moved to Centerville in 1958. I practiced law here and I got married in '49.

How do you think being in the Army changed your life?

Well, I would have been a toolmaker for General Motors all my life and that's not a bad life. And I certainly don't know whether I improved it or not. But I would say that toolmakers have a higher standing in society than do lawyers, you know. They say that there are two lawyer jokes, all the rest are true.

Robert Flohre

Robert N. Flohre and his wife Melba are the parents of eleven children, twenty-five grandchildren and two great-grandchildren. Flohre worked for forty years as a linotype operator for the Miami Valley Publishing Company in Fairborn, Ohio. He was a machine gun operator with the 398th Infantry Regiment and the 100th Division in Europe during World War II. He was wounded in France and is a member of the Order of the Purple Heart (Chapter 31), the VFW and the American Legion.

*Bob, tell us a little bit about your
life prior to military service.*

I was born at St. Ann's Hospital in Dayton, Ohio, on November 27, 1925. During my school years there was nothing-special going on. For my high school I went to Parker Co-op High School. I had two brothers and one sister—Elvera, Bill, and Jack. My mother passed away in '34 when I was nine, so I was raised by my dad, a welder at Standard Register, with help from my aunt and uncle—Rosella and Oscar Shaw. At Parker Co-op I was in the printing division when the war broke out in '41. I was in my sophomore year in high school and never thought I'd have to go in the service. But time rolled on and I had sixteen credit points and at the time that's all you needed.

So, they took me into military service at the half-year—on March 21, 1944. I was drafted out of high school and only went halfway through my high school senior year. Before that I played football, but Parker never had football so I played sandlot football. I tore my knee up in November of '43, and when I went for my Army physical it was all wrapped up. They made me unwrap it thinking I was trying to fool them. But they found out that I wasn't and they drafted me anyway. I couldn't bend my leg all the way back when I went in, but I could march. They took me anyway.

Then, on the 21st of March, I was drafted. And I was sent to Fort Thomas, Kentucky, for the pre-induction. I was inducted there and then shipped down to Camp Wheeler, Georgia, where they put me into a heavy weapons company. I did infantry training and that included the carbine, M1 rifle, 81mm mortar, machine gun, bazooka, and pistol. We had training for all of that. Oh yes, and gas mask drill. That made us cry. My biggest thrill though, being only eighteen, was when they taught me to drive a two and a half ton truck.

Did you ever get a pass?

I went to Macon, Georgia. We usually had our afternoons off on Saturday, and when we were able, we went to Macon. Once I almost got in trouble there. I got on a bus and I went to the back of the bus. And, you know, in those days the black people had to sit in the back of the bus and the white people sat in front. And of course, I didn't know that being from the north. That bus didn't move. And finally the lady I was sitting with said, "You better go up on the other side of the white line or the bus will sit here all day." They had a white line at the halfway point of the bus, so we had to go way up front. And when we got off I mentioned to the conductor, I said, "That's not right. They're just as good as we are." That was in the spring of 1944. Probably in April—April or May '44.

I finished basic training there in July and got a fourteen days' leave at home. Parker Co-op's graduation was the first week in August. My father was to get my diploma in absentia which he was happy about because he never got a diploma, but I came home in uniform and I got my diploma at the old NCR auditorium.

Anyway, from there I went to Fort Bragg, North Carolina, and was assigned to Company M, 398th Infantry Regiment, 100th Infantry Division. I was sent there because President Roosevelt, sometime in '44, decided not to send any eighteen year olds over as individual replacements. They thought it was too much stress on them to not know anybody, so they sent me to the 100th Division and we took advanced training there. We mostly took machine gun, mortar and bazooka training. When it got around October they shipped us up to Camp Kilmer to go overseas. And we left, I think it was, on the 6th of October 1944, from New York to England

We boarded on the 6th and we hit a hurricane about halfway over, and we were sicker than dogs for a few days. It took us twenty-one days to get over there, but finally we went into the English Channel and then to the White Cliffs of Dover. We were there for just a few hours and all of a sudden the ship made a turn to go back out of the channel, and they came over the loud speaker saying we were gonna be the first full division to land in Marseilles, France. And we were ordered to take all our division patches off of our shoulders, which we all did 'cause they didn't want anyone to know who was coming in. We thought we were going to England for more training, but we didn't do that, we just went back through the channel and headed south. Eventually we went past the Rock of Gibraltar, and headed right into Marseilles, France.

How many ships were in your convoy?

I don't know, but as far as I could see there were ships. And the ship I was on was called the USS *General Gordon*. It happened to be the flagship

Bob Flohre.

that General Burroughs, our commander, was on. And as far as we could see, there were ships everywhere—destroyers, aircraft carriers, everything. We went through the Mediterranean, and we ended up in Marseilles. To get on shore we had to cross sunken ships. But this was not an assault, no, no. Marseilles had already been taken. They were already up around Raon ' Tape, France, which was north of Marseilles a couple hundred miles. But that's where we had to land. It was not an assault, we could never have done that. We wasn't in assault boats or anything and we'd been on the ship fourteen days. Two weeks. We just landed there.

First, we had to go on a ten mile hike out to the fields to bivouac, put our pup tents [up] and so on. First thing we heard was an airplane, like a piper cub flying over the top saying, "Welcome 100th Infantry Division." The German propaganda was good, they knew we were coming. We bivouacked there. We got there, I'm trying to think, around the 21st of October. And we had some details there, we had to go down and unload ships in the harbor. We had to unload shells and food and stuff like that. We didn't do much training there, but we had to clean all our weapons and everything.

And then they put us on 40&8 boxcars, that's forty men or eight horses, and they shipped us out towards Raon ' Tape. They shipped us up to that area around the 1st of November of '44, and we relieved the 45th Infantry Division. I was in the 398th Regiment. And we went into combat right there at Raon ' Tape and over Moyenmoutier. There are lots of mountains through that area. A lot of walking through the mountains. That was our first bit of combat. Then they moved us up into this area around Wingen—that was way up in the mountains. And that's where I came down with frostbite pretty bad. But we just kept going anyway. We just went back, got treatment and then went on. This was the battle of the Vosges Mountains. This is our first major conflict with the Germans and, here again the 398th went into Raon ' Tape, down into Moyenmoutier and right on through it up into the mountains.

But our particular thing was being in the mountains. So, when the Germans came out of Moyenmoutier we were sitting up there waiting for them.

What was your job?

I was part of a machine gun squad. We took turns firing the gun. We had seven men in the squad. If I recall, one was the gunner who fired the machine gun and carried the tripod, the second man carried the barrel, another man carried the water for the cooler and a box of ammunition, and then you had three or four men who carried ammunition. This is a heavy machine gun. It's got the barrel surrounded by water that cooled the barrel. The water would circulate to cool the barrel down. It used a hose from our water can up into it to cool it. I fired it sometimes and other people also fired it. We all knew our jobs, and we took turns because that tripod got heavy. That was our first major encounter with the Germans.

And then our next major encounter was the Maginot line. The Maginot line, of course, was the French defense against Hitler that they thought could ward off the Germans. But it didn't work, they surrendered. The Germans came around the back of it, and they surrendered without a shot being fired. So our division was actually the first division to ever strike at the Maginot line. We had to go through Reyersville in this battle and they had a lot of pillboxes around the Camp de Bitche. We had several major battles here at Reyersville.

The gist of the whole thing was to take all of the pillboxes. There's pillboxes everywhere. And we were successful in doing this, but we had to bring the combat engineers in to blow them up. A pillbox is a concrete bunker. We would call our combat engineers up to blow the door off so we could get in. And these pillboxes went from one to another. This is pillbox six, then pillbox eight, and pillbox nine. In pillbox nine, they had this turret—and that turret used to come up and then go right back down and we could never get it. Pillboxes are heavily reinforced—it's probably about three foot thick concrete. They all were connected and they had tunnels. They had tunnels underneath from one pillbox to another and that's the reason we had to blow them up. We had to get in there—get inside. Often we had to have the engineers come up and help us. We'd start down them rows, and they'd start shooting at us, and because we didn't want to lose anybody we just blew them up. We actually used dynamite down in there and blew them up down there. Some would come out bad—some come out pretty bad. But this turret kept coming up and going down. We finally ended up getting our tanks up there on top of the hill, and finally they figured out how to get it—that is, how long it took for the turret to go up and then go back down. So, they fired at it and that's how they finally stopped it.

And Berlin Sal called us the bloody butchers of Bitche because of what we did there. Our division was famous for this major battle here at Bitche, France. At Bitche, France, I was made a battalion messenger on account of my feet—they didn't want me out in the weather all the time. I don't know if being the messenger was as bad as being a machine gunner, 'cause you never knew where you was going. One time I got through the lines, me and another fellow, and we got awful close to the Germans. We could hear them talking, but we didn't understand them because it was at night. So we just laid down and started crawling back. When we got back it was the next morning.

Were you scared—frightened?

Well, you just do what you have to do. I mean, I was just eighteen, well I was nineteen by this time, and you just didn't think of it—didn't think about it. We just did it. We lost our first man, our lieutenant, back around Moyenmoutier. You just did it without thinking, you know, you could always be killed. I had a carbine shot right out of my hand. I had it leaning against a tree while we were digging in and they started shooting. As I reached for it, the shot just took the barrel right out of my hand. See, the machine gunner and the one who carried the barrel had forty-five caliber pistols. Otherwise we carried carbines.

Our next major battle, after we went through the Maginot line, occurred when we went into Germany. The Battle of the Bulge was going on. But we had our own battle down where we were, I forget the name of it, but we had a battle too although it was not like they had up there.

And when it got towards April, we went off again from Bitche, France, and went across the Rhine River. Our next major battle was at Heilbronn, Germany, which started around the 2nd of April. And it was another major battle in an industrial town—like the city of Dayton. We had to go across the Neckar River. We went across there in assault boats. The engineers, combat engineers again, had the boats and they took us across. We had to do that because the Germans had the bridges zeroed in and they could easily blow them up. We'd try to build a bridge and they'd blow it up before we could get across. So we had to go downstream and go across in these boats.

It was at this point that we lost more men in battle than any of the battles we were in. As you can see, we were only in combat about six months, all total, when it ended. But this particular battle was bad because we had to go across open fields towards factories and the Germans were really laying for us. I had taken ammunition and messages over and came back across the river.

Well, we had a medic by the name of Apple, and he told me, after I ate, to urinate. He said, "How was it." And I said, "It burned." He said, "That's what I thought, you've got jaundice." That was the end of my combat. I went back to the Grand Hotel in France sicker than a dog two days before Roosevelt passed away in April—and that's when my combat ended. When the war ended, I was in the hospital.

Were you wounded?

I was wounded in the battle of Bitche, France. There was a little town there where I had to take messages. But the Germans started shelling with their 88s and I was hit. It wasn't bad, but the shrapnel hit my arm, my right arm, and I bled a lot. This happened when me and the first sergeant were heading for a building and the Germans started shelling with those screaming mimis—the 88s. We hit the top of the steps and something hit me in the front of the head and something hit me in the back of the head, and we both ended up down in the basement. Now, how long we were there I don't know. But we got up and we both were bleeding pretty good. I had a pretty good cut here on my hand, but that was the extent of it. I was really lucky there. I didn't get it too bad.

This map is the whole overview of all our battles, with a few of the commendations that we received. It's an overview of the whole outfit and all the battles that we were in. As you can see, we were only in for six months. I forget how many days we had straight combat. After I retired in '87, I'd told my son-in-law about my medals, and he made this case for me. Then one of my daughter-in-laws knew I hadn't received all my medals. So she knew Representative Tony Hall, and she talked to him about it. This is the Purple Heart and this is the Good Conduct Medal. It was in '92, I believe it was, that Tony Hall got my other medals for me at VFW Post 2800—they had me down there. This blue one is a Combat Infantryman Badge. That was worth ten dollars in pay. That's what we got for being in ground combat with the armed enemy. Ernie Pyle's the one who's behind that. You know Ernie Pyle. The only people who have that are the combat soldiers. Nobody else has that. They can get the other medals but not that one. That one there is strictly for combat veterans. And here's my dog tags. This is my 100th Division patch. After the war I went into the 6th Corps to work on linotype for the 6th Corps newspaper for several months. Then I came home on furlough, later went back over, and they changed the constabulary which was the occupation forces, and I was in that group until I was discharged in August of '46. This paper here is the order for the Purple Heart. This one over here is a presidential unit citation for the battle of Bitche, France, up by the Maginot line. This is a prayer book my grandmother give to me and I always wore it over my heart all through the years. And later on, my one son went in the navy for four years and he wore it also. And this is the Bronze Star which I received back in '92. That was given to me along with the Purple Heart and the Good Conduct Medal. This ribbon is the European Theater with the two major campaigns on it and this is the Victory Medal, and this is the Occupation Medal.

What are these things you brought?

Well, this picture was taken on Memorial Day of 1999 in a Springboro, Ohio, parade. I'm a member of the color guard for chapter 31, the military order of the Purple Heart. And that's my wife, Melba, with me—we were in that parade down there. And this is the *Stars and Stripes* newspaper of Tuesday, May 8, 1945, when the victory was announced. I laminated it because it was protected that way. This is also *Stars and Stripes*, Wednesday, February 2, 1945, before Hitler died. There's quite a bit of interesting material in there.

When were you discharged from the service?

I was discharged on August 26, 1946. After that I came home and met my wife at my aunt's wedding. She was a bridesmaid and I was the best man in my aunt's wedding. That's how I met my wife. She lived next door to my grandmother. She was from New Orleans and she was there with her aunt and uncle. And we got married on February 12, 1949. We just celebrated our 50th wedding anniversary back in February. Then I took a refresher course on the GI Bill in linotype down in English, Indiana, and then went to Miami Valley Publishing Company in Fairborn, Ohio. I put in forty years there as a linotype operator, foreman, and supervisor. And I retired in '87. We are the parents of eleven children. We have twenty-five grandchildren and two great-grandchildren as of this moment. Our oldest grandchildren are twin boys. Our youngest grandchildren will be a year old next year, they're twin girls.

Do you still meet with your old comrades from your 100th Division?

I've gone to two conventions in the past few years. We went to one in Pennsylvania, and then we went to one down in Charlotte, North Carolina. And we went to Charlotte, North Carolina, last year and had a side trip down to Fort Bragg, North Carolina. Our old barracks was still there. We got to go see our old barracks in Fort Bragg. If you want to go back a few steps, when the war ended in Europe I went back to my outfit and we took training to go to the Pacific. We were scheduled to go to Le Havre, France, come home to New York, go home on furlough while our ships went through the Panama Canal and then be picked up in San Diego. And we were headed for the Pacific. But, it ended. We'd been in on the invasion of Japan.

How did you feel about the atomic bomb?

I thought it was justified. You know, a youngster like me at that time, we were glad because we knew no more of us were gonna die. We had lost so many men. I don't know of any from my outfit that are still living. My sergeant, my first sergeant, he just died a couple weeks ago, so I don't know of any of them that are still living. I go to the conventions and there's nobody I know. This little card I'm holding in my hand is my membership card to the 100th Division association now. I received this in '45 as a regional member of the society and it says, "The society of the 100th Division, Sons of Bitche, France." Now, we call it Bitche [bitchy]. This was given to us because of Berlin Sal—she thought we did something we shouldn't by blowing up some of their people down in those pillboxes. That's our society now. We're still active but our members are going down of course—but we're still active.

Clarence Evans

Clarence Evans was born and raised in Tuscaloosa, Alabama, and enlisted in the Army Air Corps where he served from May of 1943 to September of 1945. He was a navigator on a B-17 operating out of Foggia, Italy, and participated in thirty-four sorties over enemy territory. After the war he attended the University of Alabama under the GI Bill of Rights, taught school for a few years and then worked in marketing services with the National Cash Register Company of Dayton, Ohio, for thirty-three years. He and his wife Polly have four children—three daughters and a son— that all live in the area.

Could you tell our readers something about your life prior to the military?

Well, I was born in Tuscaloosa, Alabama, a little suburb of Tuscaloosa called Alberta City. And I went to school there and started first grade there. During the Depression my father and mother lost their home and we had to move out into the country where we could have a cow and pigs and raise corn. We did that and survived it. And about two years later we moved back to town into Northport, Alabama, and there I went to grammar school and high school. I finished the eleventh grade on May the 19th of 1943 and I was already eighteen years old. I was scheduled to be drafted.

I had never been in an airplane, but some of the guys had flown before and they really liked to fly. So they talked me into going with them out to the airport to take the entrance exam for air cadet training. Lo and behold, I was the only guy out of the bunch that passed the entrance test. So I wound up going into the Air Corps. So I finished the eleventh grade May the 19th and I was sworn into the air cadet program on May the 21st, two days later.

Where did you do your basic training?

My wife's brother, Horace, and I were the only two that went to Fort McClellan, Alabama, to be inducted into the army. And we rode a train from Tuscaloosa, Alabama, to Biloxi, Mississippi. And that's where I went to basic training—at Keesler Field in Biloxi, Mississippi.

There we fought the skeeters, we learned how to march, we learned how to take orders, and discipline, and things of that nature. And sand, that place was decked out in hot sand and it was hot weather. But anyway, we left there to go to what was called College Training Detachment—CTD

What kind of work did you do at CTD?

Well, the basic thing there is you fly an airplane for the first time. They had little Piper Cubs and that's the first time I'd ever been in an airplane. There they separate the sheep from the goats, if you know what I'm talking about—about flying. And so anyway, we took courses in math, trigonometry, weather, code—we had to learn the Morse code—the ditty dot, ditty dot, ditty dot. And a lot of people kidded me because I had a southern accent and I spoke very slowly, and these guys from Minnesota and New York with their little fast tongues, they kidded me. They said, "Man, you never will pass that Morse code. You just never will make it." But I did. In the CTD we were required to get ten hours of flight time. And we had an instructor with us—a civilian instructor. But anyway, I didn't get to fly my ten hours because I got fed up with it. In the last flight I made with the instructor we were supposed to put it in a tailspin. And there we were going down, the ground was getting closer and closer and closer, and he said pull it out. And I felt like if I pulled that thing out it would tear apart. I just froze—I could not do anything. And he cussed me for everything you can think of about pulling that thing out. He finally let me go as far as he could and then he pulled it out himself. And then he cussed me all the way back to the airport about that. I didn't fly anymore and I didn't want to be a pilot. That was my last flying.

Anyway, we went from there to Santa Ana, California. That's where they test you very rigorously to classify you either as a pilot, co-pilot, navigator, or bombardier. Now, if you don't pass the exams, the physical exam, the mental exams and all the scholastic stuff you're washed out. And then you have a choice of going to gunnery school and being a gunner on an airplane—if you still want to fly. I kept a diary all the time from 1943 'til I was discharged, and you can look in that diary and you'll see that I made a comment that I didn't want to be a pilot. I'm the youngest guy in my class and I didn't even finish high school, and some of these guys have taught trigonometry and they know all about navigation, so I knew good and well I can't be a navigator. I hoped that they would make me a bombardier. So I couldn't believe it when they classified me as a navigator.

That was on a Friday we finished, and on Saturday we were to graduate—get our wings. And some of us were fooling around out on a tarmac playing touch football. I was running out to catch a pass and I stumbled and fell and caught myself on my hands on the pavement. Shortly my left wrist begin to hurt. So I went to the barracks and got in the bed. And the only comfortable way I could get would be to hang that thing off of the bed. Well, the first thing that next morning I went on sick call. They x-rayed it and I fractured a bunch of little bones in my hand. They put it in a cast from my fingers up to my elbow and I had to stay in the hospital. That was my home for nine weeks. And so my class got ahead of me and went to Hondo, Texas.

When I got discharged from the hospital I went from Las Vegas to Hondo, Texas. They had a big sign there that said, "This is God's country, He's the only one that will have it." And that was just about true too. But anyway, I graduated there and was made a flight officer. I was the youngest one in my class and I just barely made it, I barely made it through navigation school, as far as grades go—but I passed. And there was, oh, several hundred of us in the class, and a certain percentage of us made flight officer which is a step below second lieutenant. So I was a flight officer when I finished there.

Then I went to Plant Park, Florida. On the 15th of September of 1944 I joined my crew. This was a transition school where you joined a crew. You form a combat crew there. And then on 30th of October of '44 we went to Hunter Field in Savannah, Georgia. That's where they issued us a brand new sparkling clean B-17. And that's the way they got new airplanes into combat. They issued it to a crew that's going overseas and you fly this brand new airplane over there to be in combat.

So we flew from Hunter Field to Fort Dix, New Jersey. Later we left there and went to Bangor, Maine, where we were issued our orders. Now we weren't allowed to open our orders until we got halfway to Newfoundland— outside the continental United States. And we opened them up and we were ordered to Italy, to the 15th Air Force. But we got stranded in Newfoundland, iced in, and couldn't go anywhere. So we just ate pancakes and played poker, cribbage, threw snowballs, and ate pancakes and popcorn. The weather was too bad. The runways were frozen over and they had no way of defrosting them so we're stuck there for thirty days.

Eventually we finally left Newfoundland and went to the Azores—to Legens in the Azores. This was in November of '44. And on the first of December we hit Africa. Then we flew across Africa to Tunis, and then over to Gioia, Italy. And that's where the commander of the 99th Bomber Group came down there and got us and flew us to Foggia, Italy. And that's where I did my work with the 15th Air Force—at Foggia, Italy. That's in the heel of the boot. There's a Lake Lucerne right in the heel of the boot and we were up a little bit from Lake Lucerne.

What did you do to get combat ready?

All that was done to get the plane ready was to put a lot of sheet metal in it to make it combat ready. And that's what they did before they put it into action. They also painted it. See, it was a bright silver, I guess it was the aluminum it was built out of. But it was nice and shiny. A lot of people think that a combat crew flies in the same airplane all the time, but they don't. I flew in thirty-four sorties, or missions, and I flew in sixteen different airplanes. Some of them two or three times.

Why wouldn't they keep the crew together?

The crew stays together, but a lot of times certain conditions demand change—maybe they're short of navigators. And so to keep the same crew from flying together all the time they would pull a navigator off, or a pilot, and put him with another group to fly with. But every time that your crew flies, when your pilot and co-pilot fly, I would fly with them—we'd fly as a crew. So that's the reason it wound up that I flew about fifteen or sixteen missions with my crew and the rest of my missions with other crews.

I guess I was too young to be scared at first. I couldn't go through it today without being scared, but I really wasn't afraid. And one thing that sustained me while I was over there was the night before we left Tampa, Florida, I went to a

Clarence Evans.

Southern Baptist church. They had a special program that night for young people, and I was the only soldier that was there that night. And everybody was nice to me. And they sang a song there that night, "Never Alone," that stuck with me through the whole thing. I knew the Lord wouldn't leave me alone, and He would sustain me and He did. I had some close calls but I never was what you'd call really afraid except once or twice. But I did everything I could to help the Lord to protect me. What I was anticipating was flak and fighter opposition. This was the latter part of the war, December of '44. That's when I flew my first mission. It was the 99th Bomber Group, 346th Bomb Squadron, B-17s and this was our crew in January of 1945.

When you go on missions there would be twenty-eight airplanes—four groups of seven each. And when you go over a target, seven airplanes would be going across it and then seven more trailing, 'til all the twenty-eight airplanes went across. The lead airplane, and each of those four groups of seven planes, had a bombsite and a bombardier. The other planes had what was called a togglier. All you do would be to watch the lead plane and the very second that he dropped his bombs, the togglier hit the trigger and dropped our bombs. The whole squadron's bombs would be dropped almost simultaneously. This was my first mission and what I was anticipating was a lot of flak. That's when the shell bursts up there and the flak out of that shell goes out at pretty rapid speed. And it could knock your airplane out. We've seen them go down often due to the flak. And then also there could be fighter opposition. But it so happened that at that point in time the Germans had lost so many of their oil refineries through bombing and so on, they didn't have enough fuel to really get many airplanes in the air. As a matter of fact, I flew thirty-four sorties over there and never saw an opposing fighter plane except over Berlin. That's the only time I ever saw enemy fighters.

This ledger I have here might be interesting. I wrote over here the date of the mission, where we left from, the number of my mission, and what was the target. For instance, this was Linz, Austria, and this is south Blechemmer, Germany. By the way, that was the hardest mission, the worst mission I was on. I'll tell a little story about that later. And this is the B-17 that I flew in. I actually flew in about sixteen different airplanes.

A lot of times you go over a target and we had a device on the lead airplane called a Mickey. And it could sense the target through clouds. But some of the areas that we bombed, for instance in Vienna, would have to be a visual target because we didn't want to destroy the city if it could be prevented. So sometimes it had to be visual. And if it was cloud covered we had to take an alternate target and find one we could go over and visually bomb it. But anyway, as the navigator, I had to keep notes on this, and my prime responsibility was to make sure I knew where that airplane was at all times in reference to the ground. I had to know in case we developed a problem of some kind and had to go back home; I had to know where we were in order to give directions how to get back home. Also a lot of the cities over there had anti-aircraft guns and we had to dodge those cities—we had maps that showed us where the flak was. Then when we got back to our home base the navigator would be interrogated by the security people as to the weather conditions and whether we thought we hit the target. Of course we had bomb photos that they analyzed later, and also what the flak situation was and if there was any fighter opposition. I tried to evaluate the flak situation. Here was the worst one—heavy, intense and accurate. This was my second mission. You see, the first one was what we called a milk run. I mean a little flak way out somewhere, but nowhere around us. No fighters, no nothing—drop your bombs and come back home. But the second one we went on was to Blechemmer and it was like a hornet's nest.

Now the navigator had a piece of sheet metal to squat down on when we went over a target. Well that first one was such a milk run I said to myself, "Clarence, there's no use you sitting on that thing—just be comfortable." I sat in my chair and I was working on my table. And all of a sudden all hell broke loose, just like somebody was shelling corn and throwing it on the side of the airplane. We were getting holes everywhere, and a piece of flak came up through the bottom of the airplane and came right through my table. This piece of flak went up, hit the top of the airplane and fell down on my shoulder. I immediately got on that sheet metal and nobody had to beg me to do it. But in the meantime we had one plane shot down that day and I remember pressing my nose to the window to look down as far as I could to see it. I wanted to see if anybody got out. Some of them did get out, but I saw the plane just completely explode. It just dissolved. That was my second mission. That was near Vienna. But we weren't fortunate enough to go over the target that day. When we were approaching Vienna to drop our bombs we had two engines go out. And with ten bombs in there, ten five hundred pound bombs, you can't maintain that level very long with two engines. So what we did, the pilot called me and asked me if we had an alternate target anywhere close by. Well, it so happened on the south side of the Danube River there was a railroad track and on that railroad track there was a bridge, and that bridge was one of our alternate targets. We didn't have a bombardier, but we had that togglier and he was in the nose with me. We both looked down at the railroad track and sort of estimated when he ought to drop the bombs. And we called the tail gunner and told him to look and see if we came anywhere close. And he said he thought we hit it. But anyway, we called for fighter escort and the P-51s that were in northern Italy came to our rescue and escorted us back home.

This came in the mail to me about two years ago from my co-pilot who lives in Thousand Oaks, California, right outside of Los Angeles. He was an engineer—a mechanical engineer. Didn't know he was this much of an artist, but he painted this picture when we bombed Berlin. Now normally Berlin was bombed by the 8th Air Force out of England and it was out of the range of the B-17s flying out of Foggia, Italy. But it so happened that this was right at the end of the war and they needed an all out effort to wipe out the Daimler-Benz plant in Berlin. And that was our prime target that day. But anyway the Germans had fighters in the air, flak was everywhere, these big blotches are the explosions of the flak. The P-51s up here are our fighter escorts. This is a ME-262 which is the first jet airplane that any of us had ever seen. It was a German plane and it came right in on us and it was gone, and we couldn't believe it.

Could you comment on the red tail on the P-51s?

Well, that was a group of fighter pilots called the Tuskegee Airmen. There's been a movie made of them. They were stationed north of us in Italy, and they would join us there and go to the target with us. And a lot of times they would go down on the ground and do a little strafing or something like that to protect us while we were going across the target. Then they'd follow us back until we got out of enemy territory. Then they'd land at their base and we'd go on down to ours. My co-pilot painted this picture and I think he captured exactly what we saw on that trip. They were black airmen in the P-51s.

A friend of mine discovered that he had a talent for painting airplanes. And he painted this one for me—a replica of the plane where the flak came up through my table, and the fifty-three holes that it made in the airplane. That is the plane, the Vicious Vixen, you can see VV up here. He captured it here because I gave him a photograph to go by in order to paint that picture. And I had a print made of that and mailed it to each of our crew. Six of our crew are still living and we have a reunion every year with the 99th Bomb Group.

My wife Polly was working in Washington for the FBI. Polly and I had known each other from the third grade in school, and we got married about a year after I came back out of the service. But anyway, she had a picture made in Washington and sent me up a copy of it—a colored photograph. I found an artist in Foggia, Italy, name of Elestici, and he was doing oil paintings for soldiers or airmen of their girlfriends, wives, or whoever, from photographs. I found out about it and he said he'd do it if I'd bring him a piece of canvas—said he couldn't get canvas. So we tore up an old tent and got a piece of canvas and that's what he painted her picture on. This is painted on an army tent canvas.

I was in Foggia, Italy, one night and the United Service Organizations had a big building leased there. It was like a day room in the Air Force on base where you go to relax—and they have coffee, pop, candy and radios to listen to. And they had an artist in there that day and he was doing caricatures and he had several themes that he carried out. And I thought it was pretty neat. One of the waist gunners took this picture on a bomb run—clearly shows ten bombs dropping. Those are ten five hundred pounders going down. That's the maximum.

What's this map and target plan?

Well, on each mission the navigator received a flight plan. Up here is the route that you take with some of the key points that we would cross on our way to the target. And then this would be the target down here and then this would be coming back home. And down here would be the alternate targets. You get one of these for each mission that you flew and I just saved a bunch of these things and the one that I'm proudest of is the one when we flew to Berlin. That was the longest mission that was ever attempted in a B-17. A lot of times wind at different levels is running in different directions and different speeds. The weather people, the meteorologists, had determined that it was going to be a perfect time to maintain a certain altitude going and a certain altitude coming back to take advantage of the winds and to reduce fuel consumption. And we made it to Berlin and did our bombing mission. That was sort of toward the tail end of the war.

I had been flying extra as a navigator and I was really pooped out. When my regular crew got up one morning to fly this mission, I had flown four consecutive days prior to that while they stayed in the sack and slept. One of the places we went was to Ruhland, Germany, which is not too far south of Berlin. We thought that that was the longest mission we'd ever have to do. They usually had this great big pedestal in the briefing room with a great big map on it, and when we walked in that day they had put an extension on that map and put another big map on top of it. And it had a big word up there—BERLIN. We couldn't believe it, you know, that was unheard of—going all the way to Berlin. But we went, we conquered, and we came back home. It was a nine-hour mission. And most of them were like five, six and seven hours. Prior to this Berlin mission I had been on an eight-hour mission to Ruhland—went there twice, and the other one was to Vienna. But Ruhland was almost to Berlin so I was pooped out but my crew was relaxed, you know, 'cause they hadn't been flying in those days. But we really couldn't believe we were going to Berlin. Particularly me because eight hours is long enough.

What are these medals you've brought?

These are automatic awards that you get for the job that you're doing. Now the others like the Silver Cross and the others are given for victorious service. And this is the ribbon for that theater of operations, the Mediterranean Theater of Operations. It has four stars and they represent the four campaigns that were fought on the ground and [in] the air that the 15th Air Force participated in. These are the navigator wings and this is the Air Medal which is an automatic thing you get if you fly one mission. The oak leaf clusters on it, I had three, signifies that I flew over thirty missions—each one is for ten missions. And I had thirty-four, so I had three clusters.

And the reason I didn't fly my thirty-five mission was the war ended. Up to this point in time I had thirty-four sorties. And the next man on my crew, the most he had was twenty-two.

When I was over there they changed concepts—you didn't fly fifty missions but you had to fly thirty-five sorties. And a sortie was defined as crossing a target and dropping your bombs. Now I guess it's a well known fact that sometimes a crew would cross a target or for some reason they didn't get to the target and had to return to the base. And they didn't want to come back with the plane loaded with bombs. So they'd drop them in the Adriatic Sea. Now this was legitimate and you got credit for the mission.

If we went out on a mission with fragmentary bombs or incendiary bombs to give troop support, and you didn't get to drop those bombs, they were still ready to fire. With the big bombs you could replace the pins, but not with the fragmentary bombs. The people that unloaded the planes, the armament men, didn't want us to come back with those fragmentary bombs in the plane 'cause they didn't want to run the risk of unloading them. So we'd drop them in the Adriatic Sea. But I don't know of one mission that we went on that that happened. It wasn't a frequent thing. The big five hundred pound bombs had pins in them and you take off with the pins in there so the bombs won't explode until that pin is pulled. So when you get fairly near the target, the armament men would go into the bomb bay and pull the pins out of these bombs so they would go off when we dropped them. But in the case of the incendiary bombs they wouldn't put them back in.

When the war ended what happened to your crew?

Well, they sent me home on a boat and the rest of our crew stayed over there in the army of occupation. And they'd do things because there were still some troops in northern Italy. They'd fly supplies up there. They would also ferry people to various places.

Then I headed home. I left Naples, Italy, on a boat on August the 13th in 1945. And I got to Camp Miles Standish in New Jersey the 22nd of August. And then we rode a train from there to Camp Blanding in Florida. And it was on the 25th that we got there. When I went in for the critiquing they said, "Do you want to stay in or do you want to get out?" I said, "Man, there ain't no doubt about that, I want to get out." I wanted to go back to Alabama so I could enter the University of Alabama for the fall quarter. And that's what I did, I entered the University of Alabama in the fall of '45 under the GI Bill of Rights. I was very fortunate because with the GI Bill I got my tuition and books and a subsistence allowance all the way through my undergraduate work and my graduate work. I got a B.S. in Arts and Sciences.

Eventually I wound up in sales and I sold cash registers and adding machines for the National Cash Register Company in Alabama to retail stores for eleven years. And then I got transferred to Dayton, Ohio, in 1964. And we liked it up here. And so we made this our second home. And now we've got our four kids and five grandkids all around us up here, two in Cincinnati and two here in the Dayton area. We really enjoy it up here. But we still get back to Alabama a couple times a year. I was planning on spending some time in L.A. in January because Polly feels that if we get out of Ohio for January we can make it. When I say L.A. that's Lower Alabama, it's not Los Angeles. That's what we do now.

Seth Furnas

Seth Furnas was born and raised on a farm in the Centerville-Washington Township community. When the war started in December of 1941, Furnas was deferred from the draft in order to continue farming. But in March of 1944 he received a letter from the military requesting he take a physical. He took the physical, passed and entered the Army in April of 1944. He served for twenty-eight months and was discharged in September of 1946. Furnas served in the European Theater of Operations in the 99th Division, 394th Infantry Regiment, E Company. He and his wife Marjorie were married after the war and had four children—two boys and two girls. He is a graduate of Centerville High School, a member of the VFW and American Legion and still lives and works on a farm on East Social Row Road in Washington Township.

What were you doing, Seth, just prior to your military service?

Well, after I graduated from Centerville in May of 1940 I was farming with my father and I also rented two or three farms. I rented the ground that

Ida Weller School is now on, right down the road here. You know where that's at—on Sheehan Road. I rented that from a man by the name of Bodman. I rented, oh, I don't know, four or five farms I suppose with Dad. He kind of helped and we all used his machinery, and I just farmed and was deferred until '44.

What branch of the service were you in?

I was in the infantry and I took my basic training at Camp Blanding, Florida. And it was accelerated some because they wanted us over there I guess. This was in June or July of 1944. Stayed right up 'til December in basic training. I was twenty-two years old. I met one fellow who lived in Bellbrook and I never will forget him. We went down there together on the same train. And I saw him at the PX two or three days later, and he said, "You know what, if I was home I'd shovel manure forever just to get out of this place." He hated it.

And we had one sergeant that was a cook, and he actually stole our food. They'd start a gallon of milk down the table, and of course, it wouldn't last no time and we didn't get no more. And if you was at the end of the table you didn't get any milk. So finally, we got the officer of the day to come in and he just snuck in one morning, and he seen what was happening, and he sifted it down and we found out this old sergeant was selling all the food at Starke, a little town right next to Camp Blanding. That stopped him and from then on we got food.

Everybody had to pull KP, I suppose, in basic training. I don't remember too much of it, but they treated you like dogs, these old guys. They was old army men—I mean the sergeants. I don't even think they'd been in combat, but they let on like they had, and they kept telling us if we didn't do everything just right we wouldn't last no time when we got overseas.

After your basic training what happened then?

Well, I was supposed to get a delay en route, but for some reason they didn't give it to us. See, the Battle of the Bulge was just starting when I got over there [December 1944]. It was started already, and they wanted us over there as replacements. This outfit I joined, E Company of the 394th Regiment, 99th Division, only had twenty-six men left in it when I joined. They'd all been either captured or wounded or killed. It was the last stand the Germans actually made.

They put the 99th on line when it came over from England. That was before I was in it and it was a very inexperienced company, and it took the place of the 1st Division, the 82nd Airborne, and a couple more. It was scattered out real thin. And a lot of people complained that they made guinea pigs out of them to get the Germans to attack there. But I don't know whether that's true or not. But anyhow the 1st Division, and the 4th Division, and the 82nd Airborne all moved back in when the Bulge started. And that's why so many of these fellows was killed—they was right up there in front. See, the Germans had all them tanks, they had a place there where they made tanks underground, and I don't think our American intelligence knew it. And when all them tanks come in there on the 16th of December, it was bad.

Where was the division when you joined them in Belgium?

It was a little later when I got into it. The Bulge had already started, but Elsenborn, Belgium, is where I went to and that's where we held. It wasn't too far from Bastogne.

First we went over on the *Queen Mary*. It was triple loaded, what they call triple loaded, and we went to Glasgow, Scotland. There they put us on a train, a through train, and we went to Southampton. And then from Southampton we got on an LST and crossed the channel to Le Havre, and then they put us on a 40&8 boxcar and moved us right to the front lines.

And every so often the train would stop, and some of us would get off of it. Finally, they announced my name and I got off and joined E Company of the 394th Infantry of the 99th Division. And then there was a fellow come and got us, and took us down to where they was dug in on what they call the Elsenborn Ridge. That's where I was.

At night we'd go out on patrols and try to find out where the Germans were, and the fighting slowed up considerable by the time I got in. In fact, we held there. The regional guys was all annihilated, but we held there and it wasn't until January that we left.

Where did you first come under enemy fire?

Yes, I can tell you about that. We went down a road that was plowed out, the snow was about three or four feet deep. We went down this road just wide enough for a jeep, only we was walking. And every once in awhile we'd hear artillery come over, and this guy that come and got us he dived in the snow banks. And we looked at him and thought he was nuts, you know, we just stood there kind of. Finally, the shells went clear over us and hit some guys behind us, and they started hollering for medics and everything. Well, when the next shells come in we also dove in the bank. That's how we got baptized to enemy fire. And of course, we got our combat Infantry Badges at that time. And our pay went up.

Anyway we stayed there in them holes, it looked about like a tight grave. Two guys could get in the hole—had shelter over half the front of it to keep the light in. And we'd get these C ration cans and fill them full of dirt and pour some gasoline into them, and we used them for a little bit of heat and mainly to write letters and stuff in the holes at night, you know. Three of us in a hole. Two in and one out on guard.

We sometimes took off, two hours on and four off—and there was lots of snow. I don't see how we lived. We improvised chimneys out of juice cans. You know them juice cans about that long? And we took the wire out of them cans, punched holes in them, took both ends out of them made them sort of stove pipe like, and then poked that down through the can into the hole. See we had a row of trees over the top and then a bunch of dirt and then another row of trees crossways, then another row of trees on top of that—all this on top of our holes which would take care of a light shell. It'd shake you bad in there, but if it hit over top of you, it'd get you. But we were pretty reasonably safe.

Then we had to make a hole in there. The only problem with that hole was if the Germans come through at night on their patrols, they could drop a grenade down in the hole through that pipe. I think they made us do away with it before long. For a few days there we'd spit out that black soot every morning. I don't see how we kept from dying, but we didn't. A lot of guys got trench foot. This was in December 1944.

Well, after that we went over into Belgium, went back through the line, that fortification line, what do you call it—the Siegfried Line. We fought through that and went on and we was right on the Rhine River two months later, in March of 1945 probably. And we was right there, I could see the steeples of that big double-steepled church there at Cologne, you know, it was right on the Rhine there.

All of a sudden one night we heard these big trucks coming. They stopped and we had ten minutes to get out of there. We had dug in there and we had to get out and get on them trucks, and then we went out and crossed the bridge at Remagen. And I went back fifty years later to the 50th anniversary crossing and found out a whole lot more than I did that night.

When the 9th Armored captured it, they got across and right on the other side of the river they found a tunnel. And in

Seth Furnas in Nancy, France, early 1945.

this tunnel there must have been four thousand kids from the area around there. They was still bombing them and they moved the kids into this tunnel. And also in that tunnel was one carload, a tank carload of gasoline that was leaking, and a whole bunch of artillery. Well these civilian people that was in there went crazy when we captured it.

And the next morning they come out flying on broomsticks—they had underwear, waving anything trying to surrender. There was four or five enemy officers in charge. The Germans had been left in charge of the bridge which they didn't get blowed. And they decided under the Geneva Conference that they probably should surrender. So they surrendered. And then when we went back [years later I found out that], four out of the five of them had been killed. And the one guy, and he was there at this anniversary, he got captured by the Americans. He was the only one that lived.

This bridge over the Rhine River was quite a location. There was a great big bluff and the Germans would lob in their 88mm artillery shells. They could hit the approach to it, but they couldn't hit the bridge. So the airplanes tried to get it down, and that's the first place they used jet aircraft. You know they had a few jet planes. They used these jet aircraft there and we were no match—the P-38 was no match for them. They could run a hundred mile an hour faster then we could. The next day we was up on the bluff across the river, and we watched the jets in dogfights with them P-38s.

See, they was four days getting the bridge destroyed, but they finally did destroy it after four days. By that time we had two pontoon bridges across. And the bridge fell on the fourth day. And I just delivered straw to a man down here by Lebanon the other day and his uncle was one of the engineers that welded on that bridge when it went down—and he got killed. I knew there was about one hundred men got killed when it went down, and he was on it. But that was probably the roughest time.

They told us we was going over and nobody knew what was happening. They give us two bandoleers of ammunition and we didn't even have our mortar. I don't know what happened to them, but we didn't take them and I guess they give 'em to us later on. But anyway, they also give us a bunch of cigarettes, and I didn't smoke so I didn't even take mine. They really loaded us down when we crossed. It was a railroad bridge with sheet metal over the top of it, and every time a shell would hit, especially a bomb from them airplanes, it'd blow that steel.

We crossed at two o'clock in the morning, and we didn't have anybody go down from E Company. But F Company, they were behind us, they got hit on the approach by them 88s. Killed their company commander and it really wrecked F Company, but we was pretty lucky. We got over without too much going on. This would be on March 7, 1945.

What happened to your outfit after that?

Well, we had what I call a rat race across Germany. After that we joined up with Patton's 3rd Army and started into Germany. The objective now was to go from town to town working east towards Giessen, and then wait for the next command. It was now mid March, and the resistance grew thinner and thinner. We reached a town and started going from house to house gathering up civilians and weapons. It looked as though all were clear and then we moved further down the main street.

Suddenly out from behind a church a tank appeared with a few men alongside carrying machine guns. The Germans opened fire at point blank while we ducked into buildings trying to escape. Finally after some time the German tank and machine gunners were killed. After the smoke cleared I walked out of a building. I looked around at the rest of his company, and Patterson was missing. Patterson was one of the first men I had met back on Elsenborn Ridge. We immediately became good friends and it made war a little less hellish. He was from New Jersey, and back at home he had a wife and two kids. They never found his body. All they found were a few pieces of a boot and what they thought was his pay book. That night we camped out and the next day pushed on east in what became known as the "Rat Race Across Germany."

While marching down streets, sometimes we would see dead soldiers and horses smashed in the road by tanks. Often German civilians would crowd in and march with us for protection. If the soldiers had anything to spare they would give them some food. By the end of March 1945, the 394th had reached the town called Giessen. It was located just north of Frankfurt close to the Wied River. The Germans had fortified it by digging a trench through the middle of the road and placing prisoners armed with rifles along its edge. If the young boys and old men refused to fire at the Americans the SS would shoot them in the back. Snipers were positioned in church towers and in high buildings. It took around two days before we finally defeated the Germans and captured the town.

Close to the edge of the town there was a slave labor camp. It was the first time the men had seen how horrible the Nazis treated people. They opened up one barracks and the foul smell of feces and death filled the air. It had an aisle down the middle with three rows of bunks on either side. Straw was placed on the bunks to sleep on, but most of it had already deteriorated. The people were as thin as a rail, and they had a blank look in their eyes, and a quiet smile on their faces. Some were already dead in their beds, and others were so weak they couldn't move. In the back of the barracks there were piles of dead bodies that had not yet been buried. The troops were given orders not to feed the prisoners because most were so far gone that even a little candy bar would set their body out of line and kill them. They had to be brought along slowly by who came in after the camp was liberated.

That day they continued on around town and found more prisoners. Me and another man opened up a building that looked like a chicken coop and upon seeing the prisoners inside the man looked at me and said, "Some say that there's a just god in the world." After seeing those poor people and the way they were treated—it was terrible.

The first slave labor camp we liberated was in Giessen, Germany, and I never will forget it. We walked up there, we'd run off the SS men and they were gone, and we opened the gates. And the people was in awful shape, they'd been penned up for four days and they were in what looked like chicken coops. And they had straw beds four high in that thing, or three high, and a lot of them was dead and it was awful. But then before it was over we seen the concentration camps, and they was even worse 'cause they had bodies piled up around them, you know, lots of bodies. The concentration camps were the worst. I never seen the big ones. We liberated some of the smaller ones. Then we also liberated some of the American and British POW camps. And actually we released some of our 99th Division guys that had been captured in the Bulge.

We didn't ride tanks much, but we rode tanks sometime. The trouble with riding tanks is that it'd draw the artillery fire. And I remember when President Roosevelt died there was a tanker up ahead of us and, oh, he must have been twenty men ahead of me—we was walking, and they relayed back that the president had died. We didn't believe it. Nobody believed anything you heard in the army. And finally we had this one fellow, good friend of mine, Virgil Banyon, he was from Independence, Missouri, and we couldn't remember who was vice-president. And he finally said, "Oh my, we're all took now, the old haberdasher's in there." He called him the haberdasher— Harry Truman.

But then we went on and we got over to Czechoslovakia, right on the border there at the Danube River. And that's where it ended—we met the Russians. It was about the first of May, or second or third. I think on the eighth of May they finally signed the thing didn't they? [The surrender document.]

What was that like?

It wasn't nothing like they had here in the States. See they had the ticker [tape] parade and all that. No, it wasn't nothing like that. We just went back to this place called Veitshöchheim. We got on trains and went back there. And our company had something like a boy scout place to stay in. And we was told we was going to Japan.

They de-activated the 99th and I was put in the 79th Division. And then all of a sudden they dropped the atomic bomb. Well, we thought it was great. But since then, I wondered if they couldn't have dropped that thing on a mountain somewhere and not killed all them people. I've often thought of that, but at the time it give salvation to us 'cause we would probably have been in the invasion of Japan. We were going to fly over there, so we'd gotten over there in a hurry on some island there close.

Well, when the war ended I went back to Veitshöchheim. And then they deactivated the 79th, done away with it, and I got put in the 26th Infantry Regiment of the 1st Division in L Company, and we were billeted right across the street from the Palace of Justice. And we pulled interior and exterior guard duty at the Palace of Justice in Nuremberg. Yes, right there, the main Palace of Justice itself, and you seen pictures of them fellows in the white helmets and spats and all? I was there, but you couldn't tell.

There at Nuremberg it was kind of sad in the start. They sent the infantry, us fellows, out and we had to go out in the suburbs of Nuremberg. And people that were lucky enough not to have their houses bombed, we took them out of their houses and give them about fifteen minutes to get their stuff together. They got their blankets, a few personal pictures, their Bible and a few more things and we moved them right across the street from that old amphitheater, the big theater there in Nuremberg where they held sports and things. There's an SS barracks there and we moved them people there, and they had to stay there for about a year.

And then the American civilians come in, and they stole all their stuff out of their houses, and we got the credit, the infantry got the credit for looting them. But actually those big shots took the paintings and all that. They were rich people and it was pretty hard. Then Justice Jackson found out about it—he was chief prosecutor for America. And he stayed in Nuremberg in the old walled city. He got a place kind of half way fixed up, but he wouldn't take a house away from the people.

We could get a pass and go to the trials. Course we was right in there when the trial was going on standing behind them prisoners. We had to keep people away, but of course nothing ever happened. All the Nazi leaders had to stay in the courtroom, and they made all twenty-two of them come in the courtroom and sit there. They each one had a place to sit, and one guy was being tried for killing so many people. See, back in the 30s and early 40s and right up to the end of the war, if you done something wrong, or said something wrong, even you're kids could turn you in, they'd come and knock on the door and take them and put them in the back of a truck. When they get the truck full they'd put cyanide in there and kill them and then dump them in a mass grave.

So this day I was in the trials and they was trying this one guy who was the head of that group—the one for killing all these people. Well, they had all kinds of records. And then they had records of this guy signing his name on papers and reviewing blueprints. They made up a truck, something like a garbage disposal truck, and when they got the thing full and killed the people, why they could just shove them out the back and the guys didn't even have to get out of the truck you know. Documents showed that this guy had to know about that even though he claimed he didn't know nothing about it. But he had to know about it because he signed the papers to build so many of them trucks. That was one thing I saw in the courtroom.

There was, of course, Göring. He was a smart man and he actually surrendered to the Americans. He was head of the Luftwaffe which was the German Air Force. And if anybody had a chance of getting away from the situation, he could have flown out anywhere 'cause he had access to all the planes they had left. But he didn't. He said he was an army man and they never would do nothing with him. He always told us fellows when we pulled guard on his cell, he said, "They ain't never going to hang me. They can shoot me but they're not going to hang me, and I'll never be disgraced by being hung." And you know, he got hold of a capsule and took a capsule. He committed suicide. He cheated them out of hanging him. He said they'd never hang him.

And then I got something else I'd like to say. After the war ended and I spent my years there at Nuremberg, and when I came home I'd seen enough of that destruction and everything, I went to Washington several times lobbying. And Bob Taft, he didn't agree with me much, but I was in favor of building the Europeans up. A lot of people wasn't for the Marshall Plan, but I personally thought if we done like we done from the first world war, we'd have another war in about twenty years. That's my opinion. But we built Germany up and made friends out of them and I lobbied in Washington for, oh, five, four or five years on appropriating money through the Marshall Plan.

I'm a Quaker, but I went to the service. I could have probably got off being a conscientious objector if I had wanted to, but I couldn't see it. Clear back in 1938 we had a political science teacher named Glen Duckwall up here at Centerville, and he come in one morning and he was shook up and worked up awful because the Germans had went into the Sudetenland, or Hitler had gone into the Sudetenland. And he told us fellows that was awful and that we'd probably all wind up in the Army. And there was twelve guys graduated in my class and every one of them went in the service. Not all of them in the Army, but in the service. And he was right, he predicted this in 1938. Hitler just lied to everybody.

Did the war change your life?

Well, it was something I was glad I was in, but I'd never want my kids to be in anything like that. I know they won't because they're too old now I really learned a lot, I guess. Course, I've been to Europe five times since. My wife and I took several trips to central Europe and Italy and several other trips. But I finally went back over fifty years later and went over to what they called battlefield tours. They had a great big celebration over the crossing the Rhine at Remagen and it lasted two days. Then I stayed another five or six days, and we went back through Belgium and saw the area of the battle we fought, and some of the guys thought they found their old foxholes up there on Elsenborn Ridge.

And we talked to a lot of Belgian people. The Belgian people really give us all kinds of dinners when we went over there 'cause we liberated them. And before we got there, them farmers, everything they raised, ninety percent of it was given to Hitler and to the Germans. And if they didn't give it, they shot them. And of course when the war ended that stopped. And we went right through Belgium. We liberated a lot of Belgian people. And they really thought a lot of us.

Course, we went back also because some of my buddies are buried there in Belgium. There's a big cemetery in Belgium. We went to that cemetery, and those guys, they call them diggers, they're still taking care of that cemetery. Course America's paying them. And they've got twenty-four vehicles, second world war vintage, and they just all run like new. And they took us, well, I rode in one of them to a reception or dinner that night in a town about twenty miles away, and they took us there. They really thought a lot of us, the Belgian people did.

Really, there's so many, many things that go back to the war. For instance, in the artillery when we first started they had a detonator on them shells that didn't amount to much—they had to hit the ground or something. Then they put time fuses in them and improved those shells tremendously. And I've heard a lot of stories about that, so this was really an effort, and we won that war with not only the soldiers but the civilians. The women, you know, made battleships and were riveters, and all that stuff. Everybody took a hold. We didn't have nothing when the war started. A lot of guys trained with broomsticks, I don't know if you knew that or not, in them camps [when] they started out. Yes, that's all they had. It was bad. And Pearl Harbor, if them airplane carriers hadn't been out I don't know what would have happened over there.

Arnie Crouch

Arnold L. Crouch served almost three years in the Army including sixteen months in the European Theater of Operations. He was a member of the 42nd Infantry Division in the ammunition and pioneer platoon. He was in combat for about five months and then served in the army of occupation in Austria. After the war he attended the University of Cincinnati under the GI Bill of Rights, married and had three children. He lives with his wife in Centerville, Ohio, and is an active member of the 42nd Division's Rainbow Division Veterans Association. Crouch also served in the Korean War at the White Sands Proving Grounds in New Mexico and was involved in electro-mechanical engineering, spending forty years at Bendix Corporation (later Facet Filter Products) which made products for the aerospace industry.

I was born in Toledo in 1925, and unfortunately, my mother passed away when I was born, so my grandmother and grandfather brought me down to Dayton when I was two days old. And for all practical purposes I lived in Dayton for the rest of my life with the exception of a couple of stints in the service and at college. I spent all of my teenage years in Dayton View and Riverdale. Went to Fairview High School, graduated in 1943, and was drafted immediately after graduation.

We were sent to an infantry-training center. We learned to fire all the weapons—M1 rifle, '03 rifle, 45-caliber pistol and Thompson submachine gun. We also fired the 60mm mortar, 81mm mortar, 30 caliber light machine gun, 30 caliber heavy machine gun, and the BAR—Browning automatic rifle.

Basic training was finished in the end of August of '43. And as a unit our whole battalion was sent to Fargo, North Dakota, to North Dakota Agricultural College, NDAC. We studied mechanical engineering. ASTP was an accelerated program. You went to school from eight in the morning until five in the evening five days a week. And on Saturday mornings you had some classes and physical education.

Classes started in the academic year of September '43. But along came March of '44, and the army did just what we expected them to do—they blew the whistle on ASTP. Only the top five percent in the class stayed. The rest of us were either sent to divisions that were in the States or were sent overseas immediately as replacements. Fortunately, I was sent to Muskogee, Oklahoma, to Camp Gruber—to the Rainbow Division, the 42nd Infantry Division. I was assigned to what is called an ammunition and pioneer platoon.

Most people don't have any concept of what this is. The ammunition bit applies to the fact that we maintain an ammunition supply from the rear echelon to the front line troops—literally right out to the foxholes. And the pioneer bit was we would do minor construction or destruction work—roadblocks, laying mines, digging mines, clearing roadblocks, demolishing a building or what have you. Anything that didn't require power equipment. If you could do it with a pick and a shovel, a block and tackle, or a stick of dynamite, that was what we did. I stayed with that platoon until I came home from occupation duty.

We stayed in Oklahoma from the time I got there in March, until we departed at the end of November or first of December of '44. We spent our time training as a unit, as a division, then we went overseas. We went over on the USS *General Black* which was a troop carrier. We sailed in convoy from New York City to Marseilles, France. It was about a twelve-day passage—I think it was slow by virtue of the convoy. We went past Gibraltar and saw the first lights that we had seen for ten days. Then we pulled into Marseilles. And we were fortunate because we were able to tie up at a dock so that we went down a gangplank to unload.

By the time I got there a majority of France had been liberated. But the fighting was still going on. This was right when the Battle of the Bulge had just started—around the middle of December of '44. And when we disembarked we were billeted up on a place called CP2. It was a vast plain up on a bluff above the ocean, and even though this is southern France, it was colder than billy-be-damned. We had nothing but pup tents, no fires, and the place was void of any wood at all. There was nothing to scrounge for 'cause so many troops had gone through the area. We were there for about five or six days and then the foot troops were loaded onto 40 & 8 boxcars going north.

Fortunately, being in the A and P platoon, we had a lot of equipment like picks and shovels—things like that that needed transporting. So we had a truck assigned to us. And then we had another larger vehicle. It was a GM, or a Dodge 6x6, and we had a GMC 6x6 assigned to us to carry the ammunition. We went up by truck convoy. Along the way we had little narrow roads. The two and a half ton truck that I was riding in had a 57mm anti-tank gun in tow behind us. Now the trails of the anti-tank gun split, and when you're going to fire it they are split and are spaded into the ground, and then the barrel sticks out the other way. These go together, or clamp together, when you're towing it. Well, we're driving along with the trails clamped together and one trail came loose, it swung out, caught a tree and ripped the gun right off the mounting.

We had a little bit of a problem there, but we headed up to Strasbourg which is about two hundred miles roughly from Marseilles. Strasbourg is on the Rhine River. It sounds like it's a German city, but it is French and on the other side of the Rhine is Germany. At that point this was the front, but it meant nothing right then because the Germans were on one side of the river and we were on the other, and the fighting was sporadic.

At that point there were no artillery exchanges. And we thought, "This was pretty nifty—we don't shoot at them, they don't shoot at us." And we could see them moving around on the other side of the river, and vice versa.

We had removed our patches, our Rainbow Division patch, at the orders of the commanding general. At one point, we found a radio that would work and we'd tune into Axis Sally. And one night she says, "OK, 42nd, put your rainbow patches back on. We know you're there in Strasbourg and environs."

Many people don't realize it, or don't know about it, but there was another German salient in addition to the one at the Bulge. And this one was called, by the Germans, Operation Nordwind. And it occurred just north of Strasbourg at about the time we got into the lines. We took one helluva beating there. They almost drove us back, but fortunately we were able to persevere along with the help of other divisions—the 79th, and the 14th armored division. But we suffered some tremendous casualties. In fact, one company I know of lost about eighty to eighty-five percent of their men as casualties—either killed, captured, or wounded. We were fighting the SS troopers, some of their crack troops, and some of their crack armored divisions. As I said, we were responsible for maintaining a munitions supply from the rear area up to the front. And then occasionally there'd be a bridge or something that was to be knocked out.

Was this your first time coming under enemy fire?

Yes, and I was scared as hell. I think probably one little incident explains my feelings exactly. The first night it was colder than the dickens out in the front area, in a foxhole, and my weapon was a carbine, a 30-caliber carbine—a short, light rifle. By short, I mean small. That was great during training back in the states because it weighed about half as much as an M1 rifle. But that night, out there in the foxhole, with all this activity going on you needed more power. When we went back to replenish our ammunition I found our company kitchens in the rear area and looked up one of the cooks. Their TE weapon (table of equipment) was an M1. I said, "Would you like a carbine? I'll trade you mine for your M1." And he said, "Gladly, I don't want this damn thing." And I said, "Well I want yours." And so from then on I carried an M1. I wanted

Arnie Crouch.

something that would reach out there with a little more accuracy. We had one fellow that threw away his carbine and picked up a BAR and carried it the rest of the war even though it weighed twice as much as an M1. So that kind of expresses your feelings.

As for fear, well, you really don't have much choice. I mean, you're in just as much danger if you don't operate, so you may as well go ahead and do what you have to do. Fortunately I never received a scratch. I never even cut my thumb on a C ration can or anything. My two friends were in the same regiment, but they weren't in the same platoon or company I was in. We saw each other periodically, but they weren't literally right next to me.

What was your relationship with the other men in your platoon?

Well, I was the baby of the platoon. And ironically, our platoon lieutenant was the next baby. He was about six months older then I was. When we first joined the platoon, I was nineteen and he was twenty. And the rest of the guys ranged in age up to about thirty-five. But we had a real good relationship. Some great guys.

Our lieutenant was a good leader—very good. He became just one of the guys—he didn't try to be bossy or anything like that. He simply had a job to do. He was just a nice personality, and I still maintain my friendship with him. I see him about every six months or so. He had the respect of the older men too—yes indeed. And we called him Sully to his face—Cornelius J. Sullivan. Not in front of other officers or anything. But when he'd get his liquor ration, which the officers got and the enlisted men didn't, he'd share it with the guys. He'd get a box from home and he'd split it up with the guys just like other guys would share.

Operation Nordwind lasted for about ten days to two weeks, something like that, and finally we were able to repel the Germans and get things back in order again. But the front was quite broad and we weren't the only division that was involved. It covered a front of probably twenty-five or thirty miles or more and there were several divisions involved. One of the problems that we had was that when we went over it wasn't anticipated that we would go into the front line that soon. But we did because of the salient up at the Bulge, and then obviously this other salient which nobody was aware was coming either.

Our infantry regiments had come over first and the support troops from the division, engineers, artillery, division headquarters, things of this nature, were still back in the states or en route. And so we were thrown in the line as infantry regiments, as Task Force Linden, the name coming from our division, assistant division commander, General Linden. And so we had no artillery for support. We had to rely on other units for this type of thing. Well, after things were pretty well stabilized we were pulled back for a rest period and reorganization—back into Nancy. The rest of the division caught up with us there and we got replacements, GI replacements, for those who were either killed in action or captured or wounded. And then we went into a holding position until the final drive started around the 13th of March.

And from then on we just pushed across Europe. We crossed the Rhine at Worms. The Rhine had been cleared by that time. I mean we crossed it in peaceful conditions on a pontoon bridge, but then we had a fairly decent fight around Schweinfurt which was well known for being Germany's ball bearing works.

Schweinfurt and Würzburg was just an awful lot of fighting. And around Schweinfurt particularly, the artillery was horrendous because the Germans had the famous 88. This 88mm artillery weapon served three purposes. It was used either as anti-aircraft, as artillery, or as armor piercing for anti-tank. All you hear is a sh, sh, sh, sh, like a jet going over, but it was artillery coming in—incoming mail. And in Schweinfurt the Germans had it heavily protected with anti-aircraft because of the air raids. They were trying to protect the ball bearing works there. And these same 88s could be used for anti-aircraft. And they just traversed them over, lowered them, and used them for artillery against us too.

Then we went south from Schweinfurt to Nuremberg. This wasn't where the Nazi party was founded, but it was where their big party rallies were held. And from there we turned east towards Munich. We liberated Munich and also Dachau which was adjacent to the concentration camp nearby.

Would you comment on these photographs and souvenirs?

These are German troops we captured. Here are some pictures of the concentration camp at Dachau. Piles of bodies just like cordwood stacked up. This is a photo of a flag that was captured in Schweinfurt. Our division commander sent it to the commander of the 42nd Light Bombardment Group 'cause the 42nd Light Bombardment bombed Schweinfurt and helped us occupy it. Anyway, this particular flag is out at the Air Force Museum in Dayton, Ohio, and I've walked by it many times and just happened to discover it there about a year ago.

Where were you when the war ended?

We were about ten or fifteen miles east of Munich. We had already gone through Munich, and I remember I was getting a haircut. One of the guys, he was a milkman by trade, but he gave all the guys in the platoon haircuts, was giving me a haircut when we got the word that the Germans had capitulated. I'll always remember that.

We thought this was great. Of course, things had been winding down, we saw it coming, it wasn't as though it was a great surprise, but the relief was very real—it's finally over. We can relax. But we all knew that our division, having only been in Europe for only about five months, would be redeployed to the Pacific. And so from that standpoint we weren't too elated, but at least we knew there was a few months off before that could happen.

Our division ended up as occupation troops down in the Alps—in the beautiful Austrian Alps. Most of my time was spent down in a little town called Zell am See on a lake right in the heart of the Alps. It was gorgeous country. It had not been affected by the war too drastically because there was no physical damage or anything. There really was no reason to tear it up because there were no military targets in the area.

We had all these hotels organized and staffed, so they decided to start Rainbow University, and we used U.S. textbooks. They taught various college courses which earned credit back in the States—universities back home would accept the credits. And each company in the division was allowed to send three men for a period of three months for one term. You could take four courses. I spent a total of about seven months in Zell am See and then returned to my company. By that time my company had moved to Vienna, and I spent my last 30 days overseas in Vienna before I came home.

When you heard about the A-bomb
what kind of reaction did you have?

My personal reaction was, "What is this?" I couldn't hardly believe that something like this could exist. And to me it was incomprehensible that a bomb of this nature could exist. It was something out of Buck Rogers. And that was my reaction, but I was very grateful when we found out it did exist.

We still were a little bit edgy about being in Austria. Austria, at that time, like Germany, was divided into four sections: French, British, Russian, and American zones. And Vienna was in the Russian zone in Austria like Berlin was in the Russian zone in Germany. And while Berlin and Vienna were ruled by the four powers, when I was in Vienna it was kind of hairy. The warning was, don't get caught in the Russian zone after dark, you may never be heard from again. And it happened in some instances to the American soldiers and British too for that matter. The Russians—you never knew what they were going to do. We were on edge, and some may or may not realize that George Patton got a reprimand shortly after the war was over for saying, "Don't trust the Russians. We should go in and get them right now while we're still here, still armed and ready, and get it over with because we're going to do it sooner or later." The Cold War came but it could have become a hot war. Nevertheless, we sort of lived under that duress while we were there.

I remember one time I was in the Russian zone in Vienna. I had made the acquaintance of Heinz Fleischmann who was one of the directors of the Vienna Boys' Choir, and he and his mother and father had invited me over one evening. It was very interesting because they did a little impromptu concert for me—violin, cello, and piano. Later I was heading back to my billet late at night, and it was snowing, and it was dark, and I had about a three-block walk to get out of the Russian zone. And here comes this Russian truck. He pulls up, and a Russian jumps out and he's jabbering at me in Russian. I have no idea what he's talking about at all. I tried some of my pigeon German, but he didn't understand that, and for all I knew they were going to throw me in the truck and I'd never be seen again. Fortunately, I realized that he was asking directions, and he finally became convinced that I couldn't help them so they shoved off and I breathed a sigh of relief.

I came home alone—not alone, but as an individual. Those of us that had enough points to be returned were assigned to what they called casual companies. They'd come up with some oddball name like the 222nd Motorcycle Battalion. Just an organization to use as a unit to bring you home. We assembled in Styer, Austria, and were there for a few days. Then we took 40 & 8 trains to Le Havre and I think we were in Camp Phillip Morris. All the camps that they used for returning troops were named after cigarettes—Lucky Strike, Phillip Morris, Chesterfield, and so forth. And I believe I was in Lucky Strike but I'm not sure. Since the war was over everything was open and above board—no more secrecy. They published your orders two or three days in advance, when you would ship home and what ship you were going on.

Well, our orders came out and we were going on the USS *Florence Nightingale*. We thought great—we're going home on a hospital ship and we will get good beds to sleep in. Well, that illusion didn't last long after we saw the ship—it was a liberty ship.

We landed in New York and went to Camp Kilmer in New Jersey. Incidentally, Joyce Kilmer was the poet that wrote "Trees" and he was in the Rainbow Division in World War I. In fact, he was killed during that war. Nevertheless, we came through Camp Kilmer with an evening in New York City proper, and then we headed over to Camp Atterbury, Indiana. And these two other fellows that I mentioned earlier, the three of us were discharged the same day together.

How do you think World War II changed your life?

Well, it was an interesting change to go from the Depression into the war, and then from that into a world where there was money. It was plentiful compared to what I had known prior to the war. Jobs were available. The biggest thing in my thoughts was the shortage of things—you couldn't get this and you couldn't get that for a number of years. I went to the University of Cincinnati on the GI Bill. And then also bought my first house with the GI Bill. I married a couple of years after I came back. My wife, Charlotte, Chotty, and I had been high school sweethearts.

Did you have another tour of duty?

I stayed in the reserves, and about three years later I get orders to report for active duty at Fort Knox down in Kentucky. This is during the Korean War. My orders stated that I was to be assigned to the post engineers at Fort Knox. I thought well, if I have to go back in that's not too bad. Post engineer means I'll just be working maybe as a plumber, a carpenter, or who knows what, and plus I'm only about a hundred and some miles from home. Well, I got down there and went through processing and they told me to go see this sergeant over here. I said, "Why? How come I'm going there and everybody else is going here?" Well, they said, "You're gonna get a good deal." Well, I was in the Army for three years and I haven't seen a good deal yet. But it turned out that it was. I was sent down to White Sands Proving Grounds in New Mexico just at the time that the missile concept was coming into being.

After I came home, I was in engineering, electro-mechanical engineering with Ledex and GH Leland Development Engineering. I spent eight years there in an engineering capacity. Then I decided I wanted to get into industrial technical sales, so I joined Bendix Filter Division which later became Facet Filter Products. We manufactured fluid filters for hydraulic fuel, lube oil, things of this nature, for the aerospace industry. So my experiences at White Sands were carried over into this. I spent forty years on the road for Bendix, or I should say Facet, nee Bendix, and retired four years ago at seventy.

Ernest Guenther

Ernest Guenther was born in Breslau, Germany. His father served in the German Army in World War I and emigrated to the United States after that war. When he had saved enough money he sent for his family and they settled in Dayton, Ohio. In 1939 the family moved to a farm in Darke County and then in 1943 the family moved to California. Guenther worked in San Diego until he was drafted into the Army in January of 1944. He served two years in the Army with one and one-half years in Europe where he attained the rank of staff sergeant. Guenther is fluent in the German language. After the war he married his wife Julia and they are the parents of two children. He worked for fifty years as a certified public accountant.

My dad had always told me, "Whatever you do don't tell them you speak German. You'll get the worst job in the Army." Well, that may have been true in the German Army, but as I later found out I should have said something very early. I'd have gotten a much better job. After basic training at Camp Hood, I had six weeks advanced training and then I was to report to Fort Meade, Maryland. But I got a delay en route and was allowed to come home for a few days, so I did that.

So in January of 1945 they shipped me out on the USS *Wakefield* which was a converted luxury liner. And it was jammed with GIs. If we'd have gotten torpedoed it'd have been the end because it was January, and they said you had fifteen minutes to live if you hit the water. We had no escorts because it was a fast ship. We crossed the North Atlantic and landed in Southampton, England. And from there we got on Navy LST boats and they took us across to Le Havre, France. They were in a hurry to get us to the front lines, they needed replacements. So we got to Le Havre, stayed overnight there, and then they put us on those 40&8. Forty hommes and eight cheval. And what it meant was you could put eight horses in the train or forty men. Well we got forty men in there and they shipped us to Aachen, Germany. Part of this trip we took by truck. I'm now a replacement. I was put into Easy [E] Company of the 2nd Battalion, 47th Infantry Regiment, 9th Division. Which incidentally is the same unit in which Tom Hanks served in the movie, Forest Gump. That's the Octofoil division.

But at any rate, the Germans had blown the dam on the Ruhr River, so we were at the Ruhr River and couldn't get across. So we dug in, we had foxholes on the backside of a mountain. And it was fortunate because the Germans would shell us regularly, but because we were on the backside of this mountain the shells would go over us and land in the valley. But at any rate, we're in this foxhole. Nobody knows what fear is 'til you get up there on the line. We all have an idea that we're invincible, but when you get in a situation like that and you see people getting killed and shot, you begin to realize that you're not invincible, that's when fear really takes hold of you

But when I got to the front lines, Captain Strapp called me and he said, "You were born in Germany?" I said, "Yes." He says, "Well, then obviously you can speak German." I said, "Yes." That's the first I told anybody because we had to speak German at home until my older brother and sister went to school and brought English home. So we never spoke English until they brought English home. And then we would speak German at home and English to friends. But anyway, the captain said to me, "Fine we can use an interpreter."

I was an assistant rifle grenadier assigned to a squad, and I had to carry the rifle grenades. Weighed one hundred and twenty-five pounds or so. The first thing that happened was they sent us out on an outpost to call artillery on the Ruhr River. And we had to go through a minefield at night which was dangerous—you know, you talk about being petrified. So we get to this house, and the house is right on the river. I don't think there was more than an ordinary sized backyard between the house and the river. And right on the other side of the river were the Germans. And I could hear them speaking, I knew what they were saying because I could hear them. And we were scared because here we are in this house, one squad of men trying to call in our artillery. We stayed in the basement, except for the observers and the guys who would tell our artillery where to fire, and those shells would come right over the top of the house. Sometimes we wondered if they were going to clear the house because they were landing right across the river. It was just a petrifying situation. And so one night an officer came from battalion Intelligence and he said to me, "I hear you speak German." I said, "Yes." He says, "How would you like to be in battalion intelligence?" I said, "Anything would be better than this." And he says, "I'm gonna have you transferred."

Well, to tell you another thing, we had a colonel that was something else. He was a little bit on the heavy side. One night while we were in this outpost the moon looked like it was oblong because of all the smoke from the shells. We were really bombarding the Germans with shells. We had a first scout from Tennessee whose name was Harris, and a guy by the name of Cook who was on guard duty that night. Every night we would hear these German patrols go by us, right by the house, and they would whistle because their signals were whistle signals. And so we thought one of these times they're going to find us in this house. It was probably a squad, which is about a dozen men.

But anyway, we're at this outpost and it's night, and the moon's out there, and it looks oblong, big long moon, and here comes a guy through the shadow right towards the house. Well, Cook who was on guard recognized him—it was our colonel. So he didn't say anything. So the colonel came in and he grabbed him by the lapel, and he says, "What would you have done, soldier, if I'd have been a German." And Harris who was sitting on the galvanized tub said, "I'd have gotten you, sir." Somebody spotted the colonel as he left and the Germans began firing mortar rounds at him. It was the most comical thing we saw. We were watching from the house and his short legs were just churning as hard as they could go and these mortar shells would go off, voom, voom, and he'd get up a little more speed. Anyway, the last we saw him he was heading over the mountain.

Well, then the Ruhr River went down and as I recall they built a floating bridge across it. We crossed it. Now our unit always did what we called a dawn attack. We always attacked very early in the morning. And sometimes it'd be so black at night you'd have to hold on to the pack of the guy in front of you to find your way. We got in one little town that I remember, and usually we had to battle our way into these small towns, but this one little town they had vacated. Anyway, we got in it and we were resting there. And we found a motor scooter, a motorcycle, a little small thing, so we're riding that thing around. And one of the guys takes it out and he rides it. Now the Germans have their barns attached to the houses and usually they have these cement pits with all the manure in them that they later take out. This guy that took the motorcycle went out and he hit something and went right into that manure. So that was one of the few lighter moments. I remember another night we had to take off early in the morning. It was pitch black. We walked all night and we got into this little town and there's no Germans. And light breaks. Just before dawn breaks this one bazooka man said, "Follow me," to this assistant bazooka man. They saw a German tank

Ernest Guenther in Scheyern, Bavaria, Germany, 1945.

up on the hill. So they're going up there to get this German tank, but dawn breaks, and of course the tank takes off. Then these two Germans come out of a foxhole they had. And these two Germans came up to him and they tapped him on the shoulder, and they said, "Comrade"—with their arms in the air to surrender. He took one look, saw them, and he come down that hill just as hard as he could go. His legs were just churning almost like you'd see in one of these old cartoons. But these two Germans were bound and determined to surrender and they were right on his tail, they were right after him. So he comes up there to where we are and he screeches to a halt, and he says, "I captured two Germans." So, you know, we've had some humorous incidents.

And incidentally that's where I got this Luger and the P-38. The Germans were out there and of course they quickly started to surrender 'cause now they're surrounded. But the captain said, "Come here." And he said, "There's a couple Germans in that trench out there, see if you can get them." So I started to shoot at them but, you know, I had an old rifle that they probably found at the Anzio beachhead and it was all pitted and everything else, and you only get three rounds to try to zero it in. So you're not very accurate. And of course that's really not the idea with rifles. It's trying to pin the enemy down mostly. So anyway I started shooting at these guys and all I could do was make them duck, you know. Finally the captain says, "Go out there and get them." I said, "Huh?" He says, "Yes, I'll send the lieutenant with you. You go out and get them." He knew I could speak German, so he's telling me to go out there and have them surrender. So this lieutenant says, "Come on, I'll go with you." And he's got a 45. So I get out there, and there's an orchard. I've got my M-1. So we're getting out there and I thought, I'm not gonna get out here where these guys can pick me off. So I went out in this orchard and the lieutenant is standing in the barn with a 45 covering me. And you know, these guys are a hundred yards away or more. No 45 is gonna protect you from that. So I got out behind a tree and I yelled at them to come in, you know, I said, "Kommen Sie raus ergebt," which is come out and surrender. Well, they finally did. And I found out why they kept ducking and raising their head up. They were in a trench with water up to their chest. And it's January. I mean they're freezing cold, you know. One was a first lieutenant in the German anti-aircraft and I got a Luger and I got a pair of German binoculars. So I got these guys. The other guy was a sergeant. So I got his P-38. Now the lieutenant was one of those arrogant Germans. I mean, he was really arrogant. And I told him, I had my bayonet on, I said, "Get your butt in there and sit down." And so he says (of course the windows were broken out of the house), "I want to clean the mud off my boots," and he goes to reach for a piece of glass. I said, "You touch that glass and you're gone, you know, you don't touch nothing." This was all in German. He doesn't speak English.

Was it cold?

It's brutally cold. And you deal with it the only way you can. I usually wore two pair of wool knit underwear, a couple of shirts, a pair of pants, and then you had your wool knit sweater, and your jacket. So you just did the best you could. Fortunately a lot of the time we would be in a small town and we could go in and sleep in a house, although I remember some awfully long nights sleeping in a wet trench. But the one thing an infantry guy never does is take his shoes off. You can take everything else off but you never take your shoes off because you never know when you're going to have to run. And running barefooted don't work so good. The other thing we never did is retreat. We always called them strategic withdrawals. Which is another story. We got into a place one time and there was a woods and the Germans were waiting on us. And I told you we had these two scouts, and our captain was always right up towards the front. And the Germans let the scouts into the woods before they opened up on us. Well, when they opened up on us we did a strategic withdrawal. And of course our first scout is in the woods. And he's coming out and the colonel was behind a tree there, and as the first scout is running by he reaches out and grabs him and says, "Where're you going soldier?" He says, "This way, sir." And he was gone.

We finally got to Remagen. We were in a little town and one platoon, as I recall, of the 9th Armored Division captured the bridge at Remagen. The German who was to blow it up got drunk and he didn't blow the bridge. And so one platoon captured that bridge. And of course, the Germans did everything in their power to push them back because they knew if we crossed the Rhine River they'd be in trouble. So, we were the closest infantry unit as I recall, and they quickly put us on trucks that night and shipped us to Remagen. And I recall crossing that bridge. And as I recall it we were still getting machine-gunned going across the bridge—longest bridge in the world. And when we got on the other side we got up on the hill. And the Germans attacked us every hour on the hour trying to get us out of there—you know, counter attacked us. And we captured a bunch of Germans in that town. Must have been sixty of them. You know, it's kind of comical 'cause my job was to take the prisoners and get them rounded up so that the guys from the rear echelon could then come and get them and move them out. And I had all these Germans, must have been sixty or eighty, I don't know, all lined up in this courtyard. And I had them with their hands up against the wall. And what was comical, every GI that come by there would stop, see all these Germans with their arms against this wall, and they'd go through looking for wrist watches. And they moved them out.

And then a German, we'd knocked out a German tank in the little town, came in with an armored car while we're there. He came in there, hooked up to this tank and pulled it out. We're standing there watching them. There wasn't much we could do about it. We had a guy there, got a Silver Star as I recall, who was a bazooka man. The German tank was coming towards town and he got in this house, and the house was several rooms long. And he would go to one window and he'd fire the bazooka, and then he'd run over to this other window and the tank would put a shell through that window. Then he'd shoot from this window and run to this one. They'd put a shell through that window. But anyway, as I recall he never got the tank or anything, but at least he got a Silver Star just for having enough guts to do that.

So then shortly after that they decided to send the 3rd Battalion out. A German had come up to us and he said he knew where the German Army was. And so they asked me to come in there and interrogate him. So I interrogated him and he told us that the artillery, German artillery, was in those hills. And so the powers that be decided to try to break out from our area because we were really getting pounded to pieces. And incidentally, I admire Eisenhower greatly because he came to the front line right there at Remagen, this against [the advice of] all of his advisors. And he said I want hot food brought to these troops. And of course, by the time they got the food to us it wasn't hot any more but at least it wasn't K rations, you know. But at any rate, this German told us they were dug in out there on this ridge. So they decided to have a tank attack supported by infantry. So they took the whole 3rd Battalion. I was in the 2nd Battalion and we were still in town. Incidentally, that's the first place I saw a jet because he came over and strafed us and we didn't know what it was. But anyway, they sent out this 3rd Battalion behind these tanks. The Germans sat over there and they just boom, boom, boom, knocked out several of the tanks just like that. And so the rest of them turned around and came back and left the whole 3rd Battalion out there. And they got annihilated. They came in that night, what few were left. I wouldn't have any idea what their casualties were, but they were huge. And the guys that were still out there sneaked in at night— back to our camp. Almost lost the whole battalion. But as I told you that's where they strafed us with this Messerschmitt jet, and that's the first one I've ever seen. In the infantry we weren't afraid to get hurt. We'd dive down in the cellar, head first, do anything. The other thing we'd do, we'd get into a town and sometimes there would even be stuff on the table yet. When they heard we were coming they just left it and took off. So we would take wine, whenever we found wine, hoping it was bad. We would drink it just to get out of the front lines, you know, but we never had any of that kind of luck.

So anyway, we finally broke out of Remagen and we got to this little town called Oldenburg. I had developed the GIs. Dysentery. And I had it bad. We got into this town, Oldenburg, and we got in during the afternoon, and they put us in these houses overnight. I don't know how many pair of underwear I messed up, but I messed them up.

Ernest Guenther today.

And anyway the next morning we get out and in those days battle formation was fifteen-yard intervals between men. And we would line up on each side of the roads. And you'd have fifteen-yard intervals. Well, unbeknownst to us, up on top of the mountain outside of Oldenburg the Germans were waiting. And they had this 88mm gun which was their most fearsome weapon. The 88mm was originally an anti-aircraft gun but it became one of their best artillery pieces. They were just an all-around weapon, it was just a fearsome gun. But they waited for us to line up in the street, and they were sitting up on the mountain, and then they pointed these 88s down at us point blank. And when we got all nice and lined up they opened fire. Well, fortunately they didn't have time to zero in and so the shells were hitting on the sides of the road. But the road was flat. And we hit the ground, naturally. I thought boy the first time they reload I'm getting the heck out of here because once they zero in on the street we're goners. So, at the first pause I got up and ran. There was a picket fence and the entrance to the house was at the side. So I ran around and got to the side and just as I got into the doorway this shell went off. And I felt a pain like a guy hit me in the elbow with a baseball bat, and also on my back, and it knocked me down. And there was linoleum and I went scooting into this kitchen hollering for a medic for all I was worth you know. Well, fortunately for me there was a medic in the house. And he come up and he said, "What's the matter?" I said, "I'm dying." He said, "Where are you hit?" I said, "All over my back, my arm, all over." So I thought I was dying, so he cut my shirt off of me, see. And he started to laugh. I said, "You s.o.b., you laugh, I'll kill you. I'm dying, you're laughing." He says, "You ain't hurt that bad." I said, "What do you mean?" He says, "You got hit in the elbow, the rest of it is welts from the gravel hitting you in the back." I was afraid to look for fear I'd look like a sieve. So I threw my pack, my rifle, everything away, and the medic said, "Come on, you've got to go back to battalion intelligence. Or to the battalion aid station." That's what he said. I said, "I'm not leaving." He says, "You've got to." I said, "I don't care if Eisenhower comes in here, I'm not moving." He says,

"You've got to." By this time the troops had moved forward and the shelling had sort of ceased, you know. So he says, "Come on, I'll go back with you to battalion aid." So I said, "All right." So we go back to battalion aid. And the guy says, "The first thing we're going to do with you here is give you two shots." So, they gave me a shot of penicillin and then they gave me a shot of whiskey. Those were the two shots. Then they put me in a jeep, 'cause I was ambulatory. I was hit in the elbow. You were talking about how do you keep warm, I had so many clothes on that the shrapnel went in, hit the bone and the shrapnel split instead of the bone because of all the clothing it had to go through, it went through so much clothes it slowed it enough that it didn't crush my bone. So I was an ambulatory patient. And of course by this time you're so weak you can't hardly walk, you know, somebody has to help you. This happened on March 11, 1945. I'll never forget it because my niece was born the day I almost expired. But if I'd have been a little faster I wouldn't have gotten hit. If I'd have been a little slower I probably wouldn't be here because it would have caught me in the back, you know, maybe the spine. But anyway, they put me on a jeep and then they go get these litter cases, guys that can't move. We're sitting out there in the open, not knowing if the Germans are going to start firing again or anything else. Well, then they took us back to another aid station, and then they decided to ship us to a hospital. By this time, and I have to tell you this story because it's a riot. By this time the Germans were bombing the bridge regularly—the bridge at Remagen. And we had to cross the river again to go to the hospital. And they got us on these ambulances and as we got to the river the Germans start strafing us. They strafed the ambulances. So the drivers, they jump out and they hit the ditches. And we're all in the truck, we're ambulatory but you can't get out of there, you're still too weak, you can't get out of the truck to run. So we're sitting in this truck. And there was a black anti-aircraft battalion back there and I'm telling you, those guys were a riot and they saved our lives. They couldn't seem to hit anything, but they would get out there and they had everything from 20mm to I don't know what the biggest anti-aircraft gun, 50mm, they had all kinds of stuff. They covered the sky with flak. And they would say, here he comes, here he comes, boom, boom, boom, boom, you know. They kept those German planes so high that the strafing was ineffective because one 50-caliber maybe would hit here and the next one would be many yards away. And those guys were having a ball. They were keeping those German pilots way up there. But then the bridge collapsed. And so they took us, two navy guys, and they had what I call a floating mortarboard. Now the Rhine River is swift there. It's very swift. And they put us in this floating mortarboard—it was wide and flat. And they had four outboard motors on it. And these two Navy guys couldn't get together on how to manipulate those outboards. And we went across the river like this, you know, zigzagging around. Well, when we got to the other side they put us in the ambulances and the ambulance driver says, "I've got something for you guys." And they gave each of us a fifth of cognac. So, man, we're going back to the hospital, you know, we hadn't really slept for a long time, maybe three days or so, and so we're getting bombed on this cognac. And we get back to the hospital at Aachen, Germany. And the first guy to meet us is a minister. And of course we didn't dare let on that we were drunker than a skunk so we're trying to act sober. He's got sandwiches and ain't nobody in a position to eat a sandwich. We'd have thrown up right now, you know, so we politely refused the sandwiches, and he couldn't understand it. He says, "Well, surely you guys must be hungry, surely you'd like a sandwich." "No, we said, we just couldn't eat one. Thank you." So they put us in the hospital there.

And about two o'clock in the morning they called me in to operate on me—surgery. They take you in a room, and it was a huge, a huge room just full of wounded guys. And when your turn comes they take you over and put you on this cot, knock you out, and they perform the surgery. When I woke up I'm in this room with dozens and dozens and dozens of other guys, and a sergeant is sitting there watching to make sure you were still breathing. And when he saw that I was waking up he came over and he said, "You all right?" I said, "Yes, I'm all right." He says, "Do you think you can make it back to your bunk?" So I try to get up and of course I can't. So they get some guy to take me back to my bunk. And by this time I hadn't eaten for two or three days, and I was hungry. And I said to him, "Can I possibly have some food." "We'll get you something," he said. Well, because of the anesthesia and stuff I kept passing out, you know, sleeping, so I missed breakfast, I missed lunch, I missed supper. Finally there was a lieutenant in the bunk next to me. And I said, "Man, I'm starving to death." And he finally gave me a candy bar, you know, felt sorry for me. From there they put us on trains to go to the hospital at Rheims, France. And for the first time in days I'm on this train, they got bunks on the train, it's a Pullman, a sleeper, and I'm laying up there and I finally get to sleep. I mean it's been days since I'd slept, I'm exhausted. Don't this nurse come up and wake me up and say, "Are you all right?" I just about killed me a nurse then. But anyway, then I got back to Rheims, France, in the hospital which was an old German hospital they converted. They still had all the swastikas and everything on the wall, and German writing on the wall. But anyway, I got in that hospital there and this nurse comes in and says, "You gotta start falling out for calisthenics." I said, "I'm not falling out for any calisthenics." She says, "You better." I says, "What are you gonna do to me, you gonna put me in the hoosegow or something? Hell, that's better than the front lines, you know." So finally the doctor came in and said just leave him alone. So they left me alone. And then when I was supposed to go back to the front, I said to this doctor, I said, "Doc, I don't want to go back."

He said, "Well, I can give you another week. That's the best I can do." I said, "Anything, you know, just anything." So he gave me another week in the hospital. Well, then I got out of the hospital and we went to Paris which was nice, got to see the Folies Bergère. Cost me three packs of cigarettes to get one of the overhanging balcony seats, but it was worth it. So then they put us back on those 40&8s and started shipping us back to the front. May 8th or 9th was V-E Day. So it was right around that time. So we get to Brussels, Belgium, on these 40&8s and all heck breaks loose. I mean, boom, you know, we're thinking its shells, we're thinking we're being attacked. And we opened the door of the 40&8s, getting ready to jump out, and here's all these people. The war had ended, and they were firing firecrackers. We were on our way back to the front, and the war ended and they were shooting firecrackers and everything else.

What were your feelings right then?

Oh. You'll never know. And I can't explain them. I mean, you just can't fathom the relief, you know. I was gonna live. My unit was seventy-five kilometers from Berlin on the Elbe River. We were camped there and the Germans were surrendering by the thousands, coming across the river. And the Russians kept trying to keep them from coming. If there was a German civilian that tried to cross the river they'd shoot them. There was another strange thing about the Russians. They were only given one uniform. You'd see a German walking along with a fairly decent set of clothes on, and all of a sudden some Russian would yank him into a building and out would come the Russian in his clothes. 'Cause they didn't have but one uniform. But anyway, even at that time, you know there was animosity. We had guns and everything else stationed there at the Elbe River.

So anyway, then we went to Furstenfeldbruk which is just outside of Munich. By this time I was in battalion intelligence. But anyway, at Furstenfeldbruk there was a counter intelligence agent. So he says, "Hey, I'd like for you to work for us." So I worked for counter intelligence there as an interrogator of the German prisoners in Furstenfeldbruk. They had five, ten thousand prisoners in this prison camp. And our job was to try to find any high-ranking Nazis or Germans that were involved in the Malmédy Massacre.

I did find the head of the German SS in Vienna, Austria. And he wasn't even German, he was a White Russian. But he was head of the SS. And as soon as I found him they whisked him off to lord knows where. I suppose he wound up in Nuremberg. I have no idea.

Then I got a leave and I went to Switzerland, and while I was in Switzerland I got a call. They said get your butt back here, you're going home.

Well, when I got home I decided I'd better get an education. So the first thing I did was enroll in Parker Vocational Night School. I was gonna get my high school diploma. But I eventually graduated from Brookville High School. From there I went to Ohio State, and I graduated from Ohio State with a Bachelor of Science in business administration and became a CPA. I've been a practicing CPA for about fifty years. I've retired now but I still do a little tax work on the side. So, basically that's the story.

Conclusion

World War II was a turning point, a life-changing experience, in the lives of these men. Young, naïve youths were transformed by their experiences into self-reliant adults. This generation grew up quickly. They experienced the horrors of war, loneliness, coping with battle and successfully transcended this "rite of passage." Some few may have been temporarily embittered by the experience, but the vast majority adjusted readily to civilian life and went on to be successful people after the war in their social, economic and political lives.

Almost all the men interviewed here took advantage of the GI Bill of Rights, arguably the most important piece of legislation ever enacted. It created conditions for a social mobility unseen in America's history as millions experienced higher education. Usually they were the first person in their family to attend college and they became doctors, lawyers, businessmen, professors and entrepreneurs. Many met their wives while doing their college work and all are proud to say they encouraged their children and grandchildren to continue their education beyond high school.

Fortune, providence and the impersonal character of events were a reality in the lives of these interviewees. The hand of fate, of good luck or bad, played a role in what happened to them. A short illness, a change in government policy, the alphabet, taking one's turn for a particular duty all played a role in who was wounded and who was not, who lived and who died. Taking a test or not taking a test might have tremendous consequences. There is a large measure of irrationality involved in military service. Some joined the Army instead of the Navy because they had a date. Some joined the paratroopers and assumed terrible risks because they liked the shiny boots. Still others joined the Marines because of their splendid uniforms. Others joined the Air Corps not because they loved to fly, but because they had never been in a plane.

For most interviewees, World War II was what was happening to them at a particular moment in time and space. Few comment on operations in military theaters other than their own until after V-E Day in Europe. Only at that point do some men mention the war in the Pacific and the anxiety of being shipped to the far east to participate in the planned invasion of Japan in the fall of 1945. The war was personal, in some ways private, and knowledge of events outside ones own span of consciousness was limited.

Most fought for comrade as opposed to cause. The television miniseries entitled *Band of Brothers* probably encapsulates on film as well as anything why they struggled. Esprit de corps, represented in the Marines' motto "Semper Fi," probably sketches the outer parameters of why and for whom men fought. Ideology surely played a role in the war, but in these interviews the ideological and patriotic reasons for men fighting seem very limited. Instead, it is comrade not cause that motivates men to do their duty even when their own lives are put in harm's way.

Paul Fussell, professor of English and a World War II veteran, wrote an essay entitled, "Thank God for the Atomic Bomb" and without exception the forty-two veterans interviewed during this project supported President Truman's decision to use the A-bomb. Every nation that might plausibly start a nuclear program did so (the United States, Great Britian, France, Germany, the Soviet Union and Japan). Few scholars doubt that Japan would have used the bomb if it had been available. After all, Japan employed a state suicide policy called the kamikaze—so who can doubt its willingness to employ an atomic bomb if available. Truman's decision saved millions of lives—American and Japanese—because it hastened the end of the war. Only the A-bomb was able to break the trance that held the Japanese leadership in its iron grip.

Finally, the interviews shed light on what war is really like for the common soldier, sailor, marine and airman. The stories bear witness to the daily life of Americans coming under enemy fire from bomb, bullet and artillery. They bring home graphically the fear and the lessons learned by those in the military who have endured combat. These men learned to function, to do their duty, under an angst unknown to those outside the military brotherhood.

Appendix A: Other Veterans Interviewed in This Project

Constantine, Bernard. Army: private first class; one and one-half years of service; six months of service during World War II; European Theater of Operations. Constantine was stationed in Italy helping to establish the necessary legal institutions and rules required to change military government into civilian government.

Cooper, George C. Navy: lt. j.g.; three and one-half years service; American Theater of Operations. Cooper was one of the "Golden Thirteen"—the first group of black Americans to be commissioned as ensigns in the U.S. Navy.

Farris, Harold. Army Air Corps: corporal; three years and two months; European Theater for seven months. Farris was a classroom instructor and an instructor with flying status in Sioux Falls, South Dakota, teaching how to operate the four basic radios employed by the Air Corps during the war.

Morris, Marie. Army Nurse Corps: major; seven months' service during World War II; Pacific. After Morris' husband was killed in Europe by a land mine, she enlisted in the Army as a nurse and served in the Philippines.

Morris, Marvin. Army: warrant officer; ten months' service during World War II, American Theater of Operations. An expert on refrigeration and air conditioning, Morris converted the cold storage plants from gasoline engines to electric while stationed on Saipan.

Pancoast, Robert. Army: technician fifth grade; two years and ten months; Europe for six months. Pancoast studied engineering and spent the last six months of his military service in Europe working on recalibration of the 9th Army artillery in preparation for the assault on Japan.

Prater, Harold. Army Air Corps: private first class; two and one-half years' service; one and one-half years in the Pacific Theater. Prater served in New Guinea and the Philippines in a radar unit tracking American and Japanese bombers and fighters.

Perkins, Robert. Army: first lieutenant; two years and one month; European Theater of Operations for fifteen months. Perkins served with the 79th Division in Germany "cleaning up resistance pockets" and later was assigned to a unit in Nuremberg during the occupation of Germany.

Savage, Jack. Army: technician 4th grade; two years and four months; Pacific Theater eighteen months. Savage served in New Guinea and on the island of Luzon in the Philippines as a member of JASCO (Joint Assault Signal Company) whose task was to give close support to infantry units by directing air strikes against enemy positions.

Sortman, Donald E. Army Air Corps: sergeant; three and one-half years (three years overseas); European Theater of Operations. Sortman served as a mechanic with the 8th Air Force in England working on B-17 bombers and later with the 9th Air Force working on P-47 fighters in England and France.

Stone, J. V. Army: corporal: two and one-half years; Pacific Theater of Operations for two years. Stone completed infantry training at Camp Wheeler, Georgia, then was assigned to the 868th Bomber Squadron in New Caledonia to prepare target plans for B-24 bombers, and ended up on Okinawa where he worked on targets for bombing in Japan.

Witzke, Betty. Navy WAVE: chief yeoman; two years and ten months; American Theater of Operations. Witzke did her basic training at Hunter College in New York City, went to yeoman's school in Cedar Falls, Iowa, and was stationed in Cleveland, Ohio, doing payroll, secretarial and legal transcriptions in shorthand.

Appendix B: The Organization and Weapons of American Infantry Divisions

Organization

Unit	Strength	Commander	Parent Unit
Squad	12 to 15	Sergeant	Platoon—3-4 squads
Platoon	36 to 64	Lieutenant	Company—3 platoons
Rifle Company	180	Captain	Battalion—3 companies
Battalion	1200	Lt. Col.	Regiment—3 battalions
Regiment	3,100	Colonel	Division—3 regiments
Division	13,472	Maj. Gen.	Corps—3 divisions

Divisional units included artillery, engineer, medical, signal, reconnaissance and quartermaster formations.

Weapons

Colt .45 caliber automatic pistol
Model 1903 Springfield. 30 caliber, 5 round magazine, 8.7 pounds
M-1 Garand. 30 caliber, semi-automatic, 8 round clip, 9.6 pounds
Thompson submachine gun, .45 caliber, 700 rounds per minute, 12 pounds.
BAR, .30 caliber, fully automatic, 20 round magazine, 20 pounds.
Machine gun, .30 caliber, air and water cooled
Mortar, 60mm, 2.5 pound bomb, 2,000 yards, 42 pounds
Mortar, 81mm, 7.5 pound bomb, 3,800 yards, 80+ pounds
Artillery, 105mm, 33 pound projectile, 12,000 yards, 3,750 pounds
Artillery, 155mm, 95 pound projectile, 12,530 yards, 12,750 pounds
Artillery, 37mm, anti-tank gun

Source: Bradley, Omar N. *A Soldier's Story*. New York: Henry Holt Co., 1951, p. 564.

Appendix C: Glossary of World War II Terms

Airborne Forces: The U.S. established its first parachute units in 1940. By 1945 there were four airborne divisions.

Army Air Corps: Became U.S. Air Force in 1947 via the Unification Act of 1947, and now serves under the Department of Defense.

Arnold, H. H. : Head of Army Air Corps in World War II and member, Joint Chiefs of Staff.

atomic bomb: Dropped on Hiroshima on August 6, 1945, and Nagasaki on August 9, 1945; hastens the Japanese surrender and the end of the war.

Bataan Death March: Forced 65 mile march by American and Philippine military prisoners that resulted in thousands of deaths due to Japanese cruelty on the march.

bombers, American (major only): B-17, Flying Fortress—4 engines; B-24— 4 engines; B-25—2 engines; B-29—4 engine long range bomber (called the Superfortress).

Caroline Islands: Islands held in trust by Japan after World War I and developed into major army and navy bases in the years before World War II.

Chiang Kai-shek: Leader of Nationalist Chinese forces during World War II. Later defeated by the Communists, he fled with his troops to Taiwan in 1949.

Clark, Mark: General and commander of the U.S. Fifth Army in North Africa, and later commander of the 15th Army Corps in Italy.

cruisers: Conventional cruisers of World War II were replaced by guided missile cruisers beginning in 1961.

De Gaulle, Charles: Leader of the Free French forces in the battle for Europe.

destroyers: World War II destroyers were about 376 feet long and 40 feet wide. There were three classes of destroyers—Fletcher, Sumner and Gearing. The U.S. had 350 destroyers at the end of the war.

destroyer escorts: A World War II DE was 290 feet long and had a 35 foot beam; 400 DEs were built between 1943 and 1945.

Doolittle, James: Led first raid on Tokyo with B-25s from the carrier *Hornet* in 1942.

Eisenhower, Dwight D.: General of the Army and supreme commander of Allied expeditionary forces in Europe during World War II.

enfilading fire: gunfire directed along the length of an enemy battle line.

envelopment: an attack directed toward the enemy's flanks or rear.

field of fire: the space covered by the fire of a weapon, particularly a machine gun. Interlocking fields of fire literally created a wall of steel. Terrain and ground cover could obstruct fields of fire.

fighters (airplanes): Navy—F4F, F6F; Marines—F4U Corsair; Army Air—P-38, P-39, P-40, P-47, P-51. These are the principal American fighter planes in World War II.

flamethrowers: A weapon that projects and ignites a flammable liquid. They are well suited for the destruction of bunkers or caves.

flanks: the extreme right or left side of an army or fleet or of a subdivision of an army or fleet.

Fuchida, Mitsuo: Japanese fighter pilot who led the first wave of 180 planes in the attack on Pearl Harbor on December 7, 1941.

Gilbert Islands: Site of two major battles in the central Pacific in November of 1943: Tarawa (Marines) and Makin (Army).

Great Depression: Period between 1929 and 1940 when 25 percent of the American workforce was unemployed.

Howitzer: Most common type of artillery; relatively short barrels; 105mm and 155mm are the most common in the American artillery units.

Guadalcanal: First American ground attack in World War II—August of 1942. Assault by the 1st Marine Division. A six month campaign. The location of Henderson Field.

Hirohito: Emperor of Japan during the war; deeply involved in all aspects of war planning and execution.

Hitler, Adolf: Chancellor of Germany, 1933–1945; committed suicide in 1945 in a bunker in Berlin.

Kamikaze: Member of a Japanese air corps suicide attack force who crashed their planes into American warships; very effective in the Philippines and Okinawa.

King, Ernest J.: Commander of the U.S. Fleet and member, Joint Chiefs of Staff.

Kwajalein Atoll: Seized by the 7th Infantry Division in February 1944.

landing craft: LCT (tank), LCVP (vehicle, personnel), LST (tank), LCM (mechanized).

LeMay, Curtis E.: Commander of the 20th Bomber Command on Tinian.

Lexington: Attack carrier sunk in the Battle of the Coral Sea, May 1942.

Leyte: Philippine island invaded October 20, 1944, by MacArthur's forces.

logistics: All activities related to the supply, support, movement, and evacuation of armed forces. The goal is to provide the armed forces with the correct quantity of material to do their task.

MacArthur, Douglas: General and commander of the southwest Pacific area.

Marine Corps: Formed in 1775 under the Navy and responsible for amphibious warfare. Marines have their own air support, armor and artillery units.

Marshall, George: General and chief of staff of the U.S. Army in the war.

Midway Island: Japan's attempt to seize Midway in June of 1942 resulted in their disastrous loss of four major attack carriers; the initiative in the Pacific moved to the United States after this great battle.

mortar: A weapon designed to loft a shell (called a bomb) in a high trajectory. It is the oldest form of artillery.

New Guinea: Huge island in the southwest Pacific area (1200 miles long), and the site of scores of pitched battles between American and Japanese soldiers, sailors and marines.

Nimitz, Chester W.: Admiral and commander of the central Pacific area.

Palau Islands: Western Caroline Islands group; site of battle of Peleliu in September 1944.

patrol: a detachment of men detailed for reconnaissance.

Patton, George: General, commander of the U.S. II Corps in Tunisia, the Seventh Army in Sicily, and the Third Army in Western Europe.

Pearl Harbor: Oahu, Hawaii, Naval base and target of Japanese attack on December 7, 1941.

Philippine Sea, Battle of the: The Japanese lost almost 400 planes in what is called the Great Turkey Shoot, during the battle for Saipan in 1944.

prisoners of war: American prisoners of war died at the rate of 0.7 percent in German camps and at a rate of 34 percent when held by the Japanese.

Pyle, Ernest: Surely one of the greatest American war correspondents in World War II. Killed in the Pacific in the battle for Okinawa on Ie shima.

Rommel, Erwin: Field marshall, German commander of the Afrika Korps, also German Army Group B in Europe.

Roosevelt, Franklin: President of the United States during almost all of the war.

Rundstedt, Karl R. G. von: Field marshal, German commander-in-chief in the West.

Short, Walter C.: Army general at the time of the Pearl Harbor attack, Schofield Barracks.

sniper: A rifleman particularly trained to kill individuals at long range.

sonar: Underwater microphones which receive all sounds from the waters around them. Particularly useful in locating submarines.

Stalin, Joseph: Dictator of the Soviet Union during the war; died in 1953.

Stearman Airplane: Primary trainer used by the Army Air Corps in the war.

strategy: the combining and employing of the means of war in planning and directing large military operations.

tactics: the use and deployment of troops in combat, usually implying small-scale engagements.

Tarawa: One of the Gilbert Islands, site of the first offensive in the central Pacific by Marines; the battle these resulted in over 1000 Americans killed and 5000 Japanese killed.

Tiger tank: German tank, probably the best tank of any side in World War II.

time-on target: the synchronization of artillery fire from several batteries at different points on a selected target.

Tojo, Hideki: Wartime premier of Japan; captured and banged after war trials.

Torpex: A high explosive introduced by the Navy in 1943 as a replacement for TNT in torpedo warheads.

Truman, Harry S: President of the United States; made the decision to drop the atomic bomb on Japan to hasten the end of the war. Assumed office in April of 1945.

WAAC: Women's Army Auxiliary Corps; became WACs in late 1943.

WAVES: Women Accepted for Volunteer Emergency Service, U.S. Navy.

Yamato, Isouoku: Japanese Admiral, the man who planned the Pearl Harbor attack, killed in an airplane shot down by P-38s in Bougainville.

Yamato: Japanese battleship, 64,000 tons, nine 18-inch guns, sunk by American airplanes in April of 1945.

Yorktown: U.S. attack carrier, sunk at the Battle of Midway in June of 1942 by Japanese aircraft.

Zero: Formidable Japanese fighter plane, used on land and also carrier based; very fast and maneuverable.

Index